The Lake Classical Series

ELEMENTARY GREEK

An Introduction to the Study of Attic Greek

BY

THEODORE C. BURGESS, Ph.D.

Late of Bradley Polytechnic Institute

AND

ROBERT J. BONNER, Ph.D.

The University of Chicago

SCOTT, FORESMAN AND COMPANY
CHICAGO   ATLANTA   DALLAS   NEW YORK

PREFACE

The tendency of instruction in Greek in America during the past few years has been more and more to require that the introductory book should be in the simplest and briefest form consistent with thoroughness. In recognition of this demand the authors of *Elementary Greek* have aimed to include only the facts that are essential to a book with such a purpose, and they hope that this book will prove a natural, simple, and yet thorough introduction to Attic Greek.

This demand for a brief book carries with it also the requirement that the student complete the first book of the *Anabasis* by the end of the school or college year. *Elementary Greek* aims to meet this need effectively. It is largely with this in view that the number of lessons is reduced to sixty, that the vocabulary is made that of Xenophon, and that each lesson, beginning with the ninth, contains a passage from the *Anabasis*. The earlier portions of Xenophon's narrative are modified where necessary to fit them to the state of the student's knowledge of Greek, but after the first few lessons the text of the *Anabasis* is introduced practically without alteration. There are definite advantages in this plan. From the very outset the student is given some connected narrative in each lesson, and this narrative is continuous, not merely for the individual lesson, but also for the entire series. Thus he becomes familiar with the use of Greek particles earlier than is otherwise possible. Contact with real Greek develops an ability to read which cannot be gained from working over detached sentences or simplified selections from various Greek authors. The knowledge that he is dealing with a famous piece of literature in its original form, not with sentences composed by some modern scholar for the occasion, serves to give genuineness, life, and interest to the student's work.

There is also the practical gain that upon the completion of this book the student will not only have secured the necessary drill in forms and syntax, but at the same time will have finished the first three chapters of the *Anabasis* with a thoroughness which could not be gained so readily in any other way. The order followed in presenting the material of the individual lessons has been influenced somewhat by the use of the *Anabasis* as a text, but never in an arbitrary way. μι-verbs are introduced earlier than in most elementary books. The dual is not employed in the exercises, and in learning paradigms may be omitted or not at the option of the teacher.

Under the heading, "Drill," provision is made for constant practice both in recognizing and in recalling the forms taught in the paradigms. Accordingly these exercises are largely review work. The student's attention is directed exclusively to forms, thus securing a maximum amount of practice with a minimum expenditure of time. In this way it has been possible to reduce the number of sentences in the exercises and to eliminate from them those forms which occur less frequently in ordinary reading.

The selections from the *Anabasis* used in the lessons end in lesson LX with section 2 of Chapter III. The rest of the Third Chapter follows, with unusually copious notes.

The individual vocabularies are usually brief and the book as a whole involves a small number of words. English words derived from the Greek have been introduced freely both in the special and in the general vocabularies. The authors believe that this frequent evidence of direct connection with our own language will be interesting and stimulating. It is hoped that the prominence given to the rules for transliteration will assist in securing greater ease and correctness in the use of proper names.

The Appendix is made to include much more, both in paradigm and syntax, than is incorporated into the lessons themselves. Teachers who wish to do so may make use of this material for additional work.

The illustrations have been carefully selected with a view to affording opportunity for discussions of various phases of Greek life. The student should be encouraged to familiarize himself with the concise descriptions given on page xi.

These lessons have had the advantage of being subjected to the test of use in the classroom both in high school and college for a period of several years.

The authors gratefully acknowledge their indebtedness to Professor Edward Capps of the University of Chicago, who has rendered invaluable assistance at every stage in the preparation of the book.

THEODORE C. BURGESS
ROBERT J. BONNER

August 1, 1907

CONTENTS

LIST OF ILLUSTRATIONS

teacher looks on a roll. On the right is the pedagogue, a slave who accompanied his master's sons to and from school. Cloaks (ἱμάτια) are the only garments worn. On the wall are drinking-cups, lyres, a flute case, and a receptacle for carrying rolls such as one of the teachers holds in his hand. It was customary to paint on vases the name of a popular young man. Here the "love" inscription, which can scarcely be seen, is Ἱπ(π)οδάμος καλός.

A red-figured painting on an Attic vase of the fifth century B. C. In the center of the group of three on the left sits a woman with an embroidery frame. Behind her is a woman with a work basket, while in front stands a caller, wrapped in a mantle. Next stands a woman tying her girdle. The seated woman has a brush with which to paint her face. The servant holds a jar of unguent and a toilet box. On the wall hang two fillets, a plectrum, and two indistinct objects. Observe the dress. The first, fourth, and sixth figures wear the chiton (χιτων) alone. The two seated women and the caller have cloaks as well as chitons.

This inlaid bronze dagger blade was found in a shaft grave at Mycenae. The figures are inlaid on a separate strip of enameled bronze, which is set into the blade. The nude parts of the men and the bodies of the lions are made of gold. The clothing (trunks) and shields are made of electrum. The handle was fastened on with gold rivets. Notice the weapons and the shapes of the shields, and the method of carrying them. Observe also a spear-head protruding from the attacking lion's flank.

The banqueters wear garlands and recline on cushions. Small three-legged tables hold the drinking-utensils and sweetmeats. A female musician plays a double flute for their amusement, while one of the guests beats a tambourine.

A red-figured cylix of the fifth century B. C. The drawing combines two different portions of the original design on the outside of the cup so as to show how the greaves (κνημῖδες), breastplate (θώραξ), and sword belt were put on. The design on the shield is an armed centaur.

This design is from a Panathenaic vase, given as a prize to the athletes who won the contests at the Panathenaea, the great festival in honor of Athena, at Athens. The thong (ἀγκύλη) wound around the shaft and held in the fingers gave the javelin a rotary motion and increased its range

PAGE

This scene is taken from the same vase as Fig. 3. The boy on the left is listening to his teacher as he plays a double flute. The teacher in the center is probably correcting an exercise written on tablets. To the right sits a pedagogue. On the wall are a roll and a set of tablets tied up, a lyre with plectrum attached, and an uncertain object.

This marble relief which belongs to the pedestal of a sculptured group found at Mantinea is the work of Praxiteles. On the left sits Apollo, who has just finished playing the lyre; on the right is Marsyas playing the double flute. Apollo's Phrygian servant stands in the center with his knife, ready to exact the penalty. Notice that the slave wears a garment with sleeves such as Greeks never wore. This relief belongs to the early fourth century B. C.

Ἑλλήνων ἦρχον τότε Ὀλυμπίᾳ, ἡνίκα μοι Ζεὺς
δῶκεν νικῆσαι πρῶτον Ὀλυμπιάδα
ἵπποις ἀθλοφόροις· τὸ δὲ δεύτερον αὖτις ἐφεξῆς
ἵπποις. υἱὸς δ᾽ ἦν Τρωίλος Ἀλκινόου.

This inscription, which is in metrical form, is on a bronze plate which was originally attached to a statue of Troilus in Olympia. It was found in 1879. Pausanias saw it when he visited Olympia in the second century A. D. Observe that the words are not separated from each other.

This so-called Greek razor is three and seven-eighths inches long and is made of bronze. Notice the stirrup-shaped handle and the circular blade.

From a red-figured vase of the fifth century B. C. The woman, whose name is Danaë, reclines on an elegant couch. She is dressed in a chiton (note the way in which the sleeves are formed) and a himation, and holds in her hand the ends of a fillet (similar to those on the wall in Fig. 4) which confines her hair. On the wall are a mirror and a bag (or cap). Notice the footstool. The inscription is ΔΑΝΑΕ.

A black-figured painting on an Attic vase of the sixth century B. C. A woman is having a pair of shoes cut out and fitted. She stands on a low table. The cobbler with a semi-circular knife is on the point of cutting out the soles from a piece of leather under the woman's feet. The assistant is shaping a piece of leather for the upper portion of the shoes. The white-haired man with cloak and cane is a visitor, probably the woman's husband. On the wall are awls, pincers, cutter,

INTRODUCTORY

The Greeks have the most remarkable literary history of any people. Their literature is not less notable for rich and lofty thought than for beauty of expression. Almost all the forms in which ideas have been expressed were either originated or best developed by this creative race; e. g. history, oratory, philosophical prose, and poetry in all its forms— comedy, tragedy, epic, lyric, elegiac, and bucolic. Their art, displayed at its best in sculpture and architecture (temple-building), has never been surpassed. Their theories form the basis of modern science and philosophy. In the realm of political science, both by experiment and by speculation, they have contributed more than any other people. No other race has ever come so near perfection in so many lines.

What concerns us here chiefly is their language, which was as wonderfully developed as their art and their literature. The Greeks called themselves "Hellenes" and their land "Hellas." The Romans gave them the name "Graeci," and hence came our word "Greek." There is a tendency at the present time to return to the original names. The Greeks are a branch of the Indo-European race to which we belong, and occupied at the dawn of history what we still know as the Grecian peninsula, as well as the islands of the Aegean Sea and the coast of Asia Minor. Later they spread over the whole of the coast of the Mediterranean, and their language gradually became the medium of communication among cultivated people throughout the civilized world of antiquity.

There were three main branches of the Greek race—the Aeolians, the Dorians, and the Ionians—each speaking a dialect differing slightly from that spoken by the others.

Each made its own contribution to that wonderful body of Greek literature a portion of which has come down to us. Almost all of the classical Greek literature, however (from about 500 to 300 B.C.), was written in a dialect which was an offshoot of the Ionic, namely the Attic—the language used in Attica, whose capital was Athens. It is the Attic dialect of the Greek language, therefore, which is universally studied as the standard, and upon it our Greek grammars are based.

Greek literature has an unbroken history of twenty-eight centuries, from Homer to the present time. The Greek language is still spoken by the inhabitants of continental Greece and in many parts of the Levant. Modern Greek differs from the ancient only by such changes as the lapse of time must necessarily produce.

PRELIMINARY STATEMENTS

1. The Greek alphabet has twenty-four letters:

Form		Sound	Name	
A	α	*a* in far	ἄλφα	alpha
B	β	*b*	βῆτα	beta
Γ	γ	*g* in go	γάμμα	gamma
Δ	δ	*d*	δέλτα	delta
E	ε	*ĕ* in met	εἶ, ἒ ψῑλόν	epsilon
Z	ζ	*dz*	ζῆτα	zeta
H	η	*ey* in obey	ἦτα	eta
Θ	θ	*th* in thin	θῆτα	theta
I	ι	*i* in machine	ἰῶτα	iota
K	κ	*k*	κάππα	kappa
Λ	λ	*l*	λάμβδα	lambda
M	μ	*m*	μῦ	mu
N	ν	*n*	νῦ	nu
Ξ	ξ	*ks, x* in flax	ξεῖ, ξῖ	xi
O	ο	*ŏ* in renovate	οὖ, ὂ μῑκρόν	omicron
Π	π	*p*	πεῖ, πῖ	pi
P	ρ	*r*	ῥῶ	rho
Σ	σ ς[1]	*s* in see	σίγμα	sigma
T	τ	*t* in to	ταῦ	tau
Υ	υ	French *u*, Germ. *ü*	ὖ, ὖ ψῑλόν	upsilon
Φ	φ	*ph* in physics	φεῖ, φῖ	phi
X	χ	German *ch*	χεῖ, χῖ	chi
Ψ	ψ	*ps*	ψεῖ, ψῖ	psi
Ω	ω	*ō* in no	ὦ, ὦ μέγα	omega

The initial sound of the name (last column) gives the
sound of the letter.

---

[1] At the end of a word ς is used, elsewhere σ.

2. Of the seven vowels (α, ε, η, ι, ο, υ, ω) the *e-* and *o-* sounds have separate letters to represent the long and short quantity: ε, η; ο, ω. The other vowels (α, ι, and υ) have not. In this book α, ι, and υ are short when not marked long (ᾱ, ῑ, ῡ) or accented with the circumflex (ᾶ, ῖ, ῦ). Thus in καλᾱ́ (˘ –) the first vowel is short, the second long.[1]

✓ **3.** The consonants have the sounds of the corresponding letters in English, except that γ before κ, γ, χ, ξ has the sound of *ng*, as *n* in *ink*. This is called gamma nasal. ἄγγελος angelos, *messenger*.

4. ξ (κσ), ψ (πσ), and ζ (δ and *s*-sound) are called double consonants. Observe that θ, φ, χ are not double consonants. The *h*-sound in them was not regarded as a separate letter.

5. A word has as many syllables as it has separate vowels or diphthongs. Any combination of consonants which would easily begin a word is included in the syllable with the following vowel, e. g. ἄν-θρω-πος, πά-σχω. Compound words are divided between the original parts: οὐκέτι = οὐκ-έτι, not οὐ-κέτι.

6. The diphthongs are formed by combining a vowel with either ι or υ. υι combines these two. With ᾱ, η, and ω the letter ι is written beneath the first vowel of the diphthong and is called iota-subscript. ᾳ, ῃ, ῳ are improper diphthongs.

✓ **7.** The diphthongs are:

αι	*ai*sle	ηυ	almost as ευ [3]	ᾳ	as ᾱ
αυ	s*au*erkraut	οι	t*oi*l	ῃ	as η
ει	*ei*ght [2]	ου	y*ou*th	ῳ	as ω
ευ	f*eu*d	υι	q*ui*t [3]		

---

[1] Be careful to give every long vowel twice the time of the short in pronunciation and to pronounce both consonants when two come together: μέλλω, γνῶθι. Thus νεωτέρου has the rhythm ˘ – ˘ –, not ˘ ˘ ˘ –. [2] Some teachers prefer the sound of *ei* in h*ei*ght. [3] No exact English equivalent; υι is much like Eng. *we*.

8. The last syllable of a word is called the ultima; the next to the last, the penult; the third from the last, the antepenult.

9. There are three accents used in writing: the acute (´), the grave (`), and the circumflex (^). The accent is placed directly over the vowel, unless it is a capital letter (20), and over the second vowel of a proper diphthong: τοῖς, τούς.

10. All Greek words are accented on one of the last three syllables. The place of the accent must often be learned outright, as in English; but rules can be formulated for many words. The kind of accent—acute, circumflex, or grave—will agree with the following rules:

general rules of accent

11. The acute may stand on any one of the last three syllables of a word; the circumflex, only on the penult and ultima; the grave, on the ultima only. The circumflex is confined to long syllables. Thus in ἄρα the first α is short, in ἆρα it is long. In this way the accent will often reveal the quantity of a vowel.

12. The antepenult, if accented, takes only the acute. It can receive the accent only when the ultima is short. The majority of words with short ultima are accented on the antepenult; e. g. ἄνθρωπος.

13. The penult, if accented, takes the circumflex when it is long and the ultima is short: παῖδες. In all other cases when the penult is accented it takes the acute: νέος, δῶρου.

NOTE.—When οι and αι are final they count as short for purposes of accent, except in the optative mood and in the adverb οἴκοι: e. g. λέγεται, ἄνθρωποι, but κελεύοι (optative of a verb).

14. The ultima, if accented, may take either the acute or the circumflex; the acute only when it is short, but either the acute or the circumflex when it is long: καλός, καλοῦ, καλούς.

15. In pronouncing Greek we give each of the accents exactly the same force, that is, a mere stress upon the syllable accented. In ancient times the accents represented differences in pitch. The marks of accent were invented about 200 B. C. by Aristophanes, an Alexandrian scholar, as an assistance in teaching foreigners the correct pronunciation of Greek.

16. These rules of accent may be made clearer by the following scheme, in which the quantity of the syllable is indicated by the signs – and ⌣:

Accent on the Antepenult			*On the Penult*			*On the Ultima*		
́–	–	⌣	⌣̃	⌃	⌣			
́–	⌣	⌣	⌣̃	́–	–			
⌣́	⌣	⌣	⌣̃	⌣́	–	⌣̃	⌣̃	⌣́
⌣́	–	⌣	⌣̃	⌣́	⌣	⌣̃	⌣̃	́– *or* ⌃

17. A word with the acute accent on the ultima is called oxytone. An oxytone changes its acute to the grave when used before another word in the same clause. This is practically the only occasion for the grave accent; e. g. ἐπὶ τὴν ὁδόν, ἣν ὁρᾶτε, *to the road, which you see.*

18. Accent the bold-faced syllables in ἐκεινος, τουτων, δωρον, μονον, ουδε, ἡγηται, ἐνδοθεν, ἀνθρωποι (noun). What is the quantity of the ultima in Ἕλληνας, ἐνταῦθα, χώρα, μῑκρᾶς, θάλαττα?

19. Every vowel or diphthong at the beginning of a word has a breathing. The rough breathing (ʽ) shows that the vowel is preceded by the sound of the letter *h;* the smooth (ʼ) merely marks the absence of any *h*-sound. ἐν, *en;* ἑν, *hen.*

20. The breathing is placed over the second vowel of a diphthong; e. g. **αἰ, Οἰ.** The accent with the breathing is placed thus: **αἶ, αἶς, οἴ,** etc. Accent and breathing are placed before an initial capital vowel, not over it: Ὅμηρος;

in the case of diphthongs, accent and breathing remain on the second vowel: Εὖρος, Αἰνείᾱς.   ᾳ, ῃ, and ῳ, when capitalized at the beginning of a word, are written Αι, Ηι, and Ωι, but the accents and breathings are placed as in the case of single initial letters; e. g. ῞Αιδης, *Hades*.   All words beginning with ρ or υ have the rough breathing: ὑπέρ, *hyper;* ῥήτωρ, *rhetor.*

21. A few monosyllables have no accent, but are closely attached to the word following.   They are called proclitics (πρό+κλίνω, *lean forward*): ἐν ἀρχῇ, *in a province.*

22. A word which loses its own accent and is pronounced as if it were a part of the preceding word is called an enclitic (ἐν+κλίνω, *lean on*): ἀγαθός ἐστιν, *he is good.*[1]   For the effect of an enclitic on the accent of the preceding word see 115.

23. Of the Greek marks of punctuation, the comma and the period are the same as in English.   The colon is a point above the line (·), and takes the place of both the colon and the semicolon of English.   The mark of interrogation (;) is the same as the English semicolon.

24. When reading Greek pronounce proper names with the Greek sound of the letters and the accent as written, but in translating pronounce with the English sound of the letters and the Latin accent, i. e. with the accent on the penult if long, otherwise on the antepenult: Κλέαρχος, but English *Cleárchus;* Σωκράτης, but English *Sócrates.*

25. The values of the Greek letters in transliteration (transference into English) are seen on p. 1, "Sounds." Note, however, that

---

[1] We have practically the same thing in English: in "Téll me the néws," "me" is closely attached to "tell," and "the" to "news." Thus "me" is enclitic and "the" proclitic.

Z = *z*	**Zεύς** = *Z*eus
κ = *c*	**Κῦρος** = *C*yrus
υ = *y*	**Κῦρος** = *C*yrus
αι = *ae* (pronounce *ē*)	**Ἀριαῖος** = *A*riaeus
οι = *oe* (pronounce *ē*)	**Οἰδίπους** = *O*edipus
ει = *ī* or *ē*	**Δᾱρεῖος** = *D*arius; **Αἰνείᾱς** = *A*eneas
ου = *u*	**Οὐρανίᾱ** = *U*rania

In the second declension **ος, ον, οι** (nom. plu.) = *us*, *um*, and *i;* e. g. Κῦρος = Cyrus, Ἴλιον = Ilium; Δελφοί = Delphi. Some irregular English forms have become fixed; e. g. Ἀθῆναι, *Athens;* Ἀριστοτέλης, *Aristotle;* Πλάτων, *Plato;* Ὅμηρος, *Homer.*

26. Transliterate and mark the accented syllable of the English form of Ἀμαζών, Θουκυδίδης, Ἑλλάς, Κελαιναί, Βυζάντιον, Χειρίσοφος, Εὐριδίκη, Ξενίᾱς, Μίλητος, Θύμβριον, Οἰνεύς, Ἄρτεμις, Ῥαδάμανθος (Ῥ = Rh).

27. In most modern editions capitals are used only with proper nouns (and with proper adjectives), and at the beginning of paragraphs and direct quotations.

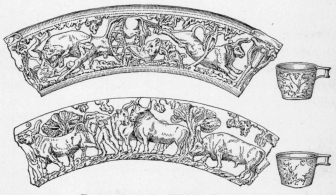

Fig. 1.—Capturing Wild Cattle

LESSON I

The Verb. Introductory

28. The verb has three voices: active, middle, and passive. The middle voice indicates that the subject acts upon himself or for his own advantage. Except in two tenses (future and aorist), the forms of the middle and passive are identical. φαίνει, *he shows;* φαίνεται (middle), *he shows himself, appears;* φαίνεται (passive), *he is shown.*

29. There are four finite moods: the indicative, subjunctive, optative, and imperative. The verb has also infinitives, participles, and verbal adjectives.

30. There are seven tenses: the present, imperfect, aorist, future, perfect, pluperfect, and future perfect. The present, future, perfect, and future perfect are called primary (or principal) tenses; the imperfect, aorist, and pluperfect refer to the past and are called secondary (or historical) tenses.

31. In general the Greek tenses correspond in meaning to those in Latin. The aorist takes the place of the historical perfect.

32. The accent of verbs is recessive, i. e. it recedes as far as possible from the end of the word. If the verb has three or more syllables, it takes the acute on the antepenult, provided the ultima is short; but if the ultima is long, it takes the acute on the penult. A verb of two syllables has the accent on the penult—the circumflex, if the penult is long and the ultima short, otherwise the acute (see 10–14).

33. There are three numbers: singular, dual, and plural. The dual[1] denotes two persons.

---

[1] As it occurs but rarely, some teachers will prefer to omit it in the paradigms. The exercises do not require a knowledge of the dual.

34. ν is added to certain words at the end of a clause or when the next word begins with a vowel. This ν is called ν-movable. The most common of these words are those ending in σι, verb forms ending in ε in the third person singular, and ἐστί; cf. Eng. aν apple.

35　　　　　The Present Indicative Active

Singular

1	λύω, *I loose*	ἔχω, *I have*	
2	λύεις, *you loose*	ἔχεις	
3	λύει, *he looses*	ἔχει	

Dual

2	λύετον, *you two loose*	ἔχετον
3	λύετον, *they two loose*	ἔχετον

Plural

1	λύομεν, *we loose*	ἔχομεν
2	λύετε, *you loose*	ἔχετε
3	λύουσι, *they loose*	ἔχουσι

Singular

1	τάττω, *I arrange*	ἀθροίζω, *I collect*
2	τάττεις	ἀθροίζεις
3	τάττει	ἀθροίζει

Dual

2	τάττετον	ἀθροίζετον
3	τάττετον	ἀθροίζετον

Plural

1	τάττομεν	ἀθροίζομεν
2	τάττετε	ἀθροίζετε
3	τάττουσι	ἀθροίζουσι

36.　　　　　　　VOCABULARY

ἀθροίζω (also ἀθροΐζω), *collect.*　　　λύω, *loose.* [ana**lysis**]
ἔχω, *have.*　　　　　　　　　　　　τάττω, *arrange, appoint.* [**tactics**]

37.　　　　　　　　EXERCISES

I. 1. λύει. 2. ἔχουσιν.[1] 3. τάττω. 4. λύομεν. 5. ἀθροίζεις. 6. ἔχετε. 7. τάττουσι. 8. ἀθροίζετε. 9. τάττει. 10. ἔχομεν.

II. 1. He has. 2. They arrange. 3. I collect. 4. We have. 5. You loose. 6. They collect. 7. He arranges. 8. We loose. 9. You collect. 10. They have.

---

[1] See 34.

LESSON II

NOUNS. THE SECOND OR o-DECLENSION

38. There are five cases: nominative, genitive, dative, accusative, and vocative. These cases express in general the same relations as the corresponding cases in Latin, except that in Greek the uses of the Latin ablative are divided between the dative and the genitive.

39. There are three genders: masculine, feminine, and neuter; and three numbers: singular, dual, and plural. There are three declensions: the First or α-Declension, the Second or o-Declension, and the Third or Consonant Declension. Compare the Latin declensions.

40. THE SECOND OR o-DECLENSION OF NOUNS AND ADJECTIVES

βίος, ὁ, *life*　　　　　　ὁ ἀγαθὸς υἱός, *the good son*

Singular

N.	βίος, *a life*	N.	ὁ ἀγαθὸς υἱός
G.	βίου, *of a life*	G.	τοῦ ἀγαθοῦ υἱοῦ
D.	βίῳ, *to* or *for a life*	D.	τῷ ἀγαθῷ υἱῷ
A.	βίον, *a life*	A.	τὸν ἀγαθὸν υἱόν
V.	βίε, *O life*	V.	ἀγαθὲ υἱέ

Dual

N. A. V.	βίω	N. A. V.	τὼ ἀγαθὼ υἱώ
G. D.	βίοιν	G. D.	τοῖν ἀγαθοῖν υἱοῖν

Plural

N.	βίοι, *lives*	N.	οἱ ἀγαθοὶ υἱοί
G.	βίων, *of lives*	G.	τῶν ἀγαθῶν υἱῶν
D.	βίοις, *to* or *for lives*	D.	τοῖς ἀγαθοῖς υἱοῖς
A.	βίους, *lives*	A.	τοὺς ἀγαθοὺς υἱούς
V.	βίοι, *O lives*	V.	ἀγαθοὶ υἱοί

πεδίον, τό, *the plain*

	Singular		*Plural*
N.	πεδίον	N.	πεδία
G.	πεδίου	G.	πεδίων
D.	πεδίῳ	D.	πεδίοις
A.	πεδίον	A.	πεδία
V.	πεδίον	V.	πεδία

Dual

N. A. V.	πεδίω	G. D.	πεδίοιν

τὸ καλὸν δῶρον, *the beautiful gift*

	Singular		*Plural*
N.	τὸ καλὸν δῶρον	N.	τὰ καλὰ δῶρα
G.	τοῦ καλοῦ δώρου	G.	τῶν καλῶν δώρων
D.	τῷ καλῷ δώρῳ	D.	τοῖς καλοῖς δώροις
A.	τὸ καλὸν δῶρον	A.	τὰ καλὰ δῶρα
V.	καλὸν δῶρον	V.	καλὰ δῶρα

Dual

N. A. V. τὼ καλὼ δώρω   G. D. τοῖν καλοῖν δώροιν

41. The stem of the second declension ends in *o*, the nominative in *os* or *ov*. Nouns in *os* are masculine, rarely feminine; those in *ov* are neuter. Compare the Latin *us* (early spelling *os*) and *um* (*om*). The accent of nouns is retentive, i. e. it remains on the same syllable as in the nominative unless the laws of accent require some change. (Cf. 10–14.)

42. When the accent falls on the ultima, it is acute in the nominative, accusative, and vocative, but circumflex in the genitive and dative, of all numbers.

43. Greek, unlike Latin, has the great advantage of possessing a definite article. ὁ, *the*, is declined like an adjective (the forms ὁ, ἡ, οἱ, and αἱ are proclitic), and agrees with its noun in gender, number, and case; as in English, it has no vocative. There is no indefinite article. It must be supplied in translation, if needed. In the vocabulary the article is placed after a noun as a convenient means of indicating gender. Thus υἱός, οὗ, ὁ is a masculine noun with genitive υἱοῦ.

44. Observe that in neuters the nominative, accusative, and vocative in each number are alike, and that in the plural these cases end in *a*. This is true of neuter nouns of all declensions. Cf. the Latin *templum, flumen, cornu*.

45. When the article is used with a noun and an attributive adjective, the adjective must be immediately preceded

by the article. Thus *the good son* is ὁ ἀγαθὸς υἱός or ὁ υἱὸς
ὁ ἀγαθός. The adjective usually stands between the article
and the noun. This is called the attributive position. A
limiting genitive may or may not be in the attributive position: ὁ Κύρου βίος or ὁ βίος Κύρου or Κύρου ὁ βίος, *the life
of Cyrus.*

46. A neuter substantive in the plural regularly takes a
verb in the singular. τὰ δῶρα ἦν καλά, *the gifts were
beautiful.*

47.   VOCABULARY

ἀγαθός, *good, honorable.* [**Agatha**]

βίος, ου, ὁ, *life.* [**bio**logy]

γυμνάζω, *exercise.* [**gymnastics**]

δῶρον, ου, τό, *gift.* [Pan**dora**]

εἰς, prep. with acc., *to, into.* [**es**-
oteric]

ἐκ, prep. with gen., *from, out of.*
[**ec**lectic]

ἐν, prep. with dat., *in.*

ἦν, *was.*

ἦσαν, *were.*

ἵππος, ου, ὁ, *horse.* [**hippo**potamus]

καλός, *beautiful,* adj. [**Calli**ope]

πεδίον, ου, τό, *plain.*

ποταμός, οῦ, ὁ, *river.*   [Meso**po**-
tamia]

στρατηγός, οῦ, ὁ, *general.* [**strategy**]

υἱός, οῦ, ὁ, *son.*

48.   DRILL

I. 1. βίων. 2. τοῦ ἵππου. 3. στρατηγοῖς. 4. τοὺς βίους. 5. πεδίῳ.
    6. οἱ ἵπποι.

II. 1. Generals. 2. From the rivers. 3. To the plains. 4. The
     horses of the general. 5. For the sons. 6. The plains.

49.   EXERCISES

I. 1. οἱ στρατηγοὶ ἔχουσι τὰ δῶρα. 2. ἵππους καλοὺς ἔχο-
    μεν τοῖς ἀγαθοῖς υἱοῖς. 3. τὰ πεδία ἦν καλά. 4. ὁ τοῦ
    στρατηγοῦ υἱὸς ἀθροίζει τοὺς ἵππους ἐκ τῶν πεδίων.
    5. γυμνάζουσι τοὺς ἵππους τῶν στρατηγῶν.

II. 1. The life of the general was honorable. 2. He has
     good gifts for the generals. 3. You are arranging the
     beautiful horses in the plain. 4. The sons of the gen-
     erals are exercising the horses. 5. There were rivers
     in the plain.

LESSON III

The **a-** or First Declension. Nouns in η. The Article

50. Nouns of the first declension end in ᾱ, ᾰ, η, feminine, and ᾱς, ης, masculine. The stem ends in ᾱ. Differences in declension are confined to the singular. The dual and plural are alike for all nouns.

51.

Singular

N.	ἀρχή, *rule*	ἡ φίλη κώμη, *the friendly village*
G.	ἀρχῆς	τῆς φίλης κώμης
D.	ἀρχῇ	τῇ φίλῃ κώμῃ
A.	ἀρχήν	τὴν φίλην κώμην
V.	ἀρχή	φίλη κώμη

Dual

N. A. V.	ἀρχά	τὼ φίλᾱ κώμᾱ
G. D.	ἀρχαῖν	τοῖν φίλαιν κώμαιν

Plural

N. V.	ἀρχαί	αἱ φίλαι κῶμαι
G.	ἀρχῶν	τῶν φίλων κωμῶν
D.	ἀρχαῖς	ταῖς φίλαις κώμαις
A.	ἀρχάς	τὰς φίλᾱς κώμᾱς

In the same manner decline τελευτή, *end;* μάχη, *battle.*

DECLENSION OF THE DEFINITE ARTICLE

Singular

	MASCULINE	FEMININE	NEUTER
N.	ὁ	ἡ	τό
G.	τοῦ	τῆς	τοῦ
D.	τῷ	τῇ	τῷ
A.	τόν	τήν	τό

Dual

N. A.	τώ	G. D.	τοῖν

Plural

N.	οἱ	αἱ	τά
G.	τῶν	τῶν	τῶν
D.	τοῖς	ταῖς	τοῖς
A.	τούς	τάς	τά

52. The article frequently has the force of a possessive pronoun: Ἀρταξέρξης ὑποπτεύει τὸν ἀδελφόν, *Artaxerxes suspects* his *brother.*

53. An acute accent on the ultima becomes a circumflex in the genitive and dative of all numbers. The genitive plural of all first-declension nouns has the circumflex on the ultima.

54.   VOCABULARY

ἄγω, *bring, lead.*

ἀδελφός,[1] οῦ, ὁ, *brother.* [Phil**adel**-**phia**]

ἀρχή, ῆς, ἡ, *rule, province.* [an-**archy**]

Δᾱρεῖος, ου, ὁ, *Darius.*

καί, *and, also, even.*

κώμη, ης, ἡ, *village.*

μάχη, ης, ἡ, *battle.* [logo**machy**]

ὁ, ἡ, τό, *the,* definite article.

πέμπω, *send.* [**pomp**]

σκηνή, ῆς, ἡ, *tent.* [**scene**]

τελευτή, ῆς, ἡ, *end.* [**tele**ology]

ὑποπτεύω, *suspect.*

φίλος, η, ον, *friendly.* [**philo**sophy]

ὦ, interj., with voc. *O.*

55.   DRILL

Give: (1) gen. sing.; (2) gen. plu.; (3) dat. sing.; (4) dat. plu.; (5) acc. sing.; (6) acc. plu.; (7) voc. sing.; (8) nom. plu., of ἡ σκηνή, ὁ ἀδελφός, τὸ πεδίον, ἡ κώμη, ὁ βίος.

56.   EXERCISES

I. 1. ἡ καλὴ σκηνὴ ἦν ἐν τῇ κώμῃ.   2. οἱ ἀδελφοὶ ἦσαν ἀγα-θοί.   3. ἄγει τοὺς ἵππους ἐκ τῶν κωμῶν.   4. ὦ υἱέ, ἔχεις σκηνὰς ἐν τοῖς πεδίοις.   5. ἡ τοῦ βίου τελευτή.   6. πέμπο-μεν τὰς σκηνὰς τοῖς Δᾱρείου υἱοῖς.   7. ἐν τῇ ἀρχῇ ἦν μάχη.

II. 1. In the province were beautiful plains.   2. They are bringing the tents to the village.   3. We are bringing gifts from the villages.   4. He arranges the tents in the plain.   5. There were battles in the villages.

---

[1] The vocative singular is irregular in accent: ἄδελφε.

LESSON IV

First Declension. Nouns in ā or a

57. Nouns ending in *a* retain the *a* throughout after ε, ι, or ρ. If preceded by any other letter, *a* becomes η in the genitive and dative singular. The accent of the nominative will usually show whether the final *a* is long or short; in the accusative and vocative it will have the same quantity as in the nominative. Final *as* is always long. *(gen. sing. + acc. pl. of first declension)*

✓ 58.

	Singular		Plural
N. V.	ἡ μῑκρὰ στρατιά, *the small army*	N. V.	αἱ μῑκραὶ στρατιαί
G.	τῆς μῑκρᾶς στρατιᾶς	G.	τῶν μῑκρῶν στρατιῶν
D.	τῇ μῑκρᾷ στρατιᾷ	D.	ταῖς μῑκραῖς στρατιαῖς
A.	τὴν μῑκρὰν στρατιάν	A.	τὰς μῑκρὰς στρατιάς

Dual

N. A. V. τὼ μῑκρὰ στρατιά
G. D. τοῖν μῑκραῖν στρατιαῖν

Singular

N. V.	καλὴ γέφῡρα, *a beautiful bridge*	θάλαττα, *sea*
G.	καλῆς γεφύρᾱς	θαλάττης
D.	καλῇ γεφύρᾳ	θαλάττῃ
A.	καλὴν γέφῡραν	θάλατταν

Dual

N. A. V.	καλὰ γεφύρᾱ	θαλάττᾱ
G. D.	καλαῖν γεφύραιν	θαλάτταιν

Plural

N. V.	καλαὶ γέφῡραι	θάλατται
G.	καλῶν γεφῡρῶν	θαλαττῶν
D.	καλαῖς γεφύραις	θαλάτταις
A.	καλὰς γεφύρᾱς	θαλάττᾱς

Thus decline ἡμέρᾱ, *day;* οἰκίᾱ, *house;* θύρᾱ, *door;* ἄμαξα, *wagon.*

59. Learn the declension of the adjectives μῑκρός, φίλος. For forms see Appendix (612).

60. Observe that in adjectives of the first and second declensions the feminine singular ends in *a* if ε, ι, or ρ precede, otherwise in η. Oxytone adjectives have the circumflex in the genitive and dative of all numbers; other adjectives follow the rules already given (see 10–14).

61.   VOCABULARY

ἀγορά, ᾶς, ἡ, *market.*

ἄμαξα, ης, ἡ, *wagon.*

γέφῡρα, ᾱς, ἡ, *bridge.*

ἡμέρᾱ, ᾱς, ἡ, *day.* [eph**emeral**]

θάλαττα, ης, ἡ, *sea.*

θύρᾱ, ᾱς, ἡ, *door.*

μῑκρός, ά, όν, *small.* [**micro**scope]

οἰκίᾱ, ᾱς. ἡ, *house.* [**eco**nomy]

στρατιά, ᾶς, ἡ, *army.*

χώρᾱ, ᾱς, ἡ, *country.*

62.   DRILL

Give: (1) gen. sing.; (2) gen. plu.; (3) dat. sing.; (4) dat. plu.; (5) acc. sing.; (6) nom. plu., of ἡ ἡμέρᾱ, ὁ ἵππος, ἡ κώμη, τὶ δῶρον, ἡ ἄμαξα.

63.   EXERCISES

I.   1. ἦν ἡ χώρᾱ τοῦ ἀδελφοῦ.   2. αἱ μῑκραὶ ἀγοραὶ ἦσαν καλαί.   3. εἰς τὴν Δᾱρείου κώμην.   4. αἱ τῶν οἰκιῶν θύραι.   5. πέμπει τὰς ἀμάξᾱς ἐκ τῆς χώρᾱς.   6. τάττουσι τὴν στρατιὰν τῷ[1] Δᾱρείῳ.   7. ἔχομεν ἀγορὰν ἐν τῇ κώμῃ.   8. πέμπουσι τοὺς ἵππους εἰς τὴν ἀγοράν.   9. ἄγει τὴν στρατιὰν εἰς τὴν θάλατταν.   10. ἔχετε δῶρα τοῖς στρατηγοῖς Δᾱρείου.

II.   1. The doors of the house were small and beautiful. 2. They are bringing wagons to the market-places of the villages.   3. There were tents in the house.   4. The general sends a beautiful horse for his son.   5. The end of the day was beautiful.

---

[1] With proper names of persons already mentioned or well known the article may be used.

LESSON V

THE IMPERFECT INDICATIVE ACTIVE. MASCULINE NOUNS OF THE FIRST DECLENSION

64. The secondary tenses of the indicative mood (30) have an augment (increase) at the beginning.

65. Augment is of two kinds:

I. All verbs beginning with a consonant prefix ε. This is called the syllabic augment; e. g. λύω, ἔλυον.

II. Verbs beginning with a vowel lengthen this vowel, if it is not already long; if a verb begins with a diphthong, the first vowel of the diphthong is lengthened. This is the temporal augment. Thus, α and ε become η: e. g. ἀθροίζω, ἤθροιζον; ι, ο, and υ become ῑ, ω, and ῡ; αι becomes ῃ, and οι becomes ῳ; but ου remains unchanged.

66. Compound verbs are formed, as in Latin, by combining a preposition and a simple verb. If the preposition ends in a vowel and the verb also begins with one, the final vowel of the preposition is dropped (elided), except in the words πρό and περί: ὑπό + ὀπτεύω = ὑπ-οπτεύω, παρά + ἦν = παρ-ῆν; περί + ἔχω = περι-έχω. The augment of compound verbs comes between the preposition and the verb: ἀνα-βαίνω, ὑπ-οπτεύω (present), ἀν-έβαινον, ὑπ-ώπτευον (imperfect). ἔχω has the irregular augment εἶχον (ἔ-εχον). The accent of compound verbs never comes before the augment: κατεῖχον.

67. The imperfect is confined to the indicative mood, and represents an action or state as in progress or as repeated in past time.

68.   THE IMPERFECT INDICATIVE ACTIVE

	Singular	Dual	Plural
1	ἔλυον, *I loosed*		ἐλύομεν, *we loosed*
2	ἔλυες, *you loosed*	ἐλύετον, *you two loosed*	ἐλύετε, *you loosed*
3	ἔλυε, *he loosed*	ἐλυέτην, *they two loosed*	ἔλυον, *they loosed*

69.   Masculine Nouns of the First Declension

Singular

N.	στρατιώτης, *soldier*		N.	σατράπης, *satrap*
→ G.	στρατιώτου		→ G.	σατράπου
D.	στρατιώτῃ		D.	σατράπῃ
A.	στρατιώτην		A.	σατράπην
→ V.	στρατιῶτα		→ V.	σατράπη

Dual

N. A. V.	στρατιώτᾱ		N. A. V.	σατράπᾱ
G. D.	στρατιώταιν		G. D.	σατράπαιν

Plural

N. V.	στρατιῶται		N. V.	σατράπαι
G.	στρατιωτῶν		G.	σατραπῶν
D.	στρατιώταις		D.	σατράπαις
A.	στρατιώτᾱς		A.	σατράπᾱς

<u>Nouns in</u> *της* have the vocative in *a.* So also Πέρσης.

Observe that all nouns of the first declension are declined alike in the dual and the plural, and that in masculines the differences are confined to the nominative, genitive, and vocative singular.

Like σατράπης decline Ἀρταξέρξης (singular only). Form the imperfect of ἄγω, *lead;* τάττω, *arrange;* πέμπω, *send;* ἁρπάζω, *plunder;* διαρπάζω, *pillage.*

70.   VOCABULARY

ἁρπάζω, *plunder.* [**harpy**]   σατράπης, ου, ὁ, *satrap.*
Ἀρταξέρξης, ου, ὁ, *Artaxerxes.*   στρατιώτης, ου, ὁ, *soldier.*
διαρπάζω, *pillage.*

71.   DRILL

Give: (1) 2 sing. pres. and imp.; (2) 2 plu. pres. and imp.; (3) 3 sing. pres. and imp.; (4) 3 plu. pres. and imp.; (5) 1 plu. pres. and imp. of τάττω, ἄγω, ἔχω, ὑποπτεύω.

72.   EXERCISES

I.   1. ἔλυεν,[1] εἴχετε, ὑπώπτευον.   2. ἐτάττομεν τὴν στρατιάν.
    3. ἠθροίζετε τοὺς στρατιώτᾱς.   4. εἶχον ἁμάξᾱς καὶ σκηνάς.

---

[1] See 34.

5. λύουσι τοὺς υἱούς. 6. ἐπέμπομεν τὸν στρατιώτην εἰς τὴν κώμην. 7. ἐν τῷ πεδίῳ ἦσαν οἰκίαι. 8. ἤγομεν τοὺς ἵππους ἐκ τοῦ ποταμοῦ. 9. αἱ τῶν στρατιωτῶν σκηναὶ ἦσαν ἐν τῇ κώμῃ. 10. ὁ τοῦ Ἀρταξέρξου ἀδελφὸς ἔπεμπε δῶρα τοῖς σατράπαις.

II. 1. We loosed. You led. He suspected. 2. I had. They sent. You were collecting. 3. He sent gifts for the soldiers of Artaxerxes. 4. He led the horse of the soldier to the tent. 5. Artaxerxes had soldiers in the market-place.

LESSON VI

THE FUTURE AND FIRST AND SECOND AORISTS INDICATIVE ACTIVE

73. Every verb has a verb-stem from which all its parts are formed. This verb-stem is often identical with the present stem, except that the present stem adds a vowel between the verb-stem and the personal ending, called the connecting or thematic vowel. In this book, when the verb-stem is given it is placed in brackets after the verb.

74. The future tense is generally formed from the verb-stem by the addition of σω, σεις, etc. Its conjugation is therefore identical with that of the present tense, except for the insertion of the σ.

75. The first aorist adds σα to the verb-stem; the *a* becomes ε in the third person singular. σα may be called the tense sign of the first aorist active.

76. The English verb as a rule forms the past tense by the addition of *ed*, but many verbs in common use form it differently; e. g. *pass, passed,* but *catch, caught; take, took,* etc. In Greek the situation is somewhat similar. Some verbs have a first and some a second aorist; a very few have both. As in English the "second aorist" is found in some of the verbs most commonly used. *(learned, learnt)*

77. The second aorist is inflected in the indicative like the imperfect. It regularly has the unmodified verb-stem, while the imperfect has the stem of the present tense. In most verbs having a second aorist the present stem is noticeably different from the verb-stem; e. g. ἐλάμβανον (imperfect), ἔλαβον (second aorist), both from λαμβάνω, whose verb-stem is λαβ.

78. When in inflection σ comes after a mute (599), euphonic changes occur:

I. A π-mute (π, β, φ) and a following σ combine to form the double consonant ψ; πέμπω, πέμψω (πέμπσω), ἔπεμψα (ἔπεμπσα). *also π τ*

II. A κ-mute (κ, γ, χ) and a following σ combine to form the double consonant ξ: λέγω, λέξω (λέγσω), ἔλεξα (ἔλεγσα). *also σσ or ττ*

III. A τ-mute (τ, δ, θ) before σ is dropped: ἀθροίζω [ἀθροιδ], ἀθροίσω (ἀθροίδσω), ἤθροισα (ἤθροιδσα). *or ζ*

79. The aorist indicative indicates merely the occurrence of an action, or a state in past time. Carefully distinguish this from the meaning of the imperfect (67). *eg. He went home.*

80. The principal parts of a verb are the first person singular indicative of all the tense systems which the verb has. Usually the principal parts will be the present active, future active, first aorist active, first perfect active, perfect middle, first aorist passive. In verbs which have the second aorist and second perfect, these take the places of the first aorist and the first perfect.

II Aorist - Augment + II aorist stem + imperfect endings

FUTURE AND FIRST AND SECOND AORISTS INDICATIVE ACTIVE

81.

FUTURE
Singular

1	λύσω, *I shall loose*	λέξω, *I shall say*
2	λύσεις	λέξεις
3	λύσει	λέξει

Dual

2	λύσετον	λέξετον
3	λύσετον	λέξετον

Plural

1	λύσομεν	λέξομεν
2	λύσετε	λέξετε
3	λύσουσι	λέξουσι

FIRST AORIST
Singular

1	ἔλῡσα, *I loosed*	ἔλεξα, *I said*
2	ἔλῡσας	ἔλεξας
3	ἔλῡσε	ἔλεξε

Dual

2	ἐλύσατον	ἐλέξατον
3	ἐλῡσάτην	ἐλεξάτην

Plural

1	ἐλύσαμεν	ἐλέξαμεν
2	ἐλύσατε	ἐλέξατε
3	ἔλῡσαν	ἔλεξαν

SECOND AORIST

	Singular	Dual		Plural
1	ἔλιπον, *I left*		1	ἐλίπομεν
2	ἔλιπες	ἐλίπετον	2	ἐλίπετε
3	ἔλιπε	ἐλιπέτην	3	ἔλιπον

Conjugate thus in the future and first aorist πέμπω, ἀθροίζω[ἀθροιδ], τάττω[ταγ] and the second aorist of ἄγω (ἤγαγον). [αγαγ]

82. ## VOCABULARY

ἄνθρωπος, ου, ὁ, *man.* [phil**an**-**thropic**]

θύω, θύσω, ἔθῡσα, *sacrifice.*

λέγω, λέξω, ἔλεξα, *say, speak.* [**lexi**-**con**] 2 ar.

λείπω, λείψω, ἔλιπον, *leave.* [el**lipsis**]

λόγος, ου, ὁ, *word.* [bio**logy**, log-arithm]

οὐ, οὐκ, οὐχ, *not:* οὐ before a consonant; οὐκ before a vowel with smooth breathing; οὐχ before a vowel with rough breathing.

πρό, prep. with gen., *before.* [**pro**-logue]

τράπεζα, ης, ἡ, *table.* [**trapeze**]

83. DRILL

Give: 1. 3 sing. of pres., fut., imp., and aor. of τάττω.
      2. 3 plu. of pres., fut., imp., and aor. of πέμπω.
      3. 1 sing. of pres., fut., imp., and aor. of ἁρπάζω.
      4. 2 plu. of pres., fut., imp., and aor. of λύω.

84. EXERCISES

I. 1. λύσει, ἔλιπεν, ἔλειπον. 2. ἄγομεν, ἤγομεν, ἄξομεν.
3. ἀθροίζουσι, ἤθροιζον, ἤθροισαν. 4. τάττεις, ἔταττες,
τάξεις, ἔταξας. 5. ἐγύμνασαν οἱ στρατιῶται τοὺς ἵππους
ἐν τῷ πεδίῳ. 6. ἤγαγε τὴν τράπεζαν εἰς τὴν οἰκίᾱν. 7. οὐκ
εἶχον σκηνὰς ἐν τῇ κώμῃ. 8. ἔταξα τοὺς στρατιώτᾱς ἐν τῇ
μάχῃ. 9. ἄξει δῶρα τῷ στρατιώτῃ. 10. οὐ θύομεν τῇ
θαλάττῃ.

II. 1. He leaves, he will leave, he left. 2. They will lead,
they were leading, they led. 3. You exercise, you ex-
ercised, you were exercising. 4. We suspected, we shall
suspect, we were suspecting. 5. The satraps did not
send the soldiers to the plain before the battle.

———

LESSON VII

THE PRESENT AND IMPERFECT MIDDLE (PASSIVE)

85. In general the middle voice indicates that the subject
is especially interested in the action of the verb. It represents the subject as acting (1) upon himself—the direct middle:
παύομαι, *I stop myself, cease;* (2) for himself or on something belonging to himself—the indirect middle: ποιοῦμαι
οἰκίᾱς, *I make myself houses,* λύεται τὸν ἀδελφόν, *he ransoms
his (own) brother.* The indirect middle is the more common,
and, through lack of means to translate it fully into English,
is often hardly to be distinguished in translation from the
active. Its force may often be best brought out by the use

of an active verb of apparently different meaning: παύω, *I put a stop to*, παύομαι, *I cease;* λύω, *I loose*, λύομαι, *I ransom;* πείθω, *I persuade*, πείθομαι, *I obey;* αἱρέω, *I take*, αἱροῦμαι, *I choose.* In such cases the English equivalent of the middle must be especially noted.

86. A verb which has the middle (passive, 246) form, but active meaning, is called a deponent verb, as in Latin. The Vocabulary indicates such verbs by giving the middle form instead of the active.

87.   PRESENT AND IMPERFECT MIDDLE (AND PASSIVE)

	Present	*Imperfect*
Sing.	λύομαι, *I ransom*	ἐλῡόμην, *I ransomed*
	λύει,	ἐλύου
	λύεται	ἐλύετο
Dual,	2 λύεσθον, 3 λύεσθον	2 ἐλύεσθον, 3 ἐλῡέσθην
Plu.	λῡόμεθα	ἐλῡόμεθα
	λύεσθε	ἐλύεσθε
	λύονται	ἐλύοντο

Thus conjugate νομίζω, ἔχω, τάττω, ἀθροίζω, βούλομαι, ἀναβαίνω.

88.   VOCABULARY

ἀναβαίνω, ἀναβήσομαι,[1] *march up.*
ἀπό, prep. with gen., *from.*
βούλομαι, βουλήσομαι, (depon.), *wish.*
γίγνομαι, γενήσομαι, ἐγενόμην (2. aor.), *become, be born.* [**genus, genitive**]
μετά, prep. with gen., *with;* with acc., *after.* [**meth**od, **meta**phor]
μεταπέμπομαι, μεταπέμψομαι, μετεπεμψάμην, (depon.), *send for, summon.*
νομίζω, νομιῶ,[2] ἐνόμισα, *think.*
πείθω, πείσω, ἔπεισα, act. *persuade;* mid. *obey* (dat.).
πορεύομαι, πορεύσομαι, (depon.), *proceed, march.*
φίλος, ου, ὁ, *friend.*

89.   DRILL

Give: (1) 3 sing.; (2) 3 plu. of pres. and imp. ind. act. and mid., of ἁρπάζω; (3) 2 sing.; (4) 1 plu. of fut. imp. and aor. ind. act., of τάττω.

---

[1] Some verbs are deponent in the future only.   [2] In Attic the future form νομιῶ is used instead of νομίσω.

90. EXERCISES

I. 1. ἔλῡον, ἐλῡ́ου, λῡ́εται. 2. λῡ́ονται, λῡ́ουσι, ἐλῡ́οντο.
3. ἀθροίζομεν, ἀθροίζομαι, ἠθροιζόμην. 4. ἔταξαν, ἐτάτ-
τετο, τάττονται. 5. οἱ στρατιῶται ἐπείθοντο τῷ σατράπῃ.
6. Κῦρος πορεύεται ἐκ τῆς ἀρχῆς. 7. μετεπέμπετο τοὺς
ἀδελφούς. 8. τὰ δῶρα ἤγετο ἐκ τῆς ἁμάξης. 9. Κῦρος
μεταπέμπεται τοὺς φίλους ἐκ τῶν μῑκρῶν κωμῶν. 10. ἀνέ-
βαινεν ἀπὸ τῆς θαλάττης εἰς τὰ πεδία.

II. 1. We wish, you proceeded, they obeyed. 2. He ransoms, they persuade, I marched up. 3. Cyrus ransomed
his friends. 4. The friends of the satrap became soldiers.
5. The tents were carried from the market to the house.

LESSON VIII

Review

91. Δᾱρείου καὶ Παρυσάτιδος[1] γίγνονται υἱοὶ δύο,
πρεσβύτερος μὲν Ἀρταξέρξης, νεώτερος δὲ Κῦρος. ἐπεὶ
δὲ Δᾱρεῖος ὑπώπτευε τελευτὴν τοῦ βίου, ἐβούλετο τοὺς
υἱοὺς ἀμφοτέρους παρεῖναι. ὁ μὲν οὖν πρεσβύτερος
παρῆν. Κῦρον δὲ μεταπέμπεται[2] ἀπὸ τῆς ἀρχῆς ἧς
σατράπης ἦν· ἀνέβαινε οὖν ὁ Κῦρος μετὰ Τισσαφέρνους[3]
ὡς φίλου.

92. VOCABULARY

ἀμφότερος, ᾱ, ον, *both.*
δέ, conj., *but, and* (postpositive).[4]
δύο, num. adj., *two* (Lat. *duo*, Eng. *two*).
ἐπεί, conj., *when, since.*
ἧς, *of which,* fem. gen. sing. of relative pronoun ὅς, ἥ, ὅ, *who, which.*

---

[1] Παρυσάτιδος, gen. of Παρύσατις, *Parysatis,* the wife of Darius. [2] The historical
present is freely used in Greek. [3] Τισσαφέρνους, gen. sing. of Τισσαφέρνης, *Tissaphernes,* a Persian satrap. [4] I. e. cannot stand first in a sentence or clause.

μέν, a particle used correlatively with δέ to show contrast or balance between sentences or parts of sentences: μέν, *on the one hand;* δέ, *on the other hand.* Sometimes with a concessive force, *while;* often, as in the text, best left untranslated or brought out by stress of voice. Postpositive.

νεώτερος, ᾱ, ον, adj. in comparative degree, *younger* (from νέος *young*). [**neophyte**]

οὖν, conj., *therefore, accordingly* (postpositive).

παρῆν, *was present* (παρά + ἦν); παρῆσαν, *were present.* Imp. ind. 3 sing. and 3 plu. of πάρειμι.

παρεῖναι, *to be present* (pres. infinitive of πάρειμι).

πρεσβύτερος, ᾱ, ον, adj. in comparative degree, *older.* [**presbyterian, priest**]

ὡς, rel. adv., *as, as if* (proclitic); conj., *when, since.*

93.   DRILL

Locate the following:

I. 1. ἀδελφῷ, βίους, στρατιώτην.
    2. ἀρχαί, σατράπου, κώμαις.
    3. πεδία, στρατιώτᾱς, ἀρχαῖν.
    4. ἀδελφώ, βίων, στρατιώτῃ.
    5. τελευτήν, υἱέ, πεδίον.
    6. λύει, ἔλῡεν, ἐλύου.
    7. ἀνεβαίνομεν, βούλεται, ἐβούλετο.
    8. ὑποπτεύουσιν, ἔλῡον, νομίζονται.
    9. ἐλύετον, ἐτάττοντο, ἀναβαίνεις.
    10. βούλεσθε, ἐλύεσθην, ἐβουλόμην.

II. 1. The houses, the plains, the lives, the wagons, the soldiers.
    2. Of the table, of the soldiers, of the son, of the satraps, of the battles.
    3. For the satraps, for the tables, for the plains, for the soldiers, for the provinces.
    4. The table and the door were brought.
    5. We are marching to the plains.

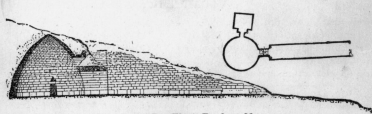

Fig. 2 —A " Bee-Hive " Tomb at Mycenae

LESSON IX

Review of the Verb. The Infinitive

94. ἐπεὶ ἀπέθανε Δαρεῖος καὶ κατέστη¹ εἰς τὴν βασι-
λείᾱν Ἀρταξέρξης, Τισσαφέρνης διαβάλλει τὸν Κῦρον
πρὸς τὸν ἀδελφὸν ὡς ἐπιβουλεύει αὐτῷ·² ὁ δὲ³ πείθεται
καὶ συλλαμβάνει Κῦρον ὡς ἀποκτενῶν,⁴ ἀποπέμπει δὲ
πάλιν ἐπὶ τὴν ἀρχήν.

95. VOCABULARY

ἀποθνῄσκω, ἀποθανοῦμαι (fut.), ἀπέθανον (2 aor.), *die.*

ἀποπέμπω, ἀποπέμψω, ἀπέπεμψα, *send away.*

αὐτός, ή, ό, *self, he, she, it.* [**autograph**]

βασιλείᾱ, ᾱς, ἡ, *sovereignty, kingdom, rule.*

διαβάλλω,⁵ διαβαλῶ (fut.), διέβαλον (2 aor.), *calumniate, slander.* [**diabolic, devil**]

ἐπί, prep., with gen., *on, upon;* with dat., *on, by, at;* with acc., *upon, to, against.* [**epi**taph, **ep**och]

ἐπιβουλεύω, ἐπιβουλεύσω, ἐπεβούλευσα, *plot.* Governs the dative.

πάλιν, adv., *back, again, a second time.* [**palim**psest, **palin**ode]

πρός, prep., with general meaning *facing;* with gen., *over against;* with dat., *at;* with acc., *to, with, against, toward.* [**pros**ody, **pros**elyte]

συλλαμβάνω, συλλήψομαι (fut.), συνέλαβον (2 aor.), *arrest.* [**syllable**]

REVIEW OF THE VERB

96. Tense stems are formed by adding suffixes to the verb stems. The suffix for the present tense stem is o in the first person singular and plural and third person plural, elsewhere ε. This double stem, e. g. λῡο and λῡε, is conveniently written λῡο/ε.   o/ε is called the thematic or connecting vowel.

---

¹ κατέστη, *was established.*   ² αὐτῷ, dat. sing. masc. of αὐτός, αὐτή, αὐτό. For declension see 629. In the oblique cases without the article it is a personal pronoun, *him, his, its, them.*   ³ ὁ δέ, *but he* or *and he;* at the beginning of a sentence or clause it usually indicates a change of subject.   ⁴ ἀποκτενῶν, fut. part. (nom. sing. masc.) to express purpose. With ὡς translate *with the (avowed) intention of putting him to death.*   ⁵ Cf. 230, 231.

97. To the present stem the personal endings are added. These unite with the stem vowel and give euphonic endings by which all regular verbs are conjugated.

EUPHONIC ENDINGS IN THE PRESENT AND IMPERFECT INDICATIVE

	PRESENT		IMPERFECT	
	Sing.	*Plu.*	*Sing.*	*Plu.*
1	-ω	-ομεν	-ον	-ομεν
2	-εις	-ετε	-ες	-ετε
3	-ει	-ουσι	-ε	-ον
	Dual		*Dual*	
2	-ετον		-ετον	
3	-ετον		-έτην	

✓**98.** Review the present, imperfect, future, and aorist active (35, 68, 81).

THE INFINITIVE

99. In the active voice the present infinitive ends in ειν, e. g. λύειν; the future infinitive in σειν, e. g. λύσειν; the first aorist infinitive in σαι, e. g. λῦσαι; the second aorist infinitive in εῖν, e. g. λιπεῖν. Observe that the aorist infinitive does not have the augment, and that the accent does not in all cases conform to the rule (32). The first aorist infinitive active is accented on the penult, and the second aorist infinitive active always has the circumflex on the ultima.

100. Except in indirect discourse, the present and aorist infinitives do not indicate time. The present is used when the action or state is represented as continuing or repeated (in the present, past, or future); otherwise the aorist is used.

101.　　　　　　　DRILL

I. Give the infinitives (pres., fut., 1 aor. or 2 aor.) of θίω, ἄγω, ὑποπτεύω, λείπω.

II. Give:
　1. 3 sing. pres. and imp. ind. act. and mid. of πείθω.
　2. 3 plu. fut. and aor. act. of λείπω.
　3. 1 sing. pres. and imp. mid. and fut. and aor. act. of ἄγω.
　4. dat. sing., dat. plu., acc. sing., acc. plu. of ἀγαθός and μικρός in all genders.

pres.　ειν　1 aor.　-σαι
fut.　σειν　2 aor.　εῖν

102. EXERCISES

I. 1. Κῦρος αὐτὸν ἔπειθε. 2. Κῦρος αὐτῷ ἐπείθετο. 3. ἀπὸ τῆς ἀρχῆς μετεπέμπετο Κῦρον. 4. οἱ ἀγαθοὶ στρατιῶται ἐβούλοντο ἀναβαίνειν. 5. ἔπεισεν Ἀρταξέρξην συλλαβεῖν τὸν νεώτερον ἀδελφόν. 6. Κῦρος οὐκ ἐπεβούλευε τῷ πρεσβυτέρῳ ἀδελφῷ.

II. 1. Artaxerxes was persuaded to arrest his younger brother. 2. Artaxerxes wished to send his brother away. 3. Tissaphernes will persuade him to arrest his brother. 4. The soldiers obey the elder brother and arrest Cyrus. 5. The kingdom was small and beautiful.

LESSON X

FUTURE AND AORIST MIDDLE

103. ὁ δὲ ὡς ἀπῆλθεν ἄτιμος, βουλεύεται ὅπως μήποτε ἔτι ἔσται[1] ἐπὶ[2] τῷ ἀδελφῷ, ἀλλὰ βασιλεύσει ἀντὶ ἐκείνου.[3]

104. VOCABULARY

ἀλλά, adversative conj., *but* (stronger than δέ; regularly used after a negative, e. g. οὐ Κῦρος, ἀλλὰ Δαρεῖος.

ἀντί, prep. (gen.), *instead of.* [**anti**dote, **ant**agonist]

ἀπέρχομαι, no fut., 2 aor. ἀπῆλθον, *go away.*

ἄτιμος,[4] ον, *dishonored, slighted.*

βασιλεύω, βασιλεύσω, ἐβασίλευσα, *be king, rule.*

βουλεύω, βουλεύσω, ἐβούλευσα, *plan,* mid. *take counsel.*

εἰμί, fut. ἔσομαι, imperf. ἦν, *be.*

ἐκεῖνος, η, ο, *that;* Lat. *ille.*

ἔτι, adv., *again, still.*

μήποτε, adv., *never.*

ὅπως, conj., *in order that, that, how.*

---

[1] The future of the verb *to be*, εἰμί, is found only in deponent form, ἔσομαι. It is conjugated regularly, except that the third person singular is ἔσται for ἔσεται (655). [2] ἐπί with the dative referring to a person, when construed with a verb signifying *to be* or *to become*, means *in the power of.* [3] ἐκεῖνος is declined like αὐτός (629). [4] A few adjectives have masculine and feminine alike.

105. The personal endings for the middle (passive, except aorist) combined with the thematic vowel, make the following euphonic endings:

	PRIMARY			SECONDARY		
	Sing.	*Dual*	*Plu.*	*Sing.*	*Dual*	*Plu.*
1	-ομαι		-όμεθα	-όμην		-όμεθα
2	-ει	-εσθον	-εσθε	-ου	-εσθον	-εσθε
3	-εται	-εσθον	-ονται	-ετο	-έσθην	-οντο

106. Review the middle and passive, present and imperfect (87).

107. Future, First Aorist Middle, Second Aorist Middle

	FUTURE	FIRST AORIST	SECOND AORIST
		Singular	
1	λύσομαι	ἐλῡσάμην	ἐλιπόμην (λείπω, *leave*)
2	λύσει	ἐλύσω	ἐλίπου
3	λύσεται	ἐλύσατο	ἐλίπετο
		Dual	
2	λύσεσθον	ἐλύσασθον	ἐλίπεσθον
3	λύσεσθον	ἐλῡσάσθην	ἐλιπέσθην
		Plural	
1	λῡσόμεθα	ἐλῡσάμεθα	ἐλιπόμεθα
2	λύσεσθε	ἐλύσασθε	ἐλίπεσθε
3	λύσονται	ἐλύσαντο	ἐλίποντο

108. The present infinitive middle (passive) is λύεσθαι; future, λύσεσθαι (mid. only); first aorist, λύσασθαι (mid. only); second aorist, λιπέσθαι (mid. only). The second aorist infinitive middle is accented on the penult.

109.　　　　　　　　DRILL

I. 1. λύσω, ἐλύσω, ἔλῡσας.
　2. λύσεται, ἐλύσατο, ἐλύετο, ἐλίπετο.
　3. λύεσθε, λύσεσθαι, ἐλύσασθε.
　4. ἐλείποντο, ἐλίποντο, λείπεσθαι, λιπέσθαι.
　5. ἔπεισαν, ἐπείσαντο, πεισόμεθα.
　6. ἐλίπου, ἔλειπον, λιπεῖν, λείψειν.

Middle Infinitive
Pres. - εσθαι
Fut - σεσθαι
1 Aor. - σασθαι
2 Aor. - έσθαι

Second aorist = augment + sec. aor. stem + ending of imperfect (active + middle)

II. Give:
  1. Act. infinitives of βασιλεύω.
  2. Mid. infinitives of βουλεύω.
  3. 3 sing. fut. and aor. act. and mid. of πέμπω.
  4. 3 plu. pres. and imp. act. and pass. of ἀθροίζω.
  5. 1 sing. 2 aor. act. and mid. of λείπω.

110.   EXERCISES

I. 1. ἄτῑμοι ἐγίγνοντο ἀλλὰ βασιλεύσουσιν. 2. ἐβούλοντο
γενέσθαι ἀγαθοὶ στρατηγοὶ καὶ στρατιώτᾱς ἔχειν. 3. Κύρῳ
φίλος ἦν ἀντὶ Ἀρταξέρξου. 4. Κῦρος ἐγένετο ἐπὶ τῷ υἱῷ
τοῦ Δαρείου.

II. 1. They wished to send them away when they became
dishonored. 2. But they summoned the younger men
from the plain. 3. So they went up instead of the older
soldiers. 4. And they were plotting against Darius.
5. Cyrus was in the power of Artaxerxes.

LESSON XI

εἰμί. Proclitics and Enclitics

111. Παρύσατις[1] μὲν δὴ ὑπῆρχε τῷ Κύρῳ, φιλοῦσα[2]
αὐτὸν μᾶλλον ἢ τὸν Ἀρταξέρξην. Κῦρος δὲ τοὺς ἀγγέλους παρὰ Ἀρταξέρξου ἀπεπέμπετο αὐτῷ[3] μᾶλλον φίλους[3]
ἢ Ἀρταξέρξῃ· καὶ οἱ βάρβαροι παρὰ αὐτῷ φίλοι ἦσαν.

112.   VOCABULARY

ἄγγελος, ου, ὁ, *messenger*. [**angel**, ev**angelist**]

βάρβαρος, ον, adj., *barbarian*. Often used in the masculine as a noun.
  [**barbarous**, rhu**barb**]

δή, intensive particle, postpositive, *indeed, you see, it is true;* its force
  is often to be expressed by the inflection of the voice.

----

[1] Nom. case, *Parysatis*, the mother of Cyrus.   [2] Pres. ppl. nom. fem., *loving;*
here has a causal force.   [3] φίλους is in predicate agreement with ἀγγέλους which it
qualifies; it governs the dative of that to which the quality is directed, as in Latin.

ἤ, conj., *than.* Used with comparatives, like Lat. *quam.*
μᾶλλον, comparative adv., *rather, more, sooner than.*
παρά, prep. (gen.), *from;* (dat.), *at, beside;* (acc.), *to, toward.* [**para**graph]
ὑπάρχω, ὑπάρξω, ὑπῆρξα, *favor* (dat.).

113. Learn the present, imperfect, and future indicative, the present and future infinitive of εἰμί (655).

114. Proclitics (21). The proclitics are the forms of the article ὁ, ἡ, οἱ, and αἱ; the prepositions εἰς, *into;* ἐν, *in;* ἐκ (ἐξ), *out of;* the conjunctions εἰ, *if,* and ὡς, *as;* the adverb οὐ (οὐκ, οὐχ), *not.* Proclitics have no effect upon the accent of the following word.

115. Enclitics (22). The most common enclitics are the indefinite pronoun, τὶς, the singular of personal pronouns (except the nominative), and the present indicative of εἰμί and φημί in all forms except the second person singular. ἐστί becomes ἔστι (1) at the beginning of a sentence; (2) when it means *exists* or *it is possible;* (3) when it follows οὐκ, μή, ὡς, ἀλλά, τοῦτο.

116. An enclitic loses its accent when it follows another word, except when a dissyllabic enclitic stands after a word with the acute on the penult: Ἀρταξέρξης τε, but Ἀρταξέρξης ἐστί.

117. The word before an enclitic, if an oxytone (17), retains the acute accent; if it is accented on the antepenult, or has the circumflex on the penult, it receives an additional accent on the ultima: στρατηγός ἐστιν, ἄγγελός ἐστιν, ἀγαθὸς ἐκεῖνός ἐστιν. A word with the circumflex on the ultima does not change its accent: ἀγγελῶ τι.

118. If the preceding word is an enclitic or a proclitic, it receives an acute accent: οὔ τε, μοί τε.

119. ἐστί may take ν-movable (34).

120.   DRILL

I. 1. ἐστί, ἦσθα, εἶναι.

   2. ἦ, ἔσεσθε, ἔσται.

   3. εἰσί, ἦτε, ἦν.

   4. ἔσει, ἔσονται, ἐστέ.

   5. ἐσόμεθα, ἦμεν, ἔσεσθαι.

II. 1. We are, I was, they were.

   2. You were, they are, you are.

   3. You will be, I shall be, they will be.

121.   EXERCISES

I. 1. τοὺς βαρβάρους ὡς ἀγγέλους εἶχον. 2. Κῦρος μὲν νεώτερος Ἀρταξέρξου[1] ἐστίν. 3. Ἀρταξέρξης δὲ αὐτῷ ἐπεβούλευεν. 4. Τισσαφέρνης οὐκ ἐβούλετο τοὺς βαρβάρους φίλους εἶναι τῷ Κύρῳ. 5. βάρβαροι οὔκ ἐσμεν. 6. εἶ φίλος τοῖς ἀγγέλοις. 7. Κύρου ἀδελφὸς οὐκ ἔστιν. 8. ἄγγελοί ἐσμεν Δαρείου. 9. τοῖς βαρβάροις μᾶλλον φίλοι ἔσεσθε ἢ Κύρῳ. 10. ἀλλὰ ἔστιν ἄτιμος.

II. 1. The barbarians, it is true, are not friends to the satrap. 2. He is not in dishonor. 3. O Cyrus, you were in dishonor. 4. Are you more friendly to Cyrus than to Artaxerxes? 5. We are messengers of Cyrus, but we are not plotting against his brother.

---

[1] The genitive is used after a comparative when ἤ, *than*, is not used.

Fig. 3.—A School Scene

LESSON XII

Pronouns

122. τὴν δὲ Ἑλληνικὴν στρατιὰν Κῦρος λάθρᾳ ἤθροι-
ζεν. ἐβούλετο γὰρ τὸν ἀδελφὸν ἀπαράσκευον λαβεῖν.
κελεύει δὲ τοὺς φρουράρχους λαμβάνειν στρατιώτας Πελοποννησίους. τούτοις δὲ ἔλεξεν ὅτι[1] Τισσαφέρνης ἐπιβουλεύει ταῖς ἐν Ἰωνίᾳ[2] Ἑλληνικαῖς ἀποικίαις.[3]

123. VOCABULARY

ἀπαράσκευος, ον, *unprepared.*

ἀποικίᾱ, ᾱς, ἡ, *colony.*

γάρ, conj. (postpositive), *for.*

Ἑλληνικός, ή, όν, *Hellenic, Greek.*

Ἰωνίᾱ, ᾱς, ἡ, *Ionia*, a region of Asia Minor.

κελεύω, κελεύσω, ἐκέλευσα, *command.*

λάθρᾳ, adv., *secretly.*

λαμβάνω, λήψομαι, ἔλαβον, *take.*

λέγω, λέξω, ἔλεξα, *say.* [dia**logue**]

ὅδε, ἥδε, τόδε, demon. pro., *this* (the following).

ὅτι, conj., *that.*

οὗτος, αὕτη, τοῦτο, demon. pro., *this* (already mentioned).

Πελοποννήσιος, ᾱ, ον, *Peloponnesian.*

φρούραρχος, ον, ὁ, *captain of a garrison, phrurarch.*

The Pronouns

124. Learn the declension of αὐτός (629), ἐκεῖνος, οὗτος, and ὅδε (632). αὐτός and ἐκεῖνος have the regular declension of adjectives of the second declension, except that the neuter singular nominative and accusative are αὐτό and ἐκεῖνο. There is no vocative.

125. ὅδε (article + δε enclitic) has the accent and declension of the article. The forms which in the article are unaccented receive the acute accent from the enclitic -δε.

---

[1] ὅτι introduces a quotation which here, though indirect, remains unchanged; this is a common form of indirect discourse. [2] A prepositional phrase with the value of an adjective may stand between the article and a noun; in English translation *Greek* (Ἑλληνικαῖς) would come between the article and its noun; *in Ionia* (ἐν Ἰωνίᾳ) would not. [3] Dative after the preposition ἐπί in composition; in general, prepositions govern the same case in composition as when used alone.

οὗτος in declension partakes of the peculiarities of both αὐτός and the article. The endings are those of αὐτός (i. e. τοῦτο, not τοῦτον, in neuter singular), while the stem has ου where the article has the o-sound (ο, ω) and αυ where it has the a-sound (α, η).

126. αὐτός is an intensive pronoun and has three uses:

I. When it stands between the article and the noun which it modifies (attributive position), it means *same:* ὁ αὐτὸς φίλος, *the same friend.* τὰ αὐτά, *the same things,* is frequently written ταὐτά, and must be carefully distinguished from ταῦτα, *these things,* which is neuter plural of οὗτος.

II. When it modifies a noun, but is not in the attributive position, it means *self* or *very,* like Lat. *ipse:* αὐτὸς ὁ φίλος or ὁ φίλος αὐτός, *the friend himself, the very friend.* When the noun to which it refers is not expressed, αὐτός is always intensive, in the nominative (cf. *ipse*): αὐτὸς ἔχει, *he himself has.* In the other cases it may be intensive, if it is given an emphatic (i. e. unusual) position: αὐτὸν μὲν λαμβάνει, οἱ δ' ἄλλοι φεύγουσι, *him he captures, but the rest escape.*

III. When used substantively without the article, it becomes in the oblique cases (i. e. other than the nominative and vocative) an unemphatic personal pronoun, *him, her, it, them:* ὁ φίλος αὐτοῦ, *his friend;* πέμπει αὐτούς, *he sends them.* This is its most frequent use. Cf. the use of *is* in Latin.

127. ὅδε (*hic*), οὗτος (*is*), ἐκεῖνος (*ille*) are the principal demonstrative pronouns. ὅδε, *this,* refers to something present or near, often to words just to be spoken. οὗτος refers to something just mentioned: ἔλεξε τάδε, *he spoke as follows;* ἔλεξε ταῦτα, *he spoke thus* (as narrated). ἐκεῖνος differs from οὗτος in indicating something more remote in time or space: ἐκεῖνος, *the former;* οὗτος, *the latter.*

128. The article regularly goes with a demonstrative pronoun used as an adjective. The demonstrative must be in the predicate position, i. e. it cannot stand between the article and the noun. οὗτος ὁ ἀδελφός, or ὁ ἀδελφὸς οὗτος, but never ὁ οὗτος ἀδελφός or ὁ ἀδελφὸς ὁ οὗτος. This is so different from the English that it must be noted most carefully.

129.   DRILL

I. Give:

   1. Acc. sing. of αὐτός and οὗτος in all genders.

   2. Gen. plu. of ἐκεῖνος and οὗτος in all genders.

   3. Dat. plu. of οὗτος and ὅδε in all genders.

II. 1. Of this soldier, of that wagon, of the garrison commander himself.

   2. For these satraps, for those armies, for the same brother.

   3. To (εἰς) this village, to those plains, to (παρά) Cyrus himself.

130.   EXERCISES

I. 1. Κῦρος δὲ ἔλεγεν ὅτι οἱ στρατηγοὶ αὐτοὶ ἀπαράσκευοι ἦσαν. 2. ἐκέλευσεν οὖν ἐκείνους τοὺς στρατιώτᾱς παρεῖναι. 3. Τισσαφέρνην αὐτῷ ἐπιβουλεύειν ἐνόμισαν. 4. ὁ αὐτὸς στρατηγὸς ἐβούλετο τοὺς Πελοποννησίους στρατιώτᾱς ἀθροίζεσθαι. 5. αὗται αἱ ἀποικίαι εἰσὶν ἐν Ἰωνίᾳ. 6. οἱ στρατηγοὶ οἱ[1] τούτων τῶν στρατιωτῶν ἀγαθοὶ ἦσαν. 7. Κῦρος αὐτὸς ἐπιβουλεύσει ταύταις ταῖς ἀποικίαις. 8. ὦ στρατιῶται, αὐτοὶ ἐσόμεθα ἀπαράσκευοι.

II. 1. Cyrus wished the garrison commanders themselves to enlist these soldiers. 2. The same garrison commanders were assembling an army. 3. Cyrus is plotting against his brother and his soldiers. 4. These were unprepared, but those were assembling an army secretly. 5. The soldiers of these colonies were unprepared.

---

[1] The article is regularly repeated with the genitive modifier. This has the effect of placing the modifier in the attributive position.

LESSON XIII

Nouns of the Third or Consonant Declension

131. Καὶ γάρ[1] Τισσαφέρνης τὸ ἀρχαῖον Ἰωνίας ἄρχων ἦν, τότε δὲ ἦν ἐπὶ Κύρῳ[2] αὕτη ἡ χώρᾱ πλὴν Μῑλήτου. Μῑλητον μὲν εἶχε Τισσαφέρνης, Κύρῳ δὲ φίλοι γενέσθαι ἐβούλοντο οἳ[3] ἐν Μῑλήτῳ.

132. VOCABULARY

ἀρχαῖος, ᾱ, ον, adj., *ancient;* τὸ ἀρχαῖον (acc.) used adverbially, *originally, formerly.* [**archaic**]

ἄρχων,[4] ἄρχοντος, ὁ, *ruler, commander.*

ἀσπίς, ίδος, ἡ, *shield.*

γέρων, οντος, ὁ, *old man.*

ἐλπίς, ίδος, ἡ, *hope.*

Μῑλητος, ον, ἡ, *Miletus,* a city of Asia Minor.

νύξ, νυκτός, ἡ, *night.*

ὄνομα, ατος, τό, *name.* [an**onymous**, syn**onym**] *ὀνόματος*

πλήν, conj. or prep. (gen.), *except.*

στράτευμα, ατος, τό, *army.*

τότε, adv., *at that time, then.*

Nouns of the Third or Consonant Declension

133. The stem of nouns of the Third Declension ends in a consonant, or in ι or υ.

134. Nouns of the Third Declension are grouped, as in Latin, according to the final letter of the stem, which may be found by dropping ος of the genitive singular.

---

[1] When a sentence begins with καὶ γάρ, a suppressed thought is indicated, an ellipsis of that for which the γάρ-clause gives the reason. The full thought here would be: "*and* (καί) it was likely that he would plot against the territory; *for* (γάρ), etc." In English there is no such simple way of indicating that a thought is suppressed, and καὶ γάρ is usually translated merely *for, and in fact.* [2] See 103, n. 2. [3] The article has the effect of making a noun of the following prepositional phrase: *those in Miletus, the people of Miletus.* In general, the article may be used to show that words other than nouns are used substantively—adverbs, participles, the infinitive, adjectives, and prepositional phrases. [4] Declined like γέρων, but retains ω in voc. sing. because originally a participle.

Lingual (τ, δ, θ) stems: The lingual disappears before
ς (78). Stems ending in οντ do not add ς to form the nominative but drop τ and lengthen ο to ω: ἀρχοντ, nominative
ἄρχων. In dative plural both ν and τ are dropped before σ
and ο becomes ου in compensation: ἄρχουσι, ἄρχοντσι.

In most masculine and feminine nouns the vocative is
like the nominative, but when the stem ends in ιδ, or in ντ
(except oxytones), the vocative singular is the stem, final δ
or τ being dropped. A Greek word can end in no consonant except ν, ρ, ς: ἀσπίς [ἀσπιδ], vocative ἀσπί and γέρων
[γεροντ], vocative γέρον.

135. Monosyllabic stems accent the ultima in the genitive
and dative of all numbers. The accent is circumflex when
the ending is long. *gen. dual + plu.*

136. ὁ γέρων [γεροντ], *old man*

	Sing.	Plu.
N.	γέρων	γέροντες
G.	γέροντος	γερόντων
D.	γέροντι	γέρουσι
A.	γέροντα	γέροντας
V.	γέρον	γέροντες

Dual
N. A. V. γέροντε
G. D. γερόντοιν

ἡ νύξ [νυκτ], *night*

	Sing.	Plu.
N.	νύξ	νύκτες
G.	νυκτός	νυκτῶν
D.	νυκτί	νυξί
A.	νύκτα	νύκτας
V.	νύξ	νύκτες

Dual
νύκτε
νυκτοῖν

ἡ ἀσπίς [ἀσπιδ], *shield*

	Sing.	Plu.
N.	ἀσπίς	ἀσπίδες
G.	ἀσπίδος	ἀσπίδων
D.	ἀσπίδι	ἀσπίσι
A.	ἀσπίδα	ἀσπίδας
V.	ἀσπί	ἀσπίδες

Dual
N. A. V. ἀσπίδε
G. D. ἀσπίδοιν

τὸ στράτευμα [στρατευματ], *army*

	Sing.	Plu.
N.	στράτευμα	στρατεύματα
G.	στρατεύματος	στρατευμάτων
D.	στρατεύματι	στρατεύμασι
A.	στράτευμα	στρατεύματα
V.	στράτευμα	στρατεύματα

Dual
στρατεύματε
στρατευμάτοιν

Decline thus ἄρχων, *commander;* ὄνομα, *name;* ἐλπίς,
hope.

137. DRILL

I. Give: (1) dat. sing., (2) dat. plu., (3) nom. plu., (4) acc. sing. of
ἄρχων, νύξ, ἐλπίς, ὄνομα; (5) 3 plu. pres., imp., and 2 aor. mid.,
of λείπω.

II. 1. ὀνόματι, ὀνόμασι, στρατιώτῃ, ἀποικίαις.

2. ἐλπίδα, στρατεύματα, πεδία.

3. τούτων τῶν ἐλπίδων, οὗτοι οἱ στρατιῶται, αὐτοὶ οἱ ἄρχοντες.

4. βουλεύουσιν, ἐγένοντο, λύσασθαι, γίγνεσθαι.

5. ἔσται, ἔλεξαν, θύσει, ἐλύσω.

138. EXERCISES

I. 1. ἐπὶ τῷ γέροντι ἦν ταῦτα τὰ στρατεύματα. 2. Κῦρος
ἄρχων τῆσδε τῆς ἀρχῆς γενέσθαι βούλεται. 3. οἱ ἄρχοντες
φίλοι ἐγένοντο τῷ στρατεύματι ἐκείνῳ. 4. ἡ Ἰωνία, πλὴν
τῶν Ἑλληνικῶν ἀποικιῶν, ἐπὶ Κύρῳ αὐτῷ ἐγένετο. 5. λέγει
δὲ ὅτι οἱ ἐν ταύτῃ τῇ χώρᾳ ἐπιβουλεύουσι τοῖς ἄρχουσιν.

II. 1. The [people[1]] in this village were plotting against
the armies of Artaxerxes. 2. For they wished to become friendly to Cyrus. 3. The commanders themselves were originally friendly to these old men. 4. That
night (dat.) they sent shields to Miletus for this army.
5. He had good hopes of life.

---

[1] Omit; cf. 131, n. 3.

FIG. 4.—Women at Home

LESSON XIV

CONTRACT VERBS IN άω.

139. Τισσαφέρνης δὲ αὐτοὺς κωλύειν ἐπειρᾶτο. Κῦρος οὖν στράτευμα συνέλεξε καὶ ἐστράτευεν ἐπὶ Μίλητον καὶ κατὰ γῆν καὶ κατὰ θάλατταν. καὶ αὕτη αὖ ἄλλη πρόφα-σις[1] ἦν αὐτῷ[2] τοῦ[3] ἀθροίζειν στράτευμα.

140.   VOCABULARY

ἄλλος, η, ο, *other, another, the rest of;* declined like αὐτός (629). [**alle**-gory, **allo**pathy]

αὖ, adv., *again, in turn.*

γῆ, γῆς, ἡ, *earth,* used in singular only. [**ge**ography, apo**gee**]

κατά, prep. (gen.), *down, down from;* (acc.), *down along, by.* κατὰ γῆν καὶ κατὰ θάλατταν, *by land and sea.* [**cata**logue, **cata**rrh]

κωλύω, κωλύσω, ἐκώλῡσα, *hinder.*

πειράω, πειράσω, ἐπείρᾱσα, *attempt.* Commonly deponent, πειράομαι, etc. [em**piri**cal, **pira**te]

στρατεύω, στρατεύσω, ἐστράτευσα, *make an expedition.* In act., of the general; in mid., of the army.

συλλέγω, συλλέξω,[4]συνέλεξα, *gather, collect.* [**syllog**ism]

τῑμάω, τῑμήσω, ἐτίμησα, *honor.* [**timo**cracy]

CONTRACT VERBS

141. Verbs ending in -άω, -έω, and -όω contract the final *a*, *ε*, and *o* of the stem with the following vowel in the present and imperfect. Such verbs are called contract verbs. Except for this contraction they are conjugated as other verbs. The following contractions occur in verbs in -άω:

$$a + \begin{Bmatrix} o \\ ov \\ ω \end{Bmatrix} = ω; \quad a + ε = \bar{a}; \quad a + ει = \bar{\alpha}$$

$a + oι = ω$
$a + η = \bar{a} \quad a + η = \bar{\alpha}$

---

[1] Fem. noun, nom. sing., *excuse, pretext.* [2] The dative is used to denote the possessor, as in Latin: Δαρείῳ ἦσαν υἱοί, *Darius had sons.* [3] The article goes with the infinitive, which is thus shown to be a noun in the genitive case (cf. 131, n. 3). The infinitive in such cases is generally best translated by a participle or verbal noun. τοῦ ἀθροίζειν is objective gen., *of (for) gathering.* [4] For συν-λέγω, assimilation.

Observe that ᾱ or ω occurs in every contract form. Contract verbs are given in the vocabulary in uncontracted form, but if the same word were used in a sentence it would be contracted: τῑμάω in vocabulary, but τῑμῶ in a sentence.

142. Learn the present and imperfect indicative, active, middle, and passive, of τῑμάω, with the present infinitive of all voices (647). *τιμάειν = τιμᾶν no ι-subscript in*

143. Accent. The general rules of accent (10–14) apply *pres. act* to contract verbs. But observe (1) that the syllable resulting from contraction is long, and (2) that if either of the syllables had an accent before contraction, the contracted syllable is accented. A contracted ultima has the circumflex. Note the application of the rules in the conjugation of τῑμάω.

Observe that contract verbs are in reality contract verbs only in the present and imperfect tenses. Outside the present system they do not differ in inflection from other verbs; but most of them lengthen the short stem-vowel in the other tenses before the tense sign, *a* and ε becoming η and ο becoming ω. Thus: τῑμάω, pres. τῑμῶ, imp. ἐτίμων, but fut. τῑμήσω, 1 aor. ἐτίμησα. *a* after ε, ι, or ρ generally becomes ᾱ instead of η: πειράω, πειράσω.

144.   DRILL

I. Locate the following forms:

  1. τῑμῶ, τῑμᾶν, ἐτῑμῶ, ἐτίμων, ἐτῑμῶντο.
  2. πειρᾶσθαι, λύσασθαι, πειρᾶσθε, τῑμᾶτε, ἐλύσατε.
  3. νυξί, ἀσπίδες, ἄδελφε, στρατιώτου, ὀνόματα.
  4. ἄρχουσι, ἀσπίδα, πεδία, νυκτί, γέρον, νυκτῶν.
  5. ἐλύσατο, θύειν, ἔλιπον, ἐνόμιζον, ἔλεξαν.

II. 1. He attempts, he will attempt, he was attempting, he attempted.
  2. He honors, he will honor, he was honoring, he honored.
  3. I am honored, I was being honored, they attempted to honor.
  4. They honored, we attempt, they will attempt, they attempted to be honored.

145. 　　　　　　　EXERCISES

I.　1. ἐπεβούλευεν αὐτῷ, Κῦρος δὲ κωλύειν ἐπειρᾶτο.　2. αὕτη
αὖ ἄλλη πρόφασις ἦν τοῦ πειρᾶσθαι τὰ στρατεύματα συλ-
λέξαι.　3. λέγει ὅτι τῑμᾷ τοὺς φίλους.　4. ἐπὶ Μίλητον
Κῦρος ἐπειρᾶτο στρατεύειν.　5. ἐβούλετο τῑμᾶν Τισσαφέρνην.

II.　1. They attempted to collect an army.　2. The people
of Miletus[1] wish to honor Cyrus.　3. We honored the
old men.　4. He attempts to make an expedition against
the colony by land and sea.　5. The commanders had
an excuse for preventing them.

LESSON XV

Contract Verbs in έω and όω

146. πρὸς δὲ ᾿Αρταξέρξην πέμπων[2] ἠξίου ἀδελφὸς ὢν[3]
αὐτοῦ σατράπης εἶναι ταύτης τῆς χώρᾱς μᾶλλον ἢ Τισσαφέρνην[4] ἄρχειν[5] αὐτῆς, καὶ ἡ Παρύσατις συνέπραττεν
αὐτῷ[6] ταῦτα· ὥστε ᾿Αρταξέρξης τὴν μὲν πρὸς ἑαυτὸν[7]
ἐπιβουλὴν οὐκ ᾐσθάνετο.

147. 　　　　　　　VOCABULARY

αἰσθάνομαι, αἰσθήσομαι, ᾐσθόμην, (depon.), *perceive, learn.* [aesthetic]

ἀξιόω, ἀξιώσω, ἠξίωσα, *deem right, expect, claim, ask.* [axiom]

ἄρχω, ἄρξω, ἦρξα, *be first, rule, command* (gen.); mid. *begin;* cf. ἀρχή.

δηλόω, δηλώσω, ἐδήλωσα, *show, make clear, explain.*

ἐπιβουλή, ῆς, ἡ, *plot;* cf. ἐπιβουλεύω.

πέμπω, πέμψω, ἔπεμψα, *send.* [pomp]

ποιέω, ποιήσω, ἐποίησα, *do, make.* [poet]

συμπράττω, συμπράξω, συνέπραξα, *act with, help in doing, help,
co-operate.*

ὥστε (ὡς + τε enclitic), conj. adv., or conj., *so that, wherefore, so as.*

---

[1] See 131, n. 3.　　[2] Pres. ppl. nom. sing. masc. of πέμπω, *sending.*　　[3] ὤν is pres.
ppl. of εἰμί. ἀδελφὸς ὢν αὐτοῦ is the equivalent of a causal clause, *since he was his brother.*
[4] The subject of the infinitive is regularly in the accusative; hence Τισσαφέρνην.
But if it is the same as the subject of the main verb (here ἠξίου), the nominative is
preferred; hence ἠξίου εἶναι σατράπης, where σατράπης is nominative not accusative.
[5] Verbs of superiority, ruling, etc., govern the genitive.　　[6] αὐτῷ is dependent upon
σύν in composition.　　[7] πρὸς ἑαυτόν, *against himself* (Artaxerxes).

CONTRACT VERBS IN ἐω AND όω

148. Verbs in -ἐω and -όω show the following contractions:

$$\epsilon + \left\{ \begin{array}{c} \text{o} \\ \text{ov} \end{array} \right\} = \text{ov}; \qquad \epsilon + \omega = \omega; \qquad \epsilon + \left\{ \begin{array}{c} \epsilon \\ \epsilon\iota \end{array} \right\} = \epsilon\iota.$$

$$\text{o} + \left\{ \begin{array}{c} \epsilon \\ \text{o} \\ \text{ov} \end{array} \right\} = \text{ov}; \qquad \text{o} + \omega = \omega; \qquad \text{o} + \epsilon\iota = \text{o}\iota.$$

[handwritten annotations: ε + οι = οι; ε + η = η; ε + η = η; ο + η = ω; ο + η = οι; *except. pres. inf.* δηλο+ειν = δηλοῦν *]*

149. Learn the present and imperfect indicative active, middle, and passive, of ποιέω and δηλόω (647, 648), with the present infinitive in all voices.

150. ὥστε introduces result. If the result did actually follow, ὥστε means *wherefore, consequently, so that,* and is generally followed by the indicative. If the result is simply expected to follow, it means *so as,* and the infinitive, with or without subject accusative, is used: εἶχε στρατιώτᾱς, ὥστε λαβεῖν Τισσαφέρνην, *he had soldiers so as to capture Tissaphernes.*

151.   DRILL

I. Locate the following:

  1. δηλοῖς, ἀξιοῦσιν, ἐδήλου, δηλοῦτε.
  2. ἀξιοῦσθε, ἀξιοῦσθαι, ἀξιοῦν, ἠξίουν, ἠξιοῦντο.
  3. δηλοῦμεν, ἐδηλούμεθα, ἀξιοῖ, ἠξιοῦτο, ἀξιοῦται.

II. Give:

  1. 3 sing. pres. and imp. act. and mid. of ἀξιόω, τῑμάω.
  2. 3 plu. pres. and imp. act. and pass. of ἀξιόω, ποιέω.

152.   EXERCISES

I. 1. ἀξιοῦμεν Κύρῳ συμπράττειν ὥστε ἄρχειν Μῑλήτου.
  2. Τισσαφέρνης δηλοῖ τὴν ἐπιβουλὴν Ἀρταξέρξῃ. 3.
  Κῦρος πειρᾶται συμπράττειν τῷ ἄρχοντι. 4. οὐκ ἠξίουν
  Τισσαφέρνην ἄρχειν ταύτης τῆς χώρᾱς. 5. Κῦρος βούλεται βασιλεύειν ἀντὶ τοῦ ἀδελφοῦ.

II. 1. The plot was explained to the brother of Cyrus. 2.
  For he thought it right to co-operate with his elder
  brother so as to collect soldiers. 3. They do not deem
  it right to suspect the army. 4. The old men perceived
  these things and attempted to rule Miletus. 5. They
  perceive this plot against the commanders.

[handwritten note at bottom: ε before a long vowel or diphthong is dropped in contraction *]*

LESSON XVI

The Participle

153. Τισσαφέρνει[1] δὲ[2] ἐνόμιζε πολεμοῦντα[3] αὐτὸν ἀμφὶ τὰ στρατεύματα δαπανᾶν·[4] ὥστε οὐκ ἤχθετο αὐτῶν πολεμούντων.[5] καὶ γὰρ ὁ Κῦρος ἀπέπεμπε τοὺς γιγνομένους δασμοὺς Ἀρταξέρξῃ ἐκ τῆς χώρᾱς ἣν Τισσαφέρνης τὸ ἀρχαῖον[6] εἶχεν.

154.   VOCABULARY

ἀμφί, prep. (acc.), *about.* [amphitheater]

ἄχθομαι, ἀχθέσομαι, (depon.), *be burdened, vexed, displeased.*

δαπανάω, δαπανήσω, ἐδαπάνησα, *spend* (money), *consume.*

δασμός, οῦ, ὁ, *tax, tribute.*

πολεμέω, πολεμήσω, ἐπολέμησα, *wage war* (dat.).

Τισσαφέρνης, ους, dat. ει, acc. ην, *Tissaphernes.*

The Participle

155. Learn the following participles: the present active, middle and passive, of λύω, τῑμάω, ποιέω, δηλόω; the future and first aorist, active and middle, of λύω; the second aorist, active and middle, of λείπω; the present and future of εἰμί (ἐσόμενος, η, ον), in 638, 641, 647, 648. Observe that the accent of the second aorist active participle is always acute on the ultima.

156. Learn the declension of ὤν, λιπών (617), λύων (618), τῑμῶν, ποιῶν, δηλῶν (624), λῡόμενος (622).

Note.—The form λύων is for λύοντς (cf. γέρων, 136). λύουσα comes by euphonic change from λύοντια.

---

[1] Dat. of indirect object with πολεμοῦντα.   [2] The contrast between this clause and the preceding is marked by the μέν and δέ. The words most sharply contrasted are πρὸς ἑαυτόν and Τισσαφέρνει.   [3] Agrees with αὐτόν, which is subj.-acc. of δαπανᾶν. πολεμοῦντα indicates cause: *he thought he was spending money because he was waging war with Tissaphernes.*   [4] δαπανᾶν, infinitive in indirect discourse; αὐτόν is subj.-acc.   [5] For syntax see 157.   [6] Adverbial accusative, *formerly, originally.*

157. The Genitive Absolute. A noun and a participle in the genitive case, and not immediately dependent on any word in the sentence, are said to be in the Genitive Absolute.

158. DRILL

I. Locate the following:

   1. τῑμῶντι, ποιοῦντι, λύοντι, δηλούσῃ, λιπούσῃ.

   2. τῑμώσᾱς, ποιουσῶν, λῡούσῃ, τῑμῶν, ποιοῦν.

   3. λῦον, λύουσαι, ποιοῦντα, δηλοῦντες.

   4. στρατιῶται, δῶρα, ἐλπίδα, γέρουσι, ἁμάξης, σατράπου.

   5. ἔλῡες, δηλοῖς, ἐτίμα, ἐτῑμῶντο, ἠξιοῦντο.

II. Give in all genders: (1) dat. sing., (2) dat. plu., (3) acc. sing., (4) nom. plu., of τῑμῶν, ἀξιῶν, ποιῶν, λιπών.

159. EXERCISES

I. 1. πολεμοῦντες οὐκ ἀπέπεμπον τοὺς δασμούς. 2. τούτων τῶν στρατευμάτων πολεμούντων ἤχθοντο. 3. Κῦρος ἀμφὶ τὸ στράτευμα ἐδαπάνᾱ. 4. ἐνόμιζον αὐτὸν τῑμᾶν Κῦρον. 5. Ἀρταξέρξης ἀξιοῖ τὸν ἀδελφὸν ἀποπέμπειν τοὺς δασμοὺς ἐκ Μῑλήτου.

II. 1. Being honored, they do not make war. 2. Cyrus, (because he was) spending money on the soldiers, did not send the tribute to his brother. 3. He is annoyed because Cyrus is honoring[1] the army. 4. They made war so as to receive (λαμβάνω) the tribute. 5. Artaxerxes thinks Cyrus is making war against this country.

---

[1] See 157.

FIG. 5.—A Lion Hunt

LESSON XVII

Third Declension. Liquid Stems

160. ἄλλο δὲ στράτευμα αὐτῷ¹ συνελέγετο² ἐν Χερρονήσῳ τῇ³ κατ᾽ ἀντιπέρᾱς Ἀβύδου τόνδε τὸν τρόπον. Κλέαρχος Λακεδαιμόνιος φυγὰς ἦν· τούτῳ⁴ συγγενόμενος ὁ
Κῦρος ἠγάσθη⁵ τε αὐτὸν καὶ παρεῖχε αὐτῷ μῡρίους
δᾱρεικούς.

161.   VOCABULARY

Ἄβῡδος, ου, ἡ, *Abydos.*

ἀγών, ῶνος, ὁ, *contest, games.* [**agony**]

ἀνήρ, ἀνδρός, ὁ, *man.*

ἀντιπέρᾱς, adv. or prep. (gen.), *opposite;* κατ᾽ ἀντιπέρᾱς forms a simple
    phrase with the same meaning, and governs the gen.

δᾱρεικός, οῦ, ὁ, *daric,* a Persian coin worth about $3.50.

Κλέαρχος, ου, ὁ, *Clearchus,* a Greek general.

Λακεδαιμόνιος, ᾱ, ον, *Lacedaemonian.*

λιμήν, ένος, ὁ, *harbor, port.*

μήν, μηνός, ὁ, *month.* [**moon**]

μήτηρ, μητρός, ἡ, *mother.*

μῡριοι, αι, α, *ten thousand.* [**myriad**]

παρέχω, παρέξω or παρασχήσω, παρέσχον, *furnish, supply, give.*

πατήρ, πατρός, ὁ, *father.*

ῥήτωρ, ορος, ὁ, *orator, speaker.* [**rhetoric**]

συγγίγνομαι, συγγενήσομαι, συνεγενόμην, *be or associate with, meet* (dat.).

τε, conj., *and* (enclitic); τε . . . . καί, *both* . . . . *and.* Postpositive.

τρόπος, ου, ὁ, *way, manner.* τόνδε τὸν τρόπον, adv. acc., *in this manner.*
    [**trope**]

φυγάς, άδος, ὁ, *fugitive, exile.*

Χερρόνησος, ου, ἡ, *Chersonnesus.*

Third Declension (*continued*). Liquid Stems

162. Learn ἀγών, λιμήν, μήν, ῥήτωρ (606). Observe that
the nominative singular of liquid stems does not add ς, but
lengthens the vowel of the last syllable, if short. ν is

---

¹ Dative of advantage.   ² Passive.   ³ This article has the effect of making
the prepositional phrase a modifier of Χερρονήσῳ.   ⁴ Dative dependent on σύν in
composition.   ⁵ *Admired,* aor. 3 sing.

dropped before σ in the dative plural. In oxytones the
vocative singular is like the nominative, in other liquid
nouns like the stem. For special rule of accent see 135.

163. Learn πατήρ, μήτηρ, ἀνήρ (607). Observe that in
ἀνήρ [ἀνερ] δ takes the place of ε of the stem in all cases
except the nominative and vocative singular. In πατήρ and
μήτηρ the ε of the stem is dropped in the genitive and dative
singular, not throughout as in Latin in *pater, mater.* In
the dative plural ερ becomes ρα. The accent is on ε except
in the genitive, dative, and vocative singular.

164. DRILL

I. Locate the following:
1. νυξί, ἀσπί, πεδία.
2. ἀσπίδα, ἀγῶσι, ἄρχοντας.
3. σατράπᾱς, βασιλείᾱς, στρατεύματα.
4. υἱῶν, ἀγών, μῆνα.
5. λιμένι, στρατιῶτα, ἁμάξῃ.
6. ἄνδρας, πατρός, μητέρα, μητέρων, πατράσι, ὀνόμασι.

II. 1. Of the father, to the mothers, the harbors.
2. The names of the men, the hopes of the orator, the contests
of the soldier.
3. For the shield, for the night, for the month.
4. To (εἰς) the man, to the harbors, to the army.
5. O satrap, O father, O men.

165. EXERCISES

I. 1. τοῖς δὲ φυγάσι Κῦρος παρέχει ἀσπίδας. 2. οἱ ἄρχοντες ἐκεῖνοι ἤθροισαν στράτευμα. 3. Κῦρος οὐκ ἐπολέμει
τῷ πατρί. 4. ἐτίμα γὰρ αὐτὸν μᾶλλον ἢ τὴν μητέρα.
5. συγγενόμενοι Κύρῳ οἱ φυγάδες συνέλεγον ἄλλα στρατεύματα.

II. 1. Cyrus met the men. 2. The commanders gave the
fugitive a daric. 3. Artaxerxes honored both his father
and his mother. 4. The fugitives collected their armies
in the following manner. 5. They deemed it right to
give shields to the soldiers.

LESSON XVIII

THIRD DECLENSION. LABIAL AND PALATAL STEMS

166. ὁ³ δὲ λαβὼν¹ τὸ χρυσίον, στράτευμα συνέλεξεν ἀπὸ τούτων τῶν χρημάτων, καὶ ἐπολέμει ἐκ Χερρονήσου ὁρμώμενος τοῖς Θρᾳξὶ τοῖς² ὑπὲρ Ἑλλήσποντον οἰκοῦσι, καὶ ὠφέλει τοὺς Ἕλληνας.

167. VOCABULARY

διῶρυξ, υχος, ἡ, *ditch, canal.*

Ἕλλην, ηνος, ὁ, *Greek.*

Ἑλλήσποντος, ου, ὁ, *Hellespont.*

Θρᾷξ, Θρᾳκός, ὁ, *Thracian, a Thracian.*

κλώψ, κλωπός, ὁ, *thief.*

οἰκέω, οἰκήσω, ᾤκησα, *inhabit, dwell;* in pass. *be situated* (generally of cities). [**eco**nomy, Green**wich** — Lat. *vicus*]

ὁρμάω, ὁρμήσω, ὥρμησα, *start, hurry;* mid. and pass., *set forth, start.*

ὑπέρ, prep. (gen.), *over, for the sake of;* (acc.), *over, beyond, above.* [**hyper**critical]

φάλαγξ, αγγος, ἡ, *phalanx, line of battle.*

φύλαξ, ακος, ὁ, *watcher, guard.*

χρῆμα, ατος, τό, *a thing one uses, things, possessions, money.* (plu.).

χρυσίον, ου, τό, *gold, money.* [**chrys**alis, **chrys**anthemum]

ὠφελέω, ὠφελήσω, ὠφέλησα, *aid, assist, help.*

THIRD DECLENSION (*continued*). LABIAL (π, β, φ) AND PALATAL (κ, γ, χ) STEMS

168. Learn κλώψ, φύλαξ, φάλαγξ, Θρᾷξ, διῶρυξ (605). Labial and palatal stems are never neuter.

169. DRILL

I. Give: (1) dat. sing.; (2) gen. plu.; (3) dat. plu.; (4) gen. sing.; (5) nom. plu.; (6) acc. sing., of νύξ, ἀνήρ, ὄνομα, κλώψ, φύλαξ.

II. 1. The phalanx of the guards, the canals of the Thracians, the gold of the thief.

---

¹ From λαμβάνω. ² τοῖς . . . . οἰκοῦσι qualifies Θρᾳξί and is best rendered by a relative clause: *who dwell* [lit. *those dwelling*]. ³ See ὁ in gen. vocab.

2. He benefits the commanders and the guards.

3. They are waging war against the Thracians and the Greeks.

4. These men are thieves, not soldiers.

5. They attempted to proceed alongside of (παρά) the ditches.

170.   EXERCISES

I. 1. οἱ ὑπὲρ Ἑλλήσποντον οἰκοῦντες ἐπολέμουν τοῖς Ἕλλησιν. 2. λαβόντες τὰ χρήματα οἱ φύλακες ὡρμῶντο. 3. οἱ
δὲ Θρᾷκες ὁρμώμενοι ἐξ Ἑλλησπόντου ὠφέλουν τοὺς ὑπὲρ
Ἑλλήσποντον οἰκοῦντας. 4. οἱ Ἕλληνες ἐτιμῶντο ἐν
Ἰωνίᾳ. 5. οἱ κλῶπες ἥρπασαν τὸ τῶν ἀνδρῶν χρῡσίον.

II. 1. The Lacedaemonian fugitives took the money and
attempted to wage war against Cyrus. 2. Cyrus started
from the Hellespont with (having) the Greeks as (ὡς)
guards. 3. The commanders assisted those who dwelt
in Ionia. 4. With this gold they collected ten thousand
soldiers. 5. In the ditches there was gold.

LESSON XIX

Third Declension. Vowel Stems

171. ὥστε[1] καὶ χρήματα ἦν αὐτῷ εἰς τὴν τροφὴν τῶν
στρατιωτῶν ἐκ τῶν Ἑλλησποντιακῶν πόλεων. τοῦτο δὲ αὖ
τὸ στράτευμα οὕτως αὐτῷ λάθρᾳ ἕτοιμον ἦν.

172.   VOCABULARY

εἷς, μία, ἕν, *one.* [hyp**hen, ace**]

Ἑλλησποντιακός, ή, όν, *Hellespontian.*

ἕτοιμος, η, ον, *ready.*

ἰχθύς, ύος, ὁ, *fish.* [**ichthy**ology]

οὕτω, adv., *thus;* before a vowel,
  οὕτως.

πόλις, εως, ἡ, *city.* [**polite**, cosmo-
  politan]

τέτταρες, α, *four.* [**tetr**archy]

τροφή, ῆς, ἡ, *nurture, support.*
  [a**troph**y]

τρεῖς, τρία, *three.* [**tri**pod]

---

[1] See 150.

THE THIRD DECLENSION (*continued*). VOWEL STEMS

173. Learn πόλις and ἰχθύς (608).

Observe that stems ending in ι and υ add ν (not a) to form the accusative singular. Stems in ι have ε in place of ι in all cases, except the nominative, accusative, and vocative singular. ως takes the place of ος in the genitive singular, but does not affect the accent. The genitive plural also has the accent on the antepenult. A few stems in υ make the same vowel changes, but most are declined like ἰχθύς.

174. Learn the declension of εἷς, δύο, τρεῖς, τέτταρες (626).

175. The names of cities or rivers are in apposition with πόλις and ποταμός: ἡ Κελαιναὶ πόλις, *the city of Celaenae;* ὁ Εὐφράτης ποταμός, *the river Euphrates.*

176. DRILL

I. Locate:

1. Θρᾳκός, πόλεως, τρισί, τρία.
2. πόλεων, ἰχθύν, ἰχθύων, τεττάρων.
3. στρατιώτῃ ἑνί, θαλάττῃ μιᾷ, νυκτί, πόλει.
4. αὐτό, αὗται, ταῦτα, ἐκεῖνα.
5. πόλεσι, τέτταρσι, πατράσι, ἰχθύος, πόλεις.

II. Give: (1) acc. sing.; (2) acc. plu.; (3) nom. plu.; (4) dat. plu., of πατήρ, πόλις, φύλαξ, τῑμῶν (in all genders), and of οὗτος (in all genders).

177. EXERCISES

I. 1. ἰχθύες ἦσαν ἐν ἀγορᾷ εἰς[2] τὴν τροφὴν τῶν Ἑλλήνων.
2. συγγενόμενος τοῖς Θρᾳξὶ αὐτοὺς ἔχειν ὡς φίλους ἐβούλετο.
3. ταῦτα τὰ χρήματα ἕτοιμα αὐτῷ ἦν ἐν τῇ Ἀβύδῳ πόλει.
4. Κλέαρχος αὐτοὺς ἀπαρασκεύους λαβεῖν ἐπειρᾶτο ὥστε τὰς Ἑλληνικὰς πόλεις ὠφελεῖν. 5. οἱ στρατιῶται ἐκ τῶν πόλεων λάθρᾳ συλλέγονται.

II. 1. He started from the city of Abydos and waged war on the fugitives. 2. In this way he aided those[1] who

---

[1] See 166, n. 2.   [2] *For.*

dwelt in the cities.   3. And the cities of the Hellespont furnished money for the support of the armies.   4. He collected another army secretly so as to make war on the Thracians.   5. There were fish in the canals and rivers of that country.

LESSON XX

Uses of the Participle

178. Ἀρίστιππος δὲ ὁ Θετταλὸς ξένος ὤν[1] ἐτύγχανεν αὐτῷ, καὶ πιεζόμενος ὑπὸ[2] τῶν οἴκοι[3] ἀντιστασιωτῶν ἔρχεται πρὸς τὸν Κῦρον καὶ αἰτεῖ[4] αὐτὸν εἰς[5] δισχιλίους ξένους καὶ τριῶν μηνῶν μισθόν, ὡς[6] οὕτω περιγενησόμενος τῶν ἀντιστασιωτῶν.[7] ὁ δὲ Κῦρος παρέχει αὐτῷ εἰς τετρακισχιλίους καὶ ἓξ μηνῶν μισθόν.

179.   VOCABULARY

αἰτέω, αἰτήσω, ἤτησα, *ask for, demand.*
ἀντιστασιώτης, ου, ὁ, *opponent, adversary.*
Ἀρίστιππος, ου, ὁ, *Aristippus.*
δισχίλιοι, αι, α, *two thousand.*
ἕξ, *six.* [**hex**agon]
ἔρχομαι, ἦλθον, *come, go.* (ελθ)
Θετταλός, οῦ, ὁ, *Thessalian.*
μισθός, οῦ, ὁ, *pay.*
ξένος, ου, ὁ, *stranger, guest-friend;* plu. *mercenaries.*
οἴκοι, adv., *at home.* See 13, note.
περιγίγνομαι, περιγενήσομαι, περιεγενόμην, (gen.), *be superior, overcome.*
πιέζω, πιέσω, ἐπίεσα, *press, oppress.* [**piezo**meter]
τετρακισχίλιοι, αι, α, *four thousand.*
τυγχάνω, τεύξομαι, ἔτυχον, *happen, happen upon, gain.*
ὑπό, prep., *under;* (gen.), *from under, by;* (dat.), *beneath;* (acc.), *down under.* [**hypo**dermic, **hypo**thesis]

---

[1] See 181, 4.   [2] ὑπό with gen. with a passive verb expresses agency.   [3] See 131, 3. [4] Governs two accusatives.   [5] εἰς with numerals means *to the number of, as many as.* [6] ὡς is very often used with a participle to show that the participle contains the thought of some other person than the speaker or the subject of the main verb. See 181, 5.   [7] Gen. governed by περί in composition.

180. Review the participles (155, 156) and learn λύσᾱς (620).

181. The participle is found far more frequently in Greek than in English. The following are its most important uses:

1. The participle is often used as an adjective: πόλις οἰκουμένη, *an inhabited city.*

2. When used alone with the article the participle becomes a noun. It is then usually best translated by a relative clause: οἱ ἐνοικοῦντες, *the inhabitants;* ὁ βουλόμενος, *the one who wishes;* τὰ γιγνόμενα, *those things which are taking place* (literally, *the happenings*).

3. In many cases the idea expressed by the participle is really co-ordinate with that of the main verb, but precedes it in time. The participle in this case is usually aorist. It is generally best translated by a finite verb, co-ordinate with the main verb: στράτευμα ἀθροίσᾱς ἐξελαύνει, *he collected an army and marched away.* This is sometimes termed the preliminary participle.

4. τυγχάνω, *happen;* λανθάνω, *escape the notice of;* φθάνω, *anticipate,* are usually followed by a predicate participle containing the main thought; ὧν ἐτύγχανεν may be translated, *happened to be,* or *was, as it happened;* ἔλαθε πέμπων, *he sent secretly* (literally, *he escaped notice sending*); ἔφθασεν αὐτὸν ἐρχόμενος, *he came before him* (literally, *he anticipated him coming*).

5. The future participle shows purpose: ἦλθον κωλύσοντες, *they came to hinder.* With ὡς an avowed purpose is expressed: ὡς οὕτω περιγενησόμενος τῶν ἀντιστασιωτῶν, *thinking that he would thus overcome his opponents.*

6. For the genitive absolute see 157.

182. The participle does not denote absolute time. The present participle expresses the same time as the verb on which it depends; the aorist, time preceding or co-ordinate with the main verb; and the future, time after it.

183. DRILL

Locate the following forms:

1. λῦσαν, ἔλῦσαν, λύσᾱσαν.
2. λῡούσαις, λῡσάσαις, ἐλύσω.
3. λύσᾱς, λῡσάσᾱς, ἔλῦσας.

4. ἀνδρός, μίαν, ταῦτα.
5. εἰσί, τρισί, πατράσι.

184. EXERCISES

I. 1. Ἀρίστιππος πρὸς τὸν Κῦρον ἦλθεν αἰτήσων τροφήν.
2. οἱ Ἕλληνες οἱ ἐν τῇ πόλει ἐτύγχανον πιεζόμενοι.
3. ἐλθὼν πρὸς τοὺς ἀντιστασιώτᾱς ᾔτει χρῡσίον. 4. οἱ
φυγάδες εἰς τετρακισχῑλίους ξένους καὶ δυοῖν μηνῶν μισθὸν
ᾔτουν. 5. Κῦρος δὲ πολεμῶν τῇ Μῑλήτῳ πόλει ἔτυχεν.

II. 1. Clearchus was hard pressed[1] by those at home, so he
became a fugitive. 2. The soldiers came to Cyrus and
asked him for three months' pay. 3. The messengers
happened to be Thessalians. 4. Those who dwelt above
the Hellespont happened to be hard pressed by the
Thracians. 5. He collected an army, thinking that he
would make war upon the city.

———

LESSON XXI

Use of Participles. Use of Prepositions

185. Review uses of the participle (Lesson XX).

186. The participle is very often used in place of a subordinate clause, either when in agreement with the subject
or object of the sentence or in the genitive absolute con-
struction. It may show:

a) Time: ταῦτα εἰπὼν ἀπῆλθεν, *when he had said this he
went away.*

b) Cause: ὑπῆρχε τῷ Κύρῳ φιλοῦσα αὐτόν, *she assisted
Cyrus because she loved him.*

---

[1] Render by a ppl.; omit "so."

c) Manner or means: διαπράττει πείσας, *he accomplishes (it) by persuasion.*

d) Purpose, shown by future participle (see 181, 5).

e) Condition: ἔχοντες τὰ ὅπλα πολεμήσομεν, *if we have our arms, we shall make war.*

f) Concession: βουλόμενος οὐκ ἦλθεν, *though he wished (to do so), he did not come.*

g) Attendant circumstances: ἦλθεν ἔχων πολὺ στράτευμα, *he came with a large army.*

187. Some prepositions govern one case only (genitive, dative, or accusative); some govern two cases (genitive and accusative); others all three cases. Observe the distinctions in the General Vocabulary.

188. Of the more common prepositions, ἀντί, *instead of;* ἀπό, *away from, from;* ἐκ, *out of, from;* πρό, *before,* govern the genitive only.

189. ἐκ (ἐξ) implies that one starts from within, ἀπό from the neighborhood of: ἐξ οἰκίας, *out of the house;* ἀπὸ οἰκίας, *from the house.* πλήν, except

190. ἐν, *in,* and σύν, *with,* govern the dative only; ἀνά, *up,* and εἰς, *into,* govern the accusative only.

191. ἀμφί, *about;* διά, *through, on account of;* κατά, *down;* μετά, *in company with, after;* ὑπέρ, *over,* govern the genitive or accusative. gen. acc.

192. ἐπί, *on, upon, at;* παρά, *alongside of, beside;* περί, *around, about;* πρός, *over against, facing, at, to;* ὑπό, *under,* govern the genitive, dative, or accusative.

193. In general, when used with prepositions the genitive expresses *motion from;* the dative, the idea of *being at* or *rest at;* the accusative, *motion toward;* e. g.: παρά w. gen. = *from the side of,* παρά w. dat. = *by the side of,* παρά w. acc. = *to the side of.* Thus, far more than in Latin, the force of the preposition is determined by the case with which it is used.

194.   DRILL

I. 1. πρὸς τῆς πόλεως, παρὰ τὴν ἀρχήν, παρὰ τῆς ἀρχῆς.

   2. διὰ τὸ χρῡσίον, περὶ χρημάτων, διὰ τῆς χώρᾱς.

   3. ἐπὶ τὴν ἀρχήν, πρὸ τῆς οἰκίᾱς, ὑπὲρ τῆς διώρυχος.

   4. ἀπὸ τοῦ ποταμοῦ, ἐκ τοῦ ποταμοῦ.

   5. ἐπὶ τῶν ἁμαξῶν, ἀμφὶ τὸ στράτευμα, σὺν τοῖς στρατιώταις.

II. Give: (1) nom. plu. (masc. fem. neut.) of the active participles
of λύω. (2) acc. sing. (masc. fem. neut.) of the middle participles of λύω.

195.   EXERCISES

I. 1. ἀπὸ τῆς πόλεως ἦλθον δισχίλιοι ἄνδρες αἰτήσοντες μισθόν.

   2. χρήματα λαβόντες ἦλθον διὰ τοῦ πεδίου μετὰ τῶν ἄλλων
στρατιωτῶν.   3. περιγενόμενος τῶν ἐν τῇ ἀρχῇ βασιλεύει
Κῦρος.   4. οἱ ποιοῦντες ταῦτα τυγχάνουσι ὄντες Ἕλληνες.

   5. λέγει ὅτι ἐβούλοντο τοὺς στρατιώτᾱς ἐκ τῆς χώρᾱς ἀθροῖσαι.

II. 1. Being dishonored, Cyrus wishes to rule instead of his
brother.   2. They came from the city to collect soldiers.
3. Since he was[1] a friend, Aristippus asked Cyrus for
money.   4. When they were present,[2] Cyrus spoke as
follows.[3]   5. Though hard pressed by his opponents, he
overcame them.

Ppl. with pred. nom.   [2] Gen. abs.   [3] Cf. 127.

Fig. 6.—A Banquet Scene

LESSON XXII

The Subjunctive

196. καὶ δεῖται[7] αὐτοῦ μὴ[1] πρόσθεν καταλῦσαι πρὸς τοὺς ἀντιστασιώτᾱς πρὶν ἂν[2] αὐτῷ συμβουλεύσηται.[3] οὕτω δὲ αὖ τὸ[4] ἐν Θετταλίᾳ ἐλάνθανεν[5] αὐτῷ τρεφόμενον στράτευμα.

197.   VOCABULARY

ἄν, see note 2 and General Vocabulary.

δέω, δεήσω, ἐδέησα, *want* (gen.); impersonally, *be necessary,* often with the value of a mere auxiliary, *must;* mid., *want for oneself, need, beg.* With gen. or with acc. of the thing, and gen. of the person.

ἐάν (εἰ + ἄν), *if* (with subjunctive).

Θετταλίᾱ, ᾱς, ἡ *Thessaly.*

ἵνα, final particle, *that, in order that.*

καταλύω, καταλύσω, κατέλῦσα, *unloose, come to terms with* (πρός).

λανθάνω, λήσω, ἔλαθον, *be hidden, escape notice.* [Lethe]

μή, adv., *not.*

πρίν (πρό), conj. adv., *before, until.*

πρόσθεν (πρός), adv., *before;* **πρόσθεν . . . . πρίν,** *before . . . . until.*

συμβουλεύω, συμβουλεύσω, συνεβούλευσα, *plan with, counsel* (dat.); mid., *consult with* (dat.).

τρέφω, θρέψω,[6] ἔθρεψα, *nourish, support.* [atrophy]

198. Only the present, aorist, and perfect tenses are found in the subjunctive. The perfect subjunctive active is very rare and may be omitted.

Learn the present subjunctive of εἰμί (655), the present and aorist, active and middle subjunctive of λύω (638, 639), and the second aorist active and middle subjunctive of λείπω (641).

---

[1] μή is the regular negative with the infinitive except in indirect discourse. [2] ἄν is a modal adv. used chiefly with subj. and opt.; it cannot be translated here. [3] When the principal clause is negative, πρίν meaning *until* is followed by the subj., if the main verb is in a primary tense; by the optative if the main verb is in a secondary (historical) tense. [4] The article belongs to στράτευμα. [5] See 181, 4. [6] When φ and σ unite, they form ψ (πσ). Sometimes, as in τρέφω, θρέψω, the aspirate in ψ is drawn into the initial consonant, giving ϑ for τ. [7] I. e. δέεται; cf. p. 80, n. 4.

199. Observe that the subjunctive has ω and η in place of o/ε of the present, and that it has the primary endings (97, 105) in all tenses. As in Latin the force of the tenses varies, but in general both present and aorist refer to future time, with the important distinction that the present represents the action as in progress or repeated, the aorist as simply occurring.

200. Purpose clauses are introduced by ἵνα, ὡς, or ὅπως, *wh* and take the subjunctive after primary tenses. After secondary tenses the subjunctive may be retained for vividness, or the verb may be in the optative. The negative is μή. *ne*

201. A more vivid future condition has in the protasis (condition) ἐάν (εἰ + ἄν, also sometimes written ἤν, ἄν) with the subjunctive, and the future indicative, or some future expression in the apodosis (conclusion). It implies considerable likelihood of fulfilment. ἐὰν κελεύσῃ, αὐτοὺς πέμψω, *if he orders it I shall send them*, or *if he will order it I shall send them.*

202. In all conditional sentences the negative in the protasis is μή, in the apodosis, οὐ.

203. A conditional sentence may state what is or will be true on a particular occasion (e. g. the sentence above, 201), or what is always true if the protasis is fulfilled. The latter is called a general condition. The present general condition always has in the protasis the same form as the vivid future particular condition, but in the apodosis it has the present indicative: ἐὰν κελεύσῃ, αὐτοὺς πέμπω, *if he orders it, I (always) send them.*

204.   DRILL

I. Locate the following:

1. καταλύσωμεν, συμβουλεύσωνται, λανθάνῃ.
2. λύσηται, λύσητε, λύσῃ (two forms), λύησθε.
3. λύσαντι, λύσᾱσα, λύουσα, λύοντα.

II. Give:
1. 3 sing. of the subjs. act. of ἀθροίζω.
2. 3 plu. of subjs. mid. of βουλεύω.
3. 3 plu. pres., fut., and aor. ind. (act. and mid.) of λύω.

205. EXERCISES

I. 1. ἐὰν ταύτας τὰς πόλεις λαβεῖν βουλώμεθα, Κῦρος κωλύσει. 2. ἐπιβουλεύσουσι τοῖς σατράπαις ἵνα βασιλεύσωσιν ἀντὶ τῶν ἄλλων. 3. ἐὰν μὴ Κῦρος χρήματα ἔχῃ, στράτευμα οὐ τρέφει. 4. συμβουλεύσομαι Κύρῳ ἵνα καταλύσωμεν πρὸς τοὺς ἐν Θετταλίᾳ. 5. ἐδέοντο Κύρου μὴ τρέφειν ταῦτα τὰ δύο στρατεύματα.

II. 1. He arrests Cyrus in order to send him away from the province. 2. They wish Artaxerxes to become their friend. 3. When he had collected an army, he came to terms with his opponents. 4. If Clearchus comes to terms with his soldiers, they will not send for Cyrus. 5. He secretly[1] begged Cyrus to support these soldiers.

3/4

LESSON XXIII

The Perfect System

206. Πρόξενον δὲ τὸν Βοιώτιον ξένον ὄντα ἐκέλευσε λαβόντα[2] ἄνδρας ὅτι πλείστους[3] παραγενέσθαι, ὡς[4] εἰς Πισίδας βουλόμενος στρατεύεσθαι, ὡς[4] πράγματα παρεχόντων[5] τῶν Πισιδῶν τῇ Ἰωνίᾳ.

207. VOCABULARY

Βοιώτιος, ᾱ, ον, *Boeotian*, an inhabitant of Boeotia.
παραγίγνομαι, παραγενήσομαι, παρεγενόμην, *be present* or *at hand, arrive*.
Πῑσίδης, ου, ὁ, *Pisidian*, an inhabitant of Pisidia.
πρᾶγμα, ματος, τό, *deed, thing, trouble* (usually plural). [**practical**] *pragmatis*
Πρόξενος, ου, ὁ, *Proxenus*.

---

[1] See 181, 4.   [2] 181, 3.   [3] ὅτι πλείστους = *the most possible*, adj. modifier of ἄνδρας; cf. Lat. *quam plurimos*.   [4] ὡς, with ppl. gives the alleged reason, *on the ground that, as if*; cf. 186, b.   [5] 157.

208. Learn the first perfect and pluperfect indicative active, the perfect subjunctive, infinitive, and participle of λύω (638), and the second perfect and pluperfect indicative active, the perfect subjunctive, infinitive, and participle of λείπω (641).

The perfect and pluperfect active have a reduplication at the beginning. If the verb begins with a single consonant (except ρ), the reduplication consists of prefixing that consonant and ε: λύω, perfect λέλυκα. A rough mute becomes the cognate smooth mute (599, 2): θαυμάζω, τεθαύμακα.

If a verb begins with two consonants (except a mute and liquid) or a double consonant (ζ, ξ, ψ), or with ρ, the syllable ε takes the place of reduplication. If a verb begins with a short vowel or diphthong, the reduplication takes the same form as the temporal augment. E. g. στρατεύω, ἐστράτευκα; ἀγγέλλω, ἤγγελκα. A long vowel remains unchanged: ὠφελέω, ὠφέληκα.

209. The pluperfect augments the perfect by prefixing ε. In verbs which begin with a vowel this augment does not have a visible effect.

210. The first perfect adds κα and the first pluperfect adds κη to the reduplicated stem. The first perfect as a rule is found only in pure,[1] liquid, and τ-stems.

211. Pure stems add the endings without changing the stem except to lengthen a final short vowel: λύω, λέλυκα, ποιέω, πεποίηκα.

212. Monosyllabic liquid stems change ε to α: στέλλω [στελ], ἔσταλκα.

213. Verbs with stems ending in a τ-mute (τ, δ, θ) drop this mute before κα, κη: θαυμάζω, τεθαύμακα.

---

[1] Verbs whose stem ends in a vowel.

214. The second perfect adds *a*, and the second pluperfect η. Most verbs with stems ending in a π-mute (π, β, φ) or a κ-mute (κ, γ, χ) have a second perfect. The final letter of the stem is usually aspirated. τρίβω, τέτριφα; πέμπω, πέπομφα. Note that the ε of monosyllabic stems is changed to ο in the second perfect.

215. The perfect tenses have primary endings (97, 105) and *a* as a characteristic vowel. In the third singular this becomes ε (cf. first aorist). The pluperfect has the secondary endings (97, 105).

216. The perfect indicative is used to denote the completion of an action or attainment of a state at the present time; the pluperfect denotes the completion of an action or the attainment of a state in the past. The force of the tense is the same whether the form is first or second perfect.

217.   DRILL

I. Locate the following verb forms:

   1. λελύκαμεν ἐλελύκη, λέλυκε.   4. λελοίπᾱσι, λιπεῖν, ἐστρατευκέναι.

   2. ἔλῡσα, λελύκᾱσι, ἐλελύκεσαν.   5. ἐλελοίπη, συγγενόμενος, λελοιπώς.

   3. ἀπέθανε, ἐπείθετο, ὑπήρχετε.

II. 1. Form first perfects of θύω, ἀθροίζω, κελεύω, κωλύω, πολεμέω, τῑμάω, στρατεύω.

   2. They had collected, we have sacrificed, you have left.

   3. He has honored, he had made war, they have ordered.

   4. He had left, you collected, they had made war.

218.   EXERCISES

I. 1. ἐκεκελεύκεμεν τὸν ἄνδρα παραγενέσθαι. 2. κεκωλύκᾱσι τοὺς στρατηγοὺς λαβεῖν ἄνδρας. 3. ἡρπάκεσαν τὴν τῶν Πῑσιδῶν χώρᾱν. 4. ἐστρατεύκη εἰς τοὺς Πῑσίδᾱς. 5. οὗτοι οἱ ἄνδρες παρεῖχον πράγματα τῇ ἀρχῇ.

II. 1. He has commanded Proxenus to make an expedition against them. 2. They had collected men on the ground that Tissaphernes wished to cause trouble to the Pisidians. 3. So he took[1] Boeotian men and came (was on hand). 4. He desired him to be present because he was a good soldier. 5. He had ordered as many generals as possible to be on hand.

LESSON XXIV

The Aorist Passive

219. Σοφαίνετον δὲ τὸν Στυμφάλιον καὶ Σωκράτην τὸν Ἀχαιόν, ξένους ὄντας καὶ τούτους, ἐκέλευσεν ἄνδρας λαβόντας ἐλθεῖν ὅτι πλείστους[2] ὡς πολεμήσων Τισσαφέρνει σὺν τοῖς φυγάσι τοῖς Μιλησίων. καὶ ἐποίουν οὕτως οὗτοι.

220.   VOCABULARY

Ἀχαιός, ά, όν, *an Achaean,* of Achaea.

γράφω, γράψω, ἔγραψα, γέγραφα, ἐγράφην, *write.* [**graphic, -graph**]

Μῑλήσιος, ᾱ, ον, *Milesian, of Miletus.*

Σοφαίνετος, ου, ὁ, *Sophaenetus,* a Greek general.

Στυμφάλιος, ᾱ, ον, *Stymphalian,* of Stymphalus.

σύν, prep. (dat.), *with.* [**syn**tax]

Σωκράτης, ου, ὁ, *Socrates,* a Greek general.

221. Except in two sets of tenses, the first and second aorist and the first and second future, the verb has the same form for the passive and middle, and one can determine which it is only by the needs of the sentence.

222. Learn the first and second aorist passive, in the indicative, subjunctive, infinitive, and participle of λύω (640) and φαίνω (642). Observe that the stem of the first aorist (also called the first passive stem) is formed by adding θε. This becomes θη except when followed by a vowel in inflection: λυθε [λυθη]. It is augmented and uses the secondary endings of the *active.* Thus the passive voice requires no new set of personal endings.

---

[1] 181, 3. [2] Modifies ἄνδρας. For translation see 206, n. 3.

223. A labial mute (π, β, φ) before θε becomes φ; a palatal mute (κ, γ, χ) becomes χ; a lingual mute (τ, δ, θ) becomes ς.

224. The second aorist stem (second passive) is formed by adding ε (η, when not followed by a vowel or two consonants in inflection) to the verb-stem. Its inflection, therefore, is like that of the first aorist except for the omission of θ. Stems containing ε change this to α.

225. The first and second future occur so rarely that they may be omitted at this time.

226. DRILL

I. Review the meanings, learn the aorist passive, and give the complete principal parts of the following verbs (consult the Greek-English vocabulary):

1. συλλαμβάνω, πορεύομαι, τάττω.   3. ἀθροίζω, ἄγω, τῑμάω.
2. πείθω, κωλύω, πέμπω.   4. κελεύω, βούλομαι, λείπω.

II. Translate, using the aorist of these verbs:
1. He obeyed, they were collected.
2. Cyrus was arrested, the soldiers proceeded.
3. He wished, you were left, he was honored.
4. They were left, we were arranged, they were ordered.

227. EXERCISES

I. 1. ἠξίου καταλύσᾱς πρὸς τοὺς στρατευομένους ἐπὶ τὸν Κῦρον ἐλθεῖν. 2. ἐπέμφθη σὺν τοῖς ἀγγέλοις εἰς Σωκράτην. 3. ἐπειρᾶτο κωλῦσαι αὐτοὺς ἵνα μὴ συλληφθῇ. 4. ἐκ Θετταλίᾱς ὁρμησάμενος[1] ἐβουλήθη στράτευμα ἀθροισθῆναι.

II. 1. He has commanded them to come that he may have good men. 2. If they do[2] these things, they will discover[3] the plot. 3. They aided those who dwelt[4] in Ionia. 4. They took counsel with the fugitives.

---

[1] 181, 3.   [2] Ppl. of ποιέω.   [3] αἰσθάνομαι.   [4] 131, n. 3.

LESSON XXV

LIQUID VERBS.   FUTURE AND FIRST AORIST

228. ἐπεὶ δ'¹ ἐδόκει² ἤδη πορεύεσθαι αὐτῷ ἄνω, τὴν μὲν
πρόφασιν ἐποιεῖτο ὡς Πισίδᾱς βουλόμενος ἐκβαλεῖν παντάπᾱσιν ἐκ τῆς χώρᾱς· καὶ ἀθροίζει ὡς ἐπὶ τούτους³ τό τε
βαρβαρικὸν καὶ τὸ Ἑλληνικόν.⁴

229.   VOCABULARY

ἄνω, adv., *up, upward;* often of a march, *inland.*

ἀποκτείνω, ἀποκτενῶ, ἀπέκτεινα, ἀπέκτονα, *kill, slay, put to death.*

βαρβαρικός, ή, όν, *barbarian, non-Greek, foreign.*

δοκέω, δόξω, ἔδοξα, δέδογμαι, ἐδόχθην, *seem, seem best* or *good, think;* often
    impersonal.   [**dogma**, ortho**dox**]

ἐκβάλλω, ἐκβαλῶ, ἐξέβαλον, ἐκβέβληκα, ἐκβέβλημαι, ἐξεβλήθην, *to throw out,
    drive out, exile.*

ἤδη, adv., *already, now.*

μένω, μενῶ, ἔμεινα, μεμένηκα, *stay, remain, wait for.*

παντάπᾱσιν, adv., *utterly, entirely, altogether.*

πορεύομαι, πορεύσομαι, πεπόρευμαι, ἐπορεύθην, pass. dep., *proceed, march.* *go*

πρόφασις, εως, ἡ, *excuse, pretext.*   [**prophet**]   *set out*

φαίνω, φανῶ, ἔφηνα, πέφαγκα and πέφηνα, πέφασμαι, ἐφάνθην and ἐφάνην, act.
    show, make appear; mid. *show oneself, appear.*   [em**phasis**,
    phenomenon]

230. Liquid verbs (i. e. verbs whose stems end in λ, μ, ν, ρ)
form the future by adding ε ο/ε instead of σ ο/ε.   The inflection then becomes like that of the present of a contract ε-verb:
μένω [μεν], future μενῶ (μενέω); βάλλω [βαλ], future βαλῶ.

231. In the first aorist *a* is added instead of σα, and the
last vowel of the stem is lengthened to compensate: *a* to η
(ᾱ after ι or ρ), ε to ει, ι to ῑ, υ to ῡ.   μένω [μεν], aor. ἔμεινα;
φαίνω [φαν], ἔφηνα; σημαίνω [σημαν], ἐσήμηνα.

---

¹ 232.   ² ἐδόκει αὐτῷ, *it seemed good to him, he decided.*   ³ *As if against these*
(*the Pisidians*).   ὡς, *as if*, shows that this is only the apparent purpose of gathering
an army.   ⁴ Sc. στράτευμα.

Learn the future and first aorist active and middle indicative, subjunctive, infinitive, and participles of φαίνω (642).

The second aorist of liquid verbs presents no peculiarities; βάλλω [βαλ], second aorist ἔβαλον.

232. Hiatus occurs when a word which ends in a vowel is followed by a word which begins with a vowel. It is avoided in two ways: (1) by the insertion of ν-movable (34), (2) by elision. Elision is the cutting-off in pronunciation of a final short vowel. The omission is indicated in writing by the apostrophe (').

233. DRILL

I. Locate the following forms:

   1. φανῶσι, φανοῦσι, μενοῦμεν.   4. ἔδοξε, ἠξίουν, ἀποκτενεῖ.

   2. βάλλει, βαλεῖ, διέβαλε.   5. ἐποίει, ποιεῖ, μενεῖν.

   3. ἐφήναμεν, ἔμειναν, ἔμεινεν.

II.—1. I remained, he will throw, they will show.

   2. He threw, they showed, we shall remain.

   3. He will traduce, they were slaying, you will remain.

   4. He collected, he has collected, they will march.

   5. They make, they will traduce, they were staying.

234. EXERCISES

I. 1. ἐκβαλοῦσι τοὺς κωλύοντας. 2. ἐὰν δοκῇ πορεύεσθαι στράτευμα συλλέξομεν. 3. ἐπορεύθησαν πρόφασιν ποιησάμενοι ὡς βουλόμενοι καταλῦσαι. 4. ἔπεισε τοῦτον τὸν ἄνδρα τοὺς στρατιώτας πρὸ τῆς πόλεως τάξαι. 5. ἦλθον μὲν ἐκβαλοῦντες[1] τοὺς Πισίδας, ἀλλ' οὐκ ἐπολέμησαν.

II. 1. They marched inland. 2. After driving the Pisidians out of the country they will remain in this city. 3. The generals decided to start out as if against them. 4. This was another excuse. 5. He collected the Greek soldiers with the intention of marching inland.

---

[1] 181, 5.

LESSON XXVI

Perfect Middle. The Relative Pronoun

235. ἐνταῦθα καὶ παραγγέλλει τῷ τε Κλεάρχῳ[1] λαβόντι[2] ἥκειν ὅσον ἦν αὐτῷ στράτευμα, καὶ τῷ Ἀριστίππῳ
συναλλαγέντι πρὸς τοὺς οἴκοι ἀποπέμψαι πρὸς ἑαυτὸν[3] ὃ
εἶχε στράτευμα.[4]

236.   VOCABULARY

ἐνταῦθα, adv., *here, there, thereupon.*

ὅς, ἥ, ὅ, rel. pro. (definite), *who, which.*

ὅσος, η, ον, rel. pro. (indefinite), *how much, many, great,* or *as much as, all that.*

παραγγέλλω, παραγγελῶ, παρήγγειλα. παρήγγελκα, παρήγγελμαι, παρηγγέλθην, *pass along an order, command, order* (dat.).

συναλλάττω, συναλλάξω, συνήλλαξα, συνήλλαχα, συνήλλαγμαι, συνηλλάχθην, and συνηλλάγην, *bring to terms, reconcile;* mid., *to become reconciled with, to come to terms with.* *change by bringing together* *make*

237. Learn the perfect and pluperfect, middle and passive in indicative, subjunctive, infinitive, and participle of λύω (639, 640).   The perfect, middle and passive of pure verbs consists merely of the reduplicated stem with personal endings, except in the subjunctive and optative where the form is compound, as in Latin perfect passive, consisting of the perfect participle and εἰμί. The pluperfect has the augment.

238. After the passive voice agency is regularly expressed by ὑπό with the genitive (178, n. 2), but with the perfect and pluperfect the dative is common.

239. Learn the declension of ὅς, ἥ, ὅ, the definite relative pronoun (634).   Its forms are like the article, except (1) ὅς for ὁ, (2) no initial τ, (3) all forms are accented.

---

[1] The dat. (indirect obj. of παραγγέλλει) displaces the subject of the infin. which would be acc.   [2] The English order is ἥκειν λαβόντι στράτευμα ὅσον ἦν αὐτῷ. στράτευμα is incorporated in the rel. clause.   [3] 146, n. 7.   [4] Cf. n. 2 end.

240. Learn the declension of λυθείς (619). In the same manner decline φανείς.

241. DRILL

I. Locate the following forms:

   1. ἐκβέβληται, ἐπεπόρευτο, ἐλέλυντο.

   2. συνηλλάγησαν, συνήλλαξαν, συναλλαγέντες.

   3. παραγγελεῖς, παραγγελθείς, παρήγγελται.

   4. ἅ, ᾗ, οἵ, φανέντι, φανεῖσι, λυθείσαις.

II. 1. We have been exiled, ordered, suspected.

   2. He has ordered, reconciled, set out.

   3. They had been proceeding, ordered, they had ransomed.

   4. Having been sent, reconciled, ordered.

   5. To whom (dat. sing. and plu. in all genders).

242. EXERCISES

I. 1. ἐὰν ἐκβάλωσι τοὺς οἴκοι, ἀποπέμψω τοὺς ἄλλους. 2. παρήγγειλε τῷ Κύρῳ ἥκειν ἔχοντι τὸ στράτευμα. 3. τοὺς στρατηγοὺς ἐλάνθανον πορευόμενοι. 4. ἐὰν Κῦρον ὠφελεῖν βούληται, ἀγαθὸς φίλος ἔσται. 5. εἴληφεν ἣν εἶχε στρατιὰν καὶ οἱ Ἕλληνες οὐκ ᾔσθοντο.

II. 1. Thereupon Clearchus took good soldiers and came. 2. For Cyrus sent word to him to collect the men whom he had. 3. If it shall seem best to Cyrus, we shall drive them from the city.

Fig. 7.—Preparing for Battle

LESSON XXVII

The Optative Active. Purpose Clauses

243. καὶ Ξενίᾳ τῷ ᾿Αρκάδι, ὃς αὐτῷ προειστήκει[1] τοῦ
ἐν ταῖς πόλεσι ξενικοῦ, ἥκειν παραγγέλλει λαβόντα[2] τοὺς
ἄνδρας πλὴν ὁπόσοι ἱκανοὶ ἦσαν τὰς ἀκροπόλεις φυλάττειν.[3]

244.   VOCABULARY

ἀκρόπολις, εως, ἡ, *acropolis, citadel.*
᾿Αρκάς, άδος, ὁ, *an Arcadian.*
ἥκω, ἥξω, only in pres. and fut., *come, be present;* usually of completed
   action: *have come, have arrived.*
ἱκανός, ή, όν, *sufficient, able.*
ξενικός, ή όν, *foreign, mercenary;* as neut. noun, *a mercenary force.* *hired troops*
ὁπόσος, η, ον, rel. pro., *as much* (*many, great*) *as;* or *how much* (*many,
   great*).
φυλάττω φυλάξω, ἐφύλαξα, πεφύλαχα, πεφύλαγμαι, ἐφυλάχθην, *watch, guard.*
Ξενίᾱς, ου, ὁ, *Xenias,* a Greek general.

245. Many verbs do not have all the tense systems (80).
In lesson vocabularies hereafter when parts are not given it
means that they are not in common use in Xenophon.

246. In the aorist tense some deponent verbs have the
middle forms and some have the passive. The former are
called middle deponents; the latter, passive deponents:
ἡγέομαι, aorist ἡγησάμην, middle deponent; πορεύομαι, aorist
ἐπορεύθην, passive deponent. This distinction is without
effect on the meaning of the verb.

247. The optative has the following tenses: present,
future, aorist, perfect, future perfect. Learn the present
optative of εἰμί (655), the second aorist optative active of
λείπω (641), and the optative active (all tenses) of λύω (638).

---

[1] *Had command of;* govs. gen.   [2] Agrees with the understood subject of ἥκειν
instead of being attracted to case of Ξενίᾳ; cf. Κλεάρχῳ λαβόντι, 235. The difference
is due to the position of the words.   [3] Infin. with ἱκανοί.

248. The force of the tenses in the optative (except in indirect discourse) is the same as in the subjunctive (199).

249. Observe that in all tenses the secondary endings are used, but that the first person singular has μι. The personal endings are preceded by a mood sign ι (ιε in the third person plural of the active and the aorist passive) which unites with the vowel of the tense stem to form οι (αι in the first aorist, a + ι = αι). Irregular forms are used in the second and third person singular, and the third plural of the first aorist active.

250. After a secondary tense purpose may be expressed by ἵνα, ὡς, or ὅπως with the optative, or the subjunctive may be retained for vividness: οἱ στρατιῶται ἦλθον ἵνα φυλάττοιεν τὴν ἀκρόπολιν (or ἵνα φυλάττωσιν), *the soldiers came to guard the acropolis.* Cf. 200. *Negative is μή*

251. DRILL

I. Locate the following:

1. ἤκοι, λελύκοι, λύοι.
2. φυλάξειεν, λύσειαν, λύσειας.
3. φυλάξαι, λάβοι, λύσαιεν.
4. λύσαιμι, φυλάξαιμεν, ἤκοιμεν.
5. εἴην, εἶεν, εἴησαν.

II. Give:

1. 3 sing. of the optatives active of λύω; 3 plu. of the optatives active of φυλάττω.
2. In order that he, you, they, might be.
3. In order that he might take, come, guard.

252. EXERCISES

I. 1. ἔταττον ἄνδρας ἱκανοὺς τὸ πεδίον φυλάξαι. 2. τὰς ἀκροπόλεις πεφυλάχασιν. 3. ἔλαβε ὅσοι ἦσαν ἄνδρες. 4. συναλλαγεὶς πρὸς τοὺς οἴκοι ἧκεν ἔχων τοὺς ἄλλους πλὴν ὁπόσοι ἐν μάχῃ ἦσαν, ἵνα Κύρῳ συμπράξειεν.

II. 1. They were capable of marching. 2. If they guard the acropolis, they will have the city. 3. After announcing these things to Cyrus, he took the army which he had. 4. They took the rest in order that they might guard the acropolis.

LESSON XXVIII

INDIRECT DISCOURSE.   CONDITIONAL SENTENCES

253. ἐκάλεσε δὲ καὶ[1] τοὺς Μίλητον πολιορκοῦντας, καὶ τοὺς φυγάδας ἐκέλευσε[2] σὺν αὐτῷ στρατεύεσθαι, ὑποσχόμενος αὐτοῖς, εἰ καλῶς καταπράξειεν ἐφ᾽ ἃ[3] ἐστρατεύετο, μὴ πρόσθεν παύσεσθαι πρὶν[4] αὐτοὺς καταγάγοι[5] οἴκαδε.

254.   VOCABULARY

ἀεί, adv., *always, ever.*

εἰ, conj. (proclitic), *if.*

καλέω, καλῶ (for καλέσω), ἐκάλεσα,[6] κέκληκα, κέκλημαι, ἐκλήθην, *call, sum-mon.* [**calendar**, ec**clesiastic**]

καλῶς, adv., *well, honorably.*   *beautifully, nobly rightly*

κατάγω, κατάξω, κατήγαγον, *lead back, restore.*   *καταπέπραχα or πραγα*

καταπράττω (κατα + πραγ), καταπράξω, κατέπρᾱξα, καταπέπρᾱγμαι, κατ-επράχθην, *do effectively, accomplish.*   *achieve, complete*

οἴκαδε, adv., *homeward.*   *home*

παύω, παύσω, ἔπαυσα, πέπαυκα, πέπαυμαι, ἐπαύθην, *cause to cease, stop;* mid., *stop oneself, cease.* [**pause, pose**]

πολιορκέω, πολιορκήσω, ἐπολιόρκησα, πεπολιόρκηκα, πεπολιόρκημαι, ἐπολιορ-κήθην, *besiege.*

ὑπισχνέομαι, ὑποσχήσομαι, ὑπεσχόμην, ὑπέσχημαι, *hold oneself under, undertake, promise.*

255. Learn the optative (all tenses), middle and passive, of λύω (639, 640), the second aorist optative middle of λείπω (641), the second aorist optative passive of φαίνω (642), and the future optative of εἰμί (655).

256. A quoted sentence (indirect discourse) may be introduced by ὅτι (*that*) or ὡς (*how*). After a primary tense an indicative does not change its mood or tense; after a secondary tense it may be changed to the optative of the same tense or retained unchanged.   πέμπω, *I send;*

---

[1] When καί follows δέ it is usually intensive, *also, as well, too.*   [2] Do not confuse this verb with καλέω.   [3] Antecedent omitted; it would be ταῦτα, object of καταπράξειεν.   [4] Note vocabulary, 197.   [5] Cf. 196, n. 3.   [6] Note that the ε in the stem is not lengthened in the aorist, as is usually the case with vowel stems.

λέγει ὅτι πέμπει, *he says that he sends;* ἔλεξεν ὅτι πέμπει (or πέμποι), *he said that he sent.*

257. Before translating English indirect discourse into Greek, the student should first find the tense of the direct form. This will always be the right tense to use in Greek.

258. The less vivid future condition has εἰ with the optative in the protasis and the optative with ἄν in the apodosis. εἰ κελεύσειε, αὐτοὺς πέμψαιμι ἄν, *if he should order it, I would send them.*

259. A general condition in past time has the optative in the protasis, but in the apodosis has the imperfect indicative. εἰ κελεύσειε, αὐτοὺς ἔπεμπον, *if ever he ordered it, I used to send them.*

260.   DRILL

I. Locate the following forms:

  1. κληθείη, παύσαιο, ἀγάγοι.

  2. ὑπόσχοιτο, καταπεπρᾱγμένοι εἶεν.

  3. ἔσοιντο, πολιορκήσοιεν, θύσειεν.

  4. παύσεσθε, ὑποσχήσοισθε, ἐσοίμην.

II. Give:

  1. (*a*) 3 sing., (*b*) 3 plu., (*c*) 2 plu. of all the middle and passive optatives of λύω.

  2. 1 plu. of the optatives middle of κελεύω.

261.   EXERCISES

I. 1. εἰ Κῦρος ὑπόσχοιτο ἐλθεῖν εἰς τὴν πόλιν, ἔλθοι ἄν. 2. ὁ δ' ἔλεξεν ὅτι καλῶς καταπράξειεν. 3. λέξει ὅτι ἐλθὼν τὴν ἀκρόπολιν ἐφύλαττεν. 4. ἔλεξεν ὅτι χρῡσίον λαβὼν πορεύοιτο. 5. ἔτυχον ὄντες ἀγαθοί.

II. 1. He said that he was restoring the fugitives. 2. If they should accomplish these things successfully, he would lead them home. 3. He promised to summon those besieging Miletus, if he made an expedition. 4. If he summoned the fugitives, they always came. 5. He says that the fugitives will not pause.

LESSON XXIX

Comparison of Adjectives

262. οἱ δὲ ἡδέως ἐπείθοντο· ἐπίστευον γὰρ αὐτῷ· καὶ λαβόντες τὰ ὅπλα παρῆσαν εἰς[1] Σάρδεις. Ξενίᾱς μὲν δὴ τοὺς ἐκ τῶν πόλεων λαβὼν παρεγένετο εἰς[1] Σάρδεις ὁπλίτᾱς εἰς[2] τετρακισχῑλίους, Πρόξενος δὲ παρῆν ἔχων ὁπλίτᾱς μὲν εἰς[2] πεντακοσίους καὶ χῑλίους, γυμνῆτας δὲ πεντακοσίους, Σοφαίνετος δὲ ὁ Στυμφάλιος ὁπλίτᾱς ἔχων χῑλίους, Σωκράτης δὲ ὁ Ἀχαιὸς ὁπλίτᾱς ἔχων ὡς[2] πεντακοσίους.

263.   VOCABULARY

γυμνής, ῆτος, ὁ, or γυμνήτης, ου, ὁ, *light-armed foot soldier.* *gymnast*

εὐδαίμων, ον, gen. ονος, adj., *of good fate, prosperous, fortunate.*

ἡδέως, adv., *sweetly, gladly.*

ἡδύς, εῖα, ύ, *sweet, pleasant.* [**hedonism**] 561⁴

ὁπλίτης, ου, ὁ, *hoplite, heavy-armed soldier.*

ὅπλον, ου, τό, *implement,* plu. *arms.* [pan**oply**] *armor*

πεντακόσιοι, αι, α, *five hundred.*

πιστεύω, πιστεύσω, ἐπίστευσα, πεπίστευμαι, ἐπιστεύθην, *trust* (dat.). *believe*

Σάρδεις, εων, αἱ, *Sardis,* a city of Asia Minor.

χῑλιοι, αι, α, *thousand.*

264. Most adjectives form the comparative and superlative by adding τερος and τατος to the stem of the positive. The declension is that of other adjectives of the first and second declensions ending in ος, η (or ᾱ), ον.

If the penult contains a short vowel not followed by two consonants, the final ο of the stem becomes ω. This is to avoid so many short syllables: νέος, νεώτερος, but πιστός, πιστότερος. The superlative, when not accompanied by the article, may be translated by *very*, as in Latin.

---

1 εἰς and the acc. are used even after παρῆσαν as though it were a verb of motion.
2 With numerals εἰς means *as many as*; ὡς means *about.*

*Stem of positive drops the s of masculine; e.g.
καλός stem in καλο*

265. A few adjectives add ἴων, ιστος, to form the comparative and superlative. These endings are added to the root: ἡδύς, ἡδίων, ἥδιστος.

266. Learn the declension of ἡδίων and εὐδαίμων (615).

267. The most common adjectives with irregular comparison are:

Positive	Comparative	Superlative
1 ἀγαθός, *good*	ἀμείνων	ἄριστος
	βελτίων	βέλτιστος
	κρείττων	κράτιστος
2 κακός, *bad*	χείρων [2]	χείριστος
	ἥττων	ἥκιστα (adv.)
3 καλός, *beautiful*	καλλίων	κάλλιστος
4 μῑκρός,[1] *small*	μείων	
5 ὀλίγος, *little*, plu. *few*	ἐλάττων	ἐλάχιστος
6 ἡδύς, *sweet*	ἡδίων	ἥδιστος
7 πολύς, *much*, plu. *many*	πλείων or πλέων	πλεῖστος
8 ταχύς, *swift*	θάττων	τάχιστος
9 μέγας, *great*	μείζων	μέγιστος

268. DRILL

I. Locate and give the meaning of the following:

1. καλλίονες, ἡδῑόνων, μείζους.   4. θάττονος, βελτίονι, κρείττονες.
2. πλεῖστοι, ἀρίστων, ἡδῑω.   5. λυθείη, κελεύσειεν, λύσειαν.
3. μέγιστος, πλείονα, κάλλιστα.

II. Give: (1) dat. sing.; (2) dat. plu.; (3) acc. sing.; (4) acc. plu.; (5) nom. plu., of εὐδαίμων ὁπλίτης, μεῖζον πεδίον.

269. EXERCISES

I. 1. Ξενίᾱς ὑπέσχετο χῑλίους γυμνῆτας καλέσαι. 2. ἐκεῖνοι καλλίους τῶνδε[3] ἦσαν. 3. εἰ ἔρχοιτο, ἀπαράσκευοι εἴημεν ἄν. 4. Ξενίᾱς ἦλθεν ἔχων στρατιώτᾱς πλείστους. 5. ἡδέως αὐτῷ πειθόμεθα, φίλος γὰρ Κύρῳ ἦν.

II. 1. Cyrus was the youngest son. 2. He had the greatest army. 3. The best soldiers did not trust their general. 4. He was younger than Artaxerxes.[3] 5. These hoplites are swifter.

---

[1] Also compared regularly, μῑκρότερος, μῑκρότατος.   [2] Also κακῑων, κάκιστος.   [3] Cf. 522.

LESSON XXX

THE IMPERATIVE MOOD

270. Πασίων δὲ ὁ Μεγαρεὺς τριᾱκοσίους μὲν ὁπλῑ́τᾱς, τριᾱκοσίους δὲ πελταστὰς ἔχων παρεγένετο· ἦν δὲ καὶ[1] οὗτος καὶ ὁ Σωκράτης τῶν ἀμφὶ Μίλητον στρατευομένων.[2] οὗτοι μὲν εἰς Σάρδεις αὐτῷ[3] ἀφίκοντο.

271. VOCABULARY

ἀφικνέομαι, ἀφίξομαι, ἀφῑκόμην, ἀφῑγμαι, *arrive, reach, come.*

διώκω, διώξω, ἐδίωξα, δεδίωχα, ἐδιώχθην, *pursue.*

δύναμις, εως, ἡ, *power, force* (of troops). [**dynamo**]

ἐάω, ἐάσω, εἴᾱσα, εἴᾱκα, εἴᾱμαι, εἰάθην, *allow, permit.*

εὖ, adv., *well.* [**eu**logy]

θεός, οῦ, ὁ or ἡ, *god, goddess.* [pan**theism, theo**logy]

κακός, ή, όν, *bad, cowardly.* [**caco**phonous]

Μεγαρεύς, έως, ὁ, *a Megarian, citizen of Megara.*

νῦν, adv., *now, just now, at present.*

Πᾱσίων, ωνος, ὁ, *Pasion,* a Greek general.

πελταστής, οῦ, ὁ, *peltast* (one equipped with the πέλτη, a small shield).

χράομαι, χρήσομαι, ἐχρησάμην, κέχρημαι, ἐχρήσθην (in pass. sense); mid. depon., *use, employ* (dat.). [cata**chresis**]

272. THE PERSONAL ENDINGS FOR THE ACTIVE IMPERATIVE

	Sing.	Dual	Plu.
2	θι	τον	τε
3	τω	των	ντων

273. Learn the imperative active of λύω in the present and aorist (638), the second aorist imperative active of λείπω (641), and the present imperative active of τῑμάω, ποιέω, δηλόω (647–49). Observe in the second person singular that θι is dropped, and that the first aorist has an irregular form, e. g. λῦσον.

274. The negative with the imperative is μή.

---

[1] Co-ordinate with καί, *both . . . . and.*   [2] Pred. gen.   [3] Dative of advantage.

275. In general, the distinction between the tenses in the imperative is the same as in the subjunctive (199).

276. The imperative expresses command. Negative commands (prohibitions) are expressed by μή with the present imperative (implying a continued action) or μή with the aorist subjunctive (implying a single act). μὴ ποίει τοῦτο, *do not keep doing this;* μὴ ποιήσῃς τοῦτο, *do not do this.*

277. Exhortations are expressed by the first person of the subjunctive. The negative is μή. καλῶς ἀποθνήσκωμεν, *let us die honorably.*

278. DRILL

I. Locate the following:
1. λῦε, λίπε, ἔλῦε.
2. ποιείτω, ἐποίει, ποιεῖτε.
3. λῦόντων, λῦσάτω, λῦσωσιν.
4. ἔλῦσαν, λῦσάντων, λῦσαιμι.
5. ἀξίου, ἠξίου, τῑμᾶτε.

II. 1. Let them have, speak, let him watch.
2. Let no one annoy Cyrus.
3. Honor the gods. Do not permit.
4. Do it now. Do not remain.

279. EXERCISES

I. 1. διώκωμεν τοὺς πελταστάς, οἳ στρατεύονται ἀμφὶ Μίλητον. 2. μὴ ἐάσῃς τὸν κακὸν ὁπλίτην λαβεῖν τὰ χρήματα. 3. νῑκήσατε καὶ διώξατε τούτους εἰς τὴν ἀκρόπολιν. 4. καλεῖ δὲ καὶ Πᾱσίωνα ἵνα στρατεύηται εἰς τοὺς Πῑσίδᾱς. 5. Κῦρος ὑπέσχετο χρῆσθαι τοῖς φυγάσι τοῖς ἐκ Μιλήτου.

II. 1. The power of the gods is not small. 2. Leave the cowardly hoplites, do not honor them. 3. Let us use this money well. 4. Pasion will be present in order that he may meet Cyrus. 5. Do not make known this plot to the brother of Cyrus.

LESSON XXXI

Nouns in εύς. μι-Verbs, ἵστημι

280. Τισσαφέρνης δὲ κατανοήσᾱς ταῦτα, καὶ μείζονα[1] ἡγησάμενος εἶναι ἢ ὡς ἐπὶ Πῑσίδᾱς τὴν παρασκευήν, πορεύεται ὡς βασιλέᾱ[2] ᾗ ἐδύνατο[3] τάχιστα ἱππέᾱς ἔχων ὡς πεντακοσίους. καὶ βασιλεὺς μὲν δή, ἐπεὶ ἤκουσε[4] Τισσαφέρνους τὸν Κύρου στόλον, ἀντιπαρεσκευάζετο.

281. VOCABULARY

\ ἀκούω, ἀκούσομαι, ἤκουσα, ἀκήκοα, ἠκούσθην, *hear.* [**acoustic**] *obey, learn, listen to, learn from (+gen)*

ἀντιπαρασκευάζομαι, ἀντιπαρασκευάσομαι, ἀντιπαρεσκευασάμην, *prepare oneself in turn* (of opposition). *make counter-preparation*

\ βασιλεύς, έως, ὁ, *king.* [**basilisk, Basil**]

\ δύναμαι, δυνήσομαι, δεδύνημαι, ἐδυνήθην, *be able, can.* [**dynamite**] *have command of (gen. obj.)*

ἡγέομαι, ἡγήσομαι, ἡγησάμην, ἥγημαι, ἡγήθην, *lead, think.* *dep. mid. lead, consider (acc. + inf.)*

\ ἱππεύς, έως, ὁ, *horseman.* (*plu.*) *cavalry*

\ ἵστημι, στήσω, ἔστησα, ἔστην, ἔστηκα, ἔσταμαι, ἐστάθην, act. (except 2 aor., perf. and plup.), *make to stand, station;* mid. and 2 aor., perf. and plup. act., *take one's stand, halt.*

κατανοέω, κατανοήσω, κατενόησα, κατανενόηκα, κατανενόημαι, κατενοήθην, *observe well, notice, consider.* *perceive*

\ μέγας, μεγάλη, μέγα, *great.* [**mega**phone, o**mega**]

παρασκευή, ῆς, ἡ, *preparation.* *equipment*

\ στόλος, ου, ὁ, *expedition.*

\ τάχιστα, adv. (s. of ταχύ), *quickly;* ᾗ ἐδύνατο τ., *as quickly as he could.*

ὡς, prep. (acc.), *to,* with names of persons only.

282. Learn βασιλεύς (608) and ταχύς (614).

283. Observe that in nouns in εύς the ν of the stem is dropped before vowel endings, i. e. in all cases except in nominative and vocative singular and dative plural.   *a* in

---

[1] Pred. adj. with εἶναι modifying παρασκευήν. μείζονα . . . . ἢ ὡς, lit. *greater than as,* i. e. *too great to be.* The expedition was professedly (ὡς) against the Pisidians. *Preparation greater than against the Pisidians* would be παρασκευὴν μείζονα ἢ ἐπὶ Πῑσίδᾱς.   [2] βασιλεύς usually means the king of Persia, and may be used without the article like a proper name.   [3] Inflected like mid. (pass.) of ἵστημι.   [4] Verbs of hearing govern the acc. of the thing heard (dir. obj.) and the gen. of the source.

accusative singular and plural is long, and the genitive singular has ως in place of ος. These nouns are masculine gender and oxytone, and express the agent or person concerned.

284. Learn ἵστημι in present and imperfect indicative, active and middle (passive) (650, 652).

285. Observe that the verb stem is στα (present stem ἱστα) and the personal endings are added directly to the stem (with vowel lengthened in the singular of the present and imperfect active).

286. DRILL

I. Locate the following:
  1. ἱππεῖ ταχεῖ, πόλεις ἡδίους, οὗτοι οἱ βασιλεῖς.
  2. βασιλέᾱ, ἰχθῦς, ταχεῖς, ταῖς πόλεσι ταύταις.
  3. ἵστησι, ἵστασαι, ἱστᾶσι, ἵστασαν.
  4. ἵσταμεν, ἵστημι, ἵσταται.
  5. ἵσταντο, ἵστανται, ἵστατο.

II. Give:
  1. (a) dat. plu., (b) gen. sing., (c) acc. sing., of βασιλεὺς οὗτος, φάλαγξ ταχεῖα, πόλις μείζων.
  2. (a) 2 sing., (b) 2 plu., (c) 3 plu. pres. and imp. ind. act. and mid., of ἵστημι and λύω.

287. EXERCISES

I. 1. Κῦρος μείζονα παρασκευὴν ἐδύνατο πέμψαι. 2. βασιλεὺς ἡγησάμενος τοὺς Ἕλληνας ἀπαρασκεύους εἶναι, ὡρμᾶτο. 3. ἔχων ὁπλίτᾱς τριᾱκοσίους ἀφίκετο εἰς Σάρδεις. 4. τῷ στρατηγῷ ἐδόκει ὡς βασιλέᾱ πορεύεσθαι. 5. οἱ τοῦ βασιλέως ἱππεῖς ἐδύναντο θᾶττον πορεύεσθαι.

II. 1. They reached the plain in the following manner. 2. His brother, noticing this, gathered an army as quickly as he could. 3. They thought the plot was against him. 4. They were able to do this. 5. The horseman is able to go to the king's satrap.

LESSON XXXII

Third Declension Stems in ϵς. Imperative Middle

288. Κῦρος δὲ ἔχων οὕς[1] εἴρηκα ὡρμᾶτο ἀπὸ Σάρδεων·
καὶ ἐξελαύνει διὰ τῆς Λῡδίᾱς σταθμοὺς τρεῖς παρασάγγᾱς
εἴκοσι καὶ δύο ἐπὶ τὸν Μαίανδρον ποταμόν.

289. VOCABULARY

διά, prep. (gen.), *through;* (acc.), *through, on account of.* [**dia**meter]

εἴκοσι, *twenty.*

ἐξελαύνω [ἐλα], ἐλῶ, ἤλασα, ἐλήλακα, ἐλήλαμαι, ἠλάθην, *drive out;* generally
intrans., *march* (of the commander, i. e. *drives his army*).

ἐρῶ (fut.), εἴρηκα, εἴρημαι, ἐρρήθην, *say, speak, tell.* Defective verb. The
present is supplied from φημί or λέγω and the 2 aor. by εἶπον.

εὖρος, ους, τό, *width, breadth.* [an**eurism**]

Λῡδίᾱ, ᾱς, ἡ, *Lydia,* a country of Asia Minor.

Μαίανδρος, ου, ὁ, *Maeander,* a river of Asia Minor. [**meander**]

Μένων, ωνος, ὁ, *Menon,* a Greek general.

παρασάγγης, ου, ὁ, *parasang,* Persian measure of distance (about 3½
miles).

σταθμός, οῦ, ὁ, *station, stopping-place, day's journey.*

290. Decline εὖρος (609). Observe that the stem ends in
ϵσ and that σ is dropped before all case endings. Contraction
then occurs. The ϵ of the stem is changed to ο in the nominative, accusative, and vocative singular. Nouns like εὖρος
are all neuter and have the recessive accent.

291. The personal endings in middle (passive) imperative:

	Singular	Dual	Plural
2	σο	σθον	σθε
3	σθω	σθων	σθων

292. In the second person singular σ is dropped and ου
results from contraction; the first aorist has the irregular form
σαι, e. g. λῦσαι. The first and second aorist passive use the
active endings, retaining θι in the second person singular.

---

[1] Antecedent (obj. of ἔχων) omitted.

293. Learn the imperative middle (passive) of the present, aorist and perfect of λύω (639, 640), of the second aorist middle of λείπω (641), of the second aorist passive of φαίνω (642), and of the present middle (passive) of τῑμάω, ποιέω, δηλόω (648).

294.   DRILL

I. Locate the following:

   1. λῦσαι, λύσαι, λέλυσαι.   4. λυθέντων, τῑμᾶσθε, ποιείσθω.
   2. λιποῦ, λίποι, ἐλύσω.   5. ποιείτω, ἠξίου, δηλοῦτε.
   3. λύσατε, λύεσθε, λύεσθαι.

II. 1. Let the city be called Sardis.
   2. Soldiers, march to the city and remain one day.
   3. Let them be conquered, not honored.

295.   EXERCISES

I. 1. εἴκοσι παρασάγγᾱς πορευθέντες ἐπὶ Κολοσσὰς ἀφίκοντο. 2. ἐξελαύνει σταθμοὺς τρεῖς ἐπὶ τὸν ποταμόν. 3. ταῦτα ἀκούσᾱς βασιλεὺς λαβὼν οὓς εἴρηκα πολεμεῖν ἐπειρᾶτο. 4. ἐπαύσαντο ἵνα Κῦρον πείσειαν. 5. ἐνόμιζον τὸ εὖρος τοῦ ποταμοῦ εἶναι μεῖζον.

II. 1. I heard of the plot from Pasion. 2. If Menon should come with boats, he would guard the acropolis. 3. The cities were small and prosperous. 4. The Maeander River is larger. 5. They reached Sardis, a prosperous city.

LESSON XXXIII

μι-VERBS, δείκνῡμι

296. τούτου¹ τὸ εὖρος² δύο πλέθρα· γέφυρα δὲ ἐπῆν ἐζευγμένη πλοίοις³ ἑπτά. τοῦτον διαπορευθεὶς ἐξελαύνει διὰ Φρυγίᾱς σταθμὸν ἕνα παρασάγγᾱς ὀκτὼ εἰς Κολοσσάς, πόλιν οἰκουμένην,⁴ εὐδαίμονα καὶ μεγάλην.

297. VOCABULARY

ἀληθής, ές, gen. οῦς, *true.*

δείκνῡμι, δείξω, ἔδειξα, δέδειχα, δέδειγμαι, ἐδείχθην, *show, point out, indicate.*

διαπορεύομαι, διαπορεύσομαι, διεπορεύθην, *march through, march over, cross.*

ἔπειμι (ἐπί, εἰμί), *be upon, be over.*

ἑπτά, *seven.* [**hept**archy]

ζεύγνῡμι, ζεύξω, ἔζευξα, ἔζευγμαι, ἐζεύχθην, *yoke, join, bridge* (with boats). [**zeugma**]

Κολοσσαί, ῶν, αἱ, *Colossae,* a city of Asia Minor.

πλέθρον, ου, τό, *plethron* (about 97 feet).

πλοῖον, ου, τό, *boat.*

Φρυγίᾱ, ᾱς, ἡ, *Phrygia,* a country in Asia Minor.

298. Learn δείκνῡμι in the present and imperfect active and middle (passive), all moods (650, 652). Observe that the verb stem is δεικ, and that the present adds νν to this stem. In the singular of the present and imperfect active the stem is δεικνῡ (not δεικνυ). In the subjunctive and optative the inflection is like that of λύω. So also outside the present system.

299. Learn μέγας (616), ἀληθής (615). μέγας has two stems, μεγα and μεγαλο/α. The latter gives the first and

---

¹It is so customary to connect Greek sentences with a conjunction that its omission has a name — asyndeton (*not bound together*). The asyndeton here is lessened by the fact that τούτου (dem. pro.) has some connective force.   ²εὖρος is subj. of ἦν understood.   ³Dat. of means.   ⁴So many cities of Asia Minor had become deserted that Xenophon often specifies that a city is inhabited.

second declension forms. μέγα gives the third declension forms—the nominative, accusative, and vocative of the masculine and neuter singular (exc. voc. masc.).

300.   DRILL

I. Locate the following:

1. δείκνῦσι, ἐδείκνῦς, ζευγνύῃς.
2. δεικνύωσι, δεικνύᾶσι, ἐζεύγνυτο.
3. δεικνύς, δεικνύῃ, ζευγνύοιντο.

4. πόλεων μεγάλων, στρατεύματι μεγάλῳ, γέρουσι εὐδαίμοσι.
5. λύσειεν, λύσειαν, λίποιεν.

II. Give:

1. (a) nom. plu., (b) acc. sing., (c) dat. plu., of γέφυρα μεγάλη, πόλις εὐδαίμων, ἐλπὶς ἀληθής.
2. (a) 3 plu., (b) 2 plu., (c) 3 sing., pres. ind., subj. and opt. act. of λύω.

301.   EXERCISES

I. 1. τοῖσδε τοῖς μεγάλοις πλοίοις ζευγνύᾶσι γέφυραν. 2. ἐὰν Κῦρος τὸν στόλον τοῦ στρατηγοῦ ἀκούσῃ ἀντιπαρασκευάσεται. 3. τούτου τοῦ πεδίου τὸ εὖρος ἦν δέκα παρασάγγαι. 4. Κῦρος ἔδειξεν τοῖς στρατιώταις ἑπτά πλοῖα. 5. ἡ πόλις ἦν εἴρηκε εὐδαίμων καὶ μεγάλη ἦν.

II. 1. They proceeded two days' journey. 2. There was a bridge made of (joined by) seven boats. 3. They started from the river when they heard this from Cyrus. 4. The cities of Phrygia were large and prosperous. 5. He took the large boats to make (ζεύγνῦμι) a bridge.

Fig. 8.—Hurling a Javelin

LESSON XXXIV

Subjunctive of Contract Verbs

302. ἐνταῦθα ἔμεινεν ἡμέρᾱς ἑπτά· καὶ ἧκε Μένων ὁ
Θετταλὸς ὁπλίτᾱς ἔχων χῑλίους καὶ πελταστὰς πεντακοσίους, Δόλοπας καὶ Αἰνιᾶνας καὶ Ὀλυνθίους. ἐντεῦθεν
ἐξελαύνει σταθμοὺς τρεῖς παρασάγγᾱς εἴκοσιν εἰς Κελαι-
νᾱ́ς, τῆς Φρυγίᾱς πόλιν οἰκουμένην, μεγάλην καὶ εὐδαίμονα.

303. VOCABULARY

Αἰνιᾶνες, ων, οἱ, *Aenianes,* a Thessalian tribe.
Δόλοπες, ων, οἱ, *Dolopians,* a people of Thessaly.
ἐντεῦθεν, adv., *from here, from there, thereupon.*
Κελαιναί, ῶν, αἱ, *Celaenae,* a city of Asia Minor.
ὀκτώ, *eight.* [**octa**gon]
Ὀλύνθιοι, ων, οἱ, *Olynthians,* the inhabitants of Olynthus.

304. Learn the present subjunctive active and middle
(passive) of τῑμάω, ποιέω, δηλόω (647, 648). Observe that

$$\alpha + \omega = \omega \qquad \epsilon + \omega = \omega \qquad o + \omega = \omega$$
$$\alpha + \eta = \bar{\alpha} \qquad \epsilon + \eta = \eta \qquad o + \eta = \omega$$
$$\alpha + \eta = ᾳ \qquad \epsilon + \eta = \eta \qquad o + \eta = οι$$

305. DRILL

I. 1. τῑμᾷ, ποιῇ, δηλοῖ.   4. μενοῦσι, μένουσι, ἔμενον.
   2. τῑμῶσι, τῑμᾶται, τῑμᾶσθε。   5. ἐτίμων, ἠξίουν, ἐπολέμει.
   3. ποιῆται, ποιῶνται, δηλῶται.

II. Give (*a*) 2 sing., (*b*) 3 plu. pres. subj. act. and mid., of λύω,
   τῑμάω, ποιέω, δηλόω.

306. EXERCISES

I. 1. ἐὰν Κῦρος τῑμᾷ τοὺς στρατιώτᾱς πολιορκήσουσι ταύτην
   τὴν πόλιν. 2. ἐξελαύνομεν ἵνα ὠφελῶμεν τοὺς Κύρου
   φίλους。 3. μεταπέμπεται τοὺς ὁπλίτᾱς ἵνα τοὺς φυγάδας
   λαβόντες ὁρμῶνται. 4. ὦ στρατιῶται, τῑμῶμεν τὸν σα-
   τράπην. 5. μενεῖ ἐν Κελαιναῖς πόλει οἰκουμένῃ.

II. 1. If the king furnishes six months' pay, the soldiers will set out. 2. The hoplites remain in order that they may be honored. 3. Let us make war on the enemies of the king. 4. The cities are large, and the inhabitants are prosperous. 5. Remain three days in this city.

LESSON XXXV

PERSONAL PRONOUNS

307. ἐνταῦθα Κύρῳ βασίλεια ἦν καὶ παράδεισος μέγας ἀγρίων θηρίων πλήρης,[1] ἃ ἐκεῖνος ἐθήρευεν ἀπὸ ἵππου, ὁπότε[2] γυμνάσαι βούλοιτο ἑαυτόν τε καὶ τοὺς ἵππους. διὰ μέσου[3] δὲ τοῦ παραδείσου ῥεῖ ὁ Μαίανδρος ποταμός· αἱ δὲ πηγαὶ αὐτοῦ εἰσιν ἐκ τῶν βασιλείων· ῥεῖ δὲ καὶ διὰ τῆς Κελαινῶν πόλεως.

308.   VOCABULARY

ἄγριος, ᾱ, ον, *of the field, wild.*

βασίλειον, ου, τό, generally plu., βασίλεια, *palace.*

ἑαυτοῦ, ῆς, reflex. pro., *of himself, herself, its.*

ἐγώ, ἐμοῦ, pers. pro., *I.*

ἐμός, ή, όν, poss. pro. of 1 pers., *my, mine.*

ἡμέτερος, ᾱ, ον, poss. pro. of 1 pers. plu., *our.*

θηρεύω, θηρεύσω, ἐθήρευσα, τεθήρευκα, *hunt.*

θηρίον, ου, τό, *wild animal, game.* [mega**therium**]

μέσος, η, ον, *middle.* [**Meso**potamia]

οἷ, dat. of 3 pers. pro., indirect reflex., *himself.*

ὁπότε, rel. adv., *when, whenever, if ever.*

παράδεισος, ου, ὁ, *park.* [**paradise**]

πηγή, ῆς, ἡ, *fountain, source.* [**peg**omancy]

πλήρης, ες, *full of, full.*

ῥέω,[4] ῥυήσομαι or ῥεύσομαι, ἐρρύηκα, ἐρρύην, *flow.* [cata**rrh, rheu**matism]

σός, σή, σόν, poss. pro., 2 pers. sing., *thy, thine.*

ὑμέτερος, ᾱ, ον, poss. pro. 2 pers. plu., *your, yours.*

---

[1] Adjs. of plenty govern the gen. [2] ὁπότε here = *if ever, if at any time;* i. e. it is in reality conditional and is so treated. Here the moods of ἐθήρευεν and βούλοιτο follow the rule given in 259. [3] Takes pred. position; trans., *middle of the park.* [4] Dissyllabic verbs in έω contract only to ει. ῥέει = ῥεῖ, but ῥέουσι is uncontracted.

309. Learn ἐγώ, σύ, οὗ (629). The singular, except the nominative and the dissyllabic forms in the first person, is enclitic. The accent may be retained for emphasis. The dissyllabic forms are also emphatic. The nominatives are seldom used except for emphasis.

310. Learn ἐμαυτοῦ, σεαυτοῦ, ἑαυτοῦ (630). Observe that the reflexive pronouns are formed from the stems of the personal pronouns + αὐτός. In the plural of the first and second persons there is of course no neuter. The plural is expressed in two words.

These are direct reflexives; i. e. refer to the subject of the clause in which they stand. οὗ is generally in a subordinate clause and refers to the subject of the principal clause; i. e., is an indirect reflexive.

311. The possessive pronouns ἐμός, σός, ἡμέτερος, ὑμέτερος are formed from the stems of the personal pronouns and are declined like adjectives in ος.

312.   DRILL

I. Locate the following:

  1. ἐμοί, ὑμῖν, οἷ.   4. αὐτούς, αὑτούς, ἡμᾶς αὐτούς.
  2. ἡμῶν, ἡμῖν, σφίσι.   5. ἱππέᾱς, μέγαν, πατράσι.
  3. ἑαυτοῖς, ὑμᾶς, ἡμεῖς.

II. 1. Me, of you, we.   4. To you, to me, to him.
  2. Us, they, them.   5. For ourselves, of ourselves,
  3. Of us, thee, to us.   myself.

313.   EXERCISES

I. 1. ἐμοὶ μὲν ἡδέως ἐπείθοντο, ὑμᾶς δὲ ἐξέβαλον. 2. ἔστι δὲ καὶ τὸ στράτευμα ἐν τῇ ἀκροπόλει. 3. εἰ ἐκεῖνοι ἀφίκοιντο ἐπὶ τὰ βασίλεια, βούλοιντο ἂν νῑκᾶν. 4. εἰ βασιλεὺς γυμνάσαιτο, ἔμενεν ἐν τῷ ἑαυτοῦ παραδείσῳ. 5. Κῦρος ἔπεισε φίλιος ὢν τοὺς υἱοὺς ἡμῶν γενέσθαι ἀγαθούς.

II. 1. These generals thought you were honorable.　2. The hoplites benefited themselves and their friends.　3. The river flows through a large and prosperous plain.　4. This city was full of men.　5. If he wishes to exercise, he hunts wild animals on (ἀπό) his own horse.

LESSON XXXVI

Review of the Third Declension

314.　ἔστι δὲ καὶ μεγάλου βασιλέως βασίλεια ἐν Κελαιναῖς ἐρυμνὰ[1] ἐπὶ ταῖς πηγαῖς τοῦ Μαρσύου ποταμοῦ ὑπὸ τῇ ἀκροπόλει.

315.　VOCABULARY

αἱρέω, αἱρήσω, εἶλον, ᾕρηκα, ᾕρημαι, ᾑρέθην, act., *take, seize, capture;* mid., *choose, prefer.* [**heresy**, di**aeresis**]

γυνή, αικός, ἡ, *woman, wife.* [miso**gyny**]

ἐρυμνός, ή, όν, *fortified.*

κῆρυξ, ῡκος, ὁ, *herald.*

Μαρσύᾱς, ου, ὁ, *Marsyas*, a satyr of Phrygia.

μάχομαι, μαχοῦμαι, ἐμαχεσάμην, μεμάχημαι, *contend, fight.*

ναῦς, νεώς, ἡ, *ship, vessel.* [**nausea**, argo**naut**]

ὄρνῑς, ῑθος, ὁ or ἡ, *bird.* [**ornith**ology]

παῖς, παιδός, ὁ or ἡ, *boy, girl, child.* [**ped**agogue, encyclo**paedia**]

πόλεμος, ου, ὁ, *war.* [**polemic**]

τριήρης, ους, ἡ, *trireme*, a ship with three banks of oars.

χείρ, ός, ἡ, *hand.* [**chiro**graphy, **sur**geon (old spelling **chir**urgeon)]

316. Nouns of this declension are classified according to the last letter of the stem as follows:

1. Labial or palatal mutes (π, β, φ; κ, γ, χ), never neuter.

2. Lingual mutes (τ, δ, θ); δ, θ, feminine; τ, of different genders, except ατ, always neuter.

3. Liquid (λ, ν, ρ), chiefly masculine.

4. σ, mostly neuters in εσ (nominative, ος).

---

[1] Nom. plu. in agreement with *Βασίλεια*

5. ι, υ, feminine; stems in ι have recessive accent.

6. ευ, masculine, oxytone, denoting the agent.

317. Observe that lingual mute stems whose nominatives end in ις (not oxytone) drop the final τ, δ, θ of the stem and add ν to form the accusative singular: χάρις [χαριτ], χάριν, but ἀσπίς [ἀσπιδ], ἀσπίδα.

318. Decline γυνή (610), ὄρνῑς (604), ναῦς, παῖς, τριήρης, χείρ (611). Κῆρυξ

319. DRILL

State gender and decline nouns formed from the following stems: ἡγεμόν, ὄρες, χρῆματ, φάλαγγ, τεῖχες, μάντι, ὄνοματ, ἀσπίδ, μήν, κῆρυκ, ἑρμηνεύ, λιμέν, γίγαντ, χάριτ, γυμνῆτ, ἀγών, φύλακ, θεράποντ, κρίσι, φῶτ, διῶρυχ.

320. EXERCISES

I. 1. ταῦτα τὰ στρατεύματα τοῖς ἄρχουσι οὓς εἵλετο πείθεται.
2. εἰ μὴ τοὺς Ἕλληνας ἐκβάλλοιμεν, πράγματα ἡμῖν παρεῖχον. 3. τούτου τοῦ ποταμοῦ τὸ εὖρος ἦν μεῖζον ἢ ἐκείνου.
4. τοῖς ἱππεῦσι ἐμάχοντο ἵνα Κῦρον βασιλέᾱ ποιήσαιντο.
5. τούτοις τοῖς ἀνδράσι ἦσαν ἄλλαι προφάσεις.

II. 1. They collected the fugitives from the cities in order that they might honor them. 2. The Greeks came from the king to Sardis and remained four months. 3. The land of the Thracians is full of large wild beasts. 4. They sent the money which Cyrus promised to the soldiers. 5. If the satrap should march through the midst of the city, the king would make war on him.

FIG. 9.—A School Scene

LESSON XXXVII

The Numerals

321. ῥεῖ δὲ καὶ οὗτος διὰ τῆς πόλεως καὶ ἐμβάλλει εἰς τὸν Μαίανδρον· τοῦ δὲ Μαρσύου τὸ εὖρός ἐστιν εἴκοσι καὶ πέντε ποδῶν.[1] ἐνταῦθα λέγεται Ἀπόλλων ἐκδεῖραι Μαρσύαν, νῑκήσᾱς ἐρίζοντά[2] οἱ περὶ σοφίᾱς, καὶ τὸ δέρμα κρεμάσαι ἐν τῷ ἄντρῳ ὅθεν αἱ πηγαί.[3]

322.　　　　　　　VOCABULARY

ἄντρον, ον, τό, *cave.*

Ἀπόλλων, ωνος, ὁ, acc. ωνα or ω, *Apollo.*

δέρμα, ατος, τό, *skin.* [epi**dermis**]

ἐκδέρω, ἐκδερῶ, ἐξέδειρα, *strip off the skin, flay.*

ἐμβάλλω, ἐμβαλῶ, ἐνέβαλον, ἐμβέβληκα, ἐμβέβλημαι, ἐνεβλήθην, *throw in* (i. e. an army), *make an attack, invasion; empty* (of rivers). [**emblem**]

ἐρίζω, only pres. and imperf., *strive, contend.* [**eristic**]

κρεμάννῡμι [κρεμα], κρεμῶ, ἐκρέμασα, ἐκρεμάσθην, *hang.*

μηδείς, μηδεμία, μηδέν, *not even one, no one.*

νῑκάω, νῑκήσω, ἐνίκησα, νενίκηκα, *conquer, surpass.* [**Nicolas**]

ὅθεν (rel. pro.+θεν, indicating source), conj. adv., *from which place, whence.*

οὐδείς, οὐδεμία, οὐδέν, *not even one, no one.*

πέντε, *five.* [**pent**agon]　περί, prep. (gen.), *concerning;* cf. 192.

πούς, ποδός, ὁ, *foot.* [**tri**pod, anti**podes**]

σοφίᾱ, ᾱς, ἡ, *wisdom, skill* (e. g. in music). [philo**sophy**, **soph**omore]

323. Learn the cardinal numbers from one to twenty-one (625). Look over the other cardinals, the ordinals, and numeral adverbs, observing the method of formation, and which ones are inflected. (Hereafter numerals will not be given in lesson vocabularies.)

324. Review declension of εἷς, δύο, τρεῖς, τέτταρες (626). Like εἷς decline οὐδείς (οὐ-δ'-εῖς) (627) and μηδείς (μή-δ'-εῖς), *no one, nothing.*

---

[1] Pred. gen.　[2] ἐρίζοντά οἱ περὶ σοφίᾱς, *who entered into a contest of musical skill with him* (Apollo); lit., *as he contended, etc.*　[3] Sc. εἰσίν.

325.   DRILL

I. Locate the following forms:

1. οὐδενί, μηδένα, οὐδέν.   4. τέτταρας, τρία, δυοῖν.
2. ὑμεῖς, μηδείς, τρεῖς.   5. οὐδεμίαν, ἐμέ, μηδεμία.
3. τρισί, σφίσι, τέτταρσι.

II. 1. One spring, three hides, two caves.
     2. No city, no war, four cities.
     3. Eleven soldiers, thirteen bridges, fifteen kings.
     4. Ten armies, eighteen heralds, twenty months.

326.   EXERCISES

I. 1. συγγενόμενος αὐτῷ περὶ χρημάτων ἤριζεν. 2. ὁ ποταμὸς ἐνέβαλε εἰς τὸν Μαρσύαν καὶ τὸ εὖρος εἴκοσι καὶ ὀκτὼ
ποδῶν ἦν. 3. ἡμῖν ἔδοξε μαχέσασθαι τόνδε τὸν τρόπον.
4. οἱ δυνάμενοι τὴν ἀκρόπολιν λαβεῖν πειράσονται ἵνα
μέγαν βασιλέᾱ ὠφελῶσι. 5. ῥέουσι δὲ ποταμοὶ μεγάλοι
τρεῖς διὰ τούτου τοῦ πεδίου.

II. 1. No one conquered the friends of the king. 2. Let
us demand a thousand darics as pay. 3. If Apollo flays
him, he will die. 4. The width of the river is twenty
feet and there is no bridge over it.[1] 5. Upon hearing
this he proceeded to the park from which the river
flowed.

---

[1] Cf. 296.

Fig. 10.—The Contest between Apollo and Marsyas

LESSON XXXVIII

Irregular Adjectives

327. διὰ δὲ τοῦτο ὁ ποταμὸς καλεῖται Μαρσύας. ἐνταῦθα Ξέρξης, ὅτε ἐκ τῆς Ἑλλάδος ἡττηθεὶς τῇ μάχῃ ἀπεχώρει, λέγεται οἰκοδομῆσαι ταῦτά τε τὰ βασίλεια καὶ τὴν Κελαινῶν ἀκρόπολιν. ἐνταῦθα ἔμεινε Κῦρος ἡμέρᾱς τριάκοντα· καὶ ἧκε Κλέαρχος ὁ Λακεδαιμόνιος φυγὰς ἔχων ὁπλίτᾱς χῑλίους καὶ πελταστὰς Θρᾷκας ὀκτακοσίους καὶ τοξότᾱς Κρῆτας διᾱκοσίους.

328.　　　　　　VOCABULARY

ἀποχωρέω, ἀποχωρήσω, ἀπεχώρησα, ἀποκεχώρηκα, *go away, withdraw.*
Ἑλλάς, άδος, ἡ, *Hellas, Greece.*
ἡττάομαι, ἡττήσομαι, ἡττήθην, *to be weaker than, be defeated.*
Κρής, Κρητός, *Cretan.*
οἰκοδομέω, οἰκοδομήσω, ᾠκοδόμησα, ᾠκοδόμηκα, *build, erect.*
ὅτε, adv. conj., *when, whenever.*
πᾶς, πᾶσα, πᾶν, adj., *all, every.* [**pan**acea, **Pan**-American]
πολύς, πολλή, πολύ, adj., *much, many.* [**poly**gamy]
τοξότης, ου, ὁ, *archer, bowman.*
Ξέρξης, ου, ὁ, *Xerxes, king of Persia.*
χαρίεις, εσσα, εν, *graceful, pleasing.*

329. Complete ἵστημι (650, 652) in present system, active, middle (passive). Learn second aorist system of ἵστημι (ἐπριάμην in middle). Note in the general vocabulary the transitive and intransitive tenses.

330. Learn πᾶς, χαρίεις (614), πολύς (616). Observe that the stem of πᾶς and of χαρίεις ends in ντ. When ς is added in the nominative masculine, ντ is dropped and the vowel lengthened, ᾰ to ᾱ, ε to ει. The ε is not lengthened in the dative plural. πάντων and πᾶσι do not obey the law for monosyllables (135).

331. These adjectives are of the first and third declensions. Like μέγας (299), πολύς has two stems, πολυ and πολλο/α. πολυ gives third declension forms—the nominative, accusative, vocative, singular, masculine and neuter. All the other forms are from πολλο/α, and are of the first (the feminine form) and second (the masculine and neuter forms) declensions.

332.   DRILL

I. Locate the following:

 1. στάντας, ἱστάναι, ἵσταται. 4. σταῖεν, σταίην, στῆναι.

 2. στάντων, ἔστησαν, ἵστασαν. 5. πολλά, πάσαις, χαριεσσῶν.

 3. στῶσι, ἱστῶσι, ἱστᾶσι.

II. 1. Give (a) acc. sing., (b) nom. plu., (c) dat. sing., (d) dat. plu., of πᾶς φυγάς, ἀγὼν πολύς, χαρίεσσα ἀκρόπολις, πᾶν στράτευμα.

 2. (a) We are placing guards. (b) He was halting (making stand) the horse. (c) The horses stood. (d) The heralds were standing. (e) I am standing.

333.   EXERCISES

I. 1. ἦλθεν λαβὼν ἄνδρας πολλοὺς ὡς πολεμήσων Κύρῳ.
 2. Ξέρξης ἐλέγετο ἡττηθῆναι τῇ μάχῃ καὶ ἐξ Ἑλλάδος ἀποχωρῆσαι. 3. ἐὰν δύνωμαι, πέμψω πάντας τοὺς ἱππέας. 4. ἀποχωρήσας ἐκ τῆς χώρας ἔστησε τὸ στράτευμα. 5. αὕτη ἡ χαρίεσσα χώρᾱ Ἑλλὰς ἐκαλεῖτο.

II. 1. The river is said to have been called Marsyas on this account. 2. When the king was conquered in battle, he came to terms. 3. Xerxes is said to have built all these cities. 4. They happened to be standing. 5. There are many large armies which will hinder them.

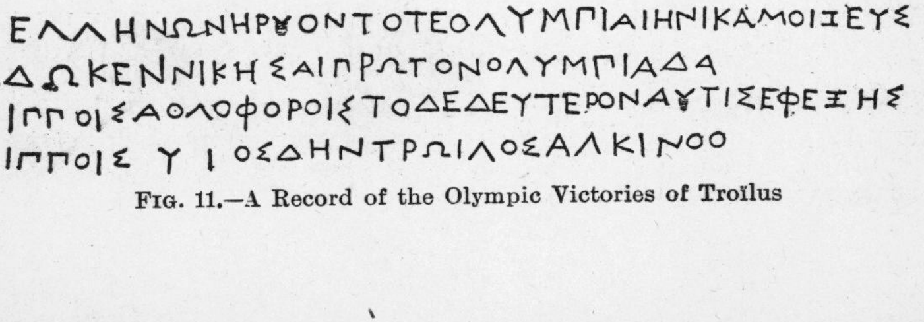

```
ΕΛΛΗΝΩΝΗΡΨΟΝΤΟΤΕΟΛΥΜΠΙΑΙΗΝΙΚΑΜΟΙΞΕΥΣ
ΔΩΚΕΝΝΙΚΗΣΑΙΠΡΩΤΟΝΟΛΥΜΠΙΑΔΑ
ΙΓΓΟΙΣΑΟΛΟΦΟΡΟΙΣΤΟΔΕΔΕΥΤΕΡΟΝΑΥΤΙΣΕΦΕΞΗΣ
ΙΓΓΟΙΣ Υ Ι ΟΣΔΗΝΤΡΩΙΛΟΣΑΛΚΙΝΟΟ
```

FIG. 11.—A Record of the Olympic Victories of Troïlus

LESSON XXXIX

Indirect Discourse. Conditional Sentences

334. ἅμα δὲ καὶ Σῶσις παρῆν ὁ Συρᾱκόσιος ἔχων ὁπλίτᾱς τριᾱκοσίους, καὶ Σοφαίνετος ὁ Ἀρκὰς ἔχων ὁπλίτᾱς χῑλίους. καὶ ἐνταῦθα Κῦρος ἐξέτασιν καὶ ἀριθμὸν τῶν Ἑλλήνων ἐποίησεν ἐν τῷ παραδείσῳ, καὶ ἐγένοντο[1] οἱ σύμπαντες[2] ὁπλῖται μὲν μύριοι καὶ χίλιοι, πελτασταὶ δὲ ἀμφὶ[3] τοὺς δισχῑλίους. ἐντεῦθεν ἐξελαύνει σταθμοὺς δύο παρασάγγᾱς δέκα εἰς Πέλτᾱς, πόλιν οἰκουμένην. ἐνταῦθ' ἔμεινεν ἡμέρᾱς τρεῖς·

335. VOCABULARY

ἅμα, adv., *at the same time.*

ἀριθμός, οῦ, ὁ, *number, numbering.* [**arithmetic,** log**arithm**]

δέχομαι, δέξομαι, ἐδεξάμην, δέδεγμαι, ἐδέχθην, *receive, accept.* [synec**doche,** pan**dect, dock**]

ἐξέτασις, εως, ἡ, *review, inspection.*

θώρᾱξ, ᾱκος, ὁ, *breastplate, corslet.* [**thorax**]

Πέλται, ῶν, αἱ, *Peltae.*

σύμπᾱς, σύμπᾱσα, σύμπαν, *all together, the whole.*

Συρᾱκόσιος, ᾱ, ον, *of Syracuse, Syracusan.*

σώζω, σώσω, ἔσωσα, σέσωκα, σέσω(σ)μαι, ἐσώθην, *save, preserve.* [creo**sote,** sozo**dont,** soterio**logy**]

Σῶσις, ιος, ὁ, *Sosis.*

τριάκοντα, *thirty.*

φημί, φήσω, ἔφησα, *say, state, declare.* [eu**phemism,** pro**phet**]

336. Review εἰμί (655). Learn εἶμι complete (656). Observe that εἶμι is used in the present system only. It usually has a future meaning and serves as a future to ἔρχομαι.

---

[1] Trans. *amounted to.* [2] Trans. *all told.* [3] ἀμφί with numerals means *about* and the numeral takes the article.

337. There are three common verbs of saying; of these (1) φημί takes the infinitive in the main verb of the quotation; (2) εἶπον (second aorist) takes ὅτι or ὡς; (3) λέγω usually takes ὅτι or ὡς after an active form, the infinitive after a passive.

338. The infinitive in indirect discourse takes the tense of the finite verb which it represents. For the mood and tense after ὅτι and ὡς see 256. οἱ ἄνδρες ἦλθον—direct form; φησὶ τοὺς ἄνδρας ἐλθεῖν—indirect form.

339. Four classes of conditional sentences have been given (201–3, 258, 259). There are two others.

I. The simple supposition has εἰ with the indicative in the protasis and any form of the verb in the apodosis. This class states a present or a past particular supposition and implies nothing as to fulfilment. εἰ Ἑλληνικός ἐστι, ἀγαθός ἐστι ἀνήρ, *if he is Greek, he is a good man.*

II. A supposition contrary to reality (present or past) has εἰ with a past tense of the indicative in the protasis and a past tense of the indicative with ἄν in the apodosis. The imperfect usually shows a condition untrue in present time; the aorist in past time. The imperfect sometimes refers to the past, denoting a continued or repeated act. εἰ Ἑλληνικὸς ἦν, ἀγαθὸς ἂν ἦν ἀνήρ, *if he were Greek, he would be a good man.*

CONDITIONAL SENTENCES IN TABULAR FORM

I. Simple supposition (particular): εἰ + present or past indicative — any form of the verb. *See above*

II. Present general: ἐάν (ἤν, ἄν) + subjunctive — present indicative. *See below*

III. Past general: εἰ + optative — imperfect indicative. *See below*

IV. Untrue supposition: εἰ + past indicative — past indicative with ἄν. *See above*

V. More vivid future: ἐάν (ἤν, ἄν) + subjunctive — future indicative or imperative. *If he orders it, I shall send them or .. he will order .. cf § 203*

VI. Less vivid future: εἰ + optative — optative with ἄν. *See below*

II e.g. If he orders it, I (always) send them. cf § 203
III e.g. If ever he ordered it, I used to send them cf § 259
VI e.g. If he should order it, I would send them cf § 259

340.　　　　　　　DRILL

I. Locate the following:

1. εἶ, εἴη, ἴη.
2. εἶσι, εἰσί, εἶτε.
3. ἴασι, ἴωσι, ὦσι.

4. ἦσαν, ἦσαν, εἴησαν.
5. ᾔει, ἔσει, ἐστί.

II. 1. He says (φησί) that the king will go.
2. They said (λέγω) that the general was in the tent.
3. I said (εἶπον) that Cyrus became satrap.

341.　　　　　　　EXERCISES

I. 1. ἅμα δὲ καὶ ὁ ἄρχων ἧκε καὶ ἔμεινεν ἡμέρᾱς τριάκοντα.
2. ταῦτα κατανοήσᾱς, ὑπέσχετο ἐξέτασιν ποιήσεσθαι.
3. ἐτάχθησαν ἐν τῷ παραδείσῳ ὥστε ἔλαθον ἐρίζοντες.
4. φημὶ σύμπαντας εἶναι ἀμφὶ τοὺς τριάκοντα στρατιώτᾱς. 5. εἶπεν ὅτι ὁ στρατηγὸς παρείη καὶ ἐξέτασιν ποιή-
σειεν. 6. ἐὰν Σῶσις τοὺς ὁπλίτᾱς ἔχῃ, ἅμα πορευσόμεθα.

II. 1. If Cyrus should make a review, he would summon
all. 2. If the peltasts were present, the number would
be ten thousand. 3. If he made a review all were
present.

LESSON XL

Present and Second Aorist of τίθημι

342. ἐν αἷς[1] Ξενίᾱς ὁ Ἀρκὰς τὰ Λύκαια ἔθῡσε καὶ
ἀγῶνα ἔθηκε· τὰ δὲ ἆθλα ἦσαν στλεγγίδες χρῡσαῖ·
ἐθεώρει δὲ τὸν ἀγῶνα καὶ[2] Κῦρος. ἐντεῦθεν ἐξελαύνει
σταθμοὺς δύο παρασάγγᾱς δώδεκα εἰς Κεράμων ἀγορᾱ́ν,
πόλιν οἰκουμένην, ἐσχάτην[3] πρὸς τῇ Μῡσίᾳ χώρᾳ.

---

[1] Sc. ἡμέραις.　[2] What position does καί occupy as regards the word which it
emphasizes?　[3] ἐσχάτην πρός, lit. *farthest in the direction of,* i. e. *on the borders of.*

343. VOCABULARY

ᾱθλον, ου, τό, *prize.* [**athlete**]

ἔσχατος, η, ον, *last, farthest.* [**eschato**logy]

θεωρέω, θεωρήσω, ἐθεώρησα, τεθεώρηκα, *look at, watch, inspect.* [**theory, theater**]

καθίστημι (see ἵστημι for prin. pts.), act., *set down;* mid., *take one's place.*

Κεράμων ἀγορά, ᾶς, ἡ, Ceramon Agora (lit. *market for tiles).*

Λύκαια, ων, τά, *Lycaean festival, festival of Zeus Lycaeus.*

Μῡσίᾱ, ᾱς, ἡ, *Mysia.*

στλεγγίς, ίδος, ἡ, *flesh-scraper, strigil.*

τίθημι, θήσω, ἔθηκα, τέθηκα, ἐτέθην, *put, establish, institute, station.* [**thesis, theme,** apo**thecary**]

χρῡσοῦς, ῆ, οῦν, *of gold, golden.* [**chrys**anthemum]

344. Learn the present and second aorist systems of τίθημι (650–53). The verb-stem is θε; present stem, τιθε (lengthened to τιθη in the singular of the present active, and in the first person of the imperfect indicative active).

345. The second and third persons of the imperfect active are from τιθέω. The second aorist lacks the singular in the indicative, and the first aorist takes its place and is itself rarely used in the dual and plural. In τίθημι, ἵημι, and δίδωμι the first aorist is an irregular form ending in κα, κας, κε.

346. DRILL

I. Locate the following forms:

1. τίθεσαι, τίθησι, ἐτίθεσο.   4. ἔθεσαν, ἔθεντο, θεῖντο.
2. τιθείη, ἐτίθει, τιθεῖτο.   5. ἔθετο, ἐτίθετο, θῶσι.
3. τίθεσθαι, τιθέναι, θεῖναι.

II. 1. He stands, he set up a prize, he stood.
2. They were setting up a prize, they institute a contest, they set up prizes.
3. If he sets up prizes all watch the contest.

347. EXERCISES

I. 1. τὰ Λύκαια θύσαντες ἀγῶνα ἔθεσαν. 2. ἔλεγεν ὅτι αὕτη ἡ πόλις εἴη ἐσχάτη πρὸς τῇ Ἑλλάδι. 3. ἐν τοῖς ἀγῶσι τὰ ἆθλα ἦν πολλά. 4. πολλὰς ἡμέρᾱς οἱ φύλακες οὐκ ἐδύναντο καθίστασθαι. 5. ἐδέοντο Κύρου μὴ ἀγῶνα τιθέναι.

II. 1. He stations guards. 2. After remaining there three days he marched two days' journey. 3. And the general also offered the Lycaean sacrifice. 4. All the other soldiers watched the contest. 5. There were not many prizes.

LESSON XLI

δίδωμι. SUPPLEMENTARY PARTICIPLE

348. ἐντεῦθεν ἐξελαύνει σταθμοὺς τρεῖς παρασάγγᾱς τριάκοντα εἰς Καΰστρου πεδίον, πόλιν οἰκουμένην. ἐνταῦθ' ἔμεινεν ἡμέρᾱς πέντε· καὶ τοῖς στρατιώταις ὠφείλετο μισθὸς πλέον[1] ἢ τριῶν μηνῶν,[2] καὶ πολλάκις ἰόντες ἐπὶ τὰς θύρᾱς ἀπῄτουν.[3] ὁ δὲ ἐλπίδας λέγων διῆγε,[4] καὶ δῆλος ἦν ἀνῑώμενος· οὐ γὰρ ἦν πρὸς[5] τοῦ Κύρου τρόπου ἔχοντα[6] μὴ ἀποδιδόναι.

349. VOCABULARY

ἀνῑάω, ἀνῑάσω, ἠνῑᾱσα, ἠνῑᾱκα, ἠνῑάθην, *grieve*; pas., *be grieved, distressed.*

ἀπαιτέω, ἀπαιτήσω, ἀπῄτησα, ἀπῄτηκα, *ask from, demand.*

ἀποδίδωμι, ἀποδώσω, ἀπέδωκα (ἀπέδοτον), ἀποδέδωκα, ἀποδέδομαι, ἀπεδόθην, *give back* (what is due), *pay.*

δῆλος, η, ον, *clear, plain, evident.*

διάγω, διάξω, διήγαγον, διῆχα, διῆγμαι, διήχθην, *lead through* or *across*; of time, *spend, continue.*

Καΰστρου πεδίον, ου, τό, *Cayster plain.*

ὀφείλω [ὀφελ], ὀφειλήσω, ὠφείλησα and ὤφελον, ὠφείληκα, ὠφειλήθην, *owe*; pas., *be due.*

πολλάκις, adv., *many times, often.*

350. Learn the present and second aorist systems of δίδωμι (650–53). The present stem is διδο from the root δο (διδω in the singular of the present tense of the active indica-

---

[1] Used as an indeclinable adj.   [2] Gen. of measure, dependent on μισθός.   [3] Note the force of the tense.   [4] Compound verbs do not allow the accent to go back of the augment.   [5] Note meanings of πρός in Vocab. Trans.: *It was not like Cyrus not to pay if he had money.*   [6] The ppl. has a conditional force; cf. 243, n. 2 for case.

tive). The singular imperfect active is as if from a contract
form διδόω. The lack of a singular in the second aorist
active is supplied by the first aorist in κα.

351. A participle sometimes forms an essential part of the
predicate, and is called a supplementary participle. When
followed by a supplementary participle, the main verb is
sometimes best translated by an adverb of manner (cf. 181,
4): ἐλπίδας λέγων, *speaking hopefully.* The participle here
defines the scope of the main verb: διῆγε ἐλπίδας λέγων,
kept speaking hopefully, or *continually spoke hopefully;*
δῆλος ἦν ἀνιώμενος, literally, *he was evident being troubled,*
i. e. *he was evidently troubled,* or *it was clear that he was
troubled.*

352. οὐ is the absolute negative; μή marks the negative
as willed or desired or conditional; so, in general, μή is used
with the infinitive (not in indirect discourse), in purpose and
conditional clauses, with the participle when it implies a condition, and with imperatives. οὐ is used elsewhere. The
same is true of compound negatives, e. g. οὐδείς, μηδείς, οὐδέ,
μηδέ, etc.

353.   DRILL

I. Locate the following:

   1. δίδως, δίδωσι, τιθῶσι.   4. δοίη, διδοῖεν, θεῖτε.

   2. ἐδίδου, ἔθου, δοῦναι.   5. τιθέασι, ἐτίθει, ἱστᾶσι.

   3. διδόναι, ἔθυσαν, ἐδίδοτο.

II. 1. They gave, I was giving, he gives.

   2. Cyrus clearly owed pay to the soldiers.

   3. If he does not give pay, the soldiers demand (it).

354.   EXERCISES

I. 1. Κῦρος δῆλος ἦν πειρώμενος ἀποχωρεῖν. 2. ὁ στρατηγὸς
ἠνιᾶτο. 3. μισθὸς πλέον ἢ τεττάρων μηνῶν τοῖς ὁπλίταις
ὠφείλετο. 4. ἐλθόντες ἐπὶ τὰς θύρας συνεβουλεύοντο. 5.
αὐτῷ πολλὰ χρήματα ἔδοσαν.

II. 1. After remaining ten days he marched to Peltae. 2.
If he remains there five days, the soldiers will demand
their pay. 3. If Cyrus had owed pay, he would have
given it. 4. They went to Cyrus many times and attempted to persuade him. 5. He gave the soldiers
many days' pay.

LESSON XLII

Passive of λύω.   Perfect of ἵστημι

355. ἐνταῦθα ἀφικνεῖται Ἐπύαξα ἡ Συεννέσιος¹ γυνὴ
τοῦ Κιλίκων βασιλέως παρὰ Κῦρον· καὶ ἐλέγετο Κύρῳ
δοῦναι χρήματα πολλά. τῇ δ' οὖν² στρατιᾷ τότε ἀπέδωκε
Κῦρος μισθὸν τεττάρων μηνῶν. εἶχε δὲ ἡ Κίλισσα καὶ
φυλακὴν περὶ αὐτὴν Κίλικας καὶ Ἀσπενδίους· ἐλέγετο³
δὲ καὶ συγγενέσθαι⁴ Κῦρον τῇ Κιλίσσῃ.

356.   VOCABULARY

Ἀσπένδιος, ᾱ, ον, *of Aspendos, Aspendian.*

δίδωμι, δώσω, ἔδωκα, δέδωκα, δέδομαι, ἐδόθην, *give.* [anti**dote**, **dose**]

Ἐπύαξα, ης, ἡ, *Epyaxa.*

Κίλιξ, ικος, *of Cilicia, Cilician.*

Κίλισσα, ης, *Cilician woman.*

πράττω [πρᾱγ], πρᾱ́ξω, ἔπρᾱξα, πέπρᾱχα or πέπρᾱγα, πέπρᾱγμαι, ἐπρᾱ́χθην,
     do, accomplish. [**practice**]

Συέννεσις, ιος, ὁ, *Syennesis.*

φυλακή, ῆς, ἡ, *guard, garrison.*

357. Learn the future perfect middle (passive) of λύω
(640). Observe that the stem of the future perfect middle
(passive) is formed by adding σο/ε to the stem of the perfect
middle. In inflection it is identical with the future middle,
except that it has the reduplication. It represents a com-

---

¹ Retains ι of the stem. Cf. πόλις, πόλεως.   ² δ' οὖν introduces known facts
after expressions of uncertainty, here after ἐλέγετο = *hearsay* or *common report;*
trans. *but at any rate.*   ³ ἐλέγετο is here impersonal, Κῦρον the subj. of infin.
⁴ Trans. συγγενέσθαι, *on terms of intimacy with.*

pleted action or state in future time, and is usually passive in force. It is rare.

358. Learn the first future passive (all moods) of λύω (640) and the second future passive of φαίνω (642). The first future passive is formed by adding the future middle endings to the stem of the first aorist passive; the forms of the second future passive bears the same relation to the second aorist passive.

359. Learn the second perfect and pluperfect active (all moods) of ἵστημι (654). Observe the declension of the perfect participle (621), and note the meaning of these tenses. (See general vocabulary.)

360. DRILL

Locate the following forms:

1. λύσεται, λέλυσαι, λελύσεται.　　4. λυθήσονται, ἐφάνησαν, φανείς.
2. φανεῖται, φανήσεται, ἑστάναι.　5. ἑστᾶσι, ἔστησαν, ἔστασαν.
3. ἑστῶσι, ἑστῶτι, ἱστᾶσι.

361. EXERCISES

I.　1. ἡ φυλακὴ εἱστήκει περὶ τὴν γυναῖκα.　2. λέγεται Ἐπύαξα πεμφθήσεσθαι εἰς Κιλικίαν.　3. εἰ μὴ ἔδωκε ἡ γυνὴ χρήματα Κύρῳ, οὐκ ἂν ἀπεδόθη τῷ στρατεύματι ὁ μισθός.　4. ἐνταῦθα ἑστῶτες ἀπῄτουν χρυσίον.　5. μὴ ἵστασθε ἐπὶ ταῖς τοῦ βασιλέως θύραις.

II.　1. If Cyrus gives money to the army, he will be honored.　2. The hoplites stood before the tent as guards.　3. They went to slay the son of the king.　4. Epyaxa, standing by the tents, reviewed the army.　5. The guard will be sent to Syennesis.

FIG. 12.—A Greek Razor

LESSON XLIII

Verbal Adjectives

362. ἐντεῦθεν δὲ ἐξελαύνει σταθμοὺς δύο παρασάγγας δέκα εἰς Θύμβριον, πόλιν οἰκουμένην. ἐνταῦθα ἦν παρὰ¹ τὴν ὁδὸν κρήνη ἡ Μίδου καλουμένη² τοῦ Φρυγῶν βασιλέως, ἐφ᾽ ᾗ λέγεται Μίδᾱς τὸν Σάτυρον θηρεῦσαι οἴνῳ³ κεράσᾱς αὐτήν. ἐντεῦθεν ἐξελαύνει σταθμοὺς δύο παρασάγγας δέκα εἰς Τυριάειον, πόλιν οἰκουμένην. ἐνταῦθα ἔμεινεν ἡμέρᾱς τρεῖς.

363.   VOCABULARY

ἀνάγκη, ης, ἡ, *necessity.*

Θύμβριον, ου, τό, *Thymbrium,* a city of Asia Minor.

κεράννῡμι [κερα], κεράσω, ἐκέρασα, κέκρᾱμαι, ἐκεράσθην, or ἐκράθην, *mix.* [crater]

κρήνη, ης, ἡ, *fountain.* [Hippocrene]

Μίδᾱς, ου, ὁ, *Midas.*

ὁδός, οῦ, ἡ, *way, road.* [exodus, method]

οἶνος, ου, ὁ, *wine.* [oenophilist]

Σάτυρος, ου, ὁ, *Satyr.*

Τυριάειον, ου, τό, *Tyriäeum,* a city of Asia Minor.

Φρύξ, Φρυγός, *Phrygian, a Phrygian.*

χρή, ἐχρῆν (imperf.), -χρήσει, -ἔχρησε, impers., *it is necessary, one must.*

364. Verbal adjectives are formed by adding τός or τέος to the verb-stem as found in the first aorist passive. φ and χ become π and κ before τ: λύω, ἐλύθην, λυτέος; ποιέω, ἐποιήθην, ποιητέος; πορεύομαι, ἐπορεύθην, πορευτέος; διώκω, ἐδιώχθην, διωκτέος; πέμπω, ἐπέμφθην, πεμπτέος.

365. The verbal in τός (ή, όν) indicates what has been done or may be done: ἡ διῶρυξ διαβατή ἐστιν, *the ditch is crossable.*

---

¹ Note in vocab. all meanings of παρά.   ² *The spring called Midas's;* i. e. *the so-called spring of Midas.*   ³ The dat. is that of association.

366. The verbal in τέος (ᾱ, ον) indicates what must be done, and is either personal or impersonal in use. The agent is in the dative (cf. Latin passive periphrastic). αἱ διώρυχες ὑμῖν διαβατέαι εἰσίν (personal), τὰς διώρυχας ὑμῖν διαβατέον ἐστίν (impersonal), *you must cross the ditches.* Observe that διαβατέον is nominative neuter singular and, though passive in form, governs διώρυχας.

367. Necessity is also expressed by δεῖ (197), or χρή, or ἀνάγκη (ἐστί) with the accusative and infinitive.

368.   DRILL

I. 1. ἐπὶ βασιλέᾱ ἡμῖν πορευτέον.   4. ἡ φυλακὴ πεμπτέᾱ.
    2. δεῖ τὰς ναῦς λαβεῖν.   5. ἀνάγκη τοὺς στρατηγοὺς ἐξέτα-
    3. οἱ πολέμιοι διωκτέοι εἰσίν.   σιν ποιήσασθαι.

II. Translate in three ways: The soldiers must proceed now.

369.   EXERCISES

I. 1. ὁ δὲ καὶ ἔλεγεν ὅτι δεῖ Κῦρον αὐτοῖς δοῦναι πολλὰ χρήματα.   2. ἐχρῆν Κῦρον ἐνταῦθα μένειν ἡμέρᾱς τρεῖς. 3. μὴ πειρώμεθα Μίλητον πολιορκῆσαι. 4. Κῦρος ποιητέος σατράπης βασιλεῖ. 5. Ἐπυάξῃ τῇ Συεννέσιος γυναικὶ πολλοὶ ὁπλῖται ἦσαν.

II. 1. The king had a park there.   2. The beautiful fountain was along the road.   3. They mingled wine with it. 4. We must proceed ten days' journey.   5. The king says that Midas hunted the Satyr.

FIG. 13.—A Greek Lady in Her Boudoir

LESSON XLIV

Perfect and Pluperfect Middle

370. καὶ λέγεται δεηθῆναι ἡ Κίλισσα Κύρου[1] ἐπιδεῖξαι
τὸ στράτευμα αὐτῇ· βουλόμενος οὖν ἐπιδεῖξαι, ἐξέτασιν
ποιεῖται ἐν τῷ πεδίῳ τῶν Ἑλλήνων καὶ τῶν βαρβάρων.
ἐκέλευσε δὲ τοὺς Ἕλληνας, ὡς νόμος[2] αὐτοῖς εἰς μάχην,
οὕτω ταχθῆναι καὶ στῆναι, συντάξαι δ' ἕκαστον[3] τοὺς
ἑαυτοῦ.[4] ἐτάχθησαν οὖν ἐπὶ τεττάρων·[5] εἶχε δὲ τὸ μὲν
δεξιὸν[6] Μένων καὶ οἱ σὺν αὐτῷ, τὸ δὲ εὐώνυμον Κλέαρχος
καὶ οἱ ἐκείνου, τὸ δὲ μέσον οἱ ἄλλοι στρατηγοί.

371.　　　　　　　VOCABULARY

δεινός, ή, όν, *terrible, severe, skilful, clever.* [**dino**therium]

δεξιός, ά, όν, *right;* cf. Lat. *dextra*, Eng. *dexterous.*

ἕκαστος, η, ον, *each.*

ἐπιδείκνυμι, ἐπιδείξω, ἐπέδειξα, ἐπιδέδειχα, ἐπιδέδειγμαι, ἐπεδείχθην, *exhibit.*

εὐώνυμος, ον, *left;* lit. *of good name;* euphemistic for *left*, the side from
　　which evil omens were supposed to come. Cf. Lat. *sinister.*

κρατέω, κρατήσω, ἐκράτησα, κεκράτηκα, ἐκρατήθην, *to be strong, rule,*
　　conquer (gen.).

νόμος, ου, ὁ, *custom, law.* [eco**nomy**]

συντάττω, συντάξω, συνέταξα, συντέταχα, συντέταγμαι, συνετάχθην, *draw up*
　　in order. [**syntax**]

372. Learn the perfect, pluperfect middle (passive) of
λείπω [λιπ], τάττω [ταγ], πείθω [πειθ] (643–45).

373. When the verb-stem ends in a vowel, the perfect
middle (passive) is the simplest tense of the verb to conjugate. When the verb-stem ends in a labial, lingual, or
palatal mute, the addition of the personal endings is attended
by euphonic changes, as follows:

---

[1] δέομαι, *to need, beg of*, governs the gen.　　[2] Sc. ἦν.　　[3] I. e. each general.　　[4] τοὺς
ἑαυτοῦ, lit. *those of himself* = *his own.*　The noun στρατιώτας or ἄνδρας is thought but
not expressed.　　[5] *Four deep*, to make the army seem as large as possible.　　[6] Sc.
κέρας, *wing.*

374. A labial mute (π, β, ϕ) before μ becomes μ;[1] with σ forms ψ; before τ or θ it assumes the same degree of roughness. See 599, 2.

A lingual mute (τ, δ, θ) before μ, τ, or θ becomes σ[2] and is dropped before σ.

A palatal mute (κ, γ, χ) before μ becomes γ; with σ forms ξ; before τ or θ it assumes the same degree of roughness.

375. Since the endings of the third plural νται, ντο could not be pronounced with consonant stems, the third person plural of such verbs in the perfect and pluperfect indicative becomes a compound form—the perfect passive participle and εἰσί in the perfect and ἦσαν in the pluperfect: λελειμμένοι εἰσί; λελειμμένοι ἦσαν.

376. DRILL

I. Locate the following:

1. ἐπιδείκνῡσι, ἐδεήθη, ἔστη.
2. τέτακται, τεταγμένοι ἦσαν, ταχθείη.
3. ἐπιδείξειαν, ἐχρῶντο, ἐδεῖτο.
4. κεκελεύκᾱσι, ἐκεκελεύκη, στάς.
5. ἐπέπειστο, ἦγμαι, ἠγμένοι ἦσαν.

II. 1. He has been left, he had left, we have obeyed.
2. They had been drawn up, they stood, he shows.
3. You have been persuaded, you had been arranged, he has persuaded.
4. They are showing, he begs Cyrus, he employs Greeks.

377. EXERCISES

I. 1. Μένων καὶ οἱ σὺν αὐτῷ ὡς νόμος[3] αὐτοῖς πεπόρευνται.
2. δεινὸς πόλεμος ἐγένετο, ἀλλὰ οἱ Ἕλληνες ἐκράτουν.
3. πέπεισται τοῦ στρατεύματος ἐξέτασιν ποιεῖσθαι. 4. βουλόμενος λαθεῖν ἐπορεύετο ἐπὶ μέγα ἄντρον. 5. οἱ μὲν Ἀσπένδιοι τὸ εὐώνυμον εἶχον, Κῦρος δὲ καὶ οἱ ἑαυτοῦ τὸ δεξιόν.

---

[1] When μμμ would result one μ is dropped.   [2] σ between two consonants is dropped.   [3] Sc. ἦν.

II.   1. The soldiers had been sent to the acropolis.   2. Epyaxa begged Cyrus to arrange his soldiers according to their custom.   3. The Greeks did not use horses in battle.   4. The soldiers were not able to hear.   5. So they arranged themselves for battle and stood.

LESSON XLV

Review of the Infinitive

378. ἐθεώρει οὖν ὁ Κῦρος πρῶτον μὲν τοὺς βαρβάρους· οἱ[1] δὲ παρήλαυνον τεταγμένοι κατ' ἴλᾱς[2] καὶ κατὰ τάξεις· εἶτα δὲ τοὺς Ἕλληνας, παρελαύνων ἐφ' ἅρματος καὶ ἡ Κίλισσα ἐφ' ἁρμαμάξης. εἶχον δὲ πάντες κράνη χαλκᾶ καὶ χιτῶνας φοινῑκοῦς καὶ κνημῖδας καὶ τὰς ἀσπίδας ἐκκεκαλυμμένᾱς.[3]

379.   VOCABULARY

ἅρμα, ατος, τό, *chariot.*

ἁρμάμαξα, ης, ἡ, *covered carriage.*

εἶτα, adv., *then, thereupon;* πρῶτον .... εἶτα, *in the first place .... in the second place.*

ἐκκαλύπτω, ἐκκαλύψω, ἐξεκάλυψα, ἐκκεκάλυμμαι, ἐξεκαλύφθην, *uncover.* [apo**calypse**]

ἴλη, ης, ἡ, *crowd, band; squadron of cavalry.* [hom**il**y]

κνημῑς, ῖδος, ἡ, *legging, greave.*

κράνος, ους, τό, *headpiece, helmet;* cf. Lat. *cranium.*

οἴομαι or οἶμαι, οἰήσομαι, ᾠήθην, *think, suppose.*

οὐδέ, conj. and adv., *and not, but not, nor yet, not even, not either.*

παρελαύνω, παρελῶ, παρήλασα, παρελήλακα, παρελήλαμαι, παρηλάθην, *ride* or *drive by, march by.*

πρῶτος, η, ον (πρό), *first, foremost;* πρῶτον as adv., *first.* [**proto**plasm, **proto**col]

τάξις, εως, ἡ, *order, arrangement, array, company, line* (of an army). [syn**tax**, **taxi**dermy]

φοινῑκοῦς, ῆ, οῦν (613), *purple-red, purple.*

χαλκοῦς, ῆ, οῦν (613), *of bronze, bronze.* [**chalco**graphy]

χιτών, ῶνος, ὁ, *an undergarment, chiton, tunic.*

---

[1] The nominative of the article with δέ regularly shows a change of subject and has the value of a pronoun.   [2] *By squadrons.*   [3] The leather coverings, to protect from the weather or injury in handling, were removed.

380. Review the infinitives of λύω (eleven in all, 638–640), and the present infinitives (all voices) of τιμάω, ποιέω, δηλόω (647, 648); the second aorist of λείπω (641).

381. Observe that:

(1) The active endings are εν and ναι. εν contracts with ε of the stem to form ειν (λύεεν, λύειν). ναι is found in the perfect active and aorist passive. The aorist active (λῦσαι) is irregular.

(2) The middle and passive (except aorist) infinitives end in σθαι.

(3) The accent is regular (recessive), except that the penult receives the accent (a) in forms ending in ναι, (b) in first aorist active, (c) the perfect middle (passive), (d) the second aorist middle and passive. The second aorist active has the circumflex on the ultima. πρίασθαι is an exception.

382. Review the infinitives of ἵστημι, τίθημι, δίδωμι, δείκνυμι, εἰμί, εἶμι (650–56) in the present and in the second aorist (when it exists). Note the accent.

383. The future and perfect infinitives may properly be said to denote differences in time, the future denoting a time after that of the verb on which it depends, the perfect a time prior to it. But the present and aorist infinitives distinguish different *kinds* of action or condition, not differences in time.

384. The present infinitive expresses an activity or state continued or repeated. The aorist expresses simply occurrence of a definite kind. ἱκανοὶ τὰς ἀκροπόλεις φυλάττειν, *men suitable to guard the acropolis* (to guard *continuously*); ἐλέγετο Κύρῳ δοῦναι χρήματα, *it was said that she gave Cyrus money* (a *single* gift; *kept giving* would be διδόναι).

385. Verbs of thinking (οἴομαι, νομίζω, ἡγοῦμαι, δοκέω) regularly take the infinitive in indirect discourse. Review the verbs introducing indirect discourse (337).

386. In indirect discourse the infinitive retains the tense which the finite verb had in the direct form; but the present represents both the present and the imperfect; the perfect, both the perfect and the pluperfect.

387. The subject of the infinitive is in the accusative case; but when it is the same as the subject of the main verb, it is usually omitted: Κῦρος οἴεται ἔσεσθαι βασιλεύς, *Cyrus thinks he will be king.*

388. Many adjectives, especially those meaning *ability, fitness, willingness,* take an infinitive to complete their meaning.

389.   DRILL

I. Locate the following forms:

    1. ἰέναι, στῆναι, λελυκέναι.   4. ἀξιοῦν, λελύσθαι, λιπέσθαι.

    2. τάξαι, θεωρεῖν, διδόναι.   5. δοῦναι, λυθῆναι, λαβεῖν.

    3. τῑμῶν, εἶναι, θεῖναι.

II. Translate:

    1. To do, to be, to be about to be.

    2. To stand, to use, to honor.

    3. To be left, to have been arranged.

    4. To leave, to go, to obey.

    5. To have ordered, to show, to place.

390.   EXERCISES

I. 1. οὐκ ἐδύναντο στῆναι οὐδὲ μεῖναι ἐν ταύτῃ τῇ πόλει.

    2. ἐβούλοντο τούτους ταχθῆναι κατ' ἴλᾱς καὶ κατὰ τάξεις.

    3. ἡγεῖται ποιήσεσθαι ἐξέτασιν τῶν βαρβάρων ἐν τῷ πεδίῳ.

    4. Κῦρος τῶν βαρβάρων δεῖται παύσασθαι.   5. ταχθέντες ὡς νόμος αὐτοῖς ἦν εἰς μάχην τὴν πόλιν ἐφυλάττοντο.

II. 1. Xenophon says that Cyrus watched the contest. 2. They beg Cyrus to ride by. 3. They thought that Cyrus gave much money. 4. The soldier stood with[1] a bronze helmet, a shield, and a purple chiton. 5. Cyrus thought he was able to give pay to all the soldiers.

---

[1] Use ἔχω.

LESSON XLVI·

ADVERBS. OPTATIVE OF CONTRACT VERBS

391. ἐπειδὴ δὲ πάντας παρήλασε,[1] στήσᾱς[2] τὸ ἅρμα
πρὸ τῆς φάλαγγος μέσης,[3] πέμψᾱς Πίγρητα τὸν ἑρμηνέᾱ
παρὰ τοὺς στρατηγοὺς τῶν Ἑλλήνων ἐκέλευσε προβαλέσθαι τὰ ὅπλα καὶ ἐπιχωρῆσαι ὅλην[4] τὴν φάλαγγα. οἱ
δὲ ταῦτα προεῖπον τοῖς στρατιώταις· καὶ ἐπεὶ ἐσάλπιγξε,[5]
προβαλλόμενοι τὰ ὅπλα ἐπῄεσαν.

392.   VOCABULARY

ἐπειδή (ἐπεί + δή), conj. adv., *when.*

ἔπειμι (ἐπί + εἶμι), *go on, advance, attack.*

ἐπιχωρέω, ἐπιχωρήσω, ἐπεχώρησα, ἐπικεχώρηκα, *move on, advance.*

ἑρμηνεύς, έως, ὁ, *interpreter.*

ὅλος, η, ον, *whole, entire, in a body.* [cat**holic**, **holo**caust]

Πίγρης, ητος, ὁ, *Pigres,* an interpreter.

προβάλλω, προβαλῶ, προύβαλον,

προβέβληκα, προβέβλημαι, προυβλήθην, *throw before* or *forward;* mid. w. **τὰ ὅπλα**, *present arms.* The **o** of **πρό** is not elided, but unites with the augment, e. g. imperf. **προύβαλλον.**

προεῖπον, 2 aor. to προαγορεύω, *proclaim.*

σαλπίζω, ἐσάλπιγξα, *sound the trumpet, signal.*

ταχέως, adv., *quickly, swiftly.*

393. Adverbs usually end in ως and are derived from
adjectives. Those derived from the vowel declensions have
the form and accent of the genitive plural neuter, but with
ς in place of ν.

πιστός, *faithful,*   genitive plural   πιστῶν,   adverb   πιστῶς
δίκαιος, *just*   "   "   δικαίων   "   δικαίως
χαλεπός, *difficult*   "   "   χαλεπῶν   "   χαλεπῶς

394. Adverbs formed from adjectives with consonant
stems add ως to the stem. This gives the same result as
though the ν of the genitive plural neuter were changed to ς.

---

[1] In subordinate clauses, especially in those of time, the aorist is often to be
translated by the English pluperfect.   [2] The 1st aor. of ἵστημι is transitive.   [3] See
307, n. 3.   [4] ὅλος takes the predicate position; it implies unity more than πᾶς, and
means *whole* rather than *all.*   [5] ὁ σαλπιγκτής, *the trumpeter,* is to be supplied as
subject.

For comparison of adjectives see §§ 264-7

395. Adverbs derived from adjectives have no separate comparison. The comparative is the same as the neuter singular accusative of the comparative in the corresponding adjective, and the superlative is the same as the accusative neuter plural of the superlative.

πιστῶς	πιστότερον	πιστότατα
καλῶς	κάλλῑον	κάλλιστα

396. The comparison of other adverbs must be learned from the dictionary. Learn from the vocabulary the meaning and comparison of the following adverbs: ἄνω, μάλα, ταχέως.

397. Learn the present optative active, middle (passive) of τῑμάω, ποιέω and δηλόω (647–48). Observe that $a + οι = ῳ$, $ε + οι = οι$, $ο + οι = οι$.

[handwritten: ἄνω, ἀνωτέρω, ἀνωτάτω — above, up, inland]

398.   DRILL

I. Locate the following forms:
  1. ποιοίη, ποιοῖεν, δηλοίμην.
  2. τῑμῷ, τῑμῴη, τῑμῷτο.
  3. δηλοίην, τῑμῶντο, τῑμήσειεν.

[handwritten: μάλα, μᾶλλον, μάλιστ — much, very greatly, exce...]

II. Give (1) 3 sing. opt. act., (2) 3 plu. opt. mid., of νῑκάω, ἐπιχωρέω.

399.   EXERCISES

I. 1. ἔλεξεν ὅτι οἱ Ἕλληνες νῑκῷεν. 2. ὡς κάλλιστα τὸ στράτευμα ἐτάχθη. 3. μετεπέμψατο τοὺς στρατηγοὺς ἵνα τοὺς φυγάδας λαβόντες ὁρμῶντο. 4. εἰ Κῦρος κελεύσειεν, οἱ στρατιῶται ἐπιχωροῖεν ἄν. 5. ἔστησε τοὺς στρατιώτᾱς πρὸ τοῦ βασιλέως καὶ ἐνταῦθα ἵσταντο.

II. 1. If the trumpet should sound, the phalanx would advance. 2. Sending the interpreter, he bade the army withdraw rapidly. 3. The soldiers gladly withdrew. 4. They presented arms in order that they might honor Cyrus. 5. He summoned the hoplite from the middle of the phalanx.

LESSON XLVII

Review of Participles

400. ἐκ δὲ τούτου θᾶττον προϊόντων[1] σὺν κραυγῇ, ἀπὸ τοῦ αὐτομάτου δρόμος[2] ἐγένετο τοῖς στρατιώταις ἐπὶ τὰς σκηνάς. τῶν δὲ βαρβάρων φόβος πολύς,[3] καὶ ἥ τε Κί-λισσα ἔφυγεν ἐπὶ τῇ ἀρμαμάξῃ καὶ οἱ[4] ἐκ τῆς ἀγορᾶς καταλιπόντες τὰ ὤνια ἔφυγον· οἱ δὲ Ἕλληνες σὺν γέλωτι ἐπὶ τὰς σκηνὰς ἦλθον.

401. VOCABULARY

αὐτόματος, η, ον, *self-prompted;* ἀπὸ or ἐκ τοῦ αὐτομάτου, *of one's own accord, voluntarily.* [**automatic**]

γέλως, ωτος, ὁ, *laughter.*

δρόμος, ου, ὁ, *a running, race.* [hippo**drome**]

καταλείπω, καταλείψω, κατέλιπον, καταλέλοιπα, καταλέλειμμαι, κατελείφθην, *leave behind, forsake.*

κραυγή, ῆς, ἡ, *cry, outcry, uproar.*

πρόειμι (πρό + εἶμι), *go forward, proceed.*

φεύγω, φεύξομαι or φευξοῦμαι, ἔφυγον, πέφευγα, *flee.*

φόβος, ου, ὁ, *fear.* [hydro**phobia**]

ὤνιος, ᾱ, ον, *purchasable;* τὰ ὤνια, *goods, wares.*

402. Review all the participles of λύω (eleven in all), the present participles of τῑμάω, ποιέω, and δηλόω, the second aorist participle of λείπω (638–41, 647, 648). Learn the declension of the perfect participle active of λύω (621) and in the same manner the second perfect active participle of φαίνω, and review the declension (617–24) and uses of participles (181, 186, 351).

---

[1] Gen. abs. with αὐτῶν omitted (as often).   [2] δρόμος . . . . στρατιώταις, *the soldiers began to run;* lit. *a running happened to the soldiers.*   [3] πολύς has frequently the translation of μέγας; cf. Eng. *much pleasure,* for *great pleasure.*
[4] See 131, n. 3.

403. DRILL

Locate the following:

1. λιπόν, λῡόντων, οὖσαι.
2. τῑμῶσαν, ποιουσῶν, λυθεῖσι.
3. λελυκότα, λῡομέναις, λυθέντι.
4. λελυκυῖαν, ποιοῦσι, λελυμέναι.
5. ὄντι, λελυκόσι, λῡσάμενα.

404. EXERCISES

I. 1. πολὺς τῶν βαρβάρων ἦν ὁ φόβος δρόμου γενομένου τοῖς Ἕλλησιν. 2. σὺν γέλωτι πορευόμενοι οἱ Ἕλληνες ἐπὶ τὴν πόλιν ἦλθον. 3. λέγεται ἀπὸ τοῦ αὐτομάτου δρόμος γενέσθαι τῇ στρατιᾷ ἐπὶ τὰς σκηνάς. 4. ἡ Κίλισσα τὴν ἁρμάμαξαν καταλιποῦσα ἔφυγεν. 5. στήσᾱς οὖν τοὺς Ἕλληνας Κῦρος αὐτὴν ἀπέπεμψεν.

II. 1. He commanded them to go forward more quickly. 2. Great fear arose among the barbarians as the Greeks presented arms. 3. The people[1] from the city fled and abandoned all their goods. 4. When the trumpet sounded, the Greeks came to their tents. 5. Cyrus came to his tent laughing, upon hearing the outcry of the barbarian.

[1] See 131, n. 3.

Fig. 14.—A Scene in a Shoemaker's Shop

LESSON XLVIII

PURPOSE AND OBJECT CLAUSES. FORMATION OF WORDS

405. ἡ δὲ Κίλισσα ἰδοῦσα τὴν λαμπρότητα καὶ τὴν
τάξιν τοῦ στρατεύματος ἐθαύμασε. Κῦρος δὲ ἥσθη τὸν[1]
ἐκ τῶν Ἑλλήνων εἰς τοὺς βαρβάρους φόβον ἰδών. ἐντεῦθεν ἐξελαύνει σταθμοὺς τρεῖς παρασάγγας εἴκοσιν εἰς
Ἰκόνιον, τῆς Φρυγίας πόλιν ἐσχάτην. ἐνταῦθα ἔμεινε
τρεῖς ἡμέρας.

406. VOCABULARY

δέδοικα 1 perf., **δέδια** 2 perf. (both used as presents), **δείσομαι,** aor. **ἔδεισα,**
fear.
ἥδομαι (*ἡδύς*), **ἡσθήσομαι, ἥσθην,** *be glad, be pleased.* *delight in (+ dat.)*
θαυμάζω, θαυμάσομαι, ἐθαύμασα, τεθαύμακα, ἐθαυμάσθην, *wonder at.*
[**thaumat**urgy]
Ἰκόνιον, ου, τό, *Iconium,* a city of Asia Minor.
λαμπρότης, ητος, ἡ, *brilliancy, splendor.* [**lamp**]
ὁράω, ὄψομαι, εἶδον, ἑόρακα or **ἑώρακα, ἑώραμαι** or **ὦμμαι, ὤφθην,** *see.*
[pan**orama, optics, idea,** spher**oid**] *(2 aor. act. stem) [8*
φοβέω, φοβήσω, ἐφόβησα, act., *frighten;* **φοβέομαι, φοβήσομαι, πεφόβημαι,**
ἐφοβήθην, pass. depon., *fear.* [hydro**phobia**]

PURPOSE AND OBJECT CLAUSES

407. Purpose and object clauses are expressed by:

1. ἵνα, ὡς, ὅπως with the subjunctive after primary tenses.
After secondary tenses the optative is used, or the subjunctive may be retained for vividness. If negative, μή is used:
ἄνδρας εἵλοντο ἵνα γέφῡραν φυλάττοιεν, *they selected men to
guard the bridge.*

---

[1] All which stands between τόν and φόβον, its noun, is in effect an adjective modifier of φόβον. The prepositions express the source and direction of the fear. Trans.:
The fear which the Greeks inspired in the barbarians. What is the literal translation?

2. The future participle (usually w. ὡς): ἄνδρας εἵλοντο γέφυραν φυλάξοντας, *they selected men to guard the bridge.*

3. A relative pronoun with the future indicative: ἄνδρας εἵλοντο οἳ γέφυραν φυλάξουσι, *they selected men to guard the bridge* (lit. *who will guard*).

4. The infinitive, especially after verbs of giving and choosing: ἄνδρας εἵλοντο γέφυραν φυλάττειν, *they selected men to guard the bridge.*

5. After verbs signifying attention, care, precaution, or effort, ὅπως is used with the future indicative (after both primary and secondary tenses): βουλεύεται ὅπως μήποτε ἔτι ἔσται ἐπὶ τῷ ἀδελφῷ, *he plans never again to be in the power of his brother* (lit., *how he shall never*).

6. Verbs of fearing take μή with the subjunctive after a primary tense, after a secondary tense μή with the optative (or subjunctive for vividness). The negative is οὐ: δεδοίκασι μὴ οὐ Κῦρος ἔλθῃ, *they are afraid that Cyrus will not come.*

The Formation of Words

408. Many of the suffixes by which nouns are formed have definite meanings.

1. The actor, i. e. doer or agent, if masculine has the endings -της, -τηρ, -τωρ, -εύς: ποιητής (ποιέω), *poet;* σωτήρ (σώζω), *savior;* ῥήτωρ (ἔρω), *orator;* γραφεύς (γράφω), *writer.*

2. The action: -τις, -σις, -σία; -σις is the most common: πρᾶξις (πράττω), *action.*

3. The result: -μα (stem ματ), all neuter: πρᾶγμα (πράττω), *deed.*

4. Quality: -της, -ία, -σύνη; ία is the most common: λαμπρότης (λαμπρός), *brightness;* σοφία (σόφος), *wisdom;* δικαιοσύνη (δίκαιος), *justice.*

5. Diminutive: -ιον, -ίσκος: παιδίον (παῖς), *small child;* νεανίσκος (νεάν), *youth.*

6. Place: -τήριον, all neuter: κοιμητήριον, *sleeping-place.*

The adjective termination -ικός implies fitness: ἀρχικός, *fit to rule.*

409. DRILL

I. Translate each sentence in as many different ways as possible:
1. They sent soldiers to ask for pay.
2. They select (αἱρέομαι) men to guard the queen.

410. EXERCISES

I. 1. οὗτοι οἱ ἄνδρες ἡδέως ἐπορεύοντο ἵνα εἰς τὴν πόλιν ὡς τάχιστα ἀφίκοιντο. 2. ἐντεῦθεν ἐξελαύνει σταθμοὺς πέντε τῶν βαρβάρων οὐ κωλυόντων. 3. ἔπειθον τὸ στράτευμα μεῖναι. 4. συνέλαβε τοὺς Ἕλληνας ὡς ἀποκτενῶν. 5. βασιλεὺς ἐφοβεῖτο μὴ Κῦρος παρείη ἔχων μέγα στράτευμα.

II. 1. Cyrus was pleased as he saw[1] those things. 2. All wondered at the brilliancy of the armor. 3. There was great laughter. 4. They stayed three days in Iconium in order to be ready. 5. The barbarians fled when they beheld the array of the Greek army. 6. They feared that the soldiers might plunder their wares. 7. They planned to fight the barbarians.

---

[1] Use a participle.

FIG. 15.—A Scene in a Blacksmith's Shop

LESSON XLIX

Review of λύω in Present System

411 ἐντεῦθεν ἐξελαύνει διὰ τῆς Λυκᾱονίᾱς σταθμοὺς πέντε παρασάγγᾱς τριάκοντα. ταύτην τὴν χώρᾱν ἐπέτρεψε διαρπάσαι¹ τοῖς Ἕλλησιν ὡς πολεμίᾱν οὖσαν.² ἐντεῦθεν Κῦρος τὴν Κίλισσαν εἰς τὴν Κιλικίᾱν ἀποπέμπει τὴν ταχίστην ὁδόν.³

412.   VOCABULARY

ἀδικέω, ἀδικήσω, ἠδίκησα, ἠδίκηκα, ἠδίκημαι, ἠδικήθην, *be unjust, wrong, injure.*

διαρπάζω, διαρπάσω, διήρπασα, διήρπακα, διήρπασμαι, διηρπάσθην, *plunder, sack.* *pillage thor...*

ἐπιτρέπω, ἐπιτρέψω, ἐπέτρεψα, ἐπέτραπον (2 aor.), ἐπιτέτροφα, ἐπιτέτραμμαι, ἐπετράπην (2 aor.), ἐπετρέφθην, *turn over to, intrust.*

ἕπομαι, ἕψομαι, ἑσπόμην, mid. depon., *follow* (dat.).

Κιλικίᾱ, ᾱς, ἡ, *Cilicia*, a country of Asia Minor.

Λυκᾱονίᾱ, ᾱς, ἡ, *Lycaonia*, a country of Asia Minor.

ξίφος, ους, τό, *sword.*

πολέμιος, ᾱ, ον, *hostile;* οἱ πολέμιοι, *the enemy.* [**polemic**]

τρέχω, δραμοῦμαι, ἔδραμον, δεδράμηκα, δεδράμημαι, *run.* [**trochee**]

χαλεπός, ή, όν, *hard, harsh.*

Review of the Verb

413. Most verbs have the following tense systems:

1. Present system—present and imperfect tenses (all voices); verb-stem + ο/ε: λῡο/ε, λύω, ἔλῡον.

2. Future system—future (active and middle); verb-stem + σο/ε: λῡσο/ε, λύσω, λύσομαι.

3. First aorist system—first aorist (active and middle); verb-stem + σα: λῦσα, ἔλῡσα, ἐλῡσάμην.

4. First perfect system—first perfect and pluperfect active; reduplicated verb-stem + κα (κε in pluperfect): λέλυκα, λέλυκε (pluperfect), λέλυκα, ἐλελύκη.

---

5. Perfect middle system — perfect, pluperfect, and future perfect, middle and passive; verb-stem reduplicated: λελυ, λελυσο/ε (future perfect), λέλυμαι, λελύσομαι.

6. First passive system — first aorist and first future passive; verb-stem + θε (θη when not followed by a vowel or two consonants); verb-stem + θησο/ε in future: λυθε, λυθησο/ε, ἐλύθην, λυθήσομαι.

414. Three other tense systems also occur:

7. Second aorist — second aorist, active and middle; verb-stem + ο/ε: λιπο/ε, ἔλιπον, ἐλιπόμην.

8. Second perfect — second perfect and pluperfect active; verb-stem reduplicated + α (ε in pluperfect): λέλοιπα, λέλοιπε, λέλοιπα, ἐλελοίπη.

9. Second passive system — second aorist and second future passive; verb-stem + ε (η when not followed by a vowel or two consonants): γραφε, ἐγράφην.

When these systems occur they usually take the place of the corresponding first tenses; thus a single verb seldom has more than six tense systems.

415. Review the present system (all moods), active, middle, and passive, of λύω (638–40).

416.   DRILL

I. 1. Locate the following:
    1. λύει, λύῃ, λῦε.
    2. ἔλῦον, λῦον, λῦου.
    3. λῦέτω, λύηται, ἐλῦετο.
    4. λύοι, λῦομαι, λῦόμεναι.
    5. λύεσθε, λύεσθαι, ἐλύεσθε.

II. Give a synopsis of λύω pres., act., and mid. (pass.) in all **moods**: (1) 3 sing., (2) 3 plu., (3) 2 sing., (4) 1 plu.

417. EXERCISES

I. 1. οἱ πολέμιοι τὴν πόλιν διαπορευθέντες τὴν χώραν διήρπασαν. 2. Κῦρος ἔμεινεν ἐν τῇ σκηνῇ ἵνα μὴ τούτους τοὺς ἄνδρας ἴδοι. 3. εἰ μὴ τὴν χώραν αὐτοῖς διαρπάσαι ἐπιτρέψειαν, οἱ ἐν τῇ πόλει πολέμιοι ἂν εἶεν. 4. ἡ Κίλισσα ἀπεπέμφθη τὴν ταχίστην ὁδόν. 5. Κῦρος μὲν ἠδίκει οὐδένα, Κλέαρχος δὲ χαλεπώτερος ἦν.

II. 1. From there Cyrus followed the enemy to Phrygia. 2. Cyrus sent the soldiers back that they might plunder the hostile country. 3. Seeing the swords, the soldiers ran to their tents. 4. After waiting one day, he turned the general over to the barbarians. 5. The country of the Cilicians was plundered by the Greeks.

Fɪɢ. 16.—Athletic Exercises

LESSON L

Pronouns. φημί

418. καὶ συνέπεμψεν αὐτῇ στρατιώτᾱς οὓς Μένων εἶχε καὶ αὐτόν.[1] Κῦρος δὲ μετὰ τῶν ἄλλων ἐξελαύνει διὰ Καππαδοκίᾱς σταθμοὺς τέτταρας παρασάγγᾱς εἴκοσι καὶ πέντε εἰς Θόανα, πόλιν οἰκουμένην, μεγάλην καὶ εὐδαίμονα. ἐνταῦθα ἔμειναν ἡμέρᾱς τρεῖς· ἐν ᾧ[2] Κῦρος ἀπέκτεινεν ἄνδρα Πέρσην Μεγαφέρνην, φοινῑκιστὴν βασίλειον, καὶ ἕτερόν τινα τῶν ὑπάρχων δυνάστην, αἰτιᾱσάμενος ἐπιβουλεύειν[3] αὐτῷ.

419. VOCABULARY

αἰτιάομαι, αἰτιάσομαι, ᾑτιᾱσάμην, ᾑτίᾱμαι, *reproach, blame, accuse.*

δυνάστης, ου, ὁ, *man of power, chief, prince.*

ἕτερος, ᾱ, ον, *other, the other* (of two). [**hetero**dox]

Θόανα, ων, τά, *Thoana,* a city of Asia Minor.

Καππαδοκίᾱ, ᾱς, ἡ, *Cappadocia,* a country of Asia Minor.

Μεγαφέρνης, ου, ὁ, *Megaphernes.*

Πέρσης, ου, *Persian.*

συμπέμπω, συμπέμψω, συνέπεμψα, συμπέπομφα, συμπέπεμμαι, συνεπέμφθην, *send with.*

τὶς, τὶ, *a certain one, anybody, someone; as adj., certain, some, any.*

ὕπαρχος, ου, ὁ, *subordinate commander, lieutenant.*

φοινῑκιστής, οῦ, ὁ, *purple-wearer, an officer of high rank; nobleman.* [**phoenix**]

χρόνος, ου, ὁ, *time.* [**chrono**logy]

420. Learn the declension of τὶς, τὶ, τίς, τί, ὅστις (633, 634).

421. Observe that ὅστις is a union of the relative and the indefinite pronouns, and that both parts retain their declension. The accent is that of the relative pronoun. In the genitive and dative abbreviated forms are sometimes used. The neuter singular is written ὅ τι, to distinguish it from ὅτι, *that.*

---

[1] Refers to Menon. [2] Sc. χρόνῳ, *meanwhile.* [3] Infin. in ind. disc. implied in αἰτιᾱσάμενος. The direct discourse was ἐπιβουλεύεις μοι, *you are plotting against me.*

422. Learn the present (in all moods), and imperfect of φημί (658). Observe that the present indicative is enclitic, except the second singular.

423. DIRECT QUESTIONS.—A question may be introduced by an interrogative word or simply indicated by the punctuation: ποῦ εἰσι οἱ ἵπποι; *where are the horses?*

424. DRILL

I. Locate the following:

1. τῷ, τινά, τίνα.
2. του, τινῶν, ᾗτινι.
3. ὅτῳ, αἷστισι, ἅττα.
4. φαίη, φάναι, ὧντινων.
5. ἔφασαν, φησί, τίσι.

II. 1. For a certain man, for a certain queen, of certain chiefs.
2. To certain cities, of a certain subordinate, a certain gift.
3. Whatever he heard, whatever soldiers, of whatever soldiers.
4. Whom did he send? To whom did he give pay?

425. EXERCISES

I. 1. εἰ τοὺς στρατιώτᾱς αὐτῷ συνέπεμψεν, Μένων στράτευμα εἶχεν ἄν. 2. Κῦρός τινας βαρβάρους ἀπέκτεινεν ὡς ἑαυτῷ ἐπιβουλεύοντας. 3. ἐπεί τις ἄνδρα ἀποκτείνειν βούλοιτι ᾐτιᾶτο ἐπιβουλεύειν τῇ πόλει. 4. πέμπει ἄνδρα ὅστις ἡμῖν ἡγήσεται. 5. τίνας ἄνδρας φησὶ πεμφθῆναι;

II. 1. He said he would send someone with the soldiers.
2. After killing all the Persians, they marched through the other city. 3. They say that the general plundered the country. 4. Meanwhile Cyrus together with Megaphernes wished to follow the cavalry of the enemy, who were rapidly fleeing. 5. Where are these men? Did Cyrus put them to death?

FIG. 17.—Scene in a Bronze Foundry

LESSON LI

REVIEW OF λύω IN FUTURE SYSTEM

426. ἐντεῦθεν ἐπειρῶντο εἰσβάλλειν εἰς τὴν Κιλικίᾱν·
ἡ δὲ εἰσβολὴ ἦν ὁδὸς ἁμαξιτὸς ὀρθίᾱ ἰσχῡρῶς, καὶ ἀμήχανος εἰσελθεῖν[1] στρατεύματι[2] εἴ τις ἐκώλῡεν.[3]

427.   VOCABULARY

ἁμαξιτός, όν, *traversable by wagon.*
  ἁμαξιτὸς ὁδός, *wagon-road.*

ἀμήχανος, ον, *without resource,
  helpless, impracticable, impossible.*

εἰσβάλλω, εἰσβαλῶ, εἰσέβαλον, εἰσβέβληκα, εἰσβέβλημαι, εἰσεβλήθην,
  throw into, enter, invade.

εἰσβολή, ῆς, ἡ, *entrance, pass.*

εἰσέρχομαι, εἰσῆλθον, εἰσελήλυθα, *go
  or come into, enter.*

ἰσχῡρῶς, adv., *strongly, violently,
  exceedingly.*

ὀλίγος, η, ον, *little, few.* [oligarchy]

ὄρθιος, ᾱ, ον, *straight up, steep.*

σκοπέω, imp. ἐσκόπουν, *look at, consider.* [microscope, episcopal]

REVIEW OF VERB—*Continued*

428. Review the future (all moods), active, middle, and
passive, of λύω (638–40). Review the method of forming
the future in liquid verbs (230, 231). Review the future
of φαίνω complete (642).

429.   DRILL

I. Locate the following:

  1. λύσοι, λύσοιο, λύσει.

  2. λύσοιμεν, λῡσόμενοι, λύσομεν.

  3. μενοῦμεν, μενοῦμαι, βαλεῖν.

  4. λύθητι, λιπών, φανῶν.

  5. λυθήσῃ, λυθήσεσθαι, λυθήσεσθε.

II. Write a synopsis of βάλλω, γράφω, ἁρπάζω in fut. in all moods
  and voices: (1) 3 sing., (2) 1 plu., (3) 2 sing., (4) 3 plu.

---

[1] Infin. complementary to ἀμήχανος.   [2] Dat. of person affected or interested
(disadvantage).   [3] Conative imperfect; the condition limits ἀμήχανος (ἦν) εἰσελθεῖν.

430. EXERCISES

I. 1. ἐὰν μή τις κωλύῃ, τὴν χώρᾱν διαρπάσει ὡς πολεμίᾱν οὖσαν. 2. ἐπεὶ ἡ ὁδὸς ὀρθίᾱ ἰσχῡρῶς ἦν, εἰσβαλεῖν οὐκ ἐπειρῶντο. 3. σκοπῶμεν ὅπως . τοὺς ἐκ τούτων τῶν πόλεων στρατιώτᾱς ἀποκτενοῦμεν. 4. ἐπορεύθησαν εἰς τὴν εἰσβολὴν ἵνα τοὺς πολεμίους κωλύσειαν εἰσελθεῖν. 5. ἀμήχανον εἰσβαλεῖν ἦν ἂν στρατεύματι, εἴ τις ἐκώλῡεν.

II. 1. If anyone attempts to hinder, the road is impassable. 2. These men are exceedingly hostile. 3. In Cilicia there are many wagon-roads. 4. He will turn them over to their enemies to kill. 5. He accused another man of attempting to plunder.

LESSON LII

Review of λύω in Aorist and Perfect Systems

431. ἐλέγετο δὲ καὶ Συέννεσις εἶναι ἐπὶ τῶν ἄκρων φυλάττων τὴν εἰσβολήν· διὸ ἔμειναν ἡμέρᾱν ἐν τῷ πεδίῳ. τῇ δ' ὑστεραίᾳ[1] ἧκεν ἄγγελος λέγων ὅτι λελοιπὼς[2] εἴη Συέννεσις τὰ ἄκρα, ἐπεὶ ᾔσθετο[3] ὅτι τὸ Μένωνος στράτευμα ἤδη ἐν Κιλικίᾳ ἦν εἴσω τῶν ὀρέων, καὶ ὅτι[4] τριήρεις ἤκουε περιπλεούσᾱς[5] ἀπ' Ἰωνίᾱς εἰς Κιλικίᾱν Ταμὼν ἔχοντα τὰς[6] Λακεδαιμονίων καὶ αὐτοῦ[7] Κύρου.

---

[1] Sc. ἡμέρᾳ. [2] The predicate ppl. with εἴη is used as the perf. opt. of λείπω for λελοίποι; the compound form is most common. [3] The same mood and tense in the original statement. The aor. ind. usually remains unchanged in subordinate clauses in indirect discourse. [4] Trans. *because;* co-ordinate with ἐπεί. [5] Ppl. agreeing with τριήρεις which is obj. of ἔχοντα. Ταμών is object of ἤκουε and is modified by ἔχοντα, but in thought noun and ppl. taken together are objects of ἤκουε and state the thing heard. The order in translation would be: ἤκουε Ταμών ἔχοντα τριήρεις τὰς Λακεδαιμονίων καὶ αὐτοῦ Κύρου περιπλεούσᾱς ἀπ' Ἰωνίᾱς εἰς Κιλικίᾱν. [6] The article has the effect of repeating τριήρεις. Apparently Xenophon saw the need of specifying what triremes they were, and added the words τὰς . . . . Κύρου as an afterthought. [7] See 126. II.

432. VOCABULARY

ἀγγέλλω, ἀγγελῶ, ἤγγειλα, ἤγγελκα, ἤγγελμαι, ἠγγέλθην, *announce, report.*

ἄκρος, ᾱ, ον, *highest, topmost;* τὸ ἄκρον, *the summit;* more often τὰ ἄκρα, *the heights.* [**acro**bat]

διό, adv. (δι' ὅ), *on which account, wherefore.*

εἴσω, adv., *within* (gen.).

ὄρος, ους, τό, *mountain.* [**oro**logy]

οὐκέτι, adv., *no longer.*

περιπλέω, περιπλεύσομαι, περιέπλευσα, περιπέπλευκα, περιπέπλευσμαι, *sail around.*

Ταμώς, gen. Ταμώ, dat. Ταμῷ, acc. Ταμών, voc. Ταμώς, *Tamos,* an Egyptian.

ὑστεραῖος, ᾱ, ον, *following, next;* τῇ ὑστεραίᾳ (ἡμέρᾳ), *on the following day.*

433. Review the first aorist, active, middle, and passive, of λύω in all moods (638–40). Review the method of forming the first aorist in liquid verbs (230, 231).

434. Review the first perfect active of λύω and νομίζω. Review the second perfect active of λείπω, πέμπω, γράφω, and πράττω.

435. After certain verbs (ἀκούω, ὁράω, γιγνώσκω, ἀγγέλλω, οἶδα, αἰσθάνομαι, etc.) the accusative of the participle may be used in indirect discourse. The tense of the participle is the same as that of the verb in the original statement. When the participle refers to the subject of the main verb, it appears in the nominative instead of in the accusative.

436. DRILL

I. Locate the following:

1. λῦσαι, λύσαι, γεγραφέναι.
2. λελύκω, λελυκώς, λελυκόσι.
3. λυθῆναι, λυθεῖεν, λυθέν.
4. λελυκέναι, πέπομφα, πέπρᾱχεν.
5. λύσειεν, λύσαιεν, λύσειαν.

II. Write synopsis (*a*) 3 sing., (*b*) 3 plu. of 1 aor. of λύω (all moods and voices) and 1 aor. act. and mid. of φαίνω.

437. EXERCISES

I. 1. τῇ δ' ὑστεραίᾳ ἐπεὶ ὁ ἄγγελος ἦλθεν αὐτοῖς ἐδόκει μεῖναι. 2. τὰ ἄκρα οὕτως ὄρθιά ἐστι ὥστε τοὺς πολεμίους μὴ

δύνασθαι τὴν χώραν ἡμῶν εἰσβάλλειν. 3. ἤθροισεν στρατιώτας πλέονας καὶ ἀμείνονας τῶν ἄλλων στρατηγῶν.
4. αἰσθόμενος τὸν βασιλέα ὄντα εἴσω τῶν ὀρέων ἐπορεύθη ᾗ
ἐδύνατο τάχιστα εἰς τὴν πόλιν. 5. ἐπεὶ ὁ ἄγγελος ἦλθεν,
Κῦρος ἐκέλευσε τοὺς ἄνδρας ταχθῆναι καὶ στῆναι ὡς εἰς
μάχην.

II. 1. If Syennesis should remain in the plain, we should
leave the heights. 2. We hear that Cyrus is proceeding against you. 3. They obeyed him gladly. 4. They
had sent men in order to drive the Greeks from the
country.

LESSON LIII

Review of Verb in Perfect System

438. Κῦρος δ' οὖν ἀνέβη[1] ἐπὶ τὰ ὄρη οὐδενὸς κωλύοντος, καὶ εἶδε τὰς σκηνὰς οὗ οἱ Κίλικες ἐφύλαττον. ἐντεῦθεν δὲ κατέβαινεν εἰς πεδίον μέγα καὶ καλόν, ἐπίρρυτον,
καὶ δένδρων παντοδαπῶν σύμπλεων[2] καὶ ἀμπέλων.

439. VOCABULARY

ἄμπελος, ου, ἡ, *grape-vine.*

δένδρον, ου, τό, *tree.* [rhodo**den**-
dron]

ἐπίρρυτος, ον (ἐπί + ῥέω), *overflowed,
well-watered.*

καταβαίνω, καταβήσομαι, κατέβην,
καταβέβηκα, καταβέβαμαι, κατεβάθην, *go down, descend.*

οὗ (ὅς), adv., *where,* originally gen.
of place.

παντοδαπός, ή, όν, *of every kind.*

σύμπλεως, ων, *quite full of, filled
with* (gen.).

---

[1] The 2d aor. of ἀναβαίνω is conjugated exactly like ἔστην (ἵστημι). [2] Decline in
mas. and fem. like Ταμώς (432); the neuter has ν in nom. and acc. sing. and α in nom.
and acc. plu. Declined:

	MAS. AND FEM.	NEU.		MAS. AND FEM.	NEU.
Sing. N. V.	σύμπλεως	σύμπλεων	*Plu.*	σύμπλεῳ	σύμπλεα
G.	σύμπλεω			σύμπλεων	
D.	σύμπλεῳ			σύμπλεῳς	
A.	σύμπλεων			σύμπλεως	σύμπλεα

Dual N. A. V. σύμπλεω

G. D. σύμπλεῳ

440. Review the perfect and pluperfect middle (passive) of all verbs (pure, lingual, palatal, labial, liquid): λύω, πείθω, τάττω, γράφω, ἀγγέλλω.

441.　　　　　　　　　DRILL

I. Locate the following:

1. πέπεισται, πεπεισμένοι εἶεν, ἤγγελτο.
2. κεκωλύκᾱσιν, ἐπεφυλάγμην, πεφυλαχώς.
3. τετάχθαι, τέτακται, ἐτέτακτο.
4. ἤγγελται, ἠγγέλκᾱσι, γεγραφώς.

II.　1. No one had prevented.
　　2. The tents have been guarded.
　　3. We have seen the Cilicians.
　　4. All the soldiers had obeyed Cyrus.
　　5. The king has been persuaded.

442.　　　　　　　　EXERCISES

I.　1. ἀναβὰς ἐπὶ τὰ ὄρη καὶ ἰδὼν τὰς σκηνὰς κατέβαινεν εἰς τὸ πεδίον.　2. τῶν Κιλίκων κωλυόντων εἰσέβαλον εἰς τὴν μεγίστην πόλιν Φρυγίᾱς.　3. ἐπέτρεψε πᾶσαν τὴν χώρᾱν τοῖς Ἕλλησι διαρπάσαι.　4. ἤγαγον ὁπλίτᾱς ὡς πλείστους.　5. εἶδον τὰ ἄκρα οὗ Κῦρος ἐφύλαττεν καὶ κατέβησαν εἰς τὸ πεδίον.

II.　1. The Greeks went up to see the tents of the Cilicians.
　2. Messengers reported that the king was not guarding the road.　3. The general persuaded the army not to go down from the mountains.　4. The trees in that plain were large.　5. If the Cilicians had been on guard Cyrus would not have descended into the plain.

Fig. 18.—Greek Ladies' Toilet

LESSON LIV

Review of Verb in Aorist Passive

443. πολὺ δὲ καὶ σήσαμον καὶ μελίνην καὶ κέγχρον καὶ πῡροὺς καὶ κρῑθᾶς φέρει. ὄρος δ᾽ αὐτὸ[1] περιέχει ὀχυρὸν καὶ ὑψηλὸν πάντῃ ἐκ θαλάττης εἰς θάλατταν.

444. VOCABULARY

κέγχρος, ου, ὁ, *millet.*

κρῑθή, ῆς, ἡ, *barley;* usually plural.

μελίνη, ης, ἡ, *panic,* a kind of millet.

ὀχυρός, όν (ἔχω), *strong.*

πάντῃ, adv., *every way, on every side.*

περιέχω, περιέξω or περισχήσω, περιέσχον, περιέσχηκα, περιέσχημαι, *surround, encompass.*

πλήττω, πλήξω, ἔπληξα, πέπληγα, πέπληγμαι, ἐπλήγην or ἐπλάγην, *strike.*
[apoplexy, **plectrum**]

πῡρός, οῦ, ὁ, *wheat;* often plural.

σήσαμον, ου, τό, *sesame;* also written σησάμη.

ὑψηλός, ή, όν, *high, lofty.*

φέρω, οἴσω, ἤνεγκα (1 aor.), ἤνεγκον (2 aor.), ἐνήνοχα, ἐνήνεγμαι, ἠνέχθην, *bear, carry, produce.* Like the Latin *fero,* φέρω contains three distinct stems; these are φερ, οἰ, ἐνεκ.

445. Review the first aorist passive of λύω, πείθω, πέμπω, ἄγω. Review the second aorist passive of φαίνω.

446. DRILL

I. Locate the following:

    1. ἠνέχθησαν, πεισθήτω, πεμφθέντες.

    2. λυθεῖσιν, ἀχθεῖν, λυθῆναι.

    3. ἀχθέντες, πεισθήσεται, ἀχθῶσι.

    4. πληγείς, πεισθείην, πληγεῖεν.

II. 1. We were persuaded.

    2. The man was frightened.

    3. The wheat and the barley were brought.

---

[1] I. e. τὸ πεδίον.

447.   EXERCISES

I.   1. οἱ ξένοι δῆλοι ἦσαν ἀνιώμενοι, τοῖς γὰρ στρατηγοῖς
οὐκ ἐπίστευον.   2. ἡττηθεὶς ἐν μάχῃ ἀπεχώρει εἰς ὄρος τι
ὑψηλόν.   3. εἰ οἱ στρατιῶται ἀγῶνα ἐν τῷ πεδίῳ θεῖεν,
Κῦρος ἂν τὰ ἆθλα παρέχοι καὶ τὸν ἀγῶνα θεωροίη.   4.
ἐλπίδας δὲ λέγοντες διῆγον, ἀλλὰ τότε οὐδενὶ χρήματα ἐδίδοσαν.   5. καὶ στήσᾱς τὸ ἑαυτοῦ στράτευμα ἔλεξεν ὅτι δέοι
ἄνδρας πέμψαι φυλάξοντας τὴν εἰσβολὴν τὴν εἰς Κιλικίᾱν.   6. οἱ πεμφθέντες ὑπὸ τοῦ ἄρχοντος ἡττήθησαν ἐν
μάχῃ.   7. τριήρεις λαβὼν πρὸς Κῦρον ἦλθε καὶ ἐπολέμει
ταῖς τῶν πόλεων φυλακαῖς.

II.   1. His own soldiers are the swiftest.   2.   And they
are capable of guarding both the market-place and the
acropolis.   3. They were sent to the doors of the king
to demand more pay.   4. For four months' pay was
due the soldiers, and they wished him to give it.   5.
This plain bears every kind of tree and vine.

Fig. 19.—Odysseus and the Sirens

LESSON LV

Review of μι-Verbs in Present System

448. καταβὰς δὲ διὰ τούτου τοῦ πεδίου ἤλασε σταθμοὺς τέτταρας παρασάγγᾱς πέντε καὶ εἴκοσιν εἰς Ταρσούς, τῆς Κιλικίᾱς πόλιν μεγάλην καὶ εὐδαίμονα. ἔνθα ἦν τὰ Συεννέσιος βασίλεια τοῦ Κιλίκων βασιλέως· διὰ μέσου δὲ τῆς πόλεως ῥεῖ ποταμὸς Κύδνος ὄνομα,[1] εὖρος[1] δύο πλέθρων.[2] ταύτην τὴν πόλιν ἐξέλιπον οἱ ἐνοικοῦντες μετὰ Συεννέσιος εἰς χωρίον ὀχυρὸν ἐπὶ τὰ ὄρη, πλὴν οἱ τὰ καπηλεῖα ἔχοντες.

449.   VOCABULARY

ἐκλείπω, ἐκλείψω, ἐξέλιπον, ἐκλέλοιπα, ἐκλέλειμμαι, ἐξελείφθην, *leave, abandon, forsake.* [**eclipse**]

ἐλαύνω, ἐλῶ, ἤλασα, ἐλήλακα, ἐλήλαμαι, ἠλάθην, *drive, ride, march.*

ἔνθα, adv., *there, here;* as rel., *where.*

ἐνοικέω, ἐνοικήσω, ἐνῴκησα, ἐνῴκηκα, *dwell in, inhabit;* οἱ ἐνοικοῦντες, *the inhabitants.*

καπηλεῖον, ου, τό, *huckster's shop, tavern.*

Κύδνος, ου, ὁ, *Cydnus,* a river in Cilicia.

Ταρσοί, ῶν, οἱ, *Tarsus,* a city of Cilicia.

φιλέω, φιλήσω, ἐφίλησα, πεφίληκα, πεφίλημαι, ἐφιλήθην, *love.* [**Phil**adelphia]

χωρίον, ου, τό, *place, spot;* cf. χώρᾱ.

450. Review the present and imperfect active and middle (passive) in all moods of ἵστημι, τίθημι, δίδωμι, δείκνῡμι (649–52).

451.   DRILL

I. Locate the following:

1. δίδωσι, δίδοσο, ἐδίδου.
2. ἐδείκνῡ, ἐδείκνυσαν, δείκνῡ.
3. ἵστασο, τίθει, τιθεῖεν.
4. ἵστασαν, τιθέντων, ἱστάντων.
5. δίδου, ἐδίδουν, ἱστᾶσι.

---

[1] Acc. of specification.   [2] Gen. of measure.

II. Write a synopsis (*a*) 3 sing., (*b*) 3 plu., of present tense (all moods) in active voice of ἵστημι, δίδωμι, τίθημι, and δείκνῡμι; (*c*) the passive of the same verbs in all moods of the **present** tense.

452. EXERCISES

I. 1. οὐκ ἐπείθοντο Κύρῳ καλοῦντι, πολέμιοι γὰρ αὐτῷ ἦσαν.
2. ἐβούλετο τοὺς μὲν ἀποκτεῖναι, τοὺς δὲ ἐκβαλεῖν. 3. ἐπεὶ δρόμος τούτοις τοῖς στρατιώταις ἐγένετο ἐπὶ τὰ ὄρη, Κῦρος ἐκέλευσε τοὺς ἄλλους τὰς σκηνὰς λιπόντας προβαλέσθαι τὰ ὅπλα καὶ ἐπιχωρῆσαι ᾗ δύναιντο τάχιστα. 4. Κῦρος μετεπέμπετο τοὺς ἱππέᾱς ἵνα τοὺς πολεμίους ἐκβάλλοι παντάπᾱσιν ἐκ τοῦ πεδίου. 5. Μένων δὲ τὸ στράτευμα ἐπεδείκνῡ Κύρῳ πρόφασιν ποιούμενος ὡς ἀριθμὸν ποιῆσαι βουλόμενος. 6. ἀγῶνας ἐτίθεσαν οἱ Ἕλληνες καὶ ἆθλα ἐδίδοσαν. 7. συνέπρᾱττον βασιλεῖ ταῦτα φιλοῦντες αὐτὸν μᾶλλον ἢ τὸν υἱόν.

II. 1. After going down through this plain, they instituted a great contest. 2. Tarsus was an inhabited city, larger than Celaenae. 3. Cyrus marched through the midst of this city and displayed his army in the plain. 4. So all the inhabitants abandoned Tarsus for the mountains except the Greeks. 5. There was a river four plethra wide whose name was Cydnus.

FIG. 20.—The Bridegroom going for the Bride

LESSON LVI

REVIEW OF μι-VERBS IN SECOND AORIST

453. ἔμειναν δὲ καὶ οἱ παρὰ τὴν θάλατταν οἰκοῦντες ἐν
Σόλοις καὶ ἐν Ἰσσοῖς. / Ἐπύαξα δὲ ἡ Συεννέσιος γυνὴ
προτέρᾳ¹ Κύρου² πέντε ἡμέραις³ εἰς Ταρσοὺς ἀφίκετο· ἐν
δὲ τῇ ὑπερβολῇ τῶν ὀρέων τῇ⁴ εἰς τὸ πεδίον δύο λόχοι τοῦ
Μένωνος στρατεύματος ἀπώλοντο.

454. VOCABULARY

ἀπόλλῡμι, ἀπολῶ, ἀπώλεσα, ἀπωλόμην, ἀπολώλεκα, ἀπόλωλα, *destroy*, mid.,
and 2 perf. (as pres.), *be destroyed, perish.*

βαίνω, βήσομαι, ἔβην (2 aor.), βέβηκα, βέβαμαι, ἐβάθην, *go.*

γιγνώσκω, γνώσομαι, ἔγνων (2 aor.), ἔγνωκα, ἔγνωσμαι, ἐγνώσθην, *know.*
[**agnostic, gnome**]

Ἰσσοί, ῶν, οἱ, *Issi* or *Issus*, a city of Cilicia.

λόχος, ου, ὁ, *company*, a division of an army.

πρότερος, ᾱ, ον (πρό, comparative), *former, earlier.* πρότερον, adv.,
before, previously. [hystern-**proteron**]

Σόλοι, ων, οἱ, *Soli*, a city of Cilicia.

ὑπερβολή, ῆς, ἡ, *crossing, passage.* [**hyperbole**]

455. Review the second aorist active of ἵστημι, τίθημι,
δίδωμι, and the second aorist middle of τίθημι and δίδωμι.
Some ω-verbs have a second aorist without connecting vowel
and are inflected like the second aorist of μι-verbs: γιγνώσκω
[γνο], *to know;* second aorist singular, ἔγνων. Learn ἔβην,
second aorist of βαίνω, and ἔγνων, second aorist of γιγνώσκω,
in all moods (662).

456. DRILL

I. Locate the following:

1. βάς, δός, στῶσι.
2. ἔγνως, ἔδοσαν, ἐδίδοσαν.
3. θείην, θεῖναι, βῇ.
4. ἔβησαν, γνῶθι, ἔγνω.
5. γνώτω, γνῶναι, σταίη.

---

¹ Pred. adj. with value of an adv. ² Gen. after comparative. ³ Dat. of
difference. ⁴ A prepositional phrase with the value of an adjective may stand
between the article and the noun or follow the noun with the article repeated.

II. Write a synopsis (*a*) 3 plu. and (*b*) 3 sing. of all the moods of
ἔγνων, ἔβην, ἔλιπον, ἐθέμην, ἐδόμην, ἐλιπόμην.

457.   EXERCISES

I. 1. ἐπεὶ ἐσάλπιγξε ἐκέλευσε πάντας στῆναι.   2. οὗτος
ὁ ἀνὴρ ἀπέθανε πρότερος τοῦ ἀδελφοῦ τρισὶ ἡμέραις.
3. τά ὄρη τῆς Κιλικίᾱς κωλύσει Κῦρον καταβῆναι εἰς τὴν
πόλιν.   4. τὸ στράτευμα ἔστησε καὶ ἐκέλευσε στῆναι προ-
βαλομένους τὰ ὅπλα.   5. ἐνόμισε ταύτᾱς τὰς πόλεις ἑαυτῷ
δοθῆναι, ὥστε ἐβούλετο τοὺς φίλους ἄρχειν αὐτῶν.   6. ἐὰν
αὐτοῖς μισθὸν ἀποδῷ ἡδέως πείθονται Κλεάρχῳ.   7. λαβὼν ὅσον ἦν αὐτῷ στράτευμα παρῆν εἰς τὸ χωρίον οὗ Κῦρος
ἐξέτασιν ἐποιεῖτο.

II. 1. Those who dwelt by the sea all perished.   2. When
Cyrus came to Tarsus, he destroyed it.   3. They reached
the tents a few days sooner than the barbarians.   4. In
the passage over the mountains they saw the heights
where Syennesis guarded.   5. The best men remained
there five days.

FIG. 21.—A Greek Parasol and Fan

LESSON LVII

ἵημι AND κάθημαι

458. οἱ μὲν[1] ἔφασαν ἁρπάζοντάς[2] τι κατακοπῆναι ὑπὸ[3] τῶν Κιλίκων, οἱ δέ,[4] ὑπολειφθέντας καὶ οὐ δυναμένους εὑρεῖν τὸ ἄλλο[5] στράτευμα οὐδὲ τὰς ὁδοὺς εἶτα πλανωμένους ἀπολέσθαι· ἦσαν δ' οὖν[6] οὗτοι ἑκατὸν ὁπλῖται. / οἱ δ' ἄλλοι ἐπεὶ ἧκον, τήν τε πόλιν διήρπασαν, διὰ τὸν ὄλεθρον τῶν συστρατιωτῶν ὀργιζόμενοι, καὶ τὰ βασίλεια[7] τὰ ἐν αὐτῇ. Κῦρος δὲ ἐπεὶ εἰσήλασεν εἰς τὴν πόλιν, μετεπέμπετο τὸν Συέννεσιν πρὸς ἑαυτόν·

459. VOCABULARY

ἁρπάζω [ἁρπαδ], ἁρπάσω, ἥρπασα, ἥρπακα, ἥρπασμαι, ἡρπάσθην, *snatch, plunder*. [**harpy**]

εἰσελαύνω, εἰσελῶ, εἰσήλασα, εἰσελήλακα, εἰσελήλαμαι, εἰσηλάθην, *ride or march into, enter*.

εὑρίσκω [εὑρ], εὑρήσω, ηὗρον, ηὕρηκα, ηὕρημαι, ηὑρέθην, *find*. [**eureka**]

κατακόπτω, κατακόψω, κατέκοψα, κατακέκοφα, κατακέκομμαι, κατεκόπην, *cut down, destroy*.

ὄλεθρος, ου, ὁ, *destruction*.

ὀργίζομαι, ὀργίσομαι or ὀργιοῦμαι, ὠργίσθην, *be angry*.

συστρατιώτης, ου, ὁ, *fellow-soldier*.

ὑπολείπω, ὑπολείψω, ὑπέλιπον, ὑπολέλοιπα, ὑπολέλειμμαι, ὑπελείφθην, *leave behind*.

460. Learn ἵημι[8](659), *send*, and κάθημαι (661), *sit down*, in the present and imperfect active and middle (passive) in all moods.

461. DRILL

I. Locate the following:

1. ἵεσαν, ἵωσι, ἱᾶσι.
2. ἵην, ἱείς, ἵεις.
3. ἵεσο, ἵεσαι, ἵετο.
4. ἱέναι, ἱεῖεν, ἱείη.
5. κάθησο, ἐκάθησο, καθοῖτο.

---

[1] ὁ μέν .... ὁ δέ means *the one .... the other*; plu., *some .... others*. [2] See 186, (a), (b); trans.: *while engaged in some act* (τι) *of plunder*. [3] See 178, n. 2. [4] Sc. ἔφασαν. [5] ἄλλος with the article means *the rest of*. [6] See 355, n. 2. [7] Obj. of διήρπασαν. [8] ἵημι(ἑ), ἥσω, ἧκα, εἷκα, εἷμαι, εἵθην, *send*; mid., *charge*.

462.   EXERCISES

I.   1. ἔφη εὑρεῖν τοὺς στρατιώτᾱς οἳ κατεκόπησαν ὑπὸ τῶν Κιλίκων.   2. οἱ μὲν ἄλλοι ἀπώλοντο, οὗτοι δὲ ἔφυγον σὺν φόβῳ πλείονι.   3. αὕτη ἦν πρόφασις τοῦ τοὺς ἄνδρας λιπεῖν ἐν Ἰωνίᾳ.   4. οἱ ὑπολειφθέντες ἵεντο ἐπὶ τὴν Κελαινᾱς πόλιν.   5. ἐπεὶ ἦλθον εἰς τὴν πόλιν, μάχῃ ἡττώμενοι τοῦ πολέμου ἐπαύσαντο.   6. ἔφασαν ἐθελῆσαι πέμπειν ληψομένους ταῦτα τὰ ὄρη.   7. παρήγγειλε τῷ ἄρχοντι πᾶν τὸ στράτευμα λαβόντα ἥκειν ὡς πολεμήσων τοῖς ἀντιστασιώταις.   8. ὑπέσχετο αὐτοὺς οἴκαδε καταγαγεῖν.

II.   1. Some were left behind and some found the rest of the army.   2. Since they could (δύναμαι) not conquer, they withdrew very rapidly.   3. The rest of the soldiers were not willing to plunder their friends.   4. If Cyrus finds the enemy in a city, he besieges it.   5. He said that these fled when the enemy charged.

LESSON LVIII

Reciprocal Pronoun. Relative Particles

463. ὁ δ' οὔτε πρότερον[1] οὐδενί[2] πω κρείττονι ἑαυτοῦ[3] εἰς χεῖρας ἐλθεῖν ἔφη οὔτε τότε Κύρῳ[2] ἰέναι[4] ἤθελε, πρὶν ἡ γυνὴ αὐτὸν ἔπεισε καὶ πίστεις ἔλαβε. / μετὰ δὲ ταῦτα ἐπεὶ συνεγένοντο ἀλλήλοις, Συέννεσις μὲν ἔδωκε Κύρῳ χρήματα πολλὰ εἰς τὴν στρατιάν, Κῦρος δὲ ἐκείνῳ δῶρα ἃ νομίζεται[5] παρὰ[6] βασιλεῖ τίμια, ἵππον[7] χρυσοχάλινον καὶ στρεπτὸν χρῡσοῦν καὶ ψέλια καὶ ἀκῑνάκην χρῡσοῦν καὶ

---

[1] Adv.   [2] Dative of association with the phrase εἰς χεῖρας ἐλθεῖν.   [3] Genitive after comparative.   [4] Sc. εἰς χεῖρας.   [5] Passive.   [6] παρὰ βασιλεῖ, *at the king's court.*
[7] δῶρα has the following appositives: ἵππον, στρεπτόν, ψέλια, ἀκῑνάκην, στολήν; and the infinitive expressions, διαρπάζεσθαι, ἀπολαμβάνειν.

στολὴν Περσικήν, καὶ τὴν χώρᾱν μηκέτι διαρπάζεσθαι,
τὰ δὲ ἡρπασμένα ἀνδράποδα,[1] ἤν που ἐντυγχάνωσιν,[2]
ἀπολαμβάνειν.

464.   VOCABULARY

ἀκῑνάκης, ου, ὁ, *short sword.*

ἀλλήλων, οις, recip. pronoun, *one another, each other.* [par**allel**]

ἀνδράποδον, ου, τό, *captive, slave.*

ἀπολαμβάνω, ἀπολήψομαι, ἀπέλαβον, ἀπείληφα, ἀπείλημμαι, ἀπελήφθην, *take back.*

ἐθέλω, ἐθελήσω, ἠθέλησα, ἠθέληκα, *be willing.*

ἐντυγχάνω, ἐντεύξομαι, ἐνέτυχον, ἐντετύχηκα, ἐντέτευχα, *happen upon, find* (dat.).   *meet*   *fall in with light upon*

ἕως, conj. adv., *while, until.*

μέχρι, conj. adv., *until.*

μηκέτι, adv., *not again, no longer.*

οὔτε, conj., *and not, nor;* οὔτε . . . . οὔτε, *neither . . . . nor.*

Περσικός, ή, όν, *Persian.*

πίστις, εως, ἡ, *faith, confidence, pledge.* [**pistic**]

πού, adv., enclitic, *somewhere, anywhere, perhaps* (qualifying a statement).

πώ, adv., enclitic, *yet, up to this time.*

στολή, ῆς, ἡ, *dress, robe.* [**stole**]

στρεπτός, ή, όν, *twisted;* neut. as a noun, *necklace.* [**strophe**]

τίμιος, ᾱ, ον, *honorable, valuable.*

χρῡσοχάλῑνος, ον, *with gold-studded bridle.*

ψέλιον, ου, τό, *bracelet, armlet.*

465. Learn the reciprocal pronoun (631).

466. Clauses introduced by ἕως, ἔστε, μέχρι, ἄχρι, *as long as, while, until,* when they refer to a definite time (usually past) have the indicative: ἔμενον ἕως Κῦρος ἧκεν, *they waited until Cyrus came.*

467. When they refer to an indefinite time (usually present or future), they take the subjunctive with ἄν after a primary tense, and the optative alone after a secondary

---

[1] Object of ἀπολαμβάνειν. τὰ . . . . ἀνδράποδα, *the slaves which had been seized* (by the Greeks).   [2] More vivid future condition. Syennesis and the Cilicians are the subject

tense: ἕως ἄν τις παρῇ, χρῶμαι, *while one is with me, I make use of him;* πορεύσεται ἔστε ἂν Κῦρος ἔλθῃ, *he will proceed until Cyrus comes;* ἔδοξε αὐτοῖς πορεύεσθαι μέχρι Κῦρος ἔλθοι, *they resolved to proceed until Cyrus should come.*

468. Clauses introduced by πρίν (meaning *before*), dependent on an affirmative clause, take the infinitive: ἰέναι ἤθελε πρὶν τὴν γύναικα αὐτὸν πεῖσαι, *he wished to go, before his wife persuaded him.*   If dependent on a negative clause, πρίν-clauses take the indicative when the time is definite (past); when the time is indefinite (present or future), they have ἄν with the subjunctive after primary tenses and the optative after secondary tenses.   ἰέναι οὐκ ἤθελε, πρὶν ἡ γυνὴ αὐτὸν ἔπεισεν, *he did not wish to go before (until) his wife persuaded him.*   For further examples see 196 and 253.

469.   EXERCISES

I. 1. Κῦρος καὶ Συέννεσις πολέμιοι ἦσαν ἕως συνεγένοντο ἀλλήλοις.   2. ὑπισχνεῖται μὴ πρόσθεν παύσασθαι πρὶν ἂν αὐτοὺς καταγάγῃ οἴκαδε.   3. Κλέαρχος Κῦρον ἔπειθε δοῦναι τῇ στρατιᾷ χρήματα πολλά.   4. τὰ ἀνδράποδα ἀπέλαβε πρὶν τῷ Κύρῳ συγγενέσθαι.   5. Μένωνι ἐδόκει στρατεύεσθαι ἕως τοῖς Πέρσαις ἐντύχοι.   6. Κῦρος ὑπίσχνεῖτο τῷ Κιλίκων βασιλεῖ μὴ τὴν χώρᾶν διαρπάσασθαι.   7. ἤκουσε τοὺς Ἕλληνας πορευομένους διὰ Φρυγίας σὺν μεγάλῃ στρατιᾷ.

II. 1. The Greeks will remain until their generals come. 2. They will not give pledges until they meet. 3. Syennesis received back his slaves before he gave pledges. 4. He said that these gifts were considered valuable. 5. If they happened upon the fugitives, they killed them.

LESSON LIX

ἵημι AND οἶδα. INDIRECT QUESTIONS

470. ἐνταῦθα ἔμεινε Κῦρος καὶ ἡ στρατιὰ¹ ἡμέρᾱς εἴ-
κοσιν· οἱ γὰρ στρατιῶται οὐκ ἔφασαν² ἰέναι τοῦ πρόσω·³
ὑπώπτευον γὰρ ἤδη ἐπὶ βασιλέᾱ ἰέναι· μισθωθῆναι δὲ
οὐκ ἐπὶ τούτῳ⁴ ἔφασαν. πρῶτος⁵ δὲ Κλέαρχος τοὺς αὐ-
τοῦ⁶ στρατιώτᾱς ἐβιάζετο⁷ ἰέναι·

471.   VOCABULARY

ἀνίστημι (ἀνά + ἵστημι, and for prin. pts. and use of tenses, see ἵστημι);
    transitive tenses, *make to stand up;* intrans., *stand up.*

ἀποκρίνομαι, ἀποκρινοῦμαι, ἀπεκρῑνάμην, ἀποκέκριμαι, mid. depon., *answer.*

ἀφίημι (ἀπὸ + ἵημι), ἀφήσω, ἀφῆκα, ἀφεῖκα, ἀφεῖμαι, ἀφείθην, *send away.*

βιάζομαι [βιαδ], βιάσομαι, ἐβιασάμην, *force, compel.*

ἐρωτάω, ἐρωτήσω, ἠρώτησα, ἠρώτηκα, *ask, inquire;* ἠρόμην (from ἔρομαι) is
    generally used for the aorist.

κίνδυνος, ου, ὁ, *danger.*

μισθόω, μισθώσω, ἐμίσθωσα, μεμίσθωκα, μεμίσθωμαι, ἐμισθώθην, *let for hire,
    hire;* pass., *be hired.*

πρόσω, adv., *forward.*

τεῖχος, ους, τό, *wall, fortification.*

472. Learn the second aorist active and middle of ἵημι
(659), and οἶδα (657) in the second perfect active system.
Observe that the second aorist of ἵημι is defective. The
singular is supplied by a first aorist in κα. Cf. τίθημι and
δίδωμι.

473. Indirect questions follow the law of indirect discourse (256). εἰ (*whether*), τίς or ὅστις (*who*), πότερον . . . .
ἤ (*whether* . . . . *or*), are common introductory words: ἠρώ-
τησεν ὅ τι ποιοῖεν, *he asked what they were doing.*

---

¹ Supply ἔμεινε.   ² οὐ φημί = *deny* (cf. *nego* in Latin), often best translated as if
the neg. modified the infin.; here, *said they would not go,* or *refused to go.*   ³ Gen.
of place, but with value of an adv., *forward.*   ⁴ *Not for this.*   ⁵ *Clearchus was the
first,* etc.   ⁶ Note rough breathing.   ⁷ The imperfect sometimes shows attempted
action.

474   DRILL

I. Locate the following:

1. ἴσāσι, ᾔδειν, εἰδείη.
2. ἴσθι, ἴθι, εἰδέναι.
3. εἶσο, ἔσει, εἰδῶσι.
4 εἷσαν, εἷεν, εἷντο.
5 εἷναι, εἶναι, εἷς.

475.   EXERCISES

I. 1. οὐκ ἴσμεν πότερον οἱ Ἕλληνες ἡττήθησαν ἢ οὔ·[1] πολέμου ἐπαύσαντο. 2. εἰ οἱ στρατιῶται δέοιντο αὐτοῦ μένειν,
Κῦρος ἐν τῷ πεδίῳ μείνειεν ἄν. 3. οἱ κήρυκες ἀπεκρίναντο ὅτι τὰ ὄρη εἴη ἰσχυρῶς ὑψηλὰ πάντη ἐκ θαλάττης
εἰς θάλατταν. 4. ἐδόκει ἡμῖν τοὺς φυγάδας καλέσαντας
ἐξελαύνειν εἴς τινα πόλιν, Ἰκόνιον ὄνομα. 5. καὶ ἐνταῦθα
Κῦρος ἐλέγετο ἀποκτεῖναι ἄνδρας Πέρσᾱς τρεῖς αἰτιᾱσάμενος πολεμίους εἶναι αὐτῷ. 6. Τισσαφέρνης οὖν
ᾔσθετο τοὺς ἐν Μῑλήτῳ τὰ αὐτὰ ταῦτα ἐπιβουλεύοντας.
7. Κλέαρχος ᾔδει ὅτι τοῖς μὲν χρήματα πολλά, τοῖς δὲ
δῶρα ἄλλα παντοδαπὰ Κῦρος δοίη. 8. τὸ μὲν ἑαυτοῦ
στράτευμα εἰς τὸ χωρίον ὀχυρὸν ἀφίκετο, οἱ δὲ ἄλλοι ἐν
ὑπερβολῇ τῶν ὀρέων ἀπώλοντο. 9. ἀναστὰς δὲ ἠρώτησέ
τις εἰ οἱ μεγάλου βασιλέως στρατιῶται φυλάττοιεν τὸ
τεῖχος.

II. 1. The army tried to march through the mountains.
2. If no one hinders, Clearchus will collect an army
and march against them. 3. They rushed from the
walls and violently attacked the besiegers. 4. Clearchus replied that he did not know whether there was
danger or not. 5. A messenger from Cyrus came to
Clearchus, but he sent him away at once.

---

[1] Observe the accent of οὐ at the end of a clause.

LESSON LX

CONDITIONAL RELATIVES

476. οἱ δὲ αὐτόν τε ἔβαλλον καὶ τὰ ὑποζύγια τὰ ἐκεί-
νου, ἐπεὶ ἄρξαιντο προϊέναι. | Κλέαρχος δὲ τότε μὲν μικρὸν[1]
ἐξέφυγε μὴ καταπετρωθῆναι, ὕστερον[1] δ', ἐπεὶ ἔγνω ὅτι οὐ
δυνήσεται[2] βιάσασθαι, συνήγαγεν ἐκκλησίαν τῶν αὐτοῦ
στρατιωτῶν.

477. VOCABULARY

ἐκκλησία (ἐκ + καλέω), ᾱς, ἡ, *assembly.* [ecclesiastic]

ἐπειδάν, conj. adv. with the subj., *whenever.*

ἐκφεύγω, ἐκφεύξομαι, ἐξέφυγον, ἐκπέφευγα, *flee forth, escape.*

καταπετρόω, κατεπετρώθην, *stone to death.*

μῑκρός, ά, όν, *small, little;* acc. neut. as adv., *for a short space or time, barely.* [microscope]

ὅταν, conj. adv. with subj., *whenever.*

συνάγω, συνάξω, συνήγαγον, συνῆχα, συνῆγμαι, συνήχθην, *lead* or *bring together.*

ὑποζύγιον (ὑπό + ζυγόν, *yoke*), ου, τό, *baggage-animal.*

ὕστερος, ᾱ, ον, *later;* neut. as adv., *later, afterward.* [hysterics]

after

478. Clauses introduced by a relative (pronoun or conjunctive adverb) with an indefinite antecedent have a conditional force. The clause upon which the relative clause (protasis) depends is the apodosis. Relative conditional sentences assume all the forms of conditional sentences, although the contrary to fact form is rare. Temporal clauses present frequent examples: ὅ τι ἂν πέμψῃ, λήψονται, *whatever he sends they will take* (more vivid fut.; ὅ τι ἄν = ἐάν τι); ὅ τι πέμψειε, λάβοιεν ἄν, *whatever he should send, they would take* (less vivid future; ὅ τι = εἴ τι); ἐπεὶ ἄρξαιντο προιέναι, αὐτὸν ἔβαλλον, *whenever they began to go forward, they threw at him.*

---

[1] Acc. neut. used as adv. [2] The mode of the original thought is retained, even after a past tense, for vividness.

479. **EXERCISES**

I. 1. ὅστις δ᾽ ἀφικνοῖτο τῶν παρὰ βασιλέως πρὸς αὐτόν,
πάντας ἀπεπέμπετο φίλους αὐτῷ μᾶλλον ἢ βασιλεῖ.
2. ἐπειδὰν βασιλεῖ ἐπιβουλεύωσι, αὐτοὺς συλλαμβάνει.
3. Κῦρον δὲ ἐλάνθανον ἀπελθόντες. 4. ὁ δ᾽ ἀγαθός ἐστι
φίλος ᾧ ἂν φίλος ᾖ. 5. οἱ δὲ ὁρῶντες ἐθαύμαζον καὶ οὐκ
ᾔσθοντο τὴν πρὸς ἑαυτοὺς ἐπιβουλήν. 6. ἐπειδὴ δὲ Κῦρος
καλέσειεν, λαβὼν ὑμᾶς ἐπορευόμην, ἵνα ὠφελοίην αὐτόν.
7. ὅταν καταβαίνῃ διὰ μέσου τοῦ πεδίου οἱ πολέμιοι ἐπὶ
τὴν ἀκρόπολιν φεύγουσιν. 8. εἴδομεν μὲν μῖκρόν τι θηρίον,
ἀλλ᾽ οὐκ ἐγιγνώσκομεν ὅ τι εἴη.

II. 1. To whomsoever he was a friend he gave gifts.
2. The Greeks knew that they could not find the way.
3. They barely escaped being cut to pieces by the
enemy. 4. Whenever he wishes to take exercise, he
hunts in the park. 5. An assembly of my own army
was brought together, and I spoke as follows:

FIG. 22.—The Gravestone of Dexileos

καὶ πρῶτον μὲν ἐδάκρυε πολὺν χρόνον ἑστώς· οἱ δὲ ὁρῶν-

3. τες ἐθαύμαζον καὶ ἐσιώπων· εἶτα δὲ ἔλεξε τοιάδε. / "Ἄνδρες
στρατιῶται, μὴ θαυμάζετε ὅτι χαλεπῶς φέρω τοῖς παροῦσι
πράγμασιν. ἐμοὶ γὰρ ξένος Κῦρος ἐγένετο καί με φεύγοντα
5 ἐκ τῆς πατρίδος τά τε ἄλλα ἐτίμησε καὶ μυρίους ἔδωκε δᾱρει-
κούς· οὓς ἐγὼ λαβὼν οὐκ εἰς τὸ ἴδιον κατεθέμην ἐμοὶ οὐδὲ

4 καθηδυπάθησα, ἀλλ᾽ εἰς ὑμᾶς ἐδαπάνων. / καὶ πρῶτον μὲν
πρὸς τοὺς Θρᾷκας ἐπολέμησα, καὶ ὑπὲρ τῆς Ἑλλάδος ἐτῑμω-
ρούμην μεθ᾽ ὑμῶν, ἐκ τῆς Χερρονήσου αὐτοὺς ἐξελαύνων
10 βουλομένους ἀφαιρεῖσθαι τοὺς ἐνοικοῦντας Ἕλληνας τὴν γῆν.

5 ἐπειδὴ δὲ Κῦρος ἐκάλει, λαβὼν ὑμᾶς ἐπορευόμην, ἵνα εἴ τι
δέοιτο ὠφελοίην αὐτὸν ἀνθ᾽ ὧν εὖ ἔπαθον ὑπ᾽ ἐκείνου. / ἐπεὶ
δὲ ὑμεῖς οὐ βούλεσθε συμπορεύεσθαι, ἀνάγκη δή μοι ἢ ὑμᾶς
προδόντα τῇ Κύρου φιλίᾳ χρῆσθαι ἢ πρὸς ἐκεῖνον ψευσά-

---

1. **πρῶτον μέν**: correlative with εἶτα δέ (l. 2). **ἐδάκρυε**: note force of
each tense in this sentence. **χρόνον**: 514. **ἑστώς**: second perfect from
ἵστημι with present meaning. 2. **τοιάδε**: less definite than τάδε.
ἄνδρες: with στρατιῶται a term of respect. 3. **μή**: 569. **χαλεπῶς φέρω**:
see vocabulary under φέρω. 4. **πράγμασιν**: 535. **ἐμοί**: 534. 5. **ἄλλα**:
513; the English would naturally reverse the order, putting the specific
before the general. 6. **ἐγώ**: 496. **ἴδιον**: adj. used as noun. **οὐδέ**: *not
even*, or *not . . . . either*. 7. **ἐδαπάνων**: note the tense. 9. **μεθ᾽ ὑμῶν**:
more complimentary than σὺν ὑμῖν. 10. **γῆν**: 512. 11. **τί**: 510.
12. **δέοιτο**: implied indirect discourse. **ὠφελοίην**: 551. **ὧν** the antecedent
(τούτων) is omitted; the relative, which would naturally be accusative,
is attracted to the case of the antecedent: ἀντὶ τούτων ἃ εὖ ἔπαθον, *in
return for the benefits I had received*. **ὑπ᾽ ἐκείνου**: gen. of agent, since
εὖ ἔπαθον is in effect passive; ἐκείνου is more emphatic than αὐτοῦ.
13. **ἀνάγκη**: sc. ἐστί. **μοί**: with ἀνάγκῃ; the person concerned may be
dat. as here, or accus. (367) subject of the infin. 14. **προδόντα**: agrees
in form with the omitted subject (μέ) of χρῆσθαι; it might have been
dat. agreeing with μοί; cf. preceding note. **φιλίᾳ**: instrumental dat.

μένον μεθ᾽ ὑμῶν εἶναι. εἰ μὲν δὴ δίκαια ποιήσω οὐκ οἶδα,
αἱρήσομαι δ᾽ οὖν ὑμᾶς καὶ σὺν ὑμῖν ὅ τι ἂν δέῃ πείσομαι.
καὶ οὔποτε ἐρεῖ οὐδεὶς ὡς ἐγὼ Ἕλληνας ἀγαγὼν εἰς τοὺς
βαρβάρους, προδοὺς τοὺς Ἕλληνας τὴν τῶν βαρβάρων φιλίαν εἱλόμην, ἀλλ᾽ ἐπεὶ ὑμεῖς ἐμοὶ οὐκ ἐθέλετε πείθεσθαι,   5
ἐγὼ σὺν ὑμῖν ἕψομαι καὶ ὅ τι ἂν δέῃ πείσομαι. / νομίζω γὰρ 6
ὑμᾶς ἐμοὶ εἶναι καὶ πατρίδα καὶ φίλους καὶ συμμάχους, καὶ
σὺν ὑμῖν μὲν ἂν οἶμαι εἶναι τίμιος ὅπου ἂν ὦ, ὑμῶν δὲ ἔρημος
ὢν οὐκ ἂν ἱκανὸς οἶμαι εἶναι οὔτ᾽ ἂν φίλον ὠφελῆσαι οὔτ᾽ ἂν
ἐχθρὸν ἀλέξασθαι. ὡς ἐμοῦ οὖν ἰόντος ὅπῃ ἂν καὶ ὑμεῖς,   10
οὕτω τὴν γνώμην ἔχετε."

ταῦτα εἶπεν· οἱ δὲ στρατιῶται οἵ τε αὐτοῦ ἐκείνου καὶ   7
οἱ ἄλλοι ταῦτα ἀκούσαντες ὅτι οὐ φαίη παρὰ βασιλέᾱ
πορεύεσθαι ἐπῄνεσαν· παρὰ δὲ Ξενίου καὶ Πασίωνος πλείους

---

with χρῆσθαι.   1. **εἰ**: 473.   **δίκαια·** 510.   **ποιήσω**: fut. indic.; what other part
of the verb has the same form?   2. **δ᾽ οὖν**: *at any rate;* cf. 355, n. 2.
δέῃ: 562, sc. **πάσχειν.** **πείσομαι**: from **πάσχω**; **πείθω** would give the same
form.   3. **οὐδείς**: when a negative (**οὔποτε**) is followed by another compound of the same negative (**οὐδείς**), the negation is strengthened; in
translation only one negative can be used.   **ὡς**: 573.   **ἀγαγών**: concessive or circumstantial ppl.   4. **προδούς**: from **προδίδωμι**, preliminary
ppl.   5. **εἱλόμην**: from **αἱρέω**; note meaning of mid. voice.   **ὑμεῖς**: 496.
ἐμοί: 533; observe that Greek like Latin tends to gather the pronouns
of a sentence.   7. **ἐμοί**: 534.   **πατρίδα**: acc. because pred. after **εἶναι.**
8. **ἄν**: goes with **εἶναι**; **ἄν** is retained with an infin. when it stands for a
finite verb which would have **ἄν**; here **ἂν εἶναι** stands for **ἂν εἴην**; the protasis is implied in **σὺν ὑμῖν** which equals **εἰ σὺν ὑμῖν ἐποίμην.** **τίμιος**: nom.
because the subj. of the infin. is not expressed, leaving **τίμιος** to agree
with the subj. of the main verb (**οἶμαι**), 577.   **ὦ**: 567.   **ὑμῶν**: gen. with
ἔρημος.   9. **ἄν**: in long sentences **ἄν** is often repeated as here; **ἂν εἶναι**
stands for **ἂν εἴην**; the protasis is in **ὤν** which stands for **εἰ εἴην.** **ὠφελῆσαι**: 596.   10. **ὡς**: suggests ind. disc., though strictly **ἐμοῦ ἰόντος** is
gen. abs. expressing cause; *therefore, since* (as I say, **ὡς**) *I am going*
(**ἰόντος** is fut. in effect) *wherever you also go, have this opinion;*
i.e. *be of this opinion, that I shall go,* etc.   **καί**: intensive, *also,*
too.   **ὑμεῖς**: sc. **ἴητε.**   12. **οἵ**: receives accent from **τέ.**   13. **οὐ**:
taken closely with **φαίη**, 470, 2.   **φαίη**: from **φημί**, 573.   14. **πλεί-**

ἢ δισχίλιοι λαβόντες τὰ ὅπλα καὶ τὰ σκευοφόρα ἐστρατοπεδεύσαντο παρὰ Κλέαρχον. Κῦρος δὲ τούτοις ἀπορῶν τε
καὶ λυπούμενος μετεπέμπετο τὸν Κλέαρχον· ὁ δὲ ἰέναι μὲν
οὐκ ἤθελε, λάθρᾳ δὲ τῶν στρατιωτῶν πέμπων αὐτῷ ἄγγελον
5 ἔλεγε θαρρεῖν ὡς καταστησομένων τούτων εἰς τὸ δέον· μετα-
πέμπεσθαι δ' ἐκέλευεν αὐτόν· αὐτὸς δ' οὐκ ἔφη ἰέναι. / μετὰ
δὲ ταῦτα συναγαγὼν τούς θ' ἑαυτοῦ στρατιώτᾱς καὶ τοὺς
προσελθόντας αὐτῷ καὶ τῶν ἄλλων τὸν βουλόμενον, ἔλεξε
τοιάδε. "Ἄνδρες στρατιῶται, τὰ μὲν δὴ Κύρου δῆλον ὅτι
10 οὕτως ἔχει πρὸς ἡμᾶς ὥσπερ τὰ ἡμέτερα πρὸς ἐκεῖνον· οὔτε
γὰρ ἡμεῖς ἐκείνου ἔτι στρατιῶται, ἐπεί γε οὐ συνεπόμεθα
αὐτῷ, οὔτε ἐκεῖνος ἔτι ἡμῖν μισθοδότης. ὅτι μέντοι ἀδικεῖσθαι νομίζει ὑφ' ἡμῶν οἶδα· ὥστε καὶ μεταπεμπομένου αὐτοῦ
οὐκ ἐθέλω ἐλθεῖν, τὸ μὲν μέγιστον αἰσχῡνόμενος ὅτι σύνοιδα
15 ἐμαυτῷ πάντα ἐψευσμένος αὐτόν, ἔπειτα καὶ δεδιὼς μὴ
λαβών με δίκην ἐπιθῇ ὧν νομίζει ὑπ' ἐμοῦ ἠδικῆσθαι. / ἐμοὶ
οὖν δοκεῖ οὐχ ὥρᾱ εἶναι ἡμῖν καθεύδειν οὐδ' ἀμελεῖν ἡμῶν

ους: contracted from πλείονες. 　　1. **ἐστρατοπεδεύσαντο**: a verb of rest,
but fol. by a prep. implying motion; cf. παρὰ Ξενίου; some texts have the
dat. παρὰ Κλεάρχῳ. 　　2. **τούτοις**: neuter, dat. of cause. **ἀπορῶν**: cause
or concession. 　　4. **στρατιωτῶν**: gen. with λάθρᾳ. 　　5. **ὡς**: *on the
ground that*, fol. by gen. abs. 　　7. **θ'**: τέ with elision of vowel and
roughening of consonant before the rough breathing of ἑαυτοῦ. 　　8. **προσελθόντας**: 490. **αὐτῷ**: dat. after πρός in composition. 　　9. **τά**: the substantive (πράγματα) is omitted. **δῆλον ὅτι**, *it is clear that*, ϝϲ. ἐστίν.
10. **ἔχει**: when modified by an adv. ἔχω is equivalent to εἰμί and an adjective of same meaning as the adv. 　　11. **ἡμεῖς**: sc. ἐσμέν. 　　12. **ἡμῖν**: 534.
ἀδικεῖσθαι: subject not expressed, as it is the same as that of νομίζει.
13: **ὑφ' ἡμῶν**: gen. of agent. **καί**: intensive with gen. abs. indicating
concession. 　　14. **μέγιστον**: 511. **σύνοιδα ἐμαυτῷ**, *conscious*; ἐμαυτῷ is
dat. after σύν in composition. 　　15. **ἐψευσμένος**: observe form of reduplication; ppl. in ind. disc.; for case see 578. **δεδιώς**: perf. with present
meaning. **μή**: 554. 　　16. **λαβών**: 581. **ὧν**: omission of antecedent and
attraction, *for that* (sc. τούτων) *in which* (ὧν for ἅ, cog. acc.) *he thinks
he has been wronged by me.* **ἠδικῆσθαι**: tense? 　　17. **δοκεῖ**, meaning
to seem, is followed by infin. in ind. disc. **καθεύδειν**: depends on ὥρᾱ; so

αὐτῶν, ἀλλὰ βουλεύεσθαι ὅ τι χρὴ ποιεῖν ἐκ τούτων. καὶ
ἕως τε μένομεν αὐτοῦ σκεπτέον μοι δοκεῖ εἶναι ὅπως ὡς ἀσφαλέστατα μενοῦμεν, εἴ τε ἤδη δοκεῖ ἀπιέναι, ὅπως ὡς ἀσφαλέστατα ἄπιμεν, καὶ ὅπως τὰ ἐπιτήδεια ἕξομεν· ἄνευ γὰρ τούτων οὔτε στρατηγοῦ οὔτε ἰδιώτου ὄφελος οὐδέν. / ὁ δ' ἀνὴρ 5
πολλοῦ μὲν ἄξιος φίλος ᾧ ἂν φίλος ᾖ, χαλεπώτατος δ' ἐχ-
θρὸς ᾧ ἂν πολέμιος ᾖ, ἔχει δὲ δύναμιν καὶ πεζὴν καὶ ἱππικὴν
καὶ ναυτικὴν ἣν πάντες ὁμοίως ὁρῶμέν τε καὶ ἐπιστάμεθα· καὶ
γὰρ οὐδὲ πόρρω δοκοῦμέν μοι αὐτοῦ καθῆσθαι. ὥστε ὥρα
λέγειν ὅ τι τις γιγνώσκει ἄριστον εἶναι." 10

ταῦτα εἰπὼν ἐπαύσατο. / ἐκ δὲ τούτου ἀνίσταντο οἱ μὲν
ἐκ τοῦ αὐτομάτου, λέξοντες ἃ ἐγίγνωσκον, οἱ δὲ καὶ ὑπ' ἐκείνου ἐγκέλευστοι, ἐπιδεικνύντες οἵα εἴη ἡ ἀπορίᾱ ἄνευ τῆς
Κύρου γνώμης καὶ μένειν καὶ ἀπιέναι. / εἷς δὲ δὴ εἶπε προσ-
ποιούμενος σπεύδειν ὡς τάχιστα πορεύεσθαι εἰς τὴν Ἑλλάδα, 15
στρατηγοὺς μὲν ἑλέσθαι ἄλλους ὡς τάχιστα, εἰ μὴ βούλεται
Κλέαρχος ἀπάγειν· τὰ δ' ἐπιτήδει' ἀγοράζεσθαι (ἡ δ' ἀγορὰ
ἦν ἐν τῷ βαρβαρικῷ στρατεύματι) καὶ συσκευάζεσθαι· ἐλθόντας δὲ Κῦρον αἰτεῖν πλοῖα, ὡς ἀποπλέοιεν· ἐὰν δὲ μὴ διδῷ
ταῦτα, ἡγεμόνα αἰτεῖν Κῦρον ὅστις διὰ φιλίᾱς τῆς χώρᾱς 20

also ἀμελεῖν and βουλεύεσθαι. 1. ἐκ τούτων: *in view of these things.*
2. ἕως: *as long as, while.* τέ (also τέ after εἰ): *both . . . . and,* frequently
rendered merely *and.* αὐτοῦ: adv. of place. σκεπτέον: 366, pred. with
εἶναι. μοί: connect with δοκεῖ. ὅπως: 553. ἀσφαλέστατα: 395. 3. ἤδη:
at once. 4. ἄπιμεν: present with future meaning. ἕξομεν: see ἔχω.
5. στρατηγοῦ: depends upon ὄφελος; sc. ἐστίν. ὁ ἀνήρ: Cyrus. 6. πολλοῦ: 531. ᾧ ἂν φίλος ᾖ: a rel. clause, present general condition. 8. τέ
. . . . καί: *both . . . . and,* with emphasis on the second member. ὁμοίως:
to be taken with πάντες, *all alike.* καὶ γάρ: ellipsis, *and (καί) I mention
this, for* (γάρ), etc. 9. αὐτοῦ: gen. with adv. πόρρω. ὥρα: sc. ἐστίν.
11. οἱ μέν . . . . οἱ δέ: 487. 12. λέξοντες: 583. ἐκείνου: Clearchus.
13. εἴη: ind. disc. 14. δή: *but one in particular* (δή) *proposed,* etc.
εἶπε: when εἶπον means *bid* or *command,* it is followed by the infin.;
hence ἑλέσθαι and the other co-ordinate infinitives. 16. εἰ: simple supposition. μή: neg. in condition. 17. ἡ δ' ἀγορά . . . . στρατεύματι: a
parenthesis inserted by the historian to show the absurdity of the plan.
19. Κῦρον . . . . πλοῖα: 512. ὡς: 551. 20. ὅστις . . . . ἀπάξει: 552. φιλίᾱς:

ἀπάξει· ἐὰν δὲ μηδὲ ἡγεμόνα διδῷ, συντάττεσθαι τὴν ταχίστην, πέμψαι δὲ καὶ προκαταληψομένους τὰ ἄκρα, ὅπως μὴ
φθάσωσι μήτε Κῦρος μήτε οἱ Κίλικες καταλαβόντες, ὧν
πολλοὺς καὶ πολλὰ χρήματα ἔχομεν ἀνηρπακότες. οὗτος
5 μὲν τοιαῦτα εἶπε· μετὰ δὲ τοῦτον Κλέαρχος εἶπε τοσοῦτον. /

"Ὡς μὲν στρατηγήσοντα ἐμὲ ταύτην τὴν στρατηγίᾶν
μηδεὶς ὑμῶν λεγέτω· πολλὰ γὰρ ἐνορῶ δι' ἃ ἐμοὶ τοῦτο οὐ
ποιητέον· ὡς δὲ τῷ ἀνδρὶ ὃν ἂν ἕλησθε πείσομαι ᾗ δυνατὸν
μάλιστα, ἵνα εἰδῆτε ὅτι καὶ ἄρχεσθαι ἐπίσταμαι ὥς τις καὶ
10 ἄλλος μάλιστα ἀνθρώπων." / μετὰ τοῦτον ἄλλος ἀνέστη,
ἐπιδεικνὺς μὲν τὴν εὐήθειαν τοῦ τὰ πλοῖα αἰτεῖν κελεύοντος,
ὥσπερ πάλιν τὸν στόλον Κύρου ποιουμένου, ἐπιδεικνὺς δὲ
ὡς εὔηθες εἴη ἡγεμόνα αἰτεῖν παρὰ τούτου ᾧ λυμαινόμεθα τὴν
πρᾶξιν. / εἰ δὲ καὶ τῷ ἡγεμόνι πιστεύσομεν ὃν ἂν Κῦρος δῷ,
15 τί κωλύει καὶ τὰ ἄκρα ἡμῖν κελεύειν Κῦρον προκαταλαβεῖν;

---

pred. adj. sc. οὔσης.   1. μηδέ: *not* .... *either*. τὴν ταχίστην: sc. ὁδόν, 511.
2. καί: intensive.   προκαταληψομένους: sc. ἄνδρας, *those who will preoccupy*, etc.; cf. λέξοντες, p. 137, l. 12. ὅπως: 551.   3. καταλαβόντες: ppl. with
φθάσωσι, 585.   ὧν: possessive gen.; ὧν .... ἀνηρπακότες is an extract from
the original speech.   4. ἀνηρπακότες: ppl. showing means or manner;
ἔχω with a pres. ppl. (sometimes perf. as here) may have the effect of a
perf. tense, *have plundered;* or ἔχομεν ἀνηρπακότες may equal ἀνηρπάκαμεν
καὶ ἔχομεν.   6. στρατηγήσοντα: ppl. ind. disc. 578.   στρατηγίᾶν: 510.
7 ἐμοί: dat. of agent.   8. ὡς δὲ τῷ ἀνδρί, etc.: dependent on words
to be supplied; e. g. οὕτω λέγετε (imperative), or ἕκαστος λεγέτω. ἀνδρί:
533.   ᾗ: sc. ὁδῷ, dat. of means. δυνατόν: sc. ἐστί.   9f. ὅτι .... ἀνθρώπων: *that I know how to submit to authority as well as any man that
lives;* μάλιστα ἀνθρώπων (part. gen.), lit. *best of all men.*   9. τις: sc.
ἐπίσταται.   10 μετὰ τοῦτον: distinguish from μετὰ ταῦτα.   11. τοῦ:
goes with κελεύοντος, ppl. used as noun.   12. Κύρου: gen. abs.   13. ὡς:
how, adv. of degree. εἴη: ind. disc. αἰτεῖν: cf. 178, where there are two
acc.; the person may be governed by a prep. as here.   13f. παρὰ ....
πρᾶξιν: exact words of the speaker.   13. ᾧ: *whose*, 538.   14. πιστεύσομεν: If we shall trust Cyrus' man, as it is proposed that we shall do,
we might as well (τί κωλύει) have him prepare our defense against him.
The apodosis is ironical, and shows the absurdity of the soldier's pro-
posal. ὅν: the rel. clause has a cond. force, hence subj. (δῷ).   15. ἡμῖν:

ἐγὼ γὰρ ὀκνοίην μὲν ἂν εἰς τὰ πλοῖα ἐμβαίνειν ἃ ἡμῖν δοίη,
μὴ ἡμᾶς ταῖς τριήρεσι καταδύσῃ, φοβοίμην δ' ἂν τῷ ἡγεμόνι
ᾧ δοίη ἕπεσθαι, μὴ ἡμᾶς ἀγάγῃ ὅθεν οὐκ ἔσται ἐξελθεῖν·
βουλοίμην δ' ἂν ἄκοντος ἀπιὼν Κύρου λαθεῖν αὐτὸν ἀπελ-
θών· ὃ οὐ δυνατόν ἐστιν. / ἀλλ' ἐγώ φημι ταῦτα μὲν φλυα- 5
οίας εἶναι· δοκεῖ δέ μοι ἄνδρας ἐλθόντας πρὸς Κῦρον οἵτινες
ἐπιτήδειοι σὺν Κλεάρχῳ ἐρωτᾶν ἐκεῖνον τί βούλεται ἡμῖν
χρῆσθαι· καὶ ἐὰν μὲν ἡ πρᾶξις ᾖ παραπλησία οἷάπερ καὶ
πρόσθεν ἐχρῆτο τοῖς ξένοις, ἕπεσθαι καὶ ἡμᾶς καὶ μὴ κακίους
εἶναι τῶν πρόσθεν τούτῳ συναναβάντων· / ἐὰν δὲ μείζων ἡ 10
πρᾶξις τῆς πρόσθεν φαίνηται καὶ ἐπιπονωτέρα καὶ ἐπικιν-
δυνοτέρα, ἀξιοῦν ἢ πείσαντα ἡμᾶς ἄγειν ἢ πεισθέντα πρὸς
φιλίαν ἀφιέναι· οὕτω γὰρ καὶ ἑπόμενοι ἂν φίλοι αὐτῷ καὶ
πρόθυμοι ἐποίμεθα καὶ ἀπιόντες ἀσφαλῶς ἂν ἀπίοιμεν· ὅ τι
δ' ἂν πρὸς ταῦτα λέγῃ ἀπαγγεῖλαι δεῦρο· ἡμᾶς δ' ἀκούσαν- 15

---

dat. of advantage or disadvantage according to the point of view.
1. ὀκνοίην: potential optative; might be regarded as apodosis of a less
vivid future cond. of which ἃ δοίη is the protasis; *I should fear*, etc.; so
also φοβοίμην and βουλοίμην.   2. τριήρεσι: 535. καταδύσῃ: 554. ἡγεμόνι: 533.
3. ᾧ: attracted from acc. (ὅν).   ὅθεν: relative, antecedent omitted; *into
a place* (ἐκεῖσε) *from which*, etc. ἔσται: fut. for vividness. ἐξελθεῖν: infin.
with ἔσται, which here means *it is possible*.   4. ἄκοντος: sc. ὄντος, 592.
ἀπιών: conditional force, equals εἰ ἀπίοιμι. ἀπελθών: supplementary
ppl. with λαθεῖν, 585; lit. *to escape his notice getting away*.   5. ὅ:
antecedent is the thought of the previous sentence. φλυαρίᾱς: plu.
(more forcible) where Eng. uses sing.   6. δοκεῖ: *it seems best*. οἵτινες:
sc. εἰσί.   7. ἐρωτᾶν: infin. with δοκεῖ; so also ἕπεσθαι, εἶναι, ἀξιοῦν, ἀπαγγεῖλαι, βουλεύεσθαι. ἐκεῖνον: Cyrus. τί, 510, *for what he desires to use us.*
8. οἷάπερ: antecedent omitted; the rel. is attracted from οἷάνπερ (cog.
acc.).   9. πρόσθεν: refers to former journey to Babylon just before the
death of Darius; cf. 91. κακίους: contracted from κακίονας.   10. τούτῳ:
gov. by σύν in comp.; more emphatic than αὐτῷ. συναναβάντων: ppl.
used as a noun.   11. πρόσθεν: full expression is τῆς πρόσθεν πράξεως.
12. πείσαντα: acc. agreeing with unexpressed subj. of ἄγειν (αὐτόν, i. e.
Cyrus).   12f. πρὸς φιλίᾱν: the phrase has the value of an adverb.
13. ἑπόμενοι: conditional; equals εἰ ἐποίμεθα; similarly ἀπιόντες (l. 14).

20. τας πρὸς ταῦτα βουλεύεσθαι. / ἔδοξε ταῦτα, καὶ ἄνδρας ἑλόμενοι σὺν Κλεάρχῳ πέμπουσιν οἳ ἠρώτων Κῦρον τὰ δόξαντα
τῇ στρατιᾷ. ὁ δ᾽ ἀπεκρίνατο ὅτι ἀκούοι ᾿Αβροκόμαν[1] ἐχθρὸν
ἄνδρα ἐπὶ τῷ Εὐφράτῃ ποταμῷ εἶναι, ἀπέχοντα δώδεκα σταθ-
5 μούς· πρὸς τοῦτον οὖν ἔφη βούλεσθαι ἐλθεῖν· κἂν μὲν ᾖ
ἐκεῖ, τὴν δίκην ἔφη χρῄζειν ἐπιθεῖναι αὐτῷ, ἢν δὲ φύγῃ,
21. ἡμεῖς ἐκεῖ πρὸς ταῦτα βουλευσόμεθα. / ἀκούσαντες δὲ ταῦτα
οἱ αἱρετοὶ ἀπαγγέλλουσι τοῖς στρατιώταις· τοῖς δὲ ὑποψίᾳ
μὲν ἦν ὅτι ἄγοι πρὸς βασιλέᾱ, ὅμως δὲ ἐδόκει ἕπεσθαι. προσ-
10 αιτοῦσι δὲ μισθόν· ὁ δὲ Κῦρος ὑπισχνεῖται ἡμιόλιον πᾶσι
δώσειν οὗ πρότερον ἔφερον, ἀντὶ δᾱρεικοῦ τρία ἡμιδᾱρεικὰ
τοῦ μηνὸς τῷ στρατιώτῃ· ὅτι δὲ ἐπὶ βασιλέᾱ ἄγοι οὐδὲ ἐνταῦθα ἤκουσεν οὐδεὶς ἕν γε τῷ φανερῷ.

---

1. **ἑλόμενοι**: from αἱρέω.   2. **ἠρώτων**: from ἐρωτάω, 512.   3. **ἀκούοι**: 573.
ἐχθρόν: a personal enemy (*inimīcus*); πολέμιος is generally used for a
public enemy (*hostis*).   4. **σταθμούς**: 514.   5. **κἄν**: by crasis for καὶ
ἐάν.   6. **αὐτῷ**: dat. after ἐπί in comp.   **ἤν**: contracted from ἐάν; ἢν ....
βουλευσόμεθα, the exact words of the speaker.   8. **αἱρετοί**: verbal used
as a noun.   **τοῖς**: the article followed by δέ at the beginning of a sentence has a demonstrative force, *but they*.   11. **δώσειν**: a verb of
promising takes fut. infin. (which gives more the impression of a quotation) or the pres. (or aor.) infin.   **οὗ**: gen. after the comparative in ἡμιόλιον; it stands for τούτου ὅν.   12. **τοῦ**: the article sometimes has a dis-
tributive force, e. g. *per man* or *a man*.   **μηνός**: 523.   **τῷ**: cf. note on τοῦ
above.   **οὐδέ — οὐδείς**: strengthened negative thought.   13. **ἐν τῷ φανερῷ**: has the value of an adv. (φανερῶς), *openly*.   **γε**: *at least*.

This chapter furnishes an excellent opportunity for the study of
prepositions. The student should consult the vocabulary, grammar,
and notes for the exact meaning, the cases which follow, etc. The following important prepositions occur in the chapter: **ἀντί, διά, εἰς, ἐν,
ἐπί, ἐκ (ἐξ), μετά, παρά, πρός, σύν, ὑπέρ, ὑπό**.

[1] ᾿Αβροκόμᾱς, ᾱ (Doric gen. for ου), ὁ, *Abrocomas*, a satrap of Phoenicia and Syria.

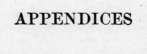

APPENDICES

APPENDIX I.—RULES OF SYNTAX

RULES OF AGREEMENT

ADJECTIVES

479. An adjective agrees with its noun in gender, number, and case: εἰς πόλιν μεγάλην, *to a large city.*

APPOSITION

480. A noun which qualifies another noun or pronoun, and denotes the same person or thing, agrees with it in case, and is called an appositive: ἔπεμψε Πίγρητα τὸν ἑρμηνέα, *he sent Pigres the interpreter.*

SUBJECT AND PREDICATE

481. A predicate noun or adjective is in the same case as the subject of the verb: ὁ ποταμὸς καλεῖται Μαίανδρος, *the river is called Maeander.*

482. A finite verb agrees with its subject in number and person, except that a neuter plural subject regularly takes a singular verb: Κῦρος ἀναβαίνει, *Cyrus marches up;* τὰ ὑποζύγια ἦν ἐν τῷ πεδίῳ, *the beasts of burden were in the plain.*

THE ARTICLE

483. With proper names of persons already mentioned or well known the article may be used: Κῦρον μεταπέμπεται· ἀναβαίνει οὖν ὁ Κῦρος, *he sends for Cyrus; Cyrus therefore goes up.*

484. With names of countries the article is generally used: ἡ Ἑλλάς, *Greece.*

485. With abstract nouns the article is frequently used: ἡ ἀρετή, *virtue.*

486. The article is regularly used with demonstrative pronouns when they qualify a noun. The demonstrative is always in the predicate position. See 495: οὗτος ὁ ἄνθρωπος or ὁ ἄνθρωπος οὗτος, *this man.*

487. The article standing alone with μέν and δέ has the force of a demonstrative: οἱ μέν .... οἱ δέ, *some .... others*, ὁ δέ, *but he;* οἱ δέ, *but they.*

488. With possessive pronouns the article is used when reference is made to a single definite object: ὁ ἐμὸς ἀδελφός, *my brother;* but ἐμὸς ἀδελφός, *a brother of mine.*

489. The article very frequently has the force of an unemphatic possessive pronoun: Κῦρος ἀθροίζει τοὺς στρατιώτᾱς, *Cyrus assembles his soldiers.*

490. A participle with the article is equivalent to a noun or to a relative clause: οἱ φεύγοντες, *those who are fleeing*, i. e. *the fugitives;* ὁ βουλόμενος, *the one who wishes.*

491. Adjectives and adverbs or their equivalents with the article are used as nouns. The use of the article with an adjective or an adverb makes the phrase in effect a noun: οἱ ἀγαθοί, *the brave;* οἱ οἶκοι, *the homefolks;* οἱ ἐκ τῆς ἀγορᾶς, *the people from the market-place.*

492. The neuter article is frequently used with the infinitive, which is a verbal noun, showing more clearly the case-relation: εἰς τὸ διώκειν ὁρμήσαντες, *hastening to the pursuit.*

493. βασιλεύς without the article is generally used to designate the Persian king.

494. If an adjective stands between the article and its noun, it is said to be in the attributive position: ὁ ἀγαθὸς ἀνήρ, or less frequently ὁ ἀνὴρ ὁ ἀγαθός and ἀνὴρ ὁ ἀγαθός, *the good man.*

495. If an adjective either precedes or follows the noun with its article, it is in the predicate position: ὁ ἀνὴρ ἀγαθός, or ἀγαθὸς ὁ ἀνήρ, *the man is good.*

PRONOUNS

496. The personal pronoun is not used as the subject of a verb except for emphasis or clearness: ταῦτα λέγεις, *you say these things;* ταῦτα μὲν δὴ σὺ λέγεις, *that is what you say.*

497. Personal pronouns in the genitive case are frequently equivalent to possessive pronouns: ὁ ἀδελφὸς ἐμοῦ = ὁ ἐμὸς ἀδελφός, *my brother.*

498. The reflexive pronoun regularly refers to the subject of the clause in which it stands; it is called the direct reflexive: ὁπότε γυμνάσαι βούλοιτο ἑαυτόν, *whenever he wished to take exercise (exercise himself).*

499. The pronoun of the third person, which occurs in Attic Greek in the forms οἷ, σφεῖς, σφῶν, σφίσι, σφᾶς, when used in a subordinate clause, or with an infinitive or participle in the principal clause, refers to the main subject; it is called the indirect reflexive: Κῦρος δεῖται αὐτοῦ δοῦναι οἷ ταύτας τὰς πόλεις, *Cyrus asked him* (the king) *to give him* (Cyrus) *these cities.*

500. αὐτός is an intensive pronoun and has three uses.

501. When it stands between the article and the noun which it modifies (attributive position), it means *same:* ὁ αὐτὸς φίλος, or more rarely ὁ φίλος ὁ αὐτός, *the same friend.*

502. When it modifies a noun, but is not in the attributive position, it means *self* or *very*, like Latin *ipse:* αὐτὸς ὁ φίλος or ὁ φίλος αὐτός, *the friend himself, the very friend.*

When the noun to which it refers is not expressed, it is always intensive in the nominative (cf. *ipse*): αὐτὸς ἔχει, *he himself has.*

In the other cases also αὐτός may be intensive, if it is placed in an emphatic (i. e. an unusual) position: αὐτὸν μὲν λαμβάνει, οἱ δὲ ἄλλοι φεύγουσιν, *him he captures, but the rest escape.*

503. When used substantively without the article, it becomes in the oblique cases (i. e. other than the nominative and vocative) an unemphatic personal pronoun, *him, her, it, them, his, hers, theirs:* ὁ φίλος αὐτοῦ, *his friend;* πέμπει αὐτούς, *he sends them.* This is its most frequent use.

504. ὅδε, *this*, refers to what follows; οὗτος, *this*, refers to what precedes; ἐκεῖνος, *that*, differs from οὗτος in indicating something more remote in time or space: ἔλεξε τάδε, *he spoke as follows;* ἔλεξε ταῦτα, *thus he spoke.*

505. ἄλλος means *another*, one of many; ἕτερος, *another*, one of two, or *the other:* ἄλλο στράτευμα, *another army;* τὸ ἕτερον στράτευμα, *the other army.* But observe τὸ ἄλλο, *the rest of.*

506. The antecedent of a relative pronoun is frequently omitted when it can be easily supplied from the context: ἔχων οὓς εἴρηκα ὡρμᾶτο ἀπὸ Σάρδεων, *he set out from Sardis with those I have mentioned.*

507. If the antecedent is a genitive or dative, a relative which would naturally be in the accusative is usually attracted into the case of the antecedent: ἀποπέμπει τοὺς δασμοὺς ἐκ τῶν πόλεων ὧν ἔχει, *he sends tribute from the cities which he has.*

THE CASES

THE VOCATIVE

508. The vocative is the case of address; ὦ usually precedes: ὦ ἄνδρες στρωτιῶται, *fellow-soldiers.*

THE ACCUSATIVE

509. The object of a transitive verb is in the accusative: ὁρῶ τὸν ἄνθρωπον, *I see the man.*

510. Many verbs are followed by an accusative of kindred meaning. This is called the cognate accusative: νίκην νῑκᾶν, *to win a victory;* τί κελεύεις; *what order do you give?*

511. The accusative is sometimes used with the value of an adverb, and is called the adverbial accusative: ἔπεμψεν αὐτοὺς τὴν ταχίστην ὁδόν, *he sent them the shortest way,*

512. Certain verbs take two accusatives, one the cognate accusative, the other the accusative of the person or thing affected. These verbs are *to ask, clothe, demand, conceal, deprive, remind, teach,* and verbs meaning to do anything to a person: ἐποίησαν ἀνήκεστα κακὰ αὐτούς, *they inflicted irreparable injury upon them;* ἀφαιρεῖσθαι αὐτοὺς τὴν γῆν, *to deprive them of their land.*

513. The accusative is used to specify the part, character, or quality to which a verb, noun, or adjective refers—the accusative of specification: ποταμὸς Κύδνος ὄνομα, *a river, Cydnus by name;* δύο πλέθρα τὸ εὖρος, *two plethra wide.*

514. *Duration of time* and *extent of space* are expressed by the accusative: ἐνταῦθα ἔμενεν ἡμέρᾱς ἑπτά, *he remained there seven days.*

515. Both a predicate accusative and an object accusative, referring to the same person or thing, may follow a verb of *naming, choosing, appointing, making, thinking, regarding:* στρατηγὸν Κῦρον ἀπέδειξεν, *he appointed Cyrus general.*

THE GENITIVE

516. The genitive denotes: (*a*) possession—the possessive genitive: ἡ Κύρου ἀρχή, *the province of Cyrus.*

517. (*b*) The subject of an action or feeling denoted by a noun—the subjective genitive: ὁ τῶν βαρβάρων φόβος, *the fear of the barbarians* (i. e. the fear which they feel).

518. (*c*) The object of an action or feeling—the objective genitive: ὁ τῶν βαρβάρων φόβος, *the fear of the barbarians* (i. e. the fear which they inspire).

519. (*d*) Measure (time, space, price): τριῶν ἡμερῶν ὁδός, *a three days' journey.*

520. (*e*) The whole to which a part belongs—the partitive genitive: τῶν μυρίων ἐλπίδων μία, *one hope in ten thousand.*

521. The genitive may be used in the predicate, generally of the verbs meaning *to be* or *to become*, to express any of the above-mentioned relations (516–520): τὸ ἄρχειν ἐστὶ τῶν νικώντων, *it is the part of those who conquer to rule.*

522. The genitive is used after an adjective or an adverb in the comparative degree when ἤ, *than*, is omitted: οὗτοι οἱ βάρβαροι πολεμιώτεροι ἔσονται τῶν παρὰ βασιλεῖ, *these barbarians will be more hostile than those with the king.*

523. *Time within which* is expressed by the genitive: δέκα ἡμερῶν, *within ten days.*

524. The genitive denotes cause with verbs of emotion: τῆς ἐλευθερίας ὑμᾶς εὐδαιμονίζω, *I congratulate you on your freedom.*

525. Certain verbs take the genitive: (*a*) Verbs of *ruling* and *leading:* ἄρχει Μιλήτου, *he rules Miletus.*

526. (*b*) Verbs of *fulness* or *want:* οὐκ ἀπορῶ ἀνδρῶν, *I do not lack men.*

527. (*c*) Verbs of *tasting, caring for, sparing, neglecting, forgetting, remembering, despising:* ὀλίγοι σίτου ἐγεύσαντο, *few tasted food.*

528. (*d*) Verbs of *separation:* τοῦ πολέμου παύεσθαι, *to give up the war.*

529. (*e*) Verbs implying comparison, e. g. *surpass, be superior:* περιγίγνεται τῶν ἀντιστασιωτῶν, *he gets the better of his opponents.*

530. (*f*) Verbs of *beginning, touching, taking hold of, aiming at, hitting, missing:* οὐδεὶς ἡμάρτανεν ἀνδρός, *no one missed his man.*

531. Many adjectives, particularly those of like meaning, with the verbs just mentioned (525–30), are followed by the genitive; e. g.: πλήρης, *full of;* ἄξιος, *worthy of;* ἔμπειρος, *skilled in;* ἐγκρατής, *master of.*

THE DATIVE

532. The indirect object of a verb is put in the dative: δίδωσι αὐτῷ μυρίους δᾱρεικούς, *he gives him ten thousand darics.*

533. Some intransitive verbs take the dative which in English are followed by the objective; e. g. *assist, trust, obey, follow, resemble, make war upon, be angry at,* and the like: τῷ ἡγεμόνι ἕπεσθαι, *to follow the leader.*

534. The dative is used with εἰμί or γίγνομαι to denote the possessor: ἄλλη πρόφασις ἦν αὐτῷ, *he had another excuse.*

535. The dative is used to denote *instrument, cause, manner,* and *means:* ἀκοντίζει τις αὐτὸν παλτῷ, *someone struck him with a lance.*

536. The dative is used to denote that by which a person or thing is accompanied: ἐλαύνει ἱδροῦντι τῷ ἵππῳ, *he rides with his horse in a sweat.*

537. *Time when* is expressed by the dative: ταύτῃ τῇ ἡμέρᾳ, *on this day.*

538. The person or thing to whom an act is an advantage or disadvantage is put in the dative: ἄλλο στράτευμα αὐτῷ συνελέγετο, *another army was being collected for him.*

539. The dative regularly denotes the agent with the verbal in -τέος, and often with the perfect and pluperfect passive: ἡ διῶρυξ ἡμῖν διαβατέᾱ, *we must cross the ditch;* πάνθ' ἡμῖν πεποίηται, *everything has been done by us.*

540. A number of adverbs and adjectives of a meaning similar to that of the verbs (533) which govern the dative are construed with the dative; e. g.: παραπλήσιος, *like;* ὠφέλιμος, *useful;* πολέμιος, *hostile.*

THE TENSES

541. The primary tenses are the present, perfect, future, and future perfect. The secondary or historical tenses are the imperfect, aorist, and pluperfect.

542. The present is often used in vivid narrative for the lively representation of the past. This is called the historical present: διαβάλλει τὸν Κῦρον, *he traduces* (i. e. *traduced*) *Cyrus.*

543. The imperfect denotes an act in progress, a customary act, and an attempted act: στρεπτὸν ἐφόρει, *he was wearing a collar;* ταῦτα τοῖς φίλοις διεδίδου, *he used to distribute these among his friends;* Κλέαρχος τοὺς αὑτοῦ στρατιώτᾱς ἐβιάζετο ἰέναι, *Clearchus tried to force his own men to advance.*

544. The perfect denotes the completion of an act at the present time: πάντα πεποίηται, *everything has been done.*

545. The pluperfect denotes an act completed in the past: ἐτετίμητο ὑπὸ Κύρου, *he had been honored by Cyrus.*

546. The aorist denotes a past action simply as a thing attained, without reference to its duration or the time of its completion: βασιλεὺς ἐγένετο τριάκοντα ἔτη, *he was king thirty years.*

547. The aorist often expresses the beginning of an action or state: ἠσθένει, *he was ill;* ἠσθένησε, *he fell ill.*

548. The aorist is often represented in English by the pluperfect, especially in temporal and relative clauses: ὡς ἀπῆλθε, *when he had returned.*

549. ἄν with the imperfect or aorist indicative in a principal clause expresses iteration: ἐκλεγόμενος τὸν ἐπιτήδειον ἔπαισεν ἄν, *selecting the proper person, he used to beat him.*

550. In the subjunctive and imperative, and in the optative and infinitive not in indirect discourse the tenses have no time significance. The present denotes an act in progress; the perfect, which is not common, an act as completed; the aorist, an act as simply brought to pass.

PURPOSE AND OBJECT CLAUSES

551. Purpose clauses are introduced by ἵνα, ὡς, or ὅπως, and take the subjunctive after primary tenses, the optative after secondary tenses; or the subjunctive may be retained after secondary tenses for vividness. The negative is μή: Κῦρος τὰς ναῦς μετεπέμψατο ὅπως ὁπλίτᾱς ἀποβιβάσειεν, *Cyrus sent for the ships in order that he might land hoplites;* Ἀβροκόμᾱς τὰ πλοῖα κατέκαυσεν ἵνα μὴ διαβαίη ὁ Κῦρος, *Abrocomas burned the vessels in order that Cyrus might not cross.*

552. A relative clause with the future indicative expresses purpose. The negative is μή: ἥκομεν ἡγεμόνας ἔχοντες οἳ ὑμᾶς ἄξουσιν, *we have come with guides to conduct you.*

553. Verbs denoting *care*, *attention*, or *effort* take ὅπως with the future indicative after both primary and secondary tenses. The negative is μή: βουλεύεται ὅπως μήποτε ἔτι ἔσται ἐπὶ τῷ ἀδελφῷ, *he plans that he may never again be in his brother's power.*

554. Verbs of *fearing* take μή with the subjunctive after a primary tense and μή with the optative after a secondary tense; or the subjunctive may be retained for vividness after secondary tenses. The negative is οὐ: φοβοῦνται μὴ οἱ Ἕλληνες ἐπιθῶνται αὐτοῖς, *they fear the Greeks will attack them;* ἐφοβεῖτο μὴ οὐ δύναιτο φυγεῖν, *he was alarmed lest he should not be able to escape.*

RESULT CLAUSES

555. ὥστε with the infinitive, with or without a subject accusative, expresses a tendency to produce a result, which may or may not be realized. The negative is μή: ἔχω τριήρεις ὥστε ἑλεῖν τὸ πλοῖον αὐτῶν, *I have triremes so as to take their ship.*

556. ὥστε with the indicative expresses a result that actually did follow; it means *wherefore, consequently, so that.* The negative is οὐ: τοσοῦτον πλήθει περιῆν ὥστε Κῦρον ἐνίκησεν, *so superior was he in numbers that he conquered Cyrus.*

557. A relative characterizing clause sometimes expresses result. The negative is οὐ: τίς οὕτω μαίνεται ὅστις οὐ βούλεται σοὶ φίλος εἶναι, *who is so mad as not to wish to be friendly with you?*

558. πρίν is used after a negative idea in the sense of *until.* The aorist indicative denotes an act or situation that is past. The subjunctive with ἄν after primary tenses, and the optative after secondary tenses (chiefly in indirect discourse), refer to an act or situation that is anticipated (i. e. in the future): οὐ διέβησαν πρὶν οἱ ἄλλοι ἀπεκρίναντο, *they did not cross until the others answered;* οὐ μενοῦσι πρὶν ἂν ἔλθητε, *they will not remain until you come;* ὑπέσχετο μὴ πρόσθεν παύσεσθαι πρὶν αὐτοὺς καταγάγοι οἴκαδε, *he promised not to stop until he should restore them to their homes.*

559. πρίν with the infinitive means *before.* It is always preceded by an affirmative idea: διέβησαν πρὶν τοὺς ἄλλους ἀποκρίνασθαι, *they crossed before the others answered.*

CONDITIONAL SENTENCES

560. The simple supposition has εἰ with the indicative in the protasis and any form of the verb in the apodosis. This form simply states a present or past particular supposition and implies nothing as to fulfilment: εἰ Ἑλληνικός ἐστι, ἀγαθός ἐστι ἀνήρ, *if he is Greek, he is a good man.*

561. A supposition contrary to fact has εἰ with the past tense of the indicative in the protasis and a past tense of the indicative with ἄν in the apodosis. The imperfect usually shows a condition untrue at the present time; the aorist in past time. The imperfect sometimes refers to the past, denoting a continued or repeated act: εἰ Ἑλληνικὸς ἦν, ἀγαθὸς ἦν ἂν ἀνήρ, *if he were Greek, he would be a good man.*

562. The more vivid future condition has in the protasis ἐάν (εἰ ἄν), also written sometimes ἤν, ἄν, with the subjunctive, and the future indicative or some future expression in the apodosis. It implies considerable likelihood of fulfilment: ἐὰν κελεύσῃ αὐτοὺς πέμψω, *if he orders it, I shall send them,* or *if he shall order it, I shall send them.*

563. The less vivid future condition has εἰ with the optative in the protasis and the optative with ἄν in the apodosis: εἰ κελεύσειε, αὐτοὺς πέμψαιμι ἄν, *if he should order it, I would send them.*

564. A conditional sentence may state what is or will be true on a particular occasion (e g. the sentences above, 560–63); or what is always true if the protasis is fulfilled. The latter is called a general condition. The protasis of the present general condition always has the same form as the more vivid future, but the apodosis has the present indicative: ἐὰν κελεύσῃ, αὐτούς πέμπω, *if he orders it, I always send them.*

565. The protasis of a general condition in past time has the same form as the less vivid future (563), but the apodosis has the imperfect indicative: εἰ κελεύσειε, αὐτοὺς ἔπεμπον, *whenever he ordered it, I used to send them.*

CONDITIONAL SENTENCES IN TABULAR FORM

566.   I. Simple supposition (particular): εἰ+present or past indicative—any appropriate form.

II. Present general: ἐάν (ἤν, ἄν)+subjunctive—present indicative.

III. Past general: εἰ+optative—imperfect indicative.

IV. Untrue supposition: εἰ+past indicative—past indicative with ἄν.

V. Future more vivid: ἐάν (ἤν, ἄν)+subjunctive—future indicative or imperative.

VI. Future less vivid: εἰ+optative—optative with ἄν.

567. Clauses introduced by a relative (pronoun or adverb) with an indefinite antecedent have a conditional force. The relative clause becomes the protasis, and that on which the relative clause depends forms the apodosis. Relative conditional sentences assume all the forms of conditional sentences. Temporal clauses present frequent examples: ὅ τι ἂν πέμψῃ λήψονται, *whatever he sends they will take* (more vivid future); ὅ τι πέμψειε λάβοιεν ἄν, *whatever he should send, they would take* (less vivid future); ἐπεὶ ἄρξαιντο προιέναι, αὐτὸν ἔβαλλον, *whenever they began to go forward, they threw at him;* ἔμενον ἕως Κῦρος ἧκεν, *they remained until Cyrus came;* ἕως μένομεν, ἀσφαλεῖς ἐσμεν, *as long as we remain we are safe;* ἕως ἄν τις παρῇ, χρῶμαι, *while one is with me I make use of him.*

COMMANDS, EXHORTATIONS, WISHES

568. Commands are expressed by the imperative: ἀνατεινάτω τὴν χεῖρα, *let him hold up his hand.*

569. Prohibitions (negative commands) are expressed by μή (or its compounds); with the present imperative, if the reference is to a continued act; with the aorist subjunctive, if the reference is to a single definite act: μὴ ποιήσῃς τοῦτο, *do not do this;* μὴ ποίει τοῦτο, *do not keep on doing this.*

570. Exhortations are expressed by the first person plural of the subjunctive. The negative is μή: καλῶς ἀποθνῄσκωμεν, *let us die gloriously.*

571. Wishes that refer to the future—i. e. that are possible of fulfilment—are expressed by the optative with or without εἴθε or εἰ γάρ. The negative is μή: μηκέτι ζῴην, *may I live no longer;* εἴθε σὺ φίλος ἡμῖν γένοιο, *would that you may become friendly to us.*

572. Wishes that are conceived of as impossible of fulfilment in present or past time are expressed by the secondary tenses of the indicative with εἴθε or εἰ γάρ; with the imperfect indicative, if it refers to the present time; with the aorist indicative, if it refers to past time. The negative is μή: εἴθε σοι τότε συνεγενόμην, *would that I had met you then.*

INDIRECT DISCOURSE

573. A quoted sentence (indirect discourse) may be introduced by ὅτι (*that*) or (less often) ὡς (*how*). When a verb of saying is in a primary tense, an indicative does not change its mood or tense; after a secondary tense it may be changed to the optative (without change of tense), or, for vividness, may retain its original mood and tense. But the imperfect and pluperfect remain unchanged after a secondary tense: πέμπω, *I am sending;* λέγει ὅτι πέμπει, *he says that he is sending;* ἔλεξεν ὅτι $\left\{ \begin{array}{l} πέμπει \\ πέμποι \end{array} \right\}$ *he said that he was sending.*

574. Subordinate clauses in indirect discourse retain the original mood and tense, always after a primary tense and sometimes (for vividness) after a secondary tense. In subordinate clauses dependent upon a secondary tense, secondary tenses of the indicative remain unchanged, but all subjunctives and primary tenses of the indicative may be changed to the same tense of the optative: ἔλεξεν ὅτι λελοιπὼς εἴη Συέννεσις τὰ ἄκρα, ἔπει ᾔσθετο ταῦτα, *he said that Syennesis had left the heights because he learned these things*—direct form, λέλοιπε (primary tense, hence changed to optative), ᾔσθετο (secondary tense, hence unchanged).

575. With a number of verbs the accusative and the infinitive are used in indirect discourse instead of ὅτι or ὡς. The infinitive retains the tense which the finite verb had in the direct form; but the present represents both the present and the imperfect, the perfect both the perfect and pluperfect. Verbs of *thinking* (οἴομαι, νομίζω, ἡγοῦμαι, δοκῶ) regularly take the infinitive: νομίζει ὑμᾶς ἑαυτοῦ εἶναι, *he considers that you are in his power.*

576. There are three common verbs of *saying;* of these (1) φημί takes the infinitive in the main verb of the quotation; (2) εἶπον (second aorist) takes ὅτι or ὡς; (3) λέγω usually takes ὅτι or ὡς after an active form, and an infinitive after the passive.

577. When the subject of the infinitive is the same as the subject of the main verb, it is usually omitted, unless it is emphatic. If expressed, it is in the nominative: ἰᾶσθαι αὐτὸς τὸ τραῦμά φησι, *he says that he himself cured the wound.* (The present infinitive is here the equivalent of an original imperfect indicative.)

578. After certain verbs (e. g. ἀκούω, ὁράω, γιγνώσκω, ἀγγέλλω, οἶδα, αἰσθάνομαι) the accusative of the participle may be used in indirect discourse. The tense of the participle is the same as that of the verb in the original statement. When the participle refers to the subject of the main verb, it appears in the nominative instead of in the accusative: ᾔσθοντο Κῦρον στράτευμα Ἑλληνικὸν ἔχοντα, *they perceived that Cyrus had a Greek army;* ἴσθι ὢν ἀνόητος, *know that you are foolish.*

THE PARTICIPLE

579. The participle very often takes the place of a relative clause in English: ὁ στρατὸς ὁ ὢν ἐν τῇ πόλει, *the army which was in the city* (lit., *being in the city*).

580. When used alone with the article, a participle becomes a noun. It is then usually best translated by a relative clause: οἱ οἰκοῦντες, *those who dwell;* τὰ γιγνόμενα, *those things which are taking place* (lit., *the happenings*).

581. In many cases the idea expressed by the participle is really co-ordinate with that of the main verb, but precedes it in time. The participle in this case is usually aorist. It is generally best translated by a finite verb, co-ordinate with the main verb. This may be termed the preliminary participle: λαβὼν τὸ χρυσίον στράτευμα συνέλεξεν, *he took the money and collected an army.*

582. The participle does not denote absolute time. The present participle expresses the same time as the verb on which it depends; the aorist, time preceding or co-ordinate with the main verb; and the future, time after it.

583. The future participle shows purpose: ἦλθον κωλύσοντες, *they came to hinder.*

584. With ὡς an alleged purpose (intention) is expressed: ὡς κωλύσοντες, *thinking that they would hinder* (lit., *as if about to hinder*).

585. τυγχάνω, *happen;* λανθάνω, *escape the notice of;* φθάνω, *anticipate,* are usually followed by a predicate participle containing the main thought: ὢν ἐτύγχανεν may be translated, *happened to be,* or *was, as it happened:* ἔλαθε πέμπων, *he sent secretly* (lit., *he escaped notice sending*); ἔφθασεν αὐτὸν ἐρχόμενος, *he came before him* (lit., *he anticipated his coming*).

The participle is very often used in place of a subordinate clause. It may show:

586. (*a*) Time: ταῦτα εἰπὼν ἀνέστη, *when he said this, he arose.*

587. (*b*) Cause: ἀδελφὸς ὤν, *since he was his brother.*

588. (*c*) Manner or means: διέπραττεν πείθων, *he accomplished it by persuasion.*

589. (*d*) Condition: ἔχοντες τὰ ὅπλα μαχούμεθα, *if we have our arms, we shall fight.*

590. (*e*) Concession: βουλόμενος οὐκ ἦλθεν, *though wishing (to do so), he did not come.*

591. (*f*) Circumstances: ἦλθεν ἔχων μέγα στράτευμα, *he came with (having) a great army.*

592. The Genitive Absolute. A noun and a participle in the genitive case, and not immediately dependent on any word in the sentence, are said to be in the genitive absolute: ἀνέβη οὐδενὸς κωλύοντος, *he marched up without opposition.*

THE INFINITIVE

593. The infinitive is a verbal noun and corresponds closely to the infinitive in English. The infinitive has five tenses—present, future, aorist, perfect, future perfect.

594. The future and perfect infinitives may properly be said to denote differences in time, the future denoting time after that of the verb on which it depends, the perfect a time prior to it. But the present and aorist infinitives distinguish different kinds of action or condition, not differences in time; cf. 550, 575.

595. The present infinitive expresses an activity or state continued or repeated. The aorist expresses simply occurrence: ἱκανοὶ τὰς ἀκροπόλεις φυλάττειν, *men suitable to guard the acropolis* (to guard continuously); οὐ γὰρ ἦν πρὸς τοῦ Κύρου τρόπον ἔχοντα μὴ ἀποδιδόναι, *for it was not like Cyrus, if he had money, not to pay his debts* (to pay his debts always); ἐδεήθη Κύρου ἐπιδεῖξαι τὸ στράτευμα, *she begged Cyrus to review his army* (single exhibition); ἐλέγετο Κύρῳ δοῦναι χρήματα, *it was said that she gave Cyrus money* (a single gift; *kept giving* would be διδόναι).

596. The infinitive is used with many adjectives, especially those meaning *ability, fitness, willingness,* to complete their meaning: οἱ Ἕλληνες ἱκανοὶ ἦσαν τὴν πόλιν φυλάττειν, *the Greeks were capable of guarding the city.*

597. The infinitive is used to express purpose after verbs of *choosing* and *giving:* τὴν χώραν ἐπέτρεψε διαρπάσαι τοῖς Ἕλλησιν, *he handed over the country to the Greeks to be plundered.*

CLASSIFICATION OF CONSONANTS

598. The Greek consonants may be divided into two classes, simple and double:

1. Simple consonants:

> Labials, π, β, φ, μ
> Linguals, τ, δ, θ, σ, λ, ν, ρ
> Palatals, κ, γ, χ

3. Double consonants:

> ζ (δ and an *s*-sound), ξ (κσ, γσ, χσ), ψ (πσ, βσ, φσ).

599. The simple consonants may be divided into two classes, semi-vowels and mutes:

1. Semi-vowels:

> *a.* Sibilant, σ.
> *b.* Liquids, λ, μ, ν, ρ.
> *c.* Nasals, μ, ν, γ-nasal (Sec. 3).

2. Mutes:

	Smooth	Middle	Rough
Labial	π	β	φ
Palatal	κ	γ	χ
Lingual	τ	δ	θ

Those in each horizontal line are called cognates, because they are produced by the same organ of speech (lips, tongue, palate). Hence the names. Those in each column are said to be co-ordinate, because they have the same degree of aspiration (roughness).

APPENDIX II

Paradigms

NOUNS

600. o-DECLENSION

	υἱός, ὁ, *son*	βίος, ὁ, *life*	ἄνθρωπος, ὁ, *man*	δῶρον, τό, *gift*	πεδίον, τό, *plain*
			SINGULAR		
N.	υἱός	βίος	ἄνθρωπος	δῶρον	πεδίον
G.	υἱοῦ	βίου	ἀνθρώπου	δώρου	πεδίου
D.	υἱῷ	βίῳ	ἀνθρώπῳ	δώρῳ	πεδίῳ
A.	υἱόν	βίον	ἄνθρωπον	δῶρον	πεδίον
V.	υἱέ	βίε	ἄνθρωπε	δῶρον	πεδίον
			DUAL		
N.A.V.	υἱώ	βίω	ἀνθρώπω	δώρω	πεδίω
G.D.	υἱοῖν	βίοιν	ἀνθρώποιν	δώροιν	πεδίοιν
			PLURAL		
N.V.	υἱοί	βίοι	ἄνθρωποι	δῶρα	πεδία
G.	υἱῶν	βίων	ἀνθρώπων	δώρων	πεδίων
D.	υἱοῖς	βίοις	ἀνθρώποις	δώροις	πεδίοις
A.	υἱούς	βίους	ἀνθρώπους	δῶρα	πεδία

601. α-DECLENSION, FEMININE

	ἀρχή, ἡ, *province*	κώμη, ἡ, *village*	στρατιά, ἡ, *army*	γέφυρα, ἡ, *bridge*	θάλαττα, ἡ, *sea*
			SINGULAR		
N.V.	ἀρχή	κώμη	στρατιά	γέφῡρα	θάλαττα
G.	ἀρχῆς	κώμης	στρατιᾶς	γεφύρᾱς	θαλάττης
D.	ἀρχῇ	κώμῃ	στρατιᾷ	γεφύρᾳ	θαλάττῃ
A.	ἀρχήν	κώμην	στρατιάν	γέφῡραν	θάλατταν
			DUAL		
N.A.V.	ἀρχά	κώμᾱ	στρατιά	γεφύρᾱ	θαλάττᾱ
G.D.	ἀρχαῖν	κώμαιν	στρατιαῖν	γεφύραιν	θαλάτταιν

PLURAL

N. V.	ἀρχαί	κῶμαι	στρατιαί	γέφῡραι	θάλατται
G.	ἀρχῶν	κωμῶν	στρατιῶν	γεφῡρῶν	θαλαττῶν
D.	ἀρχαῖς	κώμαις	στρατίαῖς	γεφύραις	θαλάτταις
A.	ἀρχάς	κώμᾱς	στρατιάς	γεφύρᾱς	θαλάττᾱς

602. α-DECLENSION, MASCULINE

νεᾱνίᾱς, ὁ,	πελταστής, ὁ,	σατράπης, ὁ,	στρατιώτης, ὅ,
young man	*targeteer*	*satrap*	*soldier*

SINGULAR

N.	νεᾱνίᾱς	πελταστής	σατράπης	στρατιώτης
G.	νεᾱνίου	πελταστοῦ	σατράπου	στρατιώτου
D.	νεᾱνίᾳ	πελταστῇ	σατράπῃ	στρατιώτῃ
A.	νεᾱνίᾱν	πελταστήν	σατράπην	στρατιώτην
V.	νεᾱνίᾱ	πελταστά	σατράπη	στρατιῶτα

DUAL

N.A.V.	νεᾱνίᾱ	πελταστά	σατράπᾱ	στρατιώτᾱ
G.D.	νεᾱνίαιν	πελτασταῖν	σατράπαιν	στρατιώταιν

PLURAL

N. V.	νεᾱνίαι	πελτασταί	σατράπαι	στρατιῶται
G.	νεᾱνιῶν	πελταστῶν	σατραπῶν	στρατιωτῶν
D.	νεᾱνίαις	πελτασταῖς	σατράπαις	στρατιώταις
A.	νεᾱνίᾱς	πελταστάς	σατράπᾱς	στρατιώτᾱς

603. CONTRACT NOUNS IN ο AND α

νοῦς, ὁ,	ὀστοῦν, τό,	μνᾶ, ἡ,
mind	*bone*	*mina*

SINGULAR

N.	(νόος)	νοῦς	(ὀστέον)	ὀστοῦν	(μνάᾱ)	μνᾶ
G.	(νόου)	νοῦ	(ὀστέου)	ὀστοῦ	(μνάᾱς)	μνᾶς
D.	(νόῳ)	νῷ	(ὀστέῳ)	ὀστῷ	(μνάᾳ)	μνᾷ
A.	(νόον)	νοῦν	(ὀστέον)	ὀστοῦν	(μνάᾱν)	μνᾶν
V.	(νόε)	νοῦ	(ὀστέον)	ὀστοῦν	(μνάᾱ)	μνᾶ

DUAL

N.A.V.	(νόω)	νώ	(ὀστέω)	ὀστώ	(μνάᾱ)	μνᾶ
G.D.	(νόοιν)	νοῖν	(ὀστέοιν)	ὀστοῖν	(μνάαιν)	μναῖν

PLURAL

N. V.	(νόοι)	νοῖ	(ὀστέα)	ὀστᾶ	(μνάαι)	μναῖ
G.	(νόων)	νῶν	(ὀστέων)	ὀστῶν	(μναῶν)	μνῶν
D.	(νόοις)	νοῖς	(ὀστέοις)	ὀστοῖς	(μνάαις)	μναῖς
A.	(νόους)	νοῦς	(ὀστέα)	ὀστᾶ	(μνάᾱς)	μνᾶς

SINGULAR

N. V.	(γέᾱ)	γῆ
G.	(γέᾱς)	γῆς
D.	(γέᾳ)	γῇ
A.	(γέᾱν)	γῆν

604. CONSONANT DECLENSION

Lingual Stems

νύξ, ἡ,	ὄρνῑς, ὁ, ἡ,	ἀσπίς, ἡ,	γέρων, ὁ,	στράτευμα, τό,
night	*bird*	*shield*	*old man*	*army*

SINGULAR

N.	νύξ	ὄρνῑς	ἀσπίς	γέρων	στράτευμα
G.	νυκτός	ὄρνῑθος	ἀσπίδος	γέροντος	στρατεύματος
D.	νυκτί	ὄρνῑθι	ἀσπίδι	γέροντι	στρατεύματι
A.	νύκτα	ὄρνῑν *cf. §317*	ἀσπίδα	γέροντα	στράτευμα
V.	νύξ	ὄρνῑς	ἀσπί	γέρον	στράτευμα

DUAL

N.A.V.	νύκτε	ὄρνῑθε	ἀσπίδε	γέροντε	στρατεύματε
G.D.	νυκτοῖν	ὀρνίθοιν	ἀσπίδοιν	γερόντοιν	στρατευμάτοιν

PLURAL

N. V.	νύκτες	ὄρνῑθες	ἀσπίδες	γέροντες	στρατεύματα
G.	νυκτῶν	ὀρνίθων	ἀσπίδων	γερόντων	στρατευμάτων
D.	νυξί	ὄρνῑσι	ἀσπίσι	γέρουσι	στρατεύμασι
A.	νύκτας	ὄρνῑθας	ἀσπίδας	γέροντας	στρατεύματα

605. *Palatal and Labial Stems*

φύλαξ, ὁ,	διῶρυξ, ἡ,	κλώψ, ὁ,	φάλαγξ, ἡ,	Θρᾷξ, ὁ,
guard	*canal*	*thief*	*phalanx*	*Thracian*

N. V.	φύλαξ	διῶρυξ	κλώψ	φάλαγξ	Θρᾷξ
G.	φύλακος	διώρυχος	κλωπός	φάλαγγος	Θρᾳκός
D.	φύλακι	διώρυχι	κλωπί	φάλαγγι	Θρᾳκί
A.	φύλακα	διώρυχα	κλῶπα	φάλαγγα	Θρᾷκα

DUAL

N.A.V.	φύλακε	διώρυχε	κλῶπε	φάλαγγε	Θρᾷκε
G.D.	φυλάκοιν	διωρύχοιν	κλωποῖν	φαλάγγοιν	Θρᾳκοῖν

Monosyllables of the third declension accent the ultima in the genitive and dative of all numbers.

PLURAL

N. V.	φύλακες	διώρυχες	κλῶπες	φάλαγγες	Θρᾷκες
G.	φυλάκων	διωρύχων	κλωπῶν	φαλάγγων	Θρᾳκῶν
D.	φύλαξι	διώρυξι	κλωψί	φάλαγξι	Θρᾳξί
A.	φύλακας	διώρυχας	κλῶπας	φάλαγγας	Θρᾷκας

606. ✓   Liquid Stems

	ἡγεμών, ὁ,	ἀγών, ὁ,	ῥήτωρ, ὁ,	μήν, ὁ,	λιμήν, ὁ,
	leader	contest	orator	month	harbor

SINGULAR

N.	ἡγεμών	ἀγών	ῥήτωρ	μήν	λιμήν
G.	ἡγεμόνος	ἀγῶνος	ῥήτορος	μηνός	λιμένος
D.	ἡγεμόνι	ἀγῶνι	ῥήτορι	μηνί	λιμένι
A.	ἡγεμόνα	ἀγῶνα	ῥήτορα	μῆνα	λιμένα
V.	ἡγεμών	ἀγών	ῥῆτορ	μήν	λιμήν

DUAL

N.A.V.	ἡγεμόνε	ἀγῶνε	ῥήτορε	μῆνε	λιμένε
G. D.	ἡγεμόνοιν	ἀγώνοιν	ῥητόροιν	μηνοῖν	λιμένοιν

PLURAL

N. V.	ἡγεμόνες	ἀγῶνες	ῥήτορες	μῆνες	λιμένες
G.	ἡγεμόνων	ἀγώνων	ῥητόρων	μηνῶν	λιμένων
D.	ἡγεμόσι	ἀγῶσι	ῥήτορσι	μησί	λιμέσι
A.	ἡγεμόνας	ἀγῶνας	ῥήτορας	μῆνας	λιμένας

607. ✓   Syncopated Liquid Stems

	θυγάτηρ, ἡ,		πατήρ, ὁ,	μήτηρ, ἡ,	ἀνήρ, ὁ,
	daughter		father	mother	man

SINGULAR

N.		θυγάτηρ	πατήρ	μήτηρ	ἀνήρ
G.	(θυγατέρος)	θυγατρός	πατρός	μητρός	ἀνδρός
D.	(θυγατέρι)	θυγατρί	πατρί	μητρί	ἀνδρί
A.		θυγατέρα	πατέρα	μητέρα	ἄνδρα
V.		θύγατερ	πάτερ	μῆτερ	ἄνερ

DUAL

N.A.V.	θυγατέρε	πατέρε	μητέρε	ἄνδρε
G. D.	θυγατέροιν	πατέροιν	μητέροιν	ἀνδροῖν

PLURAL

N. V.	θυγατέρες	πατέρες	μητέρες	ἄνδρες
G.	θυγατέρων	πατέρων	μητέρων	ἀνδρῶν
D.	θυγατράσι	πατράσι	μητράσι	ἀνδράσι
A.	θυγατέρας	πατέρας	μητέρας	ἄνδρας

✓ disappears but p remains before σι

608.   *Stems in ι and υ*

	πόλις, ἡ, *city*	πῆχυς, ὁ, *cubit*	ἄστυ, τό, *town*	ἰχθύς, ὁ, *fish*	βασιλεύς, ὁ, *king*

SINGULAR

N.	πόλις	πῆχυς	ἄστυ	ἰχθύς	βασιλεύς
G.	πόλεως	πήχεως	ἄστεως	ἰχθύος	βασιλέως
D.	(πόλεϊ) πόλει	(πήχεϊ) πήχει	(ἄστεϊ) ἄστει	ἰχθύϊ	βασιλεῖ
A.	πόλιν	πῆχυν	ἄστυ	ἰχθύν	βασιλέᾱ
V.	πόλι	πῆχυ	ἄστυ	ἰχθύ	βασιλεῦ

DUAL

N.A.V.	(πόλεε) πόλει	(πήχεε) πήχει	(ἄστεε) ἄστει	ἰχθύε	βασιλέε
G.D.	πολέοιν	πηχέοιν	ἀστέοιν	ἰχθύοιν	βασιλέοιν

PLURAL

N.V.	(πόλεες) πόλεις	(πήχεες) πήχεις	(ἄστεα) ἄστη	ἰχθύες	(βασιλέες) βασιλεῖς
G.	πόλεων	πήχεων	ἄστεων	ἰχθύων	βασιλέων
D.	πόλεσι	πήχεσι	ἄστεσι	ἰχθύσι	βασιλεῦσι
A.	πόλεις	πήχεις	(ἄστεα) ἄστη	ἰχθῦς	βασιλέᾱς

609.   *Stems in σ*

	εὖρος, τό, *breadth*	Σωκράτης, ὁ, *Socrates*	κρέας, τό, *meat*

SINGULAR

N.	εὖρος		Σωκράτης		κρέας
G.	(εὔρεος) εὔρους	(Σωκράτεος)	Σωκράτους	(κρέαος)	κρέως
D.	(εὔρεϊ) εὔρει	(Σωκράτεϊ)	Σωκράτει	(κρέαϊ)	κρέαι
A.	εὖρος	(Σωκράτεα)	Σωκράτη		κρέας
V.	εὖρος		Σώκρατες		κρέας

DUAL

N.A.V.	(εὔρεε) εὔρει	
G.D.	(εὐρέοιν) εὐροῖν	

PLURAL

N.A.V.	(εὔρεα) εὔρη		(κρέαα)	κρέᾱ
G.	(εὐρέων) εὐρῶν		(κρεάων)	κρεῶν
D.	εὔρεσι			κρέασι

[handwritten marginalia: "1. masculine; 2. σύγλωττε; 3 active or deponent for an action"]

[handwritten marginalia left: "εὖρεος / εὖρεϊ"]

[handwritten note: "Actual stem is ΕΥΡΕΣ-. σ dropped between vowels."]

[handwritten marginalia lower left: "ρεφα / ρέϟων / ἱρεϟος"]

610.　Irregular Nouns

γυνή, ἡ,	δόρυ, τό,	ἕως, ἡ,	Ζεύς, ὁ,	βοῦς, ὁ, ἡ,	κύων, ὁ, ἡ,
woman	spear	dawn	Zeus	ox, cow	dog

SINGULAR

N.	γυνή	δόρυ	ἕως	Ζεύς	βοῦς	κύων
G.	γυναικός	δόρατος	ἕω	Διός	βοός	κυνός
D.	γυναικί	δόρατι	ἕῳ	Διί	βοΐ	κυνί
A.	γυναῖκα	δόρυ	ἕω	Δία	βοῦν	κύνα
V.	γύναι	δόρυ	ἕως	Ζεῦ	βοῦ	κύον

DUAL

N.A.V.	γυναῖκε	δόρατε	ἕω		βόε	κύνε
G.D.	γυναικοῖν	δοράτοιν	ἕῳν		βοοῖν	κυνοῖν

PLURAL

N.V.	γυναῖκες	δόρατα	ἕῳ		βόες	κύνες
G.	γυναικῶν	δοράτων	ἕων		βοῶν	κυνῶν
D.	γυναιξί	δόρασι	ἕῳς		βουσί	κυσί
A.	γυναῖκας	δόρατα	ἕως		βοῦς	κύνας

611.

ναῦς, ἡ	παῖς, ὁ, ἡ,	πῦρ, τό,	τριήρης, ἡ,	ὕδωρ, τό,	χείρ, ἡ,
ship	child	fire	trireme	water	hand

SINGULAR

N.	ναῦς	παῖς	πῦρ		τριήρης	ὕδωρ	χείρ
G.	νεώς	παιδός	πυρός	(τριήρε-ος) τριήρους	ὕδατος	χειρός
D.	νηί	παιδί	πυρί	(τριήρε-ϊ) τριήρει	ὕδατι	χειρί
A.	ναῦν	παῖδα	πῦρ	(τριήρε-α) τριήρη	ὕδωρ	χεῖρα
V.	ναῦ	παῖ	πῦρ	τριήρες	ὕδωρ	χείρ

DUAL

N.A.V.	νῆε	παῖδε	πῦρε	(τριήρε-ε) τριήρει	ὕδατε	χεῖρε
G.D.	νεοῖν	παίδοιν	πυροῖν	(τριηρέ-οιν) τριήροιν	ὑδάτοιν	χεροῖν

PLURAL

N.	νῆες	παῖδες	πυρά	(τριήρε-ες) τριήρεις	ὕδατα	χεῖρες
G.	νεῶν	παίδων	πυρῶν	(τριηρέ-ων) τριήρων	ὑδάτων	χειρῶν
D.	ναυσί	παισί	πυροῖς	τριήρεσι	ὕδασι	χερσί
A.	ναῦς	παῖδας	πυρά	τριήρεις	ὕδατα	χεῖρας

ADJECTIVES

612 ADJECTIVES OF α- AND ο-DECLENSION

μῑκρός, *small, little*   φίλος, *friendly*

<table>
<tr><td colspan="4">SINGULAR</td><td colspan="3">SINGULAR</td></tr>
<tr><td></td><td>M.</td><td>F.</td><td>N.</td><td>M.</td><td>F.</td><td>N.</td></tr>
<tr><td>N.</td><td>μῑκρός</td><td>μῑκρά</td><td>μῑκρόν</td><td>φίλος</td><td>φίλη</td><td>φίλον</td></tr>
<tr><td>G.</td><td>μῑκροῦ</td><td>μῑκρᾶς</td><td>μῑκροῦ</td><td>φίλου</td><td>φίλης</td><td>φίλου</td></tr>
<tr><td>D.</td><td>μῑκρῷ</td><td>μῑκρᾷ</td><td>μῑκρῷ</td><td>φίλῳ</td><td>φίλῃ</td><td>φίλῳ</td></tr>
<tr><td>A.</td><td>μῑκρόν</td><td>μῑκράν</td><td>μῑκρόν</td><td>φίλον</td><td>φίλην</td><td>φίλον</td></tr>
<tr><td>V.</td><td>μῑκρέ</td><td>μῑκρά</td><td>μῑκρόν</td><td>φίλε</td><td>φίλη</td><td>φίλον</td></tr>
<tr><td colspan="4">DUAL</td><td colspan="3">DUAL</td></tr>
<tr><td>N.A.V.</td><td>μῑκρώ</td><td>μῑκρά</td><td>μῑκρώ</td><td>φίλω</td><td>φίλᾱ</td><td>φίλω</td></tr>
<tr><td>G.D.</td><td>μῑκροῖν</td><td>μῑκραῖν</td><td>μῑκροῖν</td><td>φίλοιν</td><td>φίλαιν</td><td>φίλοιν</td></tr>
<tr><td colspan="4">PLURAL</td><td colspan="3">PLURAL</td></tr>
<tr><td>N.V.</td><td>μῑκροί</td><td>μῑκραί</td><td>μῑκρά</td><td>φίλοι</td><td>φίλαι</td><td>φίλα</td></tr>
<tr><td>G.</td><td>μῑκρῶν</td><td>μῑκρῶν</td><td>μῑκρῶν</td><td>φίλων</td><td>φίλων</td><td>φίλων</td></tr>
<tr><td>D.</td><td>μῑκροῖς</td><td>μῑκραῖς</td><td>μῑκροῖς</td><td>φίλοις</td><td>φίλαις</td><td>φίλοις</td></tr>
<tr><td>A.</td><td>μῑκρούς</td><td>μῑκράς</td><td>μῑκρά</td><td>φίλους</td><td>φίλᾱς</td><td>φίλα</td></tr>
</table>

613. CONTRACT ADJECTIVES OF α- AND ο-DECLENSION

χρυσοῦς, *golden*

<table>
<tr><td colspan="6">SINGULAR</td></tr>
<tr><td>N.</td><td>(χρύσεος) χρῡσοῦς</td><td>(χρῡσέᾱ) χρῡσῆ</td><td>(χρύσεον) χρῡσοῦν</td></tr>
<tr><td>G.</td><td>(χρῡσέου) χρῡσοῦ</td><td>(χρῡσέᾱς) χρῡσῆς</td><td>(χρῡσέου) χρῡσοῦ</td></tr>
<tr><td>D.</td><td>(χρῡσέῳ) χρῡσῷ</td><td>(χρῡσέᾳ) χρῡσῇ</td><td>(χρῡσέῳ) χρῡσῷ</td></tr>
<tr><td>A.</td><td>(χρύσεον) χρῡσοῦν</td><td>(χρῡσέᾱν) χρῡσῆν</td><td>(χρύσεον) χρῡσοῦν</td></tr>
<tr><td colspan="6">DUAL</td></tr>
<tr><td>N.A.V.</td><td>(χρῡσέω) χρῡσώ</td><td>(χρῡσέᾱ) χρῡσᾶ</td><td>(χρῡσέω) χρῡσώ</td></tr>
<tr><td>G.D.</td><td>(χρῡσέοιν) χρῡσοῖν</td><td>(χρῡσέαιν) χρῡσαῖν</td><td>(χρῡσέοιν) χρῡσοῖν</td></tr>
<tr><td colspan="6">PLURAL</td></tr>
<tr><td>N.</td><td>(χρύσεοι) χρῡσοῖ</td><td>(χρύσεαι) χρῡσαῖ</td><td>(χρύσεα) χρῡσᾶ</td></tr>
<tr><td>G.</td><td>(χρῡσέων) χρῡσῶν</td><td>(χρῡσέων) χρῡσῶν</td><td>(χρῡσέων) χρῡσῶν</td></tr>
<tr><td>D.</td><td>(χρῡσέοις) χρῡσοῖς</td><td>(χρῡσέαις) χρῡσαῖς</td><td>(χρῡσέοις) χρῡσοῖς</td></tr>
<tr><td>A.</td><td>(χρῡσέους) χρῡσοῦς</td><td>(χρῡσέᾱς) χρῡσᾶς</td><td>(χρύσεα) χρῡσᾶ</td></tr>
</table>

In the same way decline

(ἁπλόος) ἁπλοῦς   (ἁπλέᾱ) ἁπλῆ   (ἁπλόον) ἁπλοῦν   *simple.*

Observe that

(ἀργύρεος) ἀργυροῦς   (ἀργυρέᾱ) ἀργυρᾶ   (ἀργύρεον) ἀργυροῦν   *silver*

has α throughout the feminine (έᾱ) ᾶ, (έᾱς) ᾶς, (έᾳ) ᾷ, (έᾱν) ᾶν.

614.   CONSONANT AND α-DECLENSIONS

χαρίεις, *pleasing*   ἑκών, *willing*

SINGULAR

	M.	F.	N.	M.	F.	N.
N.	χαρίεις	χαρίεσσα	χαρίεν	ἑκών	ἑκοῦσα	ἑκόν
G.	χαρίεντος	χαριέσσης	χαρίεντος	ἑκόντος	ἑκούσης	ἑκόντος
D.	χαρίεντι	χαριέσσῃ	χαρίεντι	ἑκόντι	ἑκούσῃ	ἑκόντι
A.	χαρίεντα	χαρίεσσαν	χαρίεν	ἑκόντα	ἑκοῦσαν	ἑκόν
V.	χαρίεν	χαρίεσσα	χαρίεν	ἑκών	ἑκοῦσα	ἑκόν

DUAL

	M.	F.	N.	M.	F.	N.
N. A. V.	χαρίεντε	χαριέσσᾱ	χαρίεντε	ἑκόντε	ἑκούσᾱ	ἑκόντε
G. D.	χαριέντοιν	χαριέσσαιν	χαριέντοιν	ἑκόντοιν	ἑκούσαιν	ἑκόντοιν

PLURAL

	M.	F.	N.	M.	F.	N.
N. V.	χαρίεντες	χαρίεσσαι	χαρίεντα	ἑκόντες	ἑκοῦσαι	ἑκόντα
G.	χαριέντων	χαριεσσῶν	χαριέντων	ἑκόντων	ἑκουσῶν	ἑκόντων
D.	χαρίεσι	χαριέσσαις	χαρίεσι	ἑκοῦσι	ἑκούσαις	ἑκοῦσι
A.	χαρίεντας	χαριέσσᾱς	χαρίεντα	ἑκόντας	ἑκούσᾱς	ἑκόντα

πᾶς, *all.*

SINGULAR   PLURAL

	M.	F.	N.	M.	F.	N.
N.	πᾶς	πᾶσα	πᾶν	πάντες	πᾶσαι	πάντα
G.	παντός	πάσης	παντός	πάντων	πᾱσῶν	πάντων
D.	παντί	πάσῃ	παντί	πᾶσι	πάσαις	πᾶσι
A.	πάντα	πᾶσαν	πᾶν	πάντας	πάσᾱς	πάντα

ταχύς, *swift*   μέλᾱς, *black*

SINGULAR

	M.	F.	N.	M.	F.	N.
N.	ταχύς	ταχεῖα	ταχύ	μέλᾱς	μέλαινα	μέλαν
G.	ταχέος	ταχείᾱς	ταχέος	μέλανος	μελαίνης	μέλανος
D.	ταχεῖ	ταχείᾳ	ταχεῖ	μέλανι	μελαίνῃ	μέλανι
A.	ταχύν	ταχεῖαν	ταχύ	μέλανα	μέλαιναν	μέλαν
V.	ταχύ	ταχεῖα	ταχύ	μέλαν	μέλαινα	μέλαν

DUAL

	M.	F.	N.	M.	F.	N.
N. A. V.	ταχέε	ταχείᾱ	ταχέε	μέλανε	μελαίνᾱ	μέλανε
G. D.	ταχέοιν	ταχείαιν	ταχέοιν	μελάνοιν	μελαίναιν	μελάνοιν

PLURAL

	M.	F.	N.	M.	F.	N.
N. V.	ταχεῖς	ταχεῖαι	ταχέα	μέλανες	μέλαιναι	μέλανα
G.	ταχέων	ταχειῶν	ταχέων	μελάνων	μελαινῶν	μελάνων
D.	ταχέσι	ταχείαις	ταχέσι	μέλασι	μελαίναις	μέλασι
A.	ταχεῖς	ταχείᾱς	ταχέα	μέλανας	μελαίνᾱς	μέλανα

615.   CONSONANT DECLENSION

εὐδαίμων, *prosperous*   ἡδίων, comparative of ἡδύς, *sweet*

SINGULAR

	M. AND F.	N.	M. AND F.	N.
N.	εὐδαίμων	εὔδαιμον	ἡδίων	ἥδιον
G.	εὐδαίμονος	εὐδαίμονος	ἡδίονος	ἡδίονος
D.	εὐδαίμονι	εὐδαίμονι	ἡδίονι	ἡδίονι
A.	εὐδαίμονα	εὔδαιμον	ἡδίονα, ἡδίω	ἥδιον
V.	εὔδαιμον	εὔδαιμον	ἥδιον	ἥδιον

recessive accent

DUAL

N. A. V.	εὐδαίμονε	εὐδαίμονε	ἡδίονε	ἡδίονε
G. D.	εὐδαιμόνοιν	εὐδαιμόνοιν	ἡδιόνοιν	ἡδιόνοιν

PLURAL

N. V.	εὐδαίμονες	εὐδαίμονα	ἡδίονες, ἡδίους	ἡδίονα, ἡδίω
G.	εὐδαιμόνων	εὐδαιμόνων	ἡδιόνων	ἡδιόνων
D.	εὐδαίμοσι	εὐδαίμοσι	ἡδίοσι	ἡδίοσι
A.	εὐδαίμονας	εὐδαίμονα	ἡδίονας, ἡδίους	ἡδίονα, ἡδίω

ἀληθής, *true*

SINGULAR

	M. AND F.		N.
N.		ἀληθής	ἀληθές
G.	(ἀληθέος)	ἀληθοῦς	(ἀληθέος) ἀληθοῦς
D.	(ἀληθέϊ)	ἀληθεῖ	(ἀληθέϊ) ἀληθεῖ
A.	(ἀληθέα)	ἀληθῆ	ἀληθές
V.		ἀληθές	ἀληθές

DUAL

N. A. V.	(ἀληθέε)	ἀληθεῖ	(ἀληθέε)	ἀληθεῖ
G. D.	(ἀληθέοιν)	ἀληθοῖν	(ἀληθέοιν)	ἀληθοῖν

PLURAL

N. V.	(ἀληθέες)	ἀληθεῖς	(ἀληθέα)	ἀληθῆ
G.	(ἀληθέων)	ἀληθῶν	(ἀληθέων)	ἀληθῶν
D.		ἀληθέσι		ἀληθέσι
A.		ἀληθεῖς	(ἀληθέα)	ἀληθῆ

616.   IRREGULAR ADJECTIVES

√ μέγας, *large,* great   √ πολύς, *much, many*

SINGULAR

	M.	F.	N.	M.	F.	N.
N.	μέγας	μεγάλη	μέγα	πολύς	πολλή	πολύ
G.	μεγάλου	μεγάλης	μεγάλου	πολλοῦ	πολλῆς	πολλοῦ
D.	μεγάλῳ	μεγάλῃ	μεγάλῳ	πολλῷ	πολλῇ	πολλῷ
A.	μέγαν	μεγάλην	μέγα	πολύν	πολλήν	πολύ
V.	μεγάλε	μεγάλη	μέγα	πολύ	πολλή	πολύ

DUAL

N. A. V.	μεγάλω	μεγάλᾱ	μεγάλω
G. D.	μεγάλοιν	μεγάλαιν	μεγάλοιν

PLURAL

N. V.	μεγάλοι	μεγάλαι	μεγάλα	πολλοί	πολλαί	πολλά
G.	μεγάλων	μεγάλων	μεγάλων	πολλῶν	πολλῶν	πολλῶν
D.	μεγάλοις	μεγάλαις	μεγάλοις	πολλοῖς	πολλαῖς	πολλοῖς
A.	μεγάλους	μεγάλᾱς	μεγάλα	πολλούς	πολλάς	πολλά

PARTICIPLES

617. PRES. PART. OF εἰμί.   SECOND AOR. PART. ACT. OF λείπω √

SINGULAR

	M.	F.	N.	M.	F.	N.
N.	ὤν	οὖσα	ὄν	λιπών	λιποῦσα	λιπόν
G.	ὄντος	οὔσης	ὄντος	λιπόντος	λιπούσης	λιπόντος
D.	ὄντι	οὔσῃ	ὄντι	λιπόντι	λιπούσῃ	λιπόντι
A.	ὄντα	οὖσαν	ὄν	λιπόντα	λιποῦσαν	λιπόν
V.	ὤν	οὖσα	ὄν	λιπών	λιποῦσα	λιπόν

DUAL

N. A. V.	ὄντε	οὔσᾱ	ὄντε	λιπόντε	λιπούσᾱ	λιπόντε
G. D.	ὄντοιν	οὔσαιν	ὄντοιν	λιπόντοιν	λιπούσαιν	λιπόντοιν

PLURAL

N. V.	ὄντες	οὖσαι	ὄντα	λιπόντες	λιποῦσαι	λιπόντα
G.	ὄντων	οὐσῶν	ὄντων	λιπόντων	λιπουσῶν	λιπόντων
D.	οὖσι	οὔσαις	οὖσι	λιποῦσι	λιπούσαις	λιποῦσι
A.	ὄντας	οὔσᾱς	ὄντα	λιπόντας	λιπούσᾱς	λιπόντα

618. Pres. Part. Act. of λύω and δίδωμι

SINGULAR

	M.	F.	N.	M.	F.	N.
N. V.	λύων	λύουσα	λῦον	διδούς	διδοῦσα	διδόν
G.	λύοντος	λυούσης	λύοντος	διδόντος	διδούσης	διδόντος
D.	λύοντι	λυούσῃ	λύοντι	διδόντι	διδούσῃ	διδόντι
A.	λύοντα	λύουσαν	λῦον	διδόντα	διδοῦσαν	διδόν

DUAL

	M.	F.	N.	M.	F.	N.
N. A. V.	λύοντε	λυούσᾱ	λύοντε	διδόντε	διδούσᾱ	διδόντε
G. D.	λυόντοιν	λυούσαιν	λυόντοιν	διδόντοιν	διδούσαιν	διδόντοιν

PLURAL

	M.	F.	N.	M.	F.	N.
N. V.	λύοντες	λύουσαι	λύοντα	διδόντες	διδοῦσαι	διδόντα
G.	λυόντων	λυουσῶν	λυόντων	διδόντων	διδουσῶν	διδόντων
D.	λύουσι	λυούσαις	λύουσι	διδοῦσι	διδούσαις	διδοῦσι
A.	λύοντας	λυούσᾱς	λύοντα	διδόντας	διδούσᾱς	διδόντα

619. Aor. Part. Pass. of λύω. Pres. Part. Act. of δείκνῡμι

SINGULAR

	M.	F.	N.	M.	F.	N.
N. V.	λυθείς	λυθεῖσα	λυθέν	δεικνύς	δεικνῦσα	δεικνύν
G.	λυθέντος	λυθείσης	λυθέντος	δεικνύντος	δεικνύσης	δεικνύντος
D.	λυθέντι	λυθείσῃ	λυθέντι	δεικνύντι	δεικνύσῃ	δεικνύντι
A.	λυθέντα	λυθεῖσαν	λυθέν	δεικνύντα	δεικνῦσαν	δεικνύν

DUAL

	M.	F.	N.	M.	F.	N.
N. A. V.	λυθέντε	λυθείσᾱ	λυθέντε	δεικνύντε	δεικνύσᾱ	δεικνύντε
G. D.	λυθέντοιν	λυθείσαιν	λυθέντοιν	δεικνύντοιν	δεικνύσαιν	δεικνύντοιν

PLURAL

	M.	F.	N.	M.	F.	N.
N. V.	λυθέντες	λυθεῖσαι	λυθέντα	δεικνύντες	δεικνῦσαι	δεικνύντα
G.	λυθέντων	λυθεισῶν	λυθέντων	δεικνύντων	δεικνῡσῶν	δεικνύντων
D.	λυθεῖσι	λυθείσαις	λυθεῖσι	δεικνῦσι	δεικνύσαις	δεικνῦσι
A.	λυθέντας	λυθείσᾱς	λυθέντα	δεικνύντας	δεικνύσᾱς	δεικνύντα

620. Pres. Part. Act. of ἵστημι. Aor. Part. Act. of λύω

SINGULAR

	M.	F.	N.	M.	F.	N.
N. V.	ἱστάς	ἱστᾶσα	ἱστάν	λύσᾱς	λύσᾱσα	λῦσαν
G.	ἱστάντος	ἱστάσης	ἱστάντος	λύσαντος	λῡσάσης	λύσαντος
D.	ἱστάντι	ἱστάσῃ	ἱστάντι	λύσαντι	λῡσάσῃ	λύσαντι
A.	ἱστάντα	ἱστᾶσαν	ἱστάν	λύσαντα	λύσᾱσαν	λῦσαν

DUAL

	M.	F.	N.	M.	F.	N.
N. A. V.	ἱστάντε	ἱστάσᾱ	ἱστάντε	λύσαντε	λῡσάσᾱ	λύσαντε
G. D.	ἱστάντοιν	ἱστάσαιν	ἱστάντοιν	λῡσάντοιν	λῡσάσαιν	λῡσάντοιν

PLURAL

	M.	F.	N.	M.	F.	N.
N. V.	ἱστάντες	ἱστᾶσαι	ἱστάντα	λύσαντες	λύσᾱσαι	λύσαντα
G.	ἱστάντων	ἱστᾱσῶν	ἱστάντων	λῡσάντων	λῡσᾱσῶν	λῡσάντων
D.	ἱστᾶσι	ἱστάσαις	ἱστᾶσι	λύσᾱσι	λῡσάσαις	λύσᾱσι
A.	ἱστάντας	ἱστάσᾱς	ἱστάντα	λύσαντας	λῡσάσᾱς	λύσαντα

621. Second. Perf. Part. of ἵστημι. Perf. Part. Act. of λύω

SINGULAR

	M.	F.	N.	M.	F.	N.
N. V.	ἑστώς	ἑστῶσα	ἑστός	λελυκώς	λελυκυῖα	λελυκός
G.	ἑστῶτος	ἑστώσης	ἑστῶτος	λελυκότος	λελυκυίας	λελυκότος
D.	ἑστῶτι	ἑστώσῃ	ἑστῶτι	λελυκότι	λελυκυίᾳ	λελυκότι
A.	ἑστῶτα	ἑστῶσαν	ἑστός	λελυκότα	λελυκυῖαν	λελυκός

DUAL

	M.	F.	N.	M.	F.	N.
N. A. V.	ἑστῶτε	ἑστώσᾱ	ἑστῶτε	λελυκότε	λελυκυίᾱ	λελυκότε
G. D.	ἑστώτοιν	ἑστώσαιν	ἑστώτοιν	λελυκότοιν	λελυκυίαιν	λελυκότοιν

PLURAL

	M.	F.	N.	M.	F.	N.
N. V.	ἑστῶτες	ἑστῶσαι	ἑστῶτα	λελυκότες	λελυκυῖαι	λελυκότα
G.	ἑστώτων	ἑστωσῶν	ἑστώτων	λελυκότων	λελυκυιῶν	λελυκότων
D.	ἑστῶσι	ἑστώσαις	ἑστῶσι	λελυκόσι	λελυκυίαις	λελυκόσι
A.	ἑστῶτας	ἑστώσᾱς	ἑστῶτα	λελυκότας	λελυκυίᾱς	λελυκότα

622.　　　　　　Pres. Part. Mid. (Pass.) of λύω

SINGULAR

	M.	F.	N.
N.	λῡόμενος	λῡομένη	λῡόμενον
G.	λῡομένου	λῡομένης	λῡομένου
D.	λῡομένῳ	λῡομένῃ	λῡομένῳ
A.	λῡόμενον	λῡομένην	λῡόμενον
V.	λῡόμενε	λῡομένη	λῡόμενον

DUAL

	M.	F.	N.
N. A. V.	λῡομένω	λῡομένᾱ	λῡομένω
G. D.	λῡομένοιν	λῡομέναιν	λῡομένοιν

PLURAL

	M.	F.	N.
N. V.	λῡόμενοι	λῡόμεναι	λῡόμενα
G.	λῡομένων	λῡομένων	λῡομένων
D.	λῡομένοις	λῡομέναις	λῡομένοις
A.	λῡομένους	λῡομένᾱς	λῡόμενα

623. PERF. PART. MID. (PASS.) OF λύω

SINGULAR

	M.	F.	N.
N.	λελυμένος	λελυμένη	λελυμένον
G.	λελυμένου	λελυμένης	λελυμένου
D.	λελυμένῳ	λελυμένῃ	λελυμένῳ
A.	λελυμένον	λελυμένην	λελυμένον
V.	λελυμένε	λελυμένη	λελυμένον

DUAL

	M.	F.	N.
N. A. V.	λελυμένω	λελυμένᾱ	λελυμένω
G. D.	λελυμένοιν	λελυμέναιν	λελυμένοιν

PLURAL

	M.	F.	N.
N. V.	λελυμένοι	λελυμέναι	λελυμένα
G.	λελυμένων	λελυμένων	λελυμένων
D.	λελυμένοις	λελυμέναις	λελυμένοις
A.	λελυμένους	λελυμένᾱς	λελυμένα

624. PRES. PART. ACT. OF τῑμάω AND ποιέω

SINGULAR

	M.	F.	N.	M.	F.	N.
N. V.	τῑμῶν	τῑμῶσα	τῑμῶν	ποιῶν	ποιοῦσα	ποιοῦν
G.	τῑμῶντος	τῑμώσης	τῑμῶντος	ποιοῦντος	ποιούσης	ποιοῦντος
D.	τῑμῶντι	τῑμώσῃ	τῑμῶντι	ποιοῦντι	ποιούσῃ	ποιοῦντι
A.	τῑμῶντα	τῑμῶσαν	τῑμῶν	ποιοῦντα	ποιοῦσαν	ποιοῦν

DUAL

	M.	F.	N.	M.	F.	N.
N. A. V.	τῑμῶντε	τῑμώσᾱ	τῑμῶντε	ποιοῦντε	ποιούσᾱ	ποιοῦντε
G. D.	τῑμῶντοιν	τῑμώσαιν	τῑμῶντοιν	ποιούντοιν	ποιούσαιν	ποιούντοιν

PLURAL

	M.	F.	N.	M.	F.	N.
N. V.	τῑμῶντες	τῑμῶσαι	τῑμῶντα	ποιοῦντες	ποιοῦσαι	ποιοῦντα
G.	τῑμώντων	τῑμωσῶν	τῑμώντων	ποιούντων	ποιουσῶν	ποιούντων
D.	τῑμῶσι	τῑμώσαις	τῑμῶσι	ποιοῦσι	ποιούσαις	ποιοῦσι
A.	τῑμῶντας	τῑμώσᾱς	τῑμῶντα	ποιοῦντας	ποιούσᾱς	ποιοῦντα

The present participles of verbs in όω (contracted ῶ) are declined like ποιῶν, the contracted form of ποιέω. Thus δηλῶν, δηλοῦσα, δηλοῦν.

625.   NUMERALS

	Sign	Cardinal	Ordinal	Adverb
1	α′	εἷς, μία, ἕν, *one*	πρῶτος, *first*	ἅπαξ, *once*
2	β′	δύο, *two*	δεύτερος, *second*	δίς, *twice*
3	γ′	τρεῖς, τρία	τρίτος	τρίς
4	δ′	τέτταρες, τέτταρα	τέταρτος	τετράκις
5	ε′	πέντε	πέμπτος	πεντάκις
6	ϛ′	ἕξ	ἕκτος	ἑξάκις
7	ζ′	ἑπτά	ἕβδομος	ἑπτάκις
8	η′	ὀκτώ	ὄγδοος	ὀκτάκις
9	θ′	ἐννέα	ἔνατος	ἐνάκις
10	ι′	δέκα	δέκατος	δεκάκις
11	ια′	ἕνδεκα	ἑνδέκατος	ἑνδεκάκις
12	ιβ′	δώδεκα	δωδέκατος	δωδεκάκις
13	ιγ′	τρισκαίδεκα	τρισκαιδέκατος	
14	ιδ′	τετταρεσκαίδεκα	τετταρακαιδέκατος	
15	ιε′	πεντεκαίδεκα	πεντεκαιδέκατος	
16	ιϛ′	ἑκκαίδεκα	ἑκκαιδέκατος	
17	ιζ′	ἑπτακαίδεκα	ἑπτακαιδέκατος	
18	ιη′	ὀκτωκαίδεκα	ὀκτωκαιδέκατος	
19	ιθ′	ἐννεακαίδεκα	ἐννεακαιδέκατος	
20	κ′	εἴκοσι	εἰκοστός	εἰκοσάκις
21	κα′	εἷς καὶ εἴκοσι or εἴκοσιν εἷς	πρῶτος καὶ εἰκοστός	
30	λ′	τριάκοντα	τριᾱκοστός	τριᾱκοντάκις
40	μ′	τετταράκοντα	τετταρακοστός	τετταρακοντάκις
50	ν′	πεντήκοντα	πεντηκοστός	πεντηκοντάκις
60	ξ′	ἑξήκοντα	ἑξηκοστός	ἑξηκοντάκις
70	ο′	ἑβδομήκοντα	ἑβδομηκοστός	ἑβδομηκοντάκις
80	π′	ὀγδοήκοντα	ὀγδοηκοστός	ὀγδοηκοντάκις
90	ϙ′	ἐνενήκοντα	ἐνενηκοστός	ἐνενηκοντάκις
100	ρ′	ἑκατόν	ἑκατοστός	ἑκατοντάκις
200	σ′	διᾱκόσιοι, αι, α	διᾱκοσιοστός	διακοσιάκις
300	τ′	τριᾱκόσιοι, αι, α	τριᾱκοσιοστός	
400	υ′	τετρακόσιοι, αι, α	τετρακοσιοστός	
500	φ′	πεντακόσιοι, αι, α	πεντακοσιοστός	
600	χ′	ἑξακόσιοι, αι, α	ἑξακοσιοστός	
700	ψ′	ἑπτακόσιοι, αι, α	ἑπτακοσιοστός	
800	ω′	ὀκτακόσιοι, αι, α	ὀκτακοσιοστός	
900	ϡ′	ἐνακόσιοι, αι, α	ἐνακοσιοστός	
1000	͵α	χίλιοι, αι, α	χῑλιοστός	χῑλιάκις
2000	͵β	δισχίλιοι, αι, α	δισχῑλιοστός	
3000	͵γ	τρισχίλιοι, αι, α	τρισχῑλιοστός	
10000	͵ι	μύριοι, αι, α	μῡριοστός	μῡριάκις

626.   DECLENSION OF εἷς, δύο, τρεῖς, τέτταρες

	M.	F.	N.
N.	εἷς	μία	ἕν
G.	ἑνός	μιᾶς	ἑνός
D.	ἑνί	μιᾷ	ἑνί
A.	ἕνα	μίαν	ἕν

N. A.	δύο
G. D.	δυοῖν

	M. AND F.	N.
N.	τρεῖς	τρία
G.	τριῶν	
D.	τρισί	
A.	τρεῖς	τρία

	M. AND F.	N.
	τέτταρες	τέτταρα
	τεττάρων	
	τέτταρσι	
	τέτταρας	τέτταρα

627.   οὐδείς (μηδείς), *no one*

	SINGULAR			PLURAL		
	M.	F.	N.	M.	F.	N.
N.	οὐδείς	οὐδεμία	οὐδέν	οὐδένες	οὐδεμίαι	οὐδένα
G.	οὐδενός	οὐδεμιᾶς	οὐδενός	οὐδένων	οὐδεμιῶν	οὐδένων
D.	οὐδενί	οὐδεμιᾷ	οὐδενί	οὐδέσι	οὐδεμίαις	οὐδέσι
A.	οὐδένα	οὐδεμίαν	οὐδέν	οὐδένας	οὐδεμίᾶς	οὐδένα

628.   THE ARTICLE

	SINGULAR				DUAL				PLURAL		
	M.	F.	N.		M.	F.	N.		M.	F.	N.
N.	ὁ	ἡ	τό	N. A.	τώ	τώ	τώ	N.	οἱ	αἱ	τά
G.	τοῦ	τῆς	τοῦ	G. D.	τοῖν	τοῖν	τοῖν	G.	τῶν	τῶν	τῶν
D.	τῷ	τῇ	τῷ					D.	τοῖς	ταῖς	τοῖς
A.	τόν	τήν	τό					A.	τούς	τάς	τά

PRONOUNS

629.   PERSONAL AND INTENSIVE PRONOUNS

ἐγώ, *I* σύ, *you* οὗ, *himself*   αὐτός, *self, same, him*

SINGULAR

N.	ἐγώ	σύ	—	αὐτός	αὐτή	αὐτό
G.	ἐμοῦ, μοῦ	σοῦ	οὗ	αὐτοῦ	αὐτῆς	αὐτοῦ
D.	ἐμοί, μοί	σοί	οἷ	αὐτῷ	αὐτῇ	αὐτῷ
A.	ἐμέ, μέ	σέ	ἕ	αὐτόν	αὐτήν	αὐτό

DUAL

N. A.	νώ	σφώ		αὐτώ	αὐτά	αὐτώ
G. D.	νῷν	σφῷν		αὐτοῖν	αὐταῖν	αὐτοῖν

PLURAL

N.	ἡμεῖς	ὑμεῖς	σφεῖς	αὐτοί	αὐταί	αὐτά
G.	ἡμῶν	ὑμῶν	σφῶν	αὐτῶν	αὐτῶν	αὐτῶν
D.	ἡμῖν	ὑμῖν	σφίσι	αὐτοῖς	αὐταῖς	αὐτοῖς
A.	ἡμᾶς	ὑμᾶς	σφᾶς	αὐτούς	αὐτάς	αὐτά

630.   Reflexive Pronouns

SINGULAR   PLURAL

	M.	F.		M.	F.
G.	ἐμαυτοῦ	ἐμαυτῆς		ἡμῶν αὐτῶν	ἡμῶν αὐτῶν
D.	ἐμαυτῷ	ἐμαυτῇ		ἡμῖν αὐτοῖς	ἡμῖν αὐταῖς
A.	ἐμαυτόν	ἐμαυτήν		ἡμᾶς αὐτούς	ἡμᾶς αὐτάς

	M.	F.		M.	F.
G.	σεαυτοῦ or σαυτοῦ	σεαυτῆς or σαυτῆς		ῡ̔μῶν αὐτῶν	ῡ̔μῶν αὐτῶν
D.	σεαυτῷ or σαυτῷ	σεαυτῇ or σαυτῇ		ῡ̔μῖν αὐτοῖς	ῡ̔μῖν αὐταῖς
A.	σεαυτόν or σαυτόν	σεαυτήν or σαυτήν		ῡ̔μᾶς αὐτούς	ῡ̔μᾶς αὐτάς

	M.	F.	N.		M.	F.	N.
G.	ἑαυτοῦ	ἑαυτῆς	ἑαυτοῦ		ἑαυτῶν	ἑαυτῶν	ἑαυτῶν
D.	ἑαυτῷ	ἑαυτῇ	ἑαυτῷ		ἑαυτοῖς	ἑαυταῖς	ἑαυτοῖς
A.	ἑαυτόν	ἑαυτήν	ἑαυτό		ἑαυτούς	ἑαυτάς	ἑαυτά

contracted into

	M.	F.	N.		M.	F.	N.
G.	αὑτοῦ	αὑτῆς	αὑτοῦ		αὑτῶν	αὑτῶν	αὑτῶν
D.	αὑτῷ	αὑτῇ	αὑτῷ		αὑτοῖς	αὑταῖς	αὑτοῖς
A.	αὑτόν	αὑτήν	αὑτό		αὑτούς	αὑτάς	αὑτά

631.   Reciprocal Pronoun

DUAL   PLURAL

	M.	F.	N.		M.	F.	N.
G.	ἀλλήλοιν	ἀλλήλαιν	ἀλλήλοιν		ἀλλήλων	ἀλλήλων	ἀλλήλων
D.	ἀλλήλοιν	ἀλλήλαιν	ἀλλήλοιν		ἀλλήλοις	ἀλλήλαις	ἀλλήλοις
A.	ἀλλήλω	ἀλλήλᾱ	ἀλλήλω		ἀλλήλους	ἀλλήλᾱς	ἄλληλα

632.   Demonstrative Pronouns

SINGULAR   DUAL   PLURAL

M.	F.	N.	M.	F.	N.	M.	F.	N.
οὗτος	αὕτη	τοῦτο	τούτω	τούτω	τούτω	οὗτοι	αὗται	ταῦτα
τούτου	ταύτης	τούτου	τούτοιν	τούτοιν	τούτοιν	τούτων	τούτων	τούτων
τούτῳ	ταύτῃ	τούτῳ				τούτοις	ταύταις	τούτοις
τοῦτον	ταύτην	τοῦτο				τούτους	ταύτᾱς	ταῦτα

SINGULAR

	M.	F.	N.		M.	F.	N.
N.	ὅδε	ἥδε	τόδε		ἐκεῖνος	ἐκείνη	ἐκεῖνο
G.	τοῦδε	τῆσδε	τοῦδε		ἐκείνου	ἐκείνης	ἐκείνου
D.	τῷδε	τῇδε	τῷδε		ἐκείνῳ	ἐκείνῃ	ἐκείνῳ
A.	τόνδε	τήνδε	τόδε		ἐκεῖνον	ἐκείνην	ἐκεῖνο

DUAL

	M.	F.	N.		M.	F.	N.
N. A.	τώδε	τώδε	τώδε		ἐκείνω	ἐκείνω	ἐκείνω
G. D.	τοῖνδε	τοῖνδε	τοῖνδε		ἐκείνοιν	ἐκείνοιν	ἐκείνοιν

PLURAL

	M.	F.	N.	M.	F.	N.
N.	οἵδε	αἵδε	τάδε	ἐκεῖνοι	ἐκεῖναι	ἐκεῖνα
G.	τῶνδε	τῶνδε	τῶνδε	ἐκείνων	ἐκείνων	ἐκείνων
D.	τοῖσδε	ταῖσδε	τοῖσδε	ἐκείνοις	ἐκείναις	ἐκείνοις
A.	τούσδε	τάσδε	τάδε	ἐκείνους	ἐκείνᾱς	ἐκεῖνα

633. Interrogative and Indefinite Pronouns

✓ τίς, who? what?   ✓ τὶς, some one, something, a certain one

SINGULAR

	M. AND F.	N.		M. AND F.	N.
N.	τίς	τί		τὶς	τὶ
G.	τίνος, τοῦ	τίνος, τοῦ		τινός, του	τινός, του
D.	τίνι, τῷ	τίνι, τῷ		τινί, τῳ	τινί, τῳ
A.	τίνα	τί		τινά	τὶ

DUAL

N. A.	τίνε	τίνε		τινέ	τινέ
G. D.	τίνοιν	τίνοιν		τινοῖν	τινοῖν

PLURAL

N.	τίνες	τίνα		τινές	τινά
G.	τίνων	τίνων		τινῶν	τινῶν
D.	τίσι	τίσι		τισί	τισί
A.	τίνας	τίνα		τινάς	τινά

634. Relative Pronouns

✓ ὅς, who, which   ὅστις, any one who, whoever

SINGULAR

	M.	F.	N.	M.	F.	N.
N.	ὅς	ἥ	ὅ	ὅστις	ἥτις	ὅ τι
G.	οὗ	ἧς	οὗ	οὗτινος, ὅτου	ἧστινος	οὗτινος, ὅτου
D.	ᾧ	ᾗ	ᾧ	ᾧτινι, ὅτῳ	ᾗτινι	ᾧτινι, ὅτῳ
A.	ὅν	ἥν	ὅ	ὅντινα	ἥντινα	ὅ τι

DUAL

	M.	F.	N.	M.	F.	N.
N. A.	ὥ	ὥ	ὥ	ὥτινε	ὥτινε	ὥτινε
G. D.	οἷν	οἷν	οἷν	οἷντινοιν	οἷντινοιν	οἷντινοιν

PLURAL

	M.	F.	N.	M.	F.	N.
N.	οἵ	αἵ	ἅ	οἵτινες	αἵτινες	ἅτινα, ἅττα
G.	ὧν	ὧν	ὧν	ὧντινων, ὅτων	ὧντινων	ὧντινων, ὅτων
D.	οἷς	αἷς	οἷς	οἷστισι, ὅτοις	αἷστισι	οἷστισι, ὅτοις
A.	οὕς	ἅς	ἅ	οὕστινας	ἅστινας	ἅτινα, ἅττα

VERBS

635. PERSONAL ENDINGS

I. Primary tenses of the active:

	Sing.		*Plu.*		*Dual*
1	-μι	1	-μεν		
2	-ς (σι)	2	-τε	2	-τον
3	-σι (τι)	3	-νσι	3	-τον

II. Secondary tenses:

	Sing.		*Plu.*		*Dual*
1	-ν	1	-μεν		
2	-ς	2	-τε	2	-τον
3	—	3	-ν, -σαν	3	-την

III. Middle (Passive, except aorist):

	PRIMARY			SECONDARY		
	Sing.	*Plu.*	*Dual*	*Sing.*	*Plu.*	*Dual*
1	-μαι	-μεθα		-μην	-μεθα	
2	-σαι	-σθε	-σθον	-σο	-σθε	-σθον
3	-ται	-νται	-σθον	-το	-ντο	-σθην

IV. Imperative:

	ACTIVE			MIDDLE (PASSIVE)		
	Sing.	*Plu.*	*Dual*	*Sing.*	*Plu.*	*Dual*
2	-θι	-τε	-τον	-σο	-σθε	-σθον
3	-τω	-ντων	-των	-σθω	-σθων	-σθων

V. Infinitive:

ACTIVE	MIDDLE
-εν (by combination with the thematic vowel -ειν) and -ναι	-σθαι

636. MEANING OF λύω IN EACH TENSE OF THE INDICATIVE, IMPERA-TIVE, PARTICIPLE, AND INFINITIVE ACTIVE

Λύω

	Indicative	*Imperative*	*Infinitive*	*Participle*
Pres.	I loose or am loosing.	Loose thou.	To loose or to be loosing.	Loosing.
Imp.	I loosed or was loosing.			

	Indicative	Imperative	Infinitive	Participle
Fut.	*I shall loose.*		*To be about to loose.*	*About to loose.*
Aor.	*I loosed.*	*Loose thou.*	*To loose or to have loosed.*	*Having loosed or loosing.*
Perf.	*I have loosed.*		*To have loosed.*	*Having loosed.*
Plup.	*I had loosed.*			

The middle of λύω commonly means *to release for oneself*, or *to release some one belonging to oneself*, hence *to ransom* or *to deliver*.

In the passive the meanings are changed merely to suit that voice; as *I am loosed, I was loosed, I shall be loosed, I have been loosed*, etc. The future perfect passive means *I shall have been loosed* (i. e., before some future event referred to).

637. Synopsis of λύω

λύω

ACTIVE VOICE

	Indicative	Subjunctive	Optative	Imperative	Infinitive	Participle
Pres.	λύω	λύω	λύοιμι	λῦε	λύειν	λύων
Imp.	ἔλῡον					
Fut.	λύσω		λύσοιμι		λύσειν	λύσων
Aor.	ἔλῡσα	λύσω	λύσαιμι	λῦσον	λῦσαι	λύσᾱς
Perf.	λέλυκα	λελύκω or λελυκὼς ὦ	λελύκοιμι or λελυκὼς εἴην		λελυκέναι	λελυκώς
Plup.	ἐλελύκη					

MIDDLE VOICE

	Indicative	Subjunctive	Optative	Imperative	Infinitive	Participle
Pres.	λύομαι	λύωμαι	λῡοίμην	λύου	λύεσθαι	λῡόμενος
Imp.	ἐλῡόμην					
Fut.	λύσομαι		λῡσοίμην		λύσεσθαι	λῡσόμενος
Aor.	ἐλῡσάμην	λύσωμαι	λῡσαίμην	λῦσαι	λύσασθαι	λῡσάμενος
Perf.	λέλυμαι	λελυμένος ὦ	λελυμένος εἴην	λέλυσο	λελύσθαι	λελυμένος
Plup.	ἐλελύμην					

PASSIVE VOICE[1]

	Indicative	Subjunctive	Optative	Imperative	Infinitive	Participle
Fut. } Perf. }	λελύσομαι		λελῡσοίμην		λελύσεσθαι	λελῡσόμενος
Aor.	ἐλύθην	λυθῶ	λυθείην	λύθητι	λυθῆναι	λυθείς
Fut.	λυθήσομαι		λυθησοίμην		λυθήσεσθαι	λυθησόμενος

[1] The Present and Imperfect, the Perfect and Pluperfect are the same as in the Middle Voice.

638. ACTIVE VOICE OF λύω

INDICATIVE

	Present	Imperfect	Future	Aorist	Perfect	Pluperfect
	I loose, am loosing	I loosed, was loosing, used to loose	I shall loose	I loosed	I have loosed	I had loosed
S. 1	λύω	ἔλῦον	λύσω	ἔλῦσα	λέλυκα	ἐλελύκη
2	λύεις	ἔλῦες	λύσεις	ἔλῦσας	λέλυκας	ἐλελύκης
3	λύει	ἔλῦε	λύσει	ἔλῦσε	λέλυκε	ἐλελύκει
D. 2	λύετον	ἐλύετον	λύσετον	ἐλύσατον	λελύκατον	ἐλελύκετον
3	λύετον	ἐλῦέτην	λύσετον	ἐλῦσάτην	λελύκατον	ἐλελυκέτην
P. 1	λύομεν	ἐλύομεν	λύσομεν	ἐλύσαμεν	λελύκαμεν	ἐλελύκεμεν
2	λύετε	ἐλύετε	λύσετε	ἐλύσατε	λελύκατε	ἐλελύκετε
3	λύουσι	ἔλῦον	λύσουσι	ἔλῦσαν	λελύκᾱσι	ἐλελύκεσαν

SUBJUNCTIVE

	Present		Aorist		Perfect
S. 1	λύω		λύσω		λελύκω
2	λύῃς		λύσῃς		λελύκῃς
3	λύῃ		λύσῃ		λελύκῃ
D. 2	λύητον		λύσητον		λελύκητον
3	λύητον		λύσητον		λελύκητον
P. 1	λύωμεν		λύσωμεν		λελύκωμεν
2	λύητε		λύσητε		λελύκητε
3	λύωσι		λύσωσι		λελύκωσι

OPTATIVE

	Present	Future	Aorist	Perfect
S. 1	λύοιμι	λύσοιμι	λύσαιμι	λελύκοιμι
2	λύοις	λύσοις	λύσαις, λύσειας	λελύκοις
3	λύοι	λύσοι	λύσαι, λύσειε	λελύκοι
D. 2	λύοιτον	λύσοιτον	λύσαιτον	λελύκοιτον
3	λῦοίτην	λῦσοίτην	λῦσαίτην	λελυκοίτην
P. 1	λύοιμεν	λύσοιμεν	λύσαιμεν	λελύκοιμεν
2	λύοιτε	λύσοιτε	λύσαιτε	λελύκοιτε
3	λύοιεν	λύσοιεν	λύσαιεν, λύσειαν	λελύκοιεν

IMPERATIVE

S. 2	λῦε		λῦσον
3	λυέτω		λυσάτω
D. 2	λύετον		λύσατον
3	λυέτων		λυσάτων
P. 2	λύετε		λύσατε
3	λυόντων		λυσάντων

INFINITIVE
to loose, etc. *παιδεῦσαι*

Present ✓	*Future* ✓	*Aorist* ✓	*Perfect* ✓
λύειν	λύσειν	λῦσαι	λελυκέναι

PARTICIPLE
loosing, etc.

M. λύων	λύσων ✓	λύσᾱς ✓	λελυκώς ✓
F. λύουσα	λύσουσα	λύσᾱσα	λελυκυῖα
N. λῦον *παιδεῦον*	λῦσον *παιδεῦσον*	λῦσαν	λελυκός

639.   MIDDLE VOICE OF λύω *παιδεῦσαν*

INDICATIVE

		Present ✓	*Imperfect*	*Future* ✓	*Aorist* ✓	*Perfect* ✓	*Pluperfect* ✓
S.	1	λύομαι	ἐλῡόμην	λύσομαι	ἐλῡσάμην	λέλυμαι	ἐλελύμην
	2	λύει, λύῃ	ἐλύου	λύσει, λύσῃ	ἐλύσω	λέλυσαι	ἐλέλυσο
	3	λύεται	ἐλύετο	λύσεται	ἐλύσατο	λέλυται	ἐλέλυτο
D.	2	λύεσθον	ἐλύεσθον	λύσεσθον	ἐλύσασθον	λέλυσθον	ἐλέλυσθον
	3	λύεσθον	ἐλῡέσθην	λύσεσθον	ἐλῡσάσθην	λέλυσθον	ἐλελύσθην
P.	1	λῡόμεθα	ἐλῡόμεθα	λῡσόμεθα	ἐλῡσάμεθα	λελύμεθα	ἐλελύμεθα
	2	λύεσθε	ἐλύεσθε	λύσεσθε	ἐλύσασθε	λέλυσθε	ἐλέλυσθε
	3	λύονται	ἐλύοντο	λύσονται	ἐλύσαντο	λέλυνται	ἐλέλυντο

SUBJUNCTIVE

		Present	*Aorist* ✓	*Perfect*
S.	1	λύωμαι ✓	λύσωμαι ✓	λελυμένος ὦ ✓
	2	λύῃ	λύσῃ	λελυμένος ᾖς
	3	λύηται	λύσηται	λελυμένος ᾖ
D.	2	λύησθον	λύσησθον	λελυμένω ἦτον
	3	λύησθον	λύσησθον	λελυμένω ἦτον
P.	1	λῡώμεθα	λῡσώμεθα	λελυμένοι ὦμεν
	2	λύησθε	λύσησθε	λελυμένοι ἦτε
	3	λύωνται	λύσωνται	λελυμένοι ὦσι

OPTATIVE

				Perfect
S.	1	λῡοίμην ✓	λῡσοίμην ✓	λῡσαίμην ✓	λελυμένος εἴην ✓
	2	λύοιο	λύσοιο	λύσαιο	λελυμένος εἴης
	3	λύοιτο	λύσοιτο	λύσαιτο	λελυμένος εἴη
D.	2	λύοισθον	λύσοισθον	λύσαισθον	λελυμένω εἴητον
	3	λῡοίσθην	λῡσοίσθην	λῡσαίσθην	λελυμένω εἰήτην
P.	1	λῡοίμεθα	λῡσοίμεθα	λῡσαίμεθα	λελυμένοι εἴημεν or εἶμεν
	2	λύοισθε	λύσοισθε	λύσαισθε	λελυμένοι εἴητε or εἶτε
	3	λύοιντο	λύσοιντο	λύσαιντο	λελυμένοι εἴησαν or εἶεν

παίδευσαι

IMPERATIVE

	Present	Future	Aorist	Perfect
S. 2	λύου		λῦσαι	λέλυσο
3	λυέσθω		λυσάσθω	λελύσθω
D. 2	λύεσθον		λύσασθον	λέλυσθον
3	λυέσθων		λυσάσθων	λελύσθων
P. 2	λύεσθε		λύσασθε	λέλυσθε
3	λυέσθων		λυσάσθων	λελύσθων

INFINITIVE

λύεσθαι	λύσεσθαι	λύσασθαι	λελύσθαι

§ 622

§ 623

PARTICIPLE

M.	λυόμενος	λυσόμενος	λυσάμενος	λελυμένος
F.	λυομένη	λυσομένη	λυσαμένη	λελυμένη
N.	λυόμενον	λυσόμενον	λυσάμενον	λελυμένον

640.　　　　　　PASSIVE VOICE OF λύω

Present, Imperfect, Perfect, Pluperfect, the same as the Middle, 639

INDICATIVE

	Future Perfect	Aorist	Future
S. 1	λελύσομαι	ἐλύθην	λυθήσομαι
2	λελύσει, λελύσῃ	ἐλύθης	λυθήσει, λυθήσῃ
3	λελύσεται	ἐλύθη	λυθήσεται
D. 2	λελύσεσθον	ἐλύθητον	λυθήσεσθον
3	λελύσεσθον	ἐλυθήτην	λυθήσεσθον
P. 1	λελυσόμεθα	ἐλύθημεν	λυθησόμεθα
2	λελύσεσθε	ἐλύθητε	λυθήσεσθε
3	λελύσονται	ἐλύθησαν	λυθήσονται

SUBJUNCTIVE

S. 1	λυθῶ
2	λυθῇς
3	λυθῇ
D. 2	λυθῆτον
3	λυθῆτον
P. 1	λυθῶμεν
2	λυθῆτε
3	λυθῶσι

OPTATIVE

Future Perfect	Aorist	Future
S. 1 λελῡσοίμην	λυθείην	λυθησοίμην
2 λελύσοιο	λυθείης	λυθήσοιο
3 λελύσοιτο	λυθείη	λυθήσοιτο
D. 2 λελύσοισθον	λυθείητον, λυθεῖτον	λυθήσοισθον
3 λελύσοισθην	λυθειήτην, λυθείτην	λυθησοίσθην
P. 1 λελῡσοίμεθα	λυθείημεν, λυθεῖμεν	λυθησοίμεθα
2 λελύσοισθε	λυθείητε, λυθεῖτε	λυθήσοισθε
3 λελύσοιντο	λυθείησαν, λυθεῖεν	λυθήσοιντο

IMPERATIVE

S. 2 λύθητι
3 λυθήτω

D. 2 λύθητον
3 λυθήτων

P. 2 λύθητε
3 λυθέντων

INFINITIVE

λελύσεσθαι   λυθῆναι   λυθήσεσθαι

PARTICIPLE

λελῡσόμενος, -η, -ον   λυθείς, -θεῖσα, -θέν   λυθησόμενος, -η, -ον

641. Second Aorist (Active and Middle) and Second
Perfect and Pluperfect (Active)
of λείπω (λιπ-), *leave*

	2 Aor. Act.	2 Aor. Mid.	2 Perfect	2 Pluperfect
S. 1	ἔλιπον	ἐλιπόμην	λέλοιπα	ἐλελοίπη
2	ἔλιπες	ἐλίπου	λέλοιπας	ἐλελοίπης
3	ἔλιπε	ἐλίπετο	λέλοιπε	ἐλελοίπει
D. 2	ἐλίπετον	ἐλίπεσθον	λελοίπατον	ἐλελοίπετον
3	ἐλιπέτην	ἐλιπέσθην	λελοίπατον	ἐλελοιπέτην
P. 1	ἐλίπομεν	ἐλιπόμεθα	λελοίπαμεν	ἐλελοίπεμεν
2	ἐλίπετε	ἐλίπεσθε	λελοίπατε	ἐλελοίπετε
3	ἔλιπον	ἐλίποντο	λελοίπᾱσι	ἐλελοίπεσαν

SUBJUNCTIVE

2 Aor. Act. ✓	2 Aor. Mid. ✓	2 Perfect ✓
S. 1 λίπω	λίπωμαι	λελοίπω
2 λίπῃς	λίπῃ	λελοίπῃς
3 λίπῃ	λίπηται	λελοίπῃ
D. 2 λίπητον	λίπησθον	λελοίπητον
3 λίπητον	λίπησθον	λελοίπητον
P. 1 λίπωμεν	λιπώμεθα	λελοίπωμεν
2 λίπητε	λίπησθε	λελοίπητε
3 λίπωσι	λίπωνται	λελοίπωσι

OPTATIVE

2 Aor. Act.	2 Aor. Mid.	2 Perfect
S. 1 λίποιμι ✓	λιποίμην ✓	λελοίποιμι
2 λίποις	λίποιο	λελοίποις
3 λίποι	λίποιτο	λελοίποι
D. 2 λίποιτον	λίποισθον	λελοίποιτον
3 λιποίτην	λιποίσθην	λελοιποίτην
P. 1 λίποιμεν	λιποίμεθα	λελοίποιμεν
2 λίποιτε	λίποισθε	λελοίποιτε
3 λίποιεν	λίποιντο	λελοίποιεν

IMPERATIVE

2 Aor. Act.	2 Aor. Mid.	2 Perfect
S. 2 λίπε ✓	λιποῦ ✓	
3 λιπέτω	λιπέσθω	
D. 2 λίπετον	λίπεσθον	
3 λιπέτων	λιπέσθων	
P. 2 λίπετε	λίπεσθε	
3 λιπόντων	λιπέσθων	

INFINITIVE

λιπεῖν ✓	λιπέσθαι	λελοιπέναι

PARTICIPLE

λιπών, οῦσα, όν ✓	λιπόμενος, η, ον ✓	λελοιπώς, υῖα, ός ✓

642.   LIQUID FORMS. φαίνω [φαν], *show*

INDICATIVE ✓

Future Active ✓	Fut. Mid. ✓	1 Aor. Act. ✓	1 Aor. Mid. ✓
S. 1 φανῶ	φανοῦμαι	ἔφηνα	ἐφηνάμην
2 φανεῖς	φανεῖ, φανῇ	ἔφηνας	ἐφήνω
3 φανεῖ	φανεῖται	ἔφηνε	ἐφήνατο

	Fut. Act.	Fut. Mid.	1 Aor. Act.	1 Aor. Mid.
D. 2	φανεῖτον	φανεῖσθον	ἐφήνατον	ἐφήνασθον
3	φανεῖτον	φανεῖσθον	ἐφηνάτην	ἐφηνάσθην
P. 1	φανοῦμεν	φανούμεθα	ἐφήναμεν	ἐφηνάμεθα
2	φανεῖτε	φανεῖσθε	ἐφήνατε	ἐφήνασθε
3	φανοῦσι	φανοῦνται	ἔφηναν	ἐφήναντο

SUBJUNCTIVE

S. 1	φήνω	φήνωμαι
2	φήνῃς	φήνῃ
3	φήνῃ	φήνηται
D. 2	φήνητον	φήνησθον
3	φήνητον	φήνησθον
P. 1	φήνωμεν	φηνώμεθα
2	φήνητε	φήνησθε
3	φήνωσι	φήνωνται

OPTATIVE

S. 1	φανοίην, φανοῖμι	φανοίμην	φήναιμι	φηναίμην
2	φανοίης, φανοῖς	φανοῖο	φήναις, φήνειας	φήναιο
3	φανοίη, φανοῖ	φανοῖτο	φήναι, φήνειε	φήναιτο
D. 2	φανοῖτον	φανοῖσθον	φήναιτον	φήναισθον
3	φανοίτην	φανοίσθην	φηναίτην	φηναίσθην
P. 1	φανοῖμεν	φανοίμεθα	φήναιμεν	φηναίμεθα
2	φανοῖτε	φανοῖσθε	φήναιτε	φήναισθε
3	φανοῖεν	φανοῖντο	φήναιεν, φήνειαν	φήναιντο

IMPERATIVE

S. 2	φῆνον	φῆναι
3	φηνάτω	φηνάσθω
D. 2	φήνατον	φήνασθον
3	φηνάτων	φηνάσθων
P. 2	φήνατε	φήνασθε
3	φηνάντων	φηνάσθων

INFINITIVE

φανεῖν	φανεῖσθαι	φῆναι	φήνασθαι

PARTICIPLE

φανών, οὖσα, οὖν	φανούμενος, η, ον	φήνᾱς, ᾱσα, αν	φηνάμενος, η, ον

SECOND AORIST PASSIVE

Indicative	Subjunctive	Optative	Imperative
ἐφάνην	φανῶ	φανείην	
ἐφάνης	φανῇς	φανείης	φάνηθι
ἐφάνη	φανῇ	φανείη	φανήτω
ἐφάνητον	φανῆτον	φανείητον, φανεῖτον	φάνητον
ἐφανήτην	φανῆτον	φανειήτην, φανείτην	φανήτων
ἐφάνημεν	φανῶμεν	φανείημεν, φανεῖμεν	
ἐφάνητε	φανῆτε	φανείητε, φανεῖτε	φάνητε
ἐφάνησαν	φανῶσι	φανείησαν, φανεῖεν	φανέντων

INFINITIVE	PARTICIPLE
φανῆναι	φανείς, φανεῖσα, φανέν

SECOND FUTURE PASSIVE

Indicative	Optative	Infinitive	Participle
φανήσομαι	φανησοίμην	φανήσεσθαι	φανησόμενος, η, ον
φανήσει, φανήσῃ	φανήσοιο		
φανήσεται	φανήσοιτο		
φανήσεσθον	φανήσοισθον		
φανήσεσθον	φανησοίσθην		
φανησόμεθα	φανησοίμεθα		
φανήσεσθε	φανήσοισθε		
φανήσονται	φανήσοιντο		

643.   λείπω (λιπ), *leave*, Middle or Passive

INDICATIVE

	Perfect		Pluperfect	Future Perfect
(λέ-λειπ-μαι)	λέλειμμαι	(ἐ-λε-λείπ-μην)	ἐλελείμμην	λελείψομαι
(λέ-λειπ-σαι)	λέλειψαι	(ἐ-λέ-λειπ-σο)	ἐλέλειψο	λελείψῃ
(λέ-λειπ-ται)	λέλειπται	(ἐ-λέ-λειπ-το)	ἐλέλειπτο	λελείψεται
(λέ-λειπ-σθον)	λέλειφθον	(ἐ-λέ-λειπ-σθον)	ἐλέλειφθον	λελείψεσθον
(λέ-λειπ-σθον)	λέλειφθον	(ἐ-λε-λείπ-σθην)	ἐλελείφθην	λελείψεσθον
(λε-λείπ-μεθα)	λελείμμεθα	(ἐ-λε-λείπ-μεθα)	ἐλελείμμεθα	λελειψόμεθα
(λέ-λειπ-σθε)	λέλειφθε	(ἐ-λέ-λειπ-σθε)	ἐλέλειφθε	λελείψεσθε
(λέ-λειπ-νται)	λελειμμένοι εἰσί(ν)	(ἐ-λέ-λειπ-ντο)	λελειμμένοι ἦσαν	λελείψονται

SUBJUNCTIVE

Perfect

λελειμμένος ὦ		λελειμμένοι ὦμεν
λελειμμένος ᾖς	λελειμμένω ἦτον	λελειμμένοι ἦτε
λελειμμένος ᾖ	λελειμμένω ἦτον	λελειμμένοι ὦσι(ν)

OPTATIVE

Perfect	*Future Perfect*
λελειμμένος εἴην	λελειψοίμην
λελειμμένος εἴης	λελείψοιο
λελειμμένος εἴη	λελείψοιτο
λελειμμένω εἴητον, εἴτον	λελείψοισθον
λελειμμένω εἰήτην, εἴτην	λελειψοίσθην
λελειμμένοι εἴημεν, εἶμεν	λελειψοίμεθα
λελειμμένοι εἴητε, εἶτε	λελείψοισθε
λελειμμένοι εἴησαν, εἶεν	λελείψοιντο

IMPERATIVE

λέλειψο
λελείφθω

λέλειφθον
λελείφθων

λέλειφθε
λελείφθων

INFINITIVE

λελεῖφθαι λελείψεσθαι

PARTICIPLE

λελειμμένος, η, ον

644. πείθω (πιθ), *persuade,* Middle or Passive

INDICATIVE

	Perfect		*Pluperfect*
(πέπειθ-μαι)	πέπεισμαι	(ἐπεπείθ-μην)	ἐπεπείσμην
(πέπειθ-σαι)	πέπεισαι	(ἐπέπειθ-σο)	ἐπέπεισο
(πέπειθ-ται)	πέπεισται	(ἐπέπειθ-το)	ἐπέπειστο
(πέπειθ-σθον)	πέπεισθον	(ἐπέπειθ-σθον)	ἐπέπεισθον
(πέπειθ-σθον)	πέπεισθον	(ἐπεπείθ-σθην)	ἐπεπείσθην
(πεπείθ-μεθα)	πεπείσμεθα	(ἐπεπείθ-μεθα)	ἐπεπείσμεθα
(πέπειθ-σθε)	πέπεισθε	(ἐπέπειθ-σθε)	ἐπέπεισθε
(πεπειθ-μένοι)	πεπεισμένοι εἰσί	(πεπειθ-μένοι)	πεπεισμένοι ἦσαν

SUBJUNCTIVE   OPTATIVE

Perfect

πεπεισμένος ὦ, ῇς, ῇ, etc.   πεπεισμένος εἴην, εἴης, εἴη, etc.

IMPERATIVE   INFINITIVE   PARTICIPLE

πέπεισο   πεπεῖσθαι   πεπεισμένος, η, ον
πεπείσθω

πέπεισθον
πεπείσθων

πέπεισθε
πεπείσθων

645.   τάττω (ταγ), *arrange*

INDICATIVE

Perfect   *Pluperfect*

(τέταγ-μαι)	τέταγμαι	(ἐτετάγ-μην)	ἐτετάγμην
(τέταγ-σαι)	τέταξαι	(ἐτέταγ-σο)	ἐτέταξο
(τέταγ-ται)	τέτακται	(ἐτέταγ-το)	ἐτέτακτο
(τέταγ-σθον)	τέταχθον	(ἐτέταγ-σθον)	ἐτετάχθον
(τέγαγ-σθον)	τέταχθον	(ἐτετάγ-σθην)	ἐτετάχθην
(τετάγ-μεθα)	τετάγμεθα	(ἐτετάγ-μεθα)	ἐτετάγμεθα
(τέταγ-σθε)	τέταχθε	(ἐτέταγ-σθε)	ἐτέταχθε
(τεταγ-μένοι)	τεταγμένοι εἰσί	(τεταγ-μένοι)	τεταγμένοι ἦσαν

SUBJUNCTIVE   OPTATIVE

τεταγμένος ὦ, ῇς, ῇ   τεταγμένος εἴην, εἴης, εἴη

IMPERATIVE   INFINITIVE   PARTICIPLE

| (τέταγ-σο) | τέταξο | τετάχθαι | τεταγμένος, η, ον |
| (τετάγ-σθω) | τετάχθω | | |

| (τέταγ-σθον) | τέταχθον | | |
| (τετάγ-σθων) | τετάχθων | | |

| (τέταγ-σθε) | τέταχθε | | |
| (τετάγ-σθων) | τετάχθων | | |

646.   CONTRACT VERBS

1. SYNOPSIS OF τῑμάω, ποιέω, δηλόω, IN THE INDICATIVE OF ALL VOICES

ACTIVE

Pres.	τῑμῶ	ποιῶ	δηλῶ
Imperf.	ἐτίμων	ἐποίουν	ἐδήλουν
Fut.	τῑμήσω	ποιήσω	δηλώσω
Aor.	ἐτίμησα	ἐποίησα	ἐδήλωσα
Perf.	τετίμηκα	πεποίηκα	δεδήλωκα
Plup.	ἐτετῑμήκη	ἐπεποιήκη	ἐδεδηλώκη

MIDDLE

Pres.	τῑμῶμαι	ποιοῦμαι	δηλοῦμαι
Imperf.	ἐτῑμώμην	ἐποιούμην	ἐδηλούμην
Fut.	τῑμήσομαι	ποιήσομαι	δηλώσομαι
Aor.	ἐτῑμησάμην	ἐποιησάμην	ἐδηλωσάμην
Perf.	τετίμημαι	πεποίημαι	δεδήλωμαι
Plup.	ἐτετῑμήμην	ἐπεποιήμην	ἐδεδηλώμην

PASSIVE

Pres. and Imp.: same as Middle.

Fut.	τῑμηθήσομαι	ποιηθήσομαι	δηλωθήσομαι
Aor.	ἐτῑμήθην	ἐποιήθην	ἐδηλώθην

Perf. and Plup.: same as Middle.

Fut. Perf.	τετῑμήσομαι	πεποιήσομαι	δεδηλώσομαι

2. SYNOPSIS OF CONTRACTED FORMS

ACTIVE

	Present	*Present*	*Present*
Ind.	τῑμῶ	ποιῶ	δηλῶ
Subj.	τῑμῶ	ποιῶ	δηλῶ
Opt.	τῑμῴην	ποιοίην	δηλοίην
Imp.	τίμᾱ	ποίει	δήλου
Inf.	τῑμᾶν	ποιεῖν	δηλοῦν
Part.	τῑμῶν	ποιῶν	δηλῶν
	Imperfect	*Imperfect*	*Imperfect*
	ἐτίμων	ἐποίουν	ἐδήλουν

MIDDLE AND PASSIVE

Ind.	τῑμῶμαι	ποιοῦμαι	δηλοῦμαι
Sub.	τῑμῶμαι	ποιῶμαι	δηλῶμαι
Opt.	τῑμῴμην	ποιοίμην	δηλοίμην
Imp.	τῑμῶ	ποιοῦ	δηλοῦ
Inf.	τῑμᾶσθαι	ποιεῖσθαι	δηλοῦσθαι
Part.	τῑμώμενος	ποιούμενος	δηλούμενος
	Imperfect	*Imperfect*	*Imperfect*
	ἐτῑμώμην	ἐποιούμην	ἐδηλούμην

647.

handwritten: honor　*handwritten: do, make*　*handwritten: show, explain*

ACTIVE

Present Indicative ✓

(τῑμάω)	τῑμῶ	(ποιέω)	ποιῶ	(δηλόω)	δηλῶ
(τῑμάεις)	τῑμᾷς	(ποιέεις)	ποιεῖς	(δηλόεις)	δηλοῖς
(τῑμάει)	τῑμᾷ	(ποιέει)	ποιεῖ	(δηλόει)	δηλοῖ
(τῑμάετον)	τῑμᾶτον	(ποιέετον)	ποιεῖτον	(δηλόετον)	δηλοῦτον
(τῑμάετον)	τῑμᾶτον	(ποιέετον)	ποιεῖτον	(δηλόετον)	δηλοῦτον
(τῑμάομεν)	τῑμῶμεν	(ποιέομεν)	ποιοῦμεν	(δηλόομεν)	δηλοῦμεν
(τῑμάετε)	τῑμᾶτε	(ποιέετε)	ποιεῖτε	(δηλόετε)	δηλοῦτε
(τῑμάουσι)	τῑμῶσι	(ποιέουσι)	ποιοῦσι	(δηλόουσι)	δηλοῦσι

Present Subjunctive ✓

(τῑμάω)	τῑμῶ	(ποιέω)	ποιῶ	(δηλόω)	δηλῶ
(τῑμάῃς)	τῑμᾷς	(ποιέῃς)	ποιῇς	(δηλόῃς)	δηλοῖς
(τῑμάῃ)	τῑμᾷ	(ποιέῃ)	ποιῇ	(δηλόῃ)	δηλοῖ
(τῑμάητον)	τῑμᾶτον	(ποιέητον)	ποιῆτον	(δηλόητον)	δηλῶτον
(τῑμάητον)	τῑμᾶτον	(ποιέητον)	ποιῆτον	(δηλόητον)	δηλῶτον
(τῑμάωμεν)	τῑμῶμεν	(ποιέωμεν)	ποιῶμεν	(δηλόωμεν)	δηλῶμεν
(τῑμάητε)	τῑμᾶτε	(ποιέητε)	ποιῆτε	(δηλόητε)	δηλῶτε
(τῑμάωσι)	τῑμῶσι	(ποιέωσι)	ποιῶσι	(δηλόωσι)	δηλῶσι

Present Optative[1] ✓

(τῑμάοιμι)	τῑμῷμι	(ποιέοιμι)	ποιοῖμι	(δηλόοιμι)	δηλοῖμι
(τῑμάοις)	τῑμῷς	(ποιέοις)	ποιοῖς	(δηλόοις)	δηλοῖς
(τῑμάοι)	τῑμῷ	(ποιέοι)	ποιοῖ	(δηλόοι)	δηλοῖ
(τῑμάοιτον)	τῑμῷτον	(ποιέοιτον)	ποιοῖτον	(δηλόοιτον)	δηλοῖτον
(τῑμαοίτην)	τῑμῴτην	(ποιεοίτην)	ποιοίτην	(δηλοοίτην)	δηλοίτην
(τῑμάοιμεν)	τῑμῷμεν	(ποιέοιμεν)	ποιοῖμεν	(δηλόοιμεν)	δηλοῖμεν
(τῑμάοιτε)	τῑμῷτε	(ποιέοιτε)	ποιοῖτε	(δηλόοιτε)	δηλοῖτε
(τῑμάοιεν)	τῑμῷεν	(ποιέοιεν)	ποιοῖεν	(δηλόοιεν)	δηλοῖεν
or	or	or	or	or	or
(τῑμαοίην)	τῑμῴην	(ποιεοίην)	ποιοίην	(δηλοοίην)	δηλοίην
(τῑμαοίης)	τῑμῴης	(ποιεοίης)	ποιοίης	(δηλοοίης)	δηλοίης
(τῑμαοίη)	τῑμῴη	(ποιεοίη)	ποιοίη	(δηλοοίη)	δηλοίη
(τῑμαοίητον)	τῑμῴητον	(ποιεοίητον)	ποιοίητον	(δηλοοίητον)	δηλοίητον
(τῑμαοιήτην)	τῑμῳήτην	(ποιεοιήτην)	ποιοιήτην	(δηλοοιήτην)	δηλοιήτην
(τῑμαοίημεν)	τῑμῴημεν	(ποιεοίημεν)	ποιοίημεν	(δηλοοίημεν)	δηλοίημεν
(τῑμαοίητε)	τῑμῴητε	(ποιεοίητε)	ποιοίητε	(δηλοοίητε)	δηλοίητε
(τῑμαοίησαν)	τῑμῴησαν	(ποιεοίησαν)	ποιοίησαν	(δηλοοίησαν)	δηλοίησαν

[1] In usage the -οίην forms prevail in the singular, the -οιμι in the dual and plural

handwritten: For contractions see § 141 and 148

Present Imperative

(τίμαε)	τίμᾱ	(ποίεε)	ποίει	(δήλοε)	δήλου
(τῑμαέτω)	τῑμάτω	(ποιεέτω)	ποιείτω	(δηλοέτω)	δηλούτω
(τῑμάετον)	τῑμᾶτον	(ποιέετον)	ποιεῖτον	(δηλόετον)	δηλοῦτον
(τῑμαέτων)	τῑμάτων	(ποιεέτων)	ποιείτων	(δηλοέτων)	δηλούτων
(τῑμάετε)	τῑμᾶτε	(ποιέετε)	ποιεῖτε	(δηλόετε)	δηλοῦτε
(τῑμαόντων)	τῑμώντων	(ποιεόντων)	ποιούντων	(δηλοόντων)	δηλούντων

Present Infinitive

(τῑμάειν)	τῑμᾶν	(ποιέειν)	ποιεῖν	(δηλόειν)	δηλοῦν

Present Participle (see 624)

(τῑμάων)	τῑμῶν	(ποιέων)	ποιῶν	(δηλόων)	δηλῶν

§ 624

Imperfect

(ἐτίμαον)	ἐτίμων	(ἐποίεον)	ἐποίουν	(ἐδήλοον)	ἐδήλουν
(ἐτίμαες)	ἐτίμᾱς	(ἐποίεες)	ἐποίεις	(ἐδήλοες)	ἐδήλους
(ἐτίμαε)	ἐτίμᾱ	(ἐποίεε)	ἐποίει	(ἐδήλοε)	ἐδήλου
(ἐτῑμάετον)	ἐτῑμᾶτον	(ἐποιέετον)	ἐποιεῖτον	(ἐδηλόετον)	ἐδηλοῦτον
(ἐτῑμαέτην)	ἐτῑμάτην	(ἐποιεέτην)	ἐποιείτην	(ἐδηλοέτην)	ἐδηλούτην
(ἐτῑμάομεν)	ἐτῑμῶμεν	(ἐποιέομεν)	ἐποιοῦμεν	(ἐδηλόομεν)	ἐδηλοῦμεν
(ἐτῑμάετε)	ἐτῑμᾶτε	(ἐποιέετε)	ἐποιεῖτε	(ἐδηλόετε)	ἐδηλοῦτε
(ἐτίμαον)	ἐτίμων	(ἐποίεον)	ἐποίουν	(ἐδήλοον)	ἐδήλουν

648. PASSIVE AND MIDDLE

Present Indicative

(τῑμάομαι)	τῑμῶμαι	(ποιέομαι)	ποιοῦμαι	(δηλόομαι)	δηλοῦμαι
(τῑμάει, τῑμάῃ)	τῑμᾷ	(ποιέει, ποιέῃ)	ποιεῖ, ποιῇ	(δηλόει, δηλόῃ)	δηλοῖ
(τῑμάεται)	τῑμᾶται	(ποιέεται)	ποιεῖται	(δηλόεται)	δηλοῦται
(τῑμάεσθον)	τῑμᾶσθον	(ποιέεσθον)	ποιεῖσθον	(δηλόεσθον)	δηλοῦσθον
(τῑμάεσθον)	τῑμᾶσθον	(ποιέεσθον)	ποιεῖσθον	(δηλόεσθον)	δηλοῦσθον
(τῑμαόμεθα)	τῑμώμεθα	(ποιεόμεθα)	ποιούμεθα	(δηλοόμεθα)	δηλούμεθα
(τῑμάεσθε)	τῑμᾶσθε	(ποιέεσθε)	ποιεῖσθε	(δηλόεσθε)	δηλοῦσθε
(τῑμάονται)	τῑμῶνται	(ποιέονται)	ποιοῦνται	(δηλόονται)	δηλοῦνται

Present Subjunctive

(τῑμάωμαι)	τῑμῶμαι	(ποιέωμαι)	ποιῶμαι	(δηλόωμαι)	δηλῶμαι
(τῑμάῃ)	τῑμᾷ	(ποιέῃ)	ποιῇ	(δηλόῃ)	δηλοῖ
(τῑμάηται)	τῑμᾶται	(ποιέηται)	ποιῆται	(δηλόηται)	δηλῶται
(τῑμάησθον)	τῑμᾶσθον	(ποιέησθον)	ποιῆσθον	(δηλόησθον)	δηλῶσθον
(τῑμάησθον)	τῑμᾶσθον	(ποιέησθον)	ποιῆσθον	(δηλόησθον)	δηλῶσθον
(τῑμαώμεθα)	τῑμώμεθα	(ποιεώμεθα)	ποιώμεθα	(δηλοώμεθα)	δηλώμεθα
(τῑμάησθε)	τῑμᾶσθε	(ποιέησθε)	ποιῆσθε	(δηλόησθε)	δηλῶσθε
(τῑμάωνται)	τῑμῶνται	(ποιέωνται)	ποιῶνται	(δηλόωνται)	δηλῶνται

Present Optative

(τῑμαοίμην)	τῑμῴμην	(ποιεοίμην)	ποιοίμην	(δηλοοίμην)	δηλοίμην
(τῑμάοιο)	τῑμῷο	(ποιέοιο)	ποιοῖο	(δηλόοιο)	δηλοῖο
(τῑμάοιτο)	τῑμῷτο	(ποιέοιτο)	ποιοῖτο	(δηλόοιτο)	δηλοῖτο
(τῑμάοισθον)	τῑμῷσθον	(ποιέοισθον)	ποιοῖσθον	(δηλόοισθον)	δηλοῖσθον
(τῑμαοίσθην)	τῑμῷσθην	(ποιεοίσθην)	ποιοίσθην	(δηλοοίσθην)	δηλοίσθην
(τῑμαοίμεθα)	τῑμῴμεθα	(ποιεοίμεθα)	ποιοίμεθα	(δηλοοίμεθα)	δηλοίμεθα
(τῑμάοισθε)	τῑμῷσθε	(ποιέοισθε)	ποιοῖσθε	(δηλόοισθε)	δηλοῖσθε
(τῑμάοιντο)	τῑμῷντο	(ποιέοιντο)	ποιοῖντο	(δηλόοιντο)	δηλοῖντο

Present Imperative

(τῑμάου)	τῑμῶ	(ποίεου)	ποιοῦ	(δηλόου)	δηλοῦ
(τῑμαέσθω)	τῑμάσθω	(ποιεέσθω)	ποιείσθω	(δηλοέσθω)	δηλούσθω
(τῑμάεσθον)	τῑμᾶσθον	(ποιέεσθον)	ποιεῖσθον	(δηλόεσθον)	δηλοῦσθον
(τῑμαέσθων)	τῑμάσθων	(ποιεέσθων)	ποιείσθων	(δηλοέσθων)	δηλούσθων
(τῑμάεσθε)	τῑμᾶσθε	(ποιέεσθε)	ποιεῖσθε	(δηλόεσθε)	δηλοῦσθε
(τῑμαέσθων)	τῑμάσθων	(ποιεέσθων)	ποιείσθων	(δηλοέσθων)	δηλούσθων

Present Infinitive

(τῑμάεσθαι)	τῑμᾶσθαι	(ποιέεσθαι)	ποιεῖσθαι	(δηλόεσθαι)	δηλοῦσθαι

Present Participle

(τῑμαόμενος)	τῑμώμενος	(ποιεόμενος)	ποιούμενος	(δηλοόμενος)	δηλούμενος

Imperfect

(ἐτῑμαόμην)	ἐτῑμώμην	(ἐποιεόμην)	ἐποιούμην	(ἐδηλοόμην)	ἐδηλούμην
(ἐτῑμάου)	ἐτῑμῶ	(ἐποιέου)	ἐποιοῦ	(ἐδηλόου)	ἐδηλοῦ
(ἐτῑμάετο)	ἐτῑμᾶτο	(ἐποιέετο)	ἐποιεῖτο	(ἐδηλόετο)	ἐδηλοῦτο
(ἐτῑμάεσθον)	ἐτῑμᾶσθον	(ἐποιέεσθον)	ἐποιεῖσθον	(ἐδηλόεσθον)	ἐδηλοῦσθον
(ἐτῑμαέσθην)	ἐτῑμάσθην	(ἐποιεέσθην)	ἐποιείσθην	(ἐδηλοέσθην)	ἐδηλούσθην
(ἐτῑμαόμεθα)	ἐτῑμώμεθα	(ἐποιεόμεθα)	ἐποιούμεθα	(ἐδηλοόμεθα)	ἐδηλούμεθα
(ἐτῑμάεσθε)	ἐτῑμᾶσθε	(ἐποιέεσθε)	ἐποιεῖσθε	(ἐδηλόεσθε)	ἐδηλοῦσθε
(ἐτῑμάοντο)	ἐτῑμῶντο	(ἐποιέοντο)	ἐποιοῦντο	(ἐδηλόοντο)	ἐδηλοῦντο

649. SYNOPSIS OF IRREGULAR FORMS OF VERBS IN μι

	Indicative	Subjunctive	Optative	Imperative	Infinitive	Participle
Present	ἵστημι	ἱστῶ	ἱσταίην	ἵστη	ἱστάναι	ἱστάς
	τίθημι	τιθῶ	τιθείην	τίθει	τιθέναι	τιθείς
	δίδωμι	διδῶ	διδοίην	δίδου	διδόναι	διδούς
	δείκνῡμι	δεικνύω	δεικνύοιμι	δείκνῡ	δεικνύναι	δεικνύς
Imperfect	ἵστην					
	ἐτίθην					
	ἐδίδουν					
	ἐδείκνῡν					

Indicative	Subjunctive	Optative	Imperative	Infinitive	Participle
ἔστην	στῶ	σταίην	στῆθι	στῆναι	στάς
(ἔθην)	θῶ	θείην	θές	θεῖναι	θείς
(ἔδων)	δῶ	δοίην	δός	δοῦναι	δούς
ἔδῦν	δύω	———	δῦθι	δῦναι	δύς

(left margin label: 2 Aorist)

PASSIVE AND MIDDLE

ἵσταμαι	ἱστῶμαι	ἱσταίμην	ἵστασο	ἵστασθαι	ἱστάμενος
τίθεμαι	τιθῶμαι	τιθείμην	τίθεσο	τίθεσθαι	τιθέμενος
δίδομαι	διδῶμαι	διδοίμην	δίδοσο	δίδοσθαι	διδόμενος
δείκνυμαι	δεικνύωμαι	δεικνυοίμην	δείκνυσο	δείκνυσθαι	δεικνύμενος

(left margin label: Present)

ἱστάμην					
ἐτιθέμην					
ἐδιδόμην					
ἐδεικνύμην					

(left margin label: Imperfect)

ἐπριάμην	πρίωμαι	πριαίμην	πρίω	πρίασθαι	πριάμενος
ἐθέμην	θῶμαι	θείμην	θοῦ	θέσθαι	θέμενος
ἐδόμην	δῶμαι	δοίμην	δοῦ	δόσθαι	δόμενος

(left margin label: 2 Aorist Middle)

650.   ACTIVE VOICE OF VERBS IN μι.

PRESENT INDICATIVE

(handwritten annotations: set make / stand, stop. — put place. — give — show, point out)

ἵστημι	τίθημι	δίδωμι	δείκνῦμι
ἵστης	τίθης	δίδως	δείκνῦς
ἵστησι	τίθησι	δίδωσι	δείκνῦσι
ἵστατον	τίθετον	δίδοτον	δείκνυτον
ἵστατον	τίθετον	δίδοτον	δείκνυτον
ἵσταμεν	τίθεμεν	δίδομεν	δείκνυμεν
ἵστατε	τίθετε	δίδοτε	δείκνυτε
ἱστᾶσι	τιθέᾱσι	διδόᾱσι	δεικνύᾱσι

IMPERFECT

ἵστην	ἐτίθην	ἐδίδουν	ἐδείκνῦν
ἵστης	ἐτίθεις	ἐδίδους	ἐδείκνῦς
ἵστη	ἐτίθει	ἐδίδου	ἐδείκνῦ
ἵστατον	ἐτίθετον	ἐδίδοτον	ἐδείκνυτον
ἱστάτην	ἐτιθέτην	ἐδιδότην	ἐδεικνύτην
ἵσταμεν	ἐτίθεμεν	ἐδίδομεν	ἐδείκνυμεν
ἵστατε	ἐτίθετε	ἐδίδοτε	ἐδείκνυτε
ἵστασαν	ἐτίθεσαν	ἐδίδοσαν	ἐδείκνυσαν

PRESENT SUBJUNCTIVE

ἱστῶ	τιθῶ	διδῶ	δεικνύω _like_
ἱστῇς	τιθῇς	διδῷς	δεικνύῃς
ἱστῇ	τιθῇ	διδῷ	δεικνύῃ
ἱστῆτον	τιθῆτον	διδῶτον	δεικνύητον
ἱστῆτον	τιθῆτον	διδῶτον	δεικνύητον
ἱστῶμεν	τιθῶμεν	διδῶμεν	δεικνύωμεν
ἱστῆτε	τιθῆτε	διδῶτε	δεικνύητε
ἱστῶσι	τιθῶσι	διδῶσι	δεικνύωσι

PRESENT OPTATIVE

ἱσταίην	τιθείην	διδοίην	δεικνύοιμι _like_
ἱσταίης	τιθείης	διδοίης	δεικνύοις
ἱσταίη	τιθείη	διδοίη	δεικνύοι
ἱσταίητον	τιθείητον	διδοίητον	δεικνύοιτον
ἱσταιήτην	τιθειήτην	διδοιήτην	δεικνυοίτην
ἱσταίημεν	τιθείημεν	διδοίημεν	δεικνύοιμεν
ἱσταίητε	τιθείητε	διδοίητε	δεικνύοιτε
ἱσταίησαν	τιθείησαν	διδοίησαν	δεικνύοιεν

or more commonly

ἱσταῖτον	τιθεῖτον	διδοῖτον
ἱσταίτην	τιθείτην	διδοίτην
ἱσταῖμεν	τιθεῖμεν	διδοῖμεν
ἱσταῖτε	τιθεῖτε	διδοῖτε
ἱσταῖεν	τιθεῖεν	διδοῖεν

PRESENT IMPERATIVE

ἵστη (ἵστα-ε)	τίθει (τίθε·ε)	δίδου (δίδο-ε)	δείκνῡ
ἱστάτω	τιθέτω	διδότω	δεικνύτω
ἵστατον	τίθετον	δίδοτον	δείκνυτον
ἱστάτων	τιθέτων	διδότων	δεικνύτων
ἵστατε	τίθετε	δίδοτε	δείκνυτε
ἱστάντων	τιθέντων	διδόντων	δεικνύντων

PRESENT INFINITIVE

ἱστάναι	τιθέναι	διδόναι	δεικνύναι

PRESENT PARTICIPLE

ἱστάς §620	τιθείς	διδούς §618	δεικνύς §619

see λυθείς
§619.

651.

SECOND AORIST INDICATIVE

ἔστην	[ἔθην] *ἔθηκα*	[ἔδων] *ἔδωκα*	ἔδῡν[1]
ἔστης	[ἔθης] *ἔθηκας*	[ἔδως] *ἔδωκας*	ἔδῡς
ἔστη	[ἔθη] *ἔθηκε*	[ἔδω] *ἔδωκε*	ἔδῡ
ἔστητον	ἔθετον	ἔδοτον	ἔδῡτον
ἐστήτην	ἐθέτην	ἐδότην	ἐδύτην
ἔστημεν	ἔθεμεν *ἐθήκαμεν*	ἔδομεν *ἐδώκαμεν*	ἔδῡμεν
ἔστητε	ἔθετε *ἐθήκατε*	ἔδοτε *ἐδώκατε*	ἔδῡτε
ἔστησαν	ἔθεσαν *ἐθήκαν*	ἔδοσαν *ἐδώκαν*	ἔδῡσαν

SECOND AORIST SUBJUNCTIVE

στῶ	θῶ	δῶ	δύω
στῇς	θῇς	δῷς	δύῃς
στῇ	θῇ	δῷ	δύῃ
στῆτον	θῆτον	δῶτον	δύητον
στῆτον	θῆτον	δῶτον	δύητον
στῶμεν	θῶμεν	δῶμεν	δύωμεν
στῆτε	θῆτε	δῶτε	δύητε
στῶσι	θῶσι	δῶσι	δύωσι

SECOND AORIST OPTATIVE

σταίην	θείην	δοίην
σταίης	θείης	δοίης
σταίη	θείη	δοίη
σταίητον	θείητον	δοίητον
σταιήτην	θειήτην	δοιήτην
σταίημεν	θείημεν	δοίημεν
σταίητε	θείητε	δοίητε
σταίησαν	θείησαν	δοίησαν

or more commonly

σταῖτον	θεῖτον	δοῖτον
σταίτην	θείτην	δοίτην
σταῖμεν	θεῖμεν	δοῖμεν
σταῖτε	θεῖτε	δοῖτε
σταῖεν	θεῖεν	δοῖεν

---

[1] Second aorist of δύω, *enter*.

SECOND AORIST IMPERATIVE

στῆθι	θές	δός	δῦθι
στήτω	θέτω	δότω	δύτω
στῆτον	θέτον	δότον	δῦτον
στήτων	θέτων	δότων	δύτων
στῆτε	θέτε	δότε	δῦτε
στάντων	θέντων	δόντων	δύντων

SECOND AORIST INFINITIVE

στῆναι	θεῖναι	δοῦναι	δῦναι

SECOND AORIST PARTICIPLE

στάς	θείς	δούς	δύς

652. MIDDLE (PASSIVE) VOICE OF VERBS IN μι

PRESENT INDICATIVE

ἵσταμαι	τίθεμαι	δίδομαι	δείκνυμαι
ἵστασαι	τίθεσαι	δίδοσαι	δείκνυσαι
ἵσταται	τίθεται	δίδοται	δείκνυται
ἵστασθον	τίθεσθον	δίδοσθον	δείκνυσθον
ἵστασθον	τίθεσθον	δίδοσθον	δείκνυσθον
ἱστάμεθα	τιθέμεθα	διδόμεθα	δεικνύμεθα
ἵστασθε	τίθεσθε	δίδοσθε	δείκνυσθε
ἵστανται	τίθενται	δίδονται	δείκνυνται

IMPERFECT

ἱστάμην	ἐτιθέμην	ἐδιδόμην	ἐδεικνύμην
ἵστασο	ἐτίθεσο	ἐδίδοσο	ἐδείκνυσο
ἵστατο	ἐτίθετο	ἐδίδοτο	ἐδείκνυτο
ἵστασθον	ἐτίθεσθον	ἐδίδοσθον	ἐδείκνυσθον
ἱστάσθην	ἐτιθέσθην	ἐδιδόσθην	ἐδεικνύσθην
ἱστάμεθα	ἐτιθέμεθα	ἐδιδόμεθα	ἐδεικνύμεθα
ἵστασθε	ἐτίθεσθε	ἐδίδοσθε	ἐδείκνυσθε
ἵσταντο	ἐτίθεντο	ἐδίδοντο	ἐδείκνυντο

PRESENT SUBJUNCTIVE

ἱστῶμαι	τιθῶμαι	διδῶμαι	δεικνύωμαι
ἱστῇ	τιθῇ	διδῷ	δεικνύῃ
ἱστῆται	τιθῆται	διδῶται	δεικνύηται
ἱστῆσθον	τιθῆσθον	διδῶσθον	δεικνύησθον
ἱστῆσθον	τιθῆσθον	διδῶσθον	δεικνύησθον
ἱστώμεθα	τιθώμεθα	διδώμεθα	δεικνυώμεθα
ἱστῆσθε	τιθῆσθε	διδῶσθε	δεικνύησθε
ἱστῶνται	τιθῶνται	διδῶνται	δεικνύωνται

The middle voice always has a short stem.

like λύω

PRESENT OPTATIVE

ἱσταίμην	τιθείμην	διδοίμην	δεικνυοίμην
ἱσταῖο	τιθεῖο	διδοῖο	δεικνύοιο
ἱσταῖτο	τιθεῖτο	διδοῖτο	δεικνύοιτο
ἱσταῖσθον	τιθεῖσθον	διδοῖσθον	δεικνύοισθον
ἱσταίσθην	τιθείσθην	διδοίσθην	δεικνυοίσθην
ἱσταίμεθα	τιθείμεθα	διδοίμεθα	δεικνυοίμεθα
ἱσταῖσθε	τιθεῖσθε	διδοῖσθε	δεικνύοισθε
ἱσταῖντο	τιθεῖντο	διδοῖντο	δεικνύοιντο

PRESENT IMPERATIVE

ἵστασο	τίθεσο	δίδοσο	δείκνυσο
ἱστάσθω	τιθέσθω	διδόσθω	δεικνύσθω
ἵστασθον	τίθεσθον	δίδοσθον	δείκνυσθον
ἱστάσθων	τιθέσθων	διδόσθων	δεικνύσθων
ἵστασθε	τίθεσθε	δίδοσθε	δείκνυσθε
ἱστάσθων	τιθέσθων	διδόσθων	δεικνύσθων

PRESENT INFINITIVE

ἐπιστά-θωσαν

ἵστασθαι	τίθεσθαι	δίδοσθαι	δείκνυσθαι

PRESENT PARTICIPLE

ἱστάμενος	τιθέμενος	διδόμενος	δεικνύμενος

δεικνυμένη
δεικνύμενον

653. SECOND AORIST MIDDLE OF VERBS IN μι

INDICATIVE

ἐπριάμην[1]	ἐθέμην	ἐδόμην
ἐπρίω	ἔθου	ἔδου
ἐπρίατο	ἔθετο	ἔδοτο
ἐπρίασθον	ἔθεσθον	ἔδοσθον
ἐπριάσθην	ἐθέσθην	ἐδόσθην
ἐπριάμεθα	ἐθέμεθα	ἐδόμεθα
ἐπρίασθε	ἔθεσθε	ἔδοσθε
ἐπρίαντο	ἔθεντο	ἔδοντο

ἔθετο = ἔθου

SUBJUNCTIVE

πρίωμαι	θῶμαι	δῶμαι
πρίῃ	θῇ	δῷ
πρίηται	θῆται	δῶται
πρίησθον	θῆσθον	δῶσθον
πρίησθον	θῆσθον	δῶσθον
πριώμεθα	θώμεθα	δώμεθα
πρίησθε	θῆσθε	δῶσθε
πρίωνται	θῶνται	δῶνται

---

[1] Used as second aorist of ὠνέομαι, *buy.*   ἵστημι lacks 2 aor. mid

OPTATIVE

πριαίμην	θείμην	δοίμην
πρίαιο	θεῖο	δοῖο
πρίαιτο	θεῖτο	δοῖτο
πρίαισθον	θεῖσθον	δοῖσθον
πριαίσθην	θείσθην	δοίσθην
πριαίμεθα	θείμεθα	δοίμεθα
πρίαισθε	θεῖσθε	δοῖσθε
πρίαιντο	θεῖντο	δοῖντο

IMPERATIVE

πρίω	θοῦ	δοῦ
πριάσθω	θέσθω	δόσθω
πρίασθον	θέσθον	δόσθον
πριάσθων	θέσθων	δόσθων
πρίασθε	θέσθε	δόσθε
πριάσθων	θέσθων	δόσθων

INFINITIVE

πρίασθαι	θέσθαι	δόσθαι

PARTICIPLE

πριάμενος, η, ον	θέμενος, η, ον	δόμενος, η, ον

654.   SECOND PERFECT ACTIVE OF ἵστημι

INDICATIVE	SUBJUNCTIVE	OPTATIVE	IMPERATIVE
(ἕστηκα)	ἑστῶ	ἑσταίην	
(ἕστηκας)	ἑστῇς	ἑσταίης	ἕσταθι
(ἕστηκε)	ἑστῇ	ἑσταίη	ἑστάτω
ἕστατον	ἑστῆτον	ἑσταῖτον, -αίητον	ἕστατον
ἕστατον	ἑστῆτον	ἑσταίτην, -αιήτην	ἑστάτων
ἕσταμεν	ἑστῶμεν	ἑσταῖμεν, -αίημεν	
ἕστατε	ἑστῆτε	ἑσταῖτε, -αίητε	ἕστατε
ἑστᾶσι	ἑστῶσι	ἑσταῖεν, -αίησαν	ἑστάντων

INFINITIVE	PARTICIPLE
ἑστάναι	ἑστώς, ῶσα, ός

SECOND PLUPERFECT

(εἰστήκη)		ἕσταμεν
(εἰστήκης)	ἕστατον	ἕστατε
(εἰστήκει)	ἑστάτην	<u>ἕστασαν</u>

655. PRESENT AND FUTURE SYSTEMS OF εἰμί [ἐσ], *be*

PRESENT   IMPERFECT

INDICATIVE	SUBJUNCTIVE	OPTATIVE	IMPERATIVE	IMPERFECT
εἰμί	ὦ	εἴην		ἦν, ἦ
εἶ	ᾖς	εἴης	ἴσθι	ἦσθα
ἐστί (ν)	ᾖ	εἴη	ἔστω	ἦν
ἐστόν	ἦτον	εἶτον, εἴητον	ἔστον	ἦστον, ἦτον
ἐστόν	ἦτον	εἴτην, εἰήτην	ἔστων	ἤστην, ἤτην
ἐσμέν	ὦμεν	εἶμεν, εἴημεν		ἦμεν
ἐστέ	ἦτε	εἶτε, εἴητε	ἔστε	ἦστε, ἦτε
εἰσί (ν)	ὦσι	εἶεν, εἴησαν	ἔστων	ἦσαν

Infinitive εἶναι, Participle ὤν, οὖσα, ὄν §617

FUTURE (MIDDLE)

INDICATIVE	OPTATIVE	INFINITIVE	PARTICIPLE
ἔσομαι	ἐσοίμην	ἔσεσθαι	ἐσόμενος
ἔσει	ἔσοιο		
ἔσται	ἔσοιτο		
ἔσεσθον	ἔσοισθον		
ἔσεσθον	ἐσοίσθην		
ἐσόμεθα	ἐσοίμεθα		
ἔσεσθε	ἔσοισθε		
ἔσονται	ἔσοιντο		

656. PRESENT SYSTEM OF εἶμι [ι], *go*

PRESENT   IMPERFECT *optional*

INDICATIVE	SUBJUNCTIVE	OPTATIVE	IMPERATIVE	IMPERFECT
εἶμι	ἴω	ἴοιμι, ἰοίην		ᾖα, ᾔειν
εἶ	ἴῃς	ἴοις	ἴθι	ᾔεις, ᾔεισθα
εἶσι	ἴῃ	ἴοι	ἴτω	ᾔει, ᾔειν
ἴτον	ἴητον	ἴοιτον	ἴτον	ἴ̈τον
ἴτον	ἴητον	ἰοίτην	ἴτων	ᾔτην
ἴμεν	ἴωμεν	ἴοιμεν		ᾖμεν
ἴτε	ἴητε	ἴοιτε	ἴτε	ᾖτε
ἴᾱσι	ἴωσι	ἴοιεν	ἰόντων	ᾖσαν, ᾔεσαν

Infinitive ἰέναι, Participle ἰών ἰοῦσα, ἰόν

IRREGULAR VERBS IN μι

657. οἶδα [ἰδ], *know*

	SECOND PERFECT			SECOND PLUPERFECT
INDICATIVE	SUBJUNCTIVE	OPTATIVE	IMPERATIVE	
οἶδα	εἰδῶ	εἰδείην		ᾔδη, ᾔδειν
οἶσθα	εἰδῇς	εἰδείης	ἴσθι	ᾔδησθα, ᾔδεισθα
οἶδε	εἰδῇ	εἰδείη	ἴστω	ᾔδει, ᾔδειν
ἴστον	εἰδῆτον	εἰδεῖτον	ἴστον	ᾖστον
ἴστον	εἰδῆτον	εἰδείτην	ἴστων	ᾖστην
ἴσμεν	εἰδῶμεν	εἰδεῖμεν, εἰδείημεν		ᾖσμεν
ἴστε	εἰδῆτε	εἰδεῖτε, εἰδείητε	ἴστε	ᾖστε
ἴσᾱσι	εἰδῶσι	εἰδεῖεν, εἰδείησαν	ἴστων	ᾖσαν, ᾔδεσαν

INFINITIVE	PARTICIPLE
εἰδέναι	εἰδώς, εἰδυῖα, εἰδός, gen. εἰδότος, *etc.*

658. φημί [φα], *say*

	PRESENT			
INDICATIVE	SUBJUNCTIVE	OPTATIVE	IMPERATIVE	INFINITIVE
φημί	φῶ	φαίην		φάναι
φής	φῇς	φαίης	φαθί, φάθι	
φησί	φῇ	φαίη	φάτω	
φατόν	φῆτον	φαῖτον, φαίητον	φάτον	
φατόν	φῆτον	φαίτην, φαιήτην	φάτων	
φαμέν	φῶμεν	φαῖμεν, φαίημεν		
φατέ	φῆτε	φαῖτε, φαίητε	φάτε	
φᾱσί	φῶσι	φαῖεν, φαίησαν	φάντων	

	IMPERFECT		
ἔφην			ἔφαμεν
ἔφησθα, ἔφης	ἔφατον		ἔφατε
ἔφη	ἐφάτην		ἔφασαν

659. ἵημι [ἑ], *send*

	PRESENT				
INDICATIVE	SUBJUNCTIVE	OPTATIVE	IMPERATIVE	INFINITIVE	PARTICIPLE
ἵημι	ἱῶ	ἱείην		ἱέναι	ἱείς, ἱεῖσα, ἱέν
ἵης	ἱῇς	ἱείης	ἵει		
ἵησι	ἱῇ	ἱείη	ἱέτω		
ἵετον	ἱῆτον	ἱεῖτον, ἱείητον	ἵετον		
ἵετον	ἱῆτον	ἱείτην, ἱειήτην	ἱέτων		
ἵεμεν	ἱῶμεν	ἱεῖμεν, ἱείημεν			
ἵετε	ἱῆτε	ἱεῖτε, ἱείητε	ἵετε		
ἱᾶσι	ἱῶσι	ἱεῖεν, ἱείησαν	ἱέντων		

IMPERFECT

ἵην		ἵεμεν
ἵεις	ἵετον	ἵετε
ἵει	ἱέτην	ἵεσαν

Future   *First Aorist*   *Perfect* (in composition)

ἥσω, etc., regular   ἧκα, ἧκας, ἧκε, only in indic.   εἷκα, etc., regular

SECOND AORIST (generally in composition)

INDICATIVE	SUBJUNCTIVE	OPTATIVE	IMPERATIVE	INFINITIVE	PARTICIPLE
	ὧ	εἵην		εἷναι	εἵς, εἷσα, ἕν
	ἧς	εἵης	ἕς		
	ῇ	εἵη	ἕτω		
εἷτον	ἧτον	εἷτον, εἵητον	ἕτον		
εἵτην	ἧτον	εἵτην, εἱήτην	ἕτων		
εἷμεν	ὧμεν	εἷμεν, εἵημεν			
εἷτε	ἧτε	εἷτε, εἵητε	ἕτε		
εἷσαν	ὧσι	εἷεν, εἵησαν	ἕντων		

MIDDLE

PRESENT

INDICATIVE	SUBJUNCTIVE	OPTATIVE	IMPERATIVE	INFINITIVE	PARTICIPLE
ἵεμαι	ἱῶμαι	ἱείμην		ἵεσθαι	ἱέμενος
ἵεσαι	ἱῇ	ἱεῖο	ἵεσο		
ἵεται	ἱῆται	ἱεῖτο	ἱέσθω		
ἵεσθον	ἱῆσθον	ἱεῖσθον	ἵεσθον		
ἵεσθον	ἱῆσθον	ἱείσθην	ἱέσθων		
ἱέμεθα	ἱώμεθα	ἱείμεθα			
ἵεσθε	ἱῆσθε	ἱεῖσθε	ἵεσθε		
ἵενται	ἱῶνται	ἱεῖντο	ἱέσθων		

IMPERFECT

ἱέμην		ἱέμεθα
ἵεσο	ἵεσθον	ἵεσθε
ἵετο	ἱέσθην	ἵεντο

Future (in composition)   *First Aorist* (in composition)

ἥσομαι, etc., regular   ἡκάμην, only in indic.

Perfect (in composition)

εἷμαι (imper. εἷσθω; infin. εἷσθαι; partic. εἱμένος)

SECOND AORIST (generally in composition)

INDICATIVE	SUBJUNCTIVE	OPTATIVE	IMPERATIVE	INFINITIVE	PARTICIPLE
εἵμην	ὦμαι	εἵμην		ἕσθαι	ἕμενος
εἷσο	ᾖ	εἷο	οὗ		
εἷτο	ἧται	εἷτο	ἕσθω		
εἷσθον	ἧσθον	εἷσθον	ἕσθον		
εἵσθην	ἧσθον	εἵσθην	ἕσθων		
εἵμεθα	ὥμεθα	εἵμεθα			
εἷσθε	ἧσθε	εἷσθε	ἕσθε		
εἷντο	ὧνται	εἷντο	ἕσθων		

Aorist Passive (in composition)　　　*Future Passive* (in composition)
εἵθην (subj. ἑθῶ; partic. ἑθείς)　　　ἑθήσομαι

IRREGULAR VERBS IN μι

660.　　　　κεῖμαι [κει], *lie*

PRESENT

INDICATIVE	SUBJUNCTIVE	OPTATIVF	IMPERATIVE	INFINITIVE	PARTICIPLE
κεῖμαι	κέωμαι	κεοίμην		κεῖσθαι	κείμενος
κεῖσαι	κέῃ	κέοιο	κεῖσο		
κεῖται	κέηται	κέοιτο	κείσθω		
κεῖσθον	κέησθον	κέοισθον	κεῖσθον		
κεῖσθον	κέησθον	κεοίσθην	κείσθων		
κείμεθα	κεώμεθα	κεοίμεθα			
κεῖσθε	κέησθε	κέοισθε	κεῖσθε		
κεῖνται	κέωνται	κέοιντο	κείσθων		

IMPERFECT

ἐκείμην		ἐκείμεθα
ἔκεισο	ἔκεισθον	ἔκεισθε
ἔκειτο	ἐκείσθην	ἔκειντο

661.　　　　κάθημαι [ησ], *sit down*

PRESENT

INDICATIVE	SUBJUNCTIVE	OPTATIVE	IMPERATIVE	INFINITIVE	PARTICIPLE
κάθημαι	καθῶμαι	καθοίμην		καθῆσθαι	καθήμενος
κάθησαι	καθῇ	καθοῖο	κάθησο		
κάθηται	καθῆται	καθοῖτο	καθήσθω		
κάθησθcν	καθῆσθον	καθοῖσθον	κάθησθον		
κάθησθον	καθῆσθον	καθοίσθην	καθήσθων		
καθήμεθα	καθώμεθα	καθοίμεθα			
κάθησθε	καθῆσθε	καθοῖσθε	κάθησθε		
κάθηνται	καθῶνται	καθοῖντο	καθήσθων		

IMPERFECT

ἐκαθήμην, καθήμην		ἐκαθήμεθα, καθήμεθα
ἐκάθησο, καθῆσο	ἐκάθησθον, καθῆσθον	ἐκάθησθε, καθῆσθε
ἐκάθητο, καθῆστο	ἐκαθήσθην, καθήσθην	ἐκάθηντο, καθῆντο

662.   SECOND AORIST OF μι-VERBS

ACTIVE

βαίνω [βα], go

INDICATIVE	SUBJUNCTIVE	OPTATIVE	IMPERATIVE	INFIN.	PART.
ἔβην	βῶ	βαίην		βῆναι	βάς
ἔβης	βῇς	βαίης	βῆθι		
ἔβη	βῇ	βαίη	βήτω		
ἔβητον	βῆτον	βαῖτον	βῆτον		
ἐβήτην	βῆτον	βαίτην	βήτων		
ἔβημεν	βῶμεν	βαῖμεν			
ἔβητε	βῆτε	βαῖτε	βῆτε		
ἔβησαν	βῶσι	βαῖεν	βάντων		

φθάνω [φθα], anticipate

ἔφθην	φθῶ	φθαίην		φθῆναι	φθάς
ἔφθης	φθῇς	φθαίης			
ἔφθη	φθῇ	φθαίη			
ἔφθητον	φθῆτον	φθαῖτον			
ἐφθήτην	φθῆτον	φθαίτην			
ἔφθημεν	φθῶμεν	φθαῖμεν			
ἔφθητε	φθῆτε	φθαῖτε			
ἔφθησαν	φθῶσι	φθαῖεν			

διδράσκω [δρα], run

ἔδρᾱν	δρῶ	δραίην		δρᾶναι	δράς
ἔδρᾱς	δρᾷς	δραίης			
ἔδρᾱ	δρᾷ	δραίη			
ἔδρᾱτον	δρᾶτον	δραῖτον			
ἐδράτην	δρᾶτον	δραίτην			
ἔδρᾱμεν	δρῶμεν	δραῖμεν			
ἔδρᾱτε	δρᾶτε	δραῖτε			
ἔδρᾱσαν	δρῶσι	δραῖεν			

ἁλίσκομαι [ἁλ, ἁλο], *catch*

INDICATIVE	SUBJUNCTIVE	OPTATIVE	IMPERATIVE	INFIN.	PART.
ἑάλων	ἁλῶ	ἁλοίην		ἁλῶναι	ἁλούς
ἑάλως	ἁλῷς	ἁλοίης			
ἑάλω	ἁλῷ	ἁλοίη			
ἑάλωτον	ἁλῶτον	ἁλοῖτον			
ἑᾱλώτην	ἁλῶτον	ἁλοίτην			
ἑάλωμεν	ἁλῶμεν	ἁλοῖμεν			
ἑάλωτε	ἁλῶτε	ἁλοῖτε			
ἑάλωσαν	ἁλῶσι	ἁλοῖεν			

γιγνώσκω [γνο], *know*

ἔγνων	γνῶ	γνοίην		γνῶναι	γνούς
ἔγνως	γνῷς	γνοίης	γνῶθι		
ἔγνω	γνῷ	γνοίη	γνώτω		
ἔγνωτον	γνῶτον	γνοῖτον	γνῶτον		
ἐγνώτην	γνῶτον	γνοίτην	γνώτων		
ἔγνωμεν	γνῶμεν	γνοῖμεν			
ἔγνωτε	γνῶτε	γνοῖτε	γνῶτε		
ἔγνωσαν	γνῶσι	γνοῖεν	γνόντων		

VOCABULARIES

ENGLISH-GREEK VOCABULARY

A

abandon, ἐκλείπω.
able, ἱκανός.
able, to be, δύναμαι.
above, ὑπέρ (gen.).
Abydus, Ἄβῡδος, ου, ἡ.
accomplish, καταπρᾱ́ττω.
accomplish, help to, συμπρᾱ́ττω.
according to, ὡς.
accordingly, οὖν.
account, on this, διὰ τοῦτο.
accuse, αἰτιάομαι.
acropolis, ἀκρόπολις, εως, ἡ.
advance, ἐπιχωρέω.
against, ἐπί, πρός (acc.).
aid, ὠφελέω.
all, πᾶς.
along side of, παρά (acc., dat.).
also, καί.
always, ἀεί.
amazed, to be, θαυμάζω.
among, ἐν (dat.).
and, καί.
animal, θηρίον, ου, τό.
announce, ἀγγέλλω.
annoy, ἀνῑάω.
annoyed, to be, ἄχθομαι.
another, ἄλλος, ἕτερος.
any one, τὶς.
Apollo, Ἀπόλλων, ωνος, ὁ.
arise, ἀνίστημι, γίγνομαι.
Aristippus, Ἀρίστιππος, ου, ὁ.
armor, ὅπλα, ων, τά.
army, στράτευμα, ατος, τό, στρατιᾱ́,
ᾶς, ἡ.
arrange, συντάττω.
array, τάξις, εως, ἡ.

arrest, συλλαμβάνω.
Artaxerxes, Ἀρταξέρξης, ου, ὁ.
as, as if, ὡς.
ask for, αἰτέω.
assemble, ἀθροίζω, συλλέγω.
assembly, ἐκκλησίᾱ, ᾶς, ἡ.
assist, ὠφελέω.
at, ἐπί (dat. w. verb of rest), εἰς.
at home, οἴκοι.
at once, εὐθύς.
at that time, τότε.
at the same time, ἅμα.
attack, make an, ἔπειμι (dat.).
attempt, πειράομαι.

B

barbarian, βάρβαρος, ου, ὁ.
barely, μῑκρόν.
barley, κρῑθή, ῆς, ἡ.
battle, μάχη, ης, ἡ.
be, εἰμί.
bear, φέρω.
beast, θηρίον, ου, τό.
beautiful, καλός.
because, ὅτι.
because of, διά (acc.).
become, γίγνομαι.
before, πρίν, πρότερος, πρό.
beg, δέομαι (gen.).
behold, ὁράω.
benefit, ὠφελέω.
besiege, πολιορκέω.
bid, κελεύω.
boat, πλοῖον, ου, τό.
Boeotian, Βοιώτιος, ου, ὁ.
both, ἀμφότερος, both . . . . and, καί
. . . . καί.

203

bridge, γέφῡρα, ᾱς, ἡ.
brightness (brilliancy), λαμπρότης,
    ητος, ἡ.
bring, ἄγω.
bring together, συλλέγω.
bronze, χαλκοῦς.
brother, ἀδελφός, οῦ, ὁ.
build, οἰκοδομέω.
but, ἀλλά, δέ.
by, ὑπό (agent, gen.), κατά (acc.)

C

call, καλέω.
calumniate, διαβάλλω.
canal, διῶρυξ, υχος, ἡ.
capable, ἱκανός.
carry, ἄγω, φέρω.
Castolus, Καστωλός, ου, ὁ.
cause trouble, πρᾱγματα παρέχω.
cavalry, ἱππεῖς, έων, οἱ.
cave, ἄντρον, ου, τό.
Celaenae, Κελαιναί, ῶν, αἱ.
center, μέσον, ου, τό.
certain, τὶς.
charge, ἀντίος εἶμι (dat.).
chariot, ἅρμα, ατος, τό.
chief, ἄρχων, οντος, ὁ.
chiton, χιτών, ῶνος, ὁ.
Cilicia, Κιλικίᾱ, ᾱς, ἡ.
Cilicians, Κίλικες, ων, οἱ.
city, πόλις, εως, ἡ.
claim, ἀξιόω.
Clearchus, Κλέαρχος, ου, ὁ.
clearly, δῆλος.
close, τελευτή, ῆς, ἡ.
collect, ἀθροίζω, συλλέγω.
colony, ἀποικίᾱ, ᾱς, ἡ.
come, ἔρχομαι.
come to terms with, συναλλάττω
    (πρός + acc.).
command, κελεύω.
commander, στρατηγός, οῦ, ὁ.

conquer, νῑκάω.
conquered, to be, ἡττάομαι.
consider, νομίζω.
consult with, συμβουλεύω (dat.).
contend, ἐρίζω.
contest, ἀγών, ῶνος, ὁ.
coöperate with, συμπρᾱττω (dat.).
counsel, to take — with, συμβου-
    λεύω (dat.).
country, χώρᾱ, ᾱς, ἡ.
cowardly, κακός.
custom, νόμος, ου, ὁ.
cut to pieces, κατακόπτω.
Cydnus, Κύδνος, ου, ὁ.
Cyrus, Κῦρος, ου, ὁ.

D

danger, κίνδῡνος, ου, ὁ.
daric, δᾱρεικός, οῦ, ὁ.
Darius, Δᾱρεῖος, ου, ὁ.
day, ἡμέρᾱ, ᾱς, ἡ.
day's journey, σταθμός, οῦ, ὁ.
death, put to, ἀποκτείνω.
decide, δοκέω (see Greek Vocab.).
deem right, ἀξιόω.
demand, ἀπαιτέω.
descend, καταβαίνω.
desire, βούλομαι.
destroy, ἀπόλλῡμι, διαρπάζω.
die, ἀποθνῄσκω.
discover, αἰσθάνομαι.
dishonor, in, ἄτῑμος.
dishonored, ἄτῑμος.
display, ἐπιδείκνῡμι.
ditch, διῶρυξ, υχος, ἡ.
do, ποιέω.
door, θύρα, ᾱς, ἡ.
draw up, τάττω.
drive by, παρελαύνω.
drive out, ἐκβάλλω.
due, to be, ὀφείλω.
dwell, οἰκέω.

E

earth, γῆ, γῆς, ἡ.
eighteen, ὀκτωκαίδεκα.
elder, πρεσβύτερος.
eleven, ἕνδεκα.
employ, χράομαι (dat.).
end, τελευτή, ῆς, ἡ.
enemy, πολέμιοι, ων, οἱ.
enlist, λαμβάνω.
enter, εἰσβάλλω.
entire, ὅλος, πᾶς.
Epyaxa, Ἐπύαξα, ης, ἡ.
escape, ἐκφεύγω.
exceedingly, ἰσχυρῶς.
except, πλήν.
excuse, πρόφασις, εως, ἡ.
exercise, γυμνάζω.
exile, φυγάς, άδος, ὁ. Vb. ἐκβάλλω.
expedition, make an, στρατεύω.
explain, δηλόω.
every sort, παντοδαπός.

F

father, πατήρ, πατρός, ὁ.
favor, ὑπάρχω (dat.).
fear, φόβος, ου, ὁ.
festival (Lycaean), Λύκαια, ων, τά.
few, ὀλίγοι.
fifteen, πεντεκαίδεκα.
fight, μάχομαι.
final, ἔσχατος.
find, εὑρίσκω.
first, πρῶτος.
fish, ἰχθύς, ύος, ὁ.
five, πέντε.
flay, ἐκδέρω.
flee, φεύγω.
flow, ῥέω.
follow, ἕπομαι (dat.).
follows, as, τάδε.
following day, the, τῇ ὑστεραίᾳ.
following manner, in the, τόνδε
  τὸν τρόπον.

foot, πούς, ποδός, ὁ.
for, conj., γάρ.
formerly, τὸ ἀρχαῖον.
forward, go, πρόειμι, προέρχομαι.
fountain, κρήνη, ης, ἡ.
four, τέτταρες.
friend, φίλος, ου, ὁ.
friendly, φίλος.
frightened, ppl. of φοβέομαι.
from, ἀπό, ἐκ.
from there, ἐντεῦθεν.
fugitive, φυγάς, άδος, ὁ.
full of, πλήρης.
furnish, παρέχω.

G

garrison commander, φρούραρχος
  ου, ὁ.
gather, ἀθροίζω, συλλέγω.
general, στρατηγός, οῦ, ὁ.
gift, δῶρον, ου, τό.
give, δίδωμι, παρέχω.
gladly, ἡδέως.
go, εἶμι, ἔρχομαι.
go away, ἀπέρχομαι.
go down, καταβαίνω.
go forward, πρόειμι.
go up, ἀναβαίνω.
god, θεός, οῦ, ὁ.
gold, χρυσίον, ου, τό.
good, ἀγαθός.
goods, τὰ ὤνια.
great, μέγας.
Greek, Ἑλληνικός; Ἕλλην, ηνος, ὁ.
ground, on the—that, ὡς.
guard, φυλάττω.
guest-friend, ξένος, ου, ὁ.

H

halt, ἵστημι.
hand, to be on, παραγίγνομαι.
happen, τυγχάνω.
happen upon, ἐντυγχάνω (dat.).

harbor, λιμήν, ένος, ό.
hard pressed, to be, πιέζομαι.
have, ἔχω.
he, ὁ δὲ, *and he, but he;* sometimes
   οὗτος or ἐκεῖνος = *he.*
hear, ἀκούω.
heavy-armed soldier, ὁπλίτης, ου, ὁ.
heights, ἄκρα, ων, τά.
Hellespont, Ἑλλήσποντος, ου, ὁ.
helmet, κράνος, ους, τό.
help to accomplish, συμπράττω.
herald, κῆρυξ, ῦκος, ὁ.
hide, δέρμα, ατος, τό.
him, αὐτός in oblique cases.
hinder, κωλύω.
hired soldier, ξένος, ου, ὁ.
his, αὐτοῦ.
hold, ἔχω.
home, at, οἴκοι.
homeward, οἴκαδε.
honor, τῑμάω.
honorable, καλός, τίμιος.
hope, ἐλπίς, ίδος, ἡ.
hoplite, ὁπλίτης, ου, ὁ.
horse, ἵππος, ου, ὁ.
horseman, ἱππεύς, έως, ὁ.
hostile, πολέμιος.
house, οἰκίᾱ, ᾱς, ἡ.
how many, πόσος.
hunt, θηρεύω.

I

I, ἐγώ.
Iconium, Ἰκόνιον, ου, τό.
if, εἰ, ἐάν.
impassable, ἀδιάβατος, ον.
in, ἐν.
inhabit, οἰκέω.
inhabitants, οἱ ἐνοικοῦντες.
inhabited, οἰκούμενος.
inland, ἄνω.
in order that, ἵνα, ὡς, ὅπως.
instead of, ἀντί.

institute, τίθημι.
intention (future of participle).
interpreter, ἑρμηνεύς, έως, ὁ.
into, εἰς (acc.).
Ionia, Ἰωνίᾱ, ᾱς, ἡ.
it, αὐτό in oblique cases.

J

join, ζεύγνῡμι.
journey, a day's, σταθμός, οῦ, ὁ.

K

kill, ἀποκτείνω.
kind, every, παντοδαπός.
king, βασιλεύς, έως, ὁ.
kingdom, βασιλείᾱ, ᾱς, ἡ.
know, γιγνώσκω.
known, to make, δηλόω.

L

Lacedaemonian, Λακεδαιμόνιος.
land, γῆ, γῆς, ἡ; χώρᾱ, ᾱς, ἡ.
large, μέγας.
laugh, γελάω.
laughter, γέλως, ωτος, ὁ.
lead, ἄγω, ἡγέομαι (dat. or gen.).
lead back home (restore), κατάγω.
leader, ἄρχων, οντος, ὁ.
leave, λείπω.
leave behind, καταλείπω.
life, βίος, ου, ὁ.
loose, λύω.
Lycaean, cf. "festival."

M

Maeander, Μαίανδρος, ου, ὁ.
make, ποιέω.
make an attack, ἔπειμι (dat.).
make a bridge, ζεύγνῡμι.
make a review, ἐπιδείκνῡμι, ἐξέτασιν
   ποιοῦμαι.
make war, πολεμέω (dat. or πρός
   with acc.).
man, ἀνήρ, ἀνδρός, ὁ; ἄνθρωπος, ου, ὁ.

manner, τρόπος, ου, ὁ.
many, πολύς. as—as possible, ὡς πλεῖστοι. —times, πολλάκις.
march, πορεύομαι, ἐξελαύνω.
march up, ἀναβαίνω.
market-place, ἀγορά, ᾶς, ἡ.
Marsyas, Μαρσύας, ου, ὁ.
meanwhile, ἐν ᾧ.
meet, go to, ἀπαντάω (dat.).
meet with, συγγίγνομαι (dat.).
Menon, Μένων, ωνος, ὁ.
messenger, ἄγγελος, ου, ὁ.
Midas, Μίδας, ου, ὁ.
middle, μέσος.
midst, in the, ἐν μέσῳ.
Miletus, Μίλητος, ου, ἡ.
mingle (mix with), κεράννυμι (acc. and dat.).
money, χρῆμα, ατος, τό.
month, μήν, μηνός, ὁ.
more, πλείων.
mother, μήτηρ, μητρός, ἡ.
mountain, ὄρος, ὄρους, τό.
much, πολύς.
myself, ἐμαυτοῦ, ῆς.

N

name, ὄνομα, ατος, τό.
night, νύξ, νυκτός, ἡ.
no one, οὐδείς, μηδείς.
not, οὐ, μή.
notice, κατανοέω.
now, νῦν, ἤδη.
number, ἀριθμός, οῦ, ὁ.

O

obey, πείθω (mid.. dat.).
offer sacrifice, θύω.
old, πρέσβυς.
old man, γέρων, οντος, ὁ.
older, πρεσβύτερος.
on, ἐπί (w. gen.).
one, εἷς.
once, at, εὐθύς.

opponent, ἀντιστασιώτης, ου, ὁ.
orator, ῥήτωρ, ορος, ὁ.
order, in—that, ἵνα, ὡς, ὅπως.
order, to, κελεύω.
originally, τὸ ἀρχαῖον.
ourselves, ἡμεῖς αὐτοί.
outcry, κραυγή, ῆς, ἡ.
over, ὑπέρ (gen. or acc.).
overcome, περιγίγνομαι (gen.).
owe, ὀφείλω.

P

palace, βασίλεια, ων, τά.
park, παράδεισος, ου, ὁ.
parasang, παρασάγγης, ου, ὁ.
Parysatis, Παρύσατις, ιδος, ἡ.
Pasion, Πασίων, ωνος, ὁ.
pass, εἰσβολή, ῆς, ἡ.
passage, ὑπερβολή, ῆς, ἡ.
pause, παύω (mid.).
pay, μισθός, οῦ, ὁ.
pay, to, ἀποδίδωμι.
pelt, to, βάλλω.
Peltae, Πέλται, ῶν, οἱ.
peltast, πελταστής, οῦ, ὁ.
perceive, αἰσθάνομαι.
perform sacrifice, θύω.
perish, ἀπόλλυμι (mid.).
permit, ἐάω.
Persian, Πέρσης, ου, ὁ.
persuade, πείθω.
phalanx, φάλαγξ, αγγος, ἡ.
Phrygia, Φρυγία, ᾶς, ἡ.
Pigres, Πίγρης, ητος, ὁ.
Pisidians, Πισίδαι, ῶν, οἱ.
place, ἵστημι.
plain, πεδίον, ου, τό.
plan, βουλεύομαι.
pleasant, χαρίεις, ἡδύς.
pleased with, to be, ἥδομαι (dat.).
pledge, πιστόν, ου, τό.
phethron, πλέθρον, ου, τό.
plot, ἐπιβουλή, ῆς, ἡ.

plot (against), to, ἐπιβουλεύω (dat.).
plunder, ἁρπάζω.
possess, ἔχω, εἰμί w. dat.
power, δύναμις, εως, ἡ.
power, come into the — of, γίγνομαι
ἐπί (dat.). in the — of, ἐπί (dat.).
present arms, προβάλλω τὰ ὅπλα.
present, to be, πάρειμι, παραγίγνομαι.
press hard, πιέζω.
prevent, κωλύω.
prize, ἆθλον, ου, τό.
proceed, πορεύομαι.
promise, ὑπισχνέομαι.
prosperous, εὐδαίμων.
province, ἀρχή, ῆς, ἡ.
Proxenus, Πρόξενος, ου, ὁ.
purple, φοινικοῦς.
put to death, ἀποκτείνω.

Q

queen, βασίλεια, ᾶς, ἡ.
quickly, ταχύ, θᾶττον, τάχιστα.

R

ransom, λύομαι.
rapidly, see "quickly."
reach, ἀφικνέομαι.
ready, ἕτοιμος, παράσκευος.
receive, λαμβάνω.
receive back, ἀπολαμβάνω.
reconcile, συναλλάττω.
region, χώρᾱ, ᾶς, ἡ.
remain, μένω.
rest of, the, οἱ ἄλλοι.
restore, κατάγω.
review, ἐξέτασις, εως, ἡ.
review, to, ἐξέτασιν ποιοῦμαι.
right, think it, ἀξιόω.
ride by, παρελαύνω.
river, ποταμός, οῦ, ὁ.
road, ὁδός, οῦ, ἡ.
rule, ἄρχω (gen.).
ruler, ἄρχων, οντος, ὁ.

run, τρέχω.
rush, ἵημι (mid.).

S

sacrifice, θύω.
same, the, ὁ αὐτός.
same things, the, τὰ αὐτά, ταὐτά.
Sardis, Σάρδεις, εων, αἱ.
satrap, σατράπης, ου, ὁ.
satyr, σάτυρος, ου, ὁ.
say, λέγω, φημί, εἶπον.
sea, θάλαττα, ης, ἡ.
secretly, λανθάνω with a ppl., λάθρᾳ
see, ὁράω.
seem best, δοκέω.
send, πέμπω.
send away or back, ἀποπέμπω.
send for, μεταπέμπομαι.
send word, παραγγέλλω.
set out, ὁρμάομαι.
set up, τίθημι.
seven, ἑπτά.
shield, ἀσπίς, ίδος, ἡ.
show, φαίνω, δείκνυμι.
since, ἐπεί.
six, ἕξ.
slay, ἀποκτείνω.
small, μικρός.
so, οὖν.
so as, ὥστε.
soldier, στρατιώτης, ου, ὁ.
someone, τὶς.
son, υἱός, οῦ, ὁ.
sooner, πρότερος.
so that, ὥστε.
sound the trumpet, σαλπίζω.
speak, λέγω, εἶπον.
spend money, δαπανάω.
spring, κρήνη, ης, ἡ.
stand, ἵστημι.
start, ὁρμάω (usually mid.).
station, τίθημι.
stay, μένω.

steep, ὄρθιος.

subordinate, ὕπαρχος, ου, ὁ.

successfully, καλῶς.

support, τροφή, ῆς, ἡ.

support, to, τρέφω, ὑπάρχω (dat.).

suppose, νομίζω.

suspect, ὑποπτεύω.

summon, μεταπέμπομαι, καλέω.

swift, ταχύς.

sword, ξίφος, ους, τό.

Syennesis, Συέννεσις, ιος, ὁ.

T

table, τράπεζα, ης, ἡ.

take, λαμβάνω.

take exercise, γυμνάζω.

Tarsus, Ταρσοί, ῶν, οἱ.

ten, δέκα.

ten thousand, μύριοι.

tent, σκηνή, ῆς, ἡ.

terms, come to, καταλύω (πρός with acc.).

territory, χώρα, ᾱς, ἡ.

than, ἤ.

that, ἐκεῖνος.   in order that, ἵνα, ὡς, ὅπως.

the, ὁ, ἡ, τό.

themselves, αὐτοί.

then, ἐνταῦθα.

there, ἐνταῦθα.   from —, ἐντεῦθεν.

thereupon, ἐνταῦθα.

these things, ταῦτα.

they, οἱ δέ, *and* or *but they*, otherwise omitted.

thief, κλώψ, κλωπός, ὁ.

think, νομίζω, οἴομαι, ἡγέομαι.

think it right, ἀξιόω.

this, οὗτος.

thirteen, τρισκαίδεκα.

though, καίπερ.

thousand, χίλιοι, ων.

Thracians, Θρᾷκες, ῶν, οἱ.

three, τρεῖς.

through, διά (gen.).

throw, βάλλω.

thus, οὕτω, οὕτως.

times, many, πολλάκις.

Tissaphernes, Τισσαφέρνης, ους, ὁ.

to, εἰς, ἐπί, πρός, παρά.

traduce, διαβάλλω.

tree, δένδρον, ου, τό.

tribute, δασμός, οῦ, ὁ.

trireme, τριήρης, ους, ἡ.

troops, στρατιῶται, ῶν, οἱ.

trouble, πράγματα, ων, τά.

true, it is, δή.

trumpet, sound the, σαλπίζω.

trust, πιστεύω (dat.).

try, πειράομαι.

turn over to, ἐπιτρέπω.

twenty, εἴκοσι.

two, δύο.

Tyriaeum, Τυριαῖον, ου, τό.

U

unprepared, ἀπαράσκευος.

until, ἕως.

upon, ἐπί (gen.).

use, χράομαι (dat.).

V

valuable, τίμιος.

very, πάνυ.

village, κώμη, ης, ἡ.

vine, ἄμπελος, ου, ἡ.

W

wage war, πολεμέω.

wagon, ἅμαξα, ης, ἡ.

wagon road, ὁδὸς ἁμαξιτός, ἡ.

wait, μένω.

wall, τεῖχος, ους, τό.

war, make, πολεμέω.

wares, ὤνια, τά.

was, were, ἦν, ἦσαν.

watch, θεωρέω, φυλάττω.

way, ὁδός, οῦ, ἡ.   in this way, οὕτως

we, ἡμεῖς.
whatever, ὅ τι.
wheat, πῦρός, οῦ, ὁ.
when, ἐπεί, ὅτε.
whenever, ἐπεί, ἐπειδάν, ὅτε, ὅταν.
where, οὗ. ποῦ (interrog.).
which, ὅς.
who, ὅς, τίς.
width (wide), εὖρος, ους, τό.
wild, ἄγριος.
willing, to be, ἐθέλω.
wine, οἶνος, ου, ὁ.
wish, βούλομαι, ἐθέλω.

with, μετά (gen.), σύν (dat.), ἔχων.
withdraw, ἀποχωρέω.
wonder, θαυμάζω.

X

Xerxes, Ξέρξης, ου, ὁ.
Xenophon, Ξενοφῶν, ῶντος, ὁ.

Y

you, ὑμεῖς.
young, νέος.
younger, νεώτερος.
youngest, νεώτατος.

GREEK-ENGLISH VOCABULARY

[Numbers in parentheses indicate the lesson in which the word first occurs.]

A

Ἄβῡδος, ου, ἡ (17), *Abydus*, a city of Asia Minor on the Hellespont. Here Xerxes built his famous bridge, and from here Leander swam across the strait to Hero.

ἀγαθός, ή, όν (2), *good, brave, upright, excellent*. καλὸς καὶ ἀγαθός, *noble and good;* τὰ ἀγαθά, *goods, possessions*. Compared irregularly: ἀμείνων, ἄριστος; βελτίων, βέλτιστος; κρείττων, κράτιστος; λῴων, λῷστος. Cf. adv. εὖ. [**Agatha**]

ἀγαγεῖν, ἀγάγῃ, etc., see ἄγω.

ἀγγέλλω [ἀγγελ], ἀγγελῶ, ἤγγειλα, ἤγγελκα, ἤγγελμαι, ἠγγέλθην (52), *bring news, announce, report.* Cf. ἄγγελος.

ἄγγελος, ου, ὁ (11), *messenger, herald.* Cf. ἀγγέλλω. [**angel**, ev**angel**ist]

ἀγορά, ᾶς, ἡ (4), *agora* (Lat. forum), *assembly, place of assembling, market-place, market.* ἀγορὰ πλήθουσα, *time of full market,* from 9 A. M. to noon.

ἀγοράζω [ἀγοραδ], ἀγοράσω, ἠγόρασα, ἠγόρακα (ch. 3), *buy, purchase;* mid., *buy for oneself.*

ἄγριος, ᾱ, ον (35), *of the fields, wild.* Lat. ager and Eng. acre are related words.

ἄγω, ἄξω, 2 aor. ἤγαγον, ἦχα, ἦγμαι, ἤχθην (3), *drive, lead, convey, bring;* intrans., *lead on, march, go.* Cf. Lat. ago, Eng. agent, agile. [ped**agogue**]

ἀγών, ῶνος, ὁ (17), *assembly, contest, games.* ἀγῶνα τιθέναι or ποιεῖν, *to hold games.* Cf. ἄγω. [**agony**]

ἀδελφός, οῦ, ὁ (3), *brother,* voc. ἄδελφε. [Phil**adelphia**]

ἀδικέω, ἀδικήσω, ἠδίκησα, ἠδίκηκα, ἠδίκημαι, ἠδικήθην (49), *be or do wrong, wrong, injure, harm.* Pres. often as perf.

ἀεί (28), adv. *always, ever, constantly.* [**ai**zoon]

ἆθλον, ου, τό (40), *prize* (of contest). [**athlete**]

ἀθροίζω [ἀθροιδ], ἀθροίσω, ἤθροισα, ἤθροικα, ἤθροισμαι, ἠθροίσθην (17), *assemble, muster, collect;* mid. intrans., *assemble.* (Also ἁθροίζω.)

αἱ, αἵ, see ὁ, ὅς.

Αἰνιᾶνες, ων, οἱ (34), *Aenianes* or *Aenianians,* a tribe in Thessaly.

αἱρέω [αἱρε, ἑλ], αἱρήσω, 2 aor. εἷλον, ᾕρηκα, ᾕρημαι, ᾑρέθην, imperf. ᾕρουν (36), *take, seize, capture;* mid., *take for oneself, choose, elect.* [**heresy**, di**aeresis**]

αἱρετός, ή, όν (ch. 3), verbal adj., *taken, chosen.* οἱ αἱρετοί, *those chosen as delegates.*

αἷς, see ὅς.

αἰσθάνομαι [αισθ], αἰσθήσομαι, 2 aor. ᾐσθόμην, ᾔσθημαι (15), *perceive, learn, see;* fol. by acc., or acc. and ppl., or by ὅτι-clause. [**aesthetic**]

αἰσχύνω, αἰσχυνῶ, ᾔσχυνα, ᾔσχυμμαι, ᾐσχύνθην (ch. 3), *shame, disgrace;* pas.

211

dep., *feel ashamed, stand in awe of.* [aeschynite]

αἰτέω, αἰτήσω, ᾔτησα, ᾔτηκα, ᾔτημαι ᾐτήθην, imperf. ᾔτουν (20), *ask for, demand;* gov. two acc. or acc. and infin.

αἰτιάομαι, αἰτιάσομαι, ᾐτιασάμην, ᾐτίαμαι (50), *blame, accuse;* with infin. clause. [aetiology]

ἀκινάκης, ου, ὁ (58), *short sword, sword,* worn by the Persians.

ἀκούω [ἄκου], ἀκούσομαι, ἤκουσα, 2 pf. ἀκήκοα, ἠκούσθην (31), *hear, learn, hear of, listen to;* fol. by ppl., ὅτι, or infin. clause; gov. gen. of pers., acc. (sometimes gen.) of the thing heard. [acoustics]

ἀκρόπολις, εως, ἡ (27), *highest part of a city, citadel, acropolis,* ἄκρος + πόλις.

ἄκρος, ᾱ, ον (52), *pointed, at the point, highest.* τὸ ἄκρον, *the summit;* τὰ ἄκρα, *the heights.* Related to Lat. acer, Eng. acme. [acrobat]

ἄκων, ἄκουσα, ἆκον, gen. ἄκοντος (ch. 3), *unwilling.*

ἀλέξω, ἀλέξομαι, ἠλεξάμην (ch. 3), *ward off, repulse.*

ἀληθής, ές, gen. οῦς (33), *not concealed, true.* ἀ + λανθάνω.

ἀλλά (10), adversative conj., stronger than δέ, *otherwise, but, still, on the other hand,* often preceded by a negative; ἀλλὰ γάρ, *but then.* Cf. ἄλλος.

ἀλλήλων, οις (58), reciprocal pro., *of one another, of each other.* [parallel]

ἄλλος, η, ο (14), *other, another;* with article, *the other, the rest, the rest of.* Cf. Lat. alius. [allegory, allopathic]

ἅμα (39), adv., *at the same time, together.* With dat., *together with, at the same time with.* ἅμα τῇ ἡμέρᾳ, *at daybreak.* ἅμα is for σάμα; cf. Lat. simul, Eng. same.

ἅμαξα, ης, ἡ (4), *wagon.* ἅμα + ἄγω.

ἁμαξιτός, όν (51), *traversable by wagons.* ἁμαξιτὸς ὁδός, *a wagonroad.* Cf. ἅμαξα.

ἀμείνων, ον, comp. of ἀγαθός.

ἀμελέω, ἀμελήσω, ἠμέλησα, ἠμέληκα (ch. 3), *be careless, neglect* (w. gen.).

ἀμήχανος, ον (51), *without resource, helpless, impracticable, impossible.*

ἄμπελος, ου, ἡ (53), *grape-vine.*

ἀμφί (16), prep. with acc. and rarely gen.: w. gen., *about* (showing source or cause); w. acc., *about;* with numerals (preceded by article), *about.* οἱ ἀμφὶ Κῦρον, *Cyrus and his men,* or *the followers of Cyrus.* [amphitheater]

ἀμφότερος, ᾱ, ον (8), *both.*

ἄν (22), adv., postpos. No English equivalent; used as a modal adv. in conditional expressions.

ἄν, contracted form of ἐάν.

ἀναβαίνω, ἀναβήσομαι, 2 aor. ἀνέβην, ἀναβέβηκα, ἀναβέβαμαι, ἀνεβάθην (7), *go up, march up* or *inland.* [Anabasis]

ἀνάγκη, ης. ἡ (43), *necessity;* with or without ἐστί, *it is necessary, one must;* often with infin., acc. and infin., or dat. and infin.

ἀναρπάζω, ἀναρπάσω, ἀνήρπασα, ἀνήρπακα, ἀνήρπασμαι, ἀνηρπάσθην (ch. 3), *snatch up, carry off, plunder.*

ἀνδράποδον, ου, τό (58), *slave, captive.*

ἄνευ (ch. 3), prep., w. gen., *without,
apart from.*

ἀνήρ, ἀνδρός, ὁ (17), *man.* ἄνδρες στρατιῶται, *fellow-soldiers;* cf. ἄνθρωπος, *man* (generic); cf. Lat. vir.
[**Andrew,** Alex**ander**]

ἄνθρωπος, ου, ὁ (6), *man, human being;* cf. Lat. homo. [phil**an-
thropist**]

ἀνιάω, ἀνιάσω, ἠνίασα, ἀνιάθην (41),
grieve, distress, w. acc. of person;
pas. (and fut. mid.), *be grieved,
be distressed,* w. dat. of pers. or
thing.

ἀνίστημι, ἀναστήσω, ἀνέστησα, 2 aor.
ἀνέστην, ἀνέστηκα, ἀνέσταμαι, ἀνεστά-
θην (59), *make stand up, rouse;* in
mid., and in perf. and 2 aor. act.,
intrans., *stand up, rise, stand.*

ἀντί (10), prep., w. gen., *facing,
against, instead of, for, in
preference to, in return for.*
[**anti**dote, **ant**agonist, **anti**septic,
anthem]

ἀντιπαρασκευάζομαι, ἀντιπαρασκευάσομαι, ἀντιπαρεσκευασάμην, ἀντιπαρ-
εσκεύασμαι (31), *prepare oneself
in turn* or *in opposition, make
counter preparations.* ἀντί +
παρά + σκευάζω.

ἀντιπέρᾱς (17), adv., *opposite, over
against;* w. gen. κατ' ἀντιπέρᾱς
forms a simple phrase with same
meaning.

ἀντιστασιώτης, ου, ὁ (20), *opponent,
adversary.*

ἄντρον, ου, τό (37), *cave;* cf. Lat. an-
trum.

ἄνω (25), adv., *above, up, upward,
inland* (of marching); c. ἀνωτέρω,
s. ἀνωτάτω.

ἄξιος, ᾱ, ον (ch. 3), *worth, worthy;*
ἄξιον, sc. ἐστί, *be worth while, fit-*

ting; w. gen., e. g. πολλοῦ, *worthy
of much, valuable;* also used w.
infin.

ἀξιόω, ἀξιώσω, ἠξίωσα, ἠξίωκα, ἠξίωμαι,
ἠξιώθην, imperf. ἠξίουν (15), *think
right, ask as one's right, claim,
deem worthy.* [**axiom**]

ἀπαγγέλλω, ἀπαγγελῶ, ἀπήγγειλα,
ἀπήγγελκα, ἀπήγγελμαι, ἀπηγγέλθην
(ch. 3), *bring back word, announce, report.*

ἀπάγω, ἀπάξω, 2 aor. ἀπήγαγον, ἀπῆχα,
ἀπῆγμαι, ἀπήχθην (ch. 3), *lead
away, lead back.*

ἀπαιτέω, ἀπαιτήσω, ἀπήτησα, ἀπήτηκα,
ἀπήτημαι, ἀπητήθην, imperf. ἀπή-
τουν (41), *ask back, demand* (what
is due); w. two acc. ἀπό + αἰτέω.

ἀπαράσκευος, ον (12), *unprepared.*
ἀ + παρασκευή.

ἄπειμι (ch. 3), *go away, depart, re-
treat.*

ἀπέρχομαι, ἀπῆλθον, ἀπελήλυθα (10),
come away, go away, return.
ἀπό + ἔρχομαι.

ἀπέχω, ἀφέξω or ἀποσχήσω, 2 aor.
ἀπέσχον, ἀπέσχηκα, ἀπέσχημαι
(ch. 3), *keep away, be away* or
distant from.

ἀπό (7), prep., w. gen., *from, away
from.* Allied to Lat. ab, Eng.
off. [**apo**stle, **apo**dosis]

ἀποδίδωμι, ἀποδώσω, ἀπέδωκα (2 aor.
ἀπέδοτον), ἀποδέδωκα, ἀποδέδομαι,
ἀπεδόθην (41), *give back, restore,
pay.* [**apodosis**]

ἀποθνῄσκω [θαν, θνη], ἀποθανοῦμαι,
2 aor. ἀπέθανον, ἀποτέθνηκα (9), *die,
be killed, perish,* used as pas. to
ἀποκτείνω. In prose ἀποθνῄσκω is
used for θνῄσκω, but the simple
form τέθνηκα in perfect.

ἀποικίᾱ, ᾱς, ἡ (12), *colony.*

ἀποκρίνομαι, ἀποκρινοῦμαι, ἀπεκρινά-
μην, ἀποκέκριμαι (59), *give a deci-
sion, answer, reply.* ἀπό + κρίνω.

ἀποκτείνω, ἀποκτενῶ, ἀπέκτεινα, 2 pf.
ἀπέκτονα (25), *kill off, put to
death.* ἀποθνήσκω is used as passive. ἀπό + κτείνω.

ἀπολαμβάνω, ἀπολήψομαι, 2 aor. ἀπέλαβον, 2 pf. ἀπείληφα, ἀπείλημμαι,
ἀπελήφθην (58), *take away* or
back, receive back, recover. ἀπό
+ λαμβάνω.

ἀπόλλῡμι, ἀπολῶ, ἀπώλεσα, 2 aor. ἀπωλόμην, ἀπολώλεκα, 2 pf. ἀπόλωλα (56),
utterly destroy, kill, lose, mid.
and 2 perf. system, *perish.* ἀπό
+ ὄλλῡμι. [ὀλ]

Ἀπόλλων, ωνος, ὁ (37), dat. ᾿Απόλ-
λωνι, acc. ᾿Απόλλωνα or ᾿Απόλλω,
voc. ῎Απολλον, *Apollo.*

ἀπολώλεκα, see ἀπόλλῡμι.

ἀποπέμπω, ἀποπέμψω, ἀπέπεμψα, ἀπο-
πέπομφα, ἀπέπεμμαι, ἀπεπέμφθην
(9), *send off* or *back, dismiss.*

ἀποπλέω, ἀποπλεύσομαι, ἀπέπλευσα,
ἀποπέπλευκα, ἀποπέπλευσμαι (ch. 3),
sail away, sail back, sail home.

ἀπορέω, ἀπορήσω, ἠπόρησα, ἠπόρηκα
(ch. 3), *be in doubt, be at a loss,
be perplexed* (w. dat.).

ἀπορίᾱ, ᾱς, ἡ (ch. 3), *lack of means*
or *resource, difficulty.*

ἀποχωρέω, ἀποχωρήσω, ἀπεχώρησα,
ἀποκεχώρηκα, ἀποκεχώρημαι, ἀπεχω-
ρήθην (38), *go away, depart, withdraw.* ἀπό + χωρέω.

ἀριθμός, οῦ, ὁ (39), *number, numbering.* [**arith**metic, log**arithm**]

Ἀρίστιππος, ον, ὁ (20), *Aristippus,*
a Greek general.

ἄριστος, η, ον, superl. of ἀγαθός.
[**aristo**cracy]

᾿Αρκάς, άδος, ὁ (27), *an Arcadian,*
inhabitant of Arcadia, a division
of Greece.

ἅρμα, ατος, τό (45), *chariot, war-
chariot.*

ἁρμάμαξα, ης, ἡ (45), *covered carriage.* ἅρμα + ἅμαξα.

ἁρπάζω [ἁρπαδ], ἁρπάσω, ἥρπασα,
ἥρπακα, ἥρπασμαι, ἡρπάσθην (57),
sieze, capture, plunder. Cf. Lat.
rapio, Eng. rapid. [**harpy**]

᾿Αρταξέρξης, ου, ὁ (5), *Artaxerxes,* a
king of Persia.

ἀρχαῖος, ᾱ, ον (13), *from the beginning, ancient, old.* τὸ ἀρχαῖον,
adv. acc., *originally, anciently,
formerly.* Cf. ἀρχή. [**archae-
ology**]

ἀρχή, ῆς, ἡ (3), *beginning, rule,
province, satrapy.* Cf. ἄρχω.
[an**archy**, **archaic**]

ἄρχω [ἀρχ], ἄρξω, ἦρξα, ἦργμαι, ἤρχθην
(15), *be first, begin, rule, command,* gov. gen. [**arch**angel
patri**arch**]

ἄρχων, οντος, ὁ (13), ppl. used as
noun, *ruler, commander, leader*
(higher title than στρατηγός). Cf.
ἄρχω. [**archon**]

᾿Ασπένδιος, ᾱ, ον (42), *an Aspendian,*
inhabitant of Aspendus, a city of
Pamphylia.

ἀσπίς, ίδος, ἡ (13), *shield.* [**asp**]

ἀσφαλής, ες (ch. 3), *safe, secure;* c.
ἀσφαλέστερος, s. ἀσφαλέστατος.

ἄτῑμος, ον (10), *dishonored, slighted.*
ἀ + τίμη.

αὖ (14), adv., postpos., *again, in
turn, moreover.* Cf. Lat. autem.

αὐτόματος, η, ον (47) *of one's own
accord, spontaneously.* [**automatic**]

αὐτός, ή, ό (9), intensive pro., *self;* in
pred. position or alone, in nom.,
self; in attrib. position, *same,
very;* alone in oblique cases,
him, her, it, them. Cf. Lat. ipse.
[**auto**graph]

αὐτοῦ, adv. (ch. 3), *here, in this
place, there.*

αὐτοῦ = ἐαυτοῦ.

ἀφαιρέω, ἀφαιρήσω, 2 aor. ἀφεῖλον, ἀφ-
ῄρηκα, ἀφῄρημαι, ἀφηρέθην (ch. 3),
take away from; mid., *take away
for oneself, deprive, rob,* gov.
two acc.

ἀφίημι, ἀφήσω, ἀφῆκα (2 aor. ἀφεῖμεν),
ἀφεῖκα, ἀφεῖμαι (59), *send off* or
away, let go, set free. ἀπό + ἵημι.

ἀφικνέομαι [ἀφικ], ἀφίξομαι, 2 aor. ἀφ-
ικόμην, ἀφῖγμαι (30), *come from,
come, arrive (at), reach.*

Ἀχαιός, οῦ, ὁ (24), *an Achaean,*
inhabitant of Achaea, a division
of Greece.

ἀφ' see ἀπό.

ἄχθομαι [ἀχθ], ἀχθέσομαι, ἤχθημαι,
ἠχθέσθην (16), *be burdened, vexed,
displeased.*

B

βαίνω [βα], βήσομαι, 2 aor. ἔβην, βέβηκα, βέβαμαι, ἐβάθην (56), *go, walk.*
[**basis**]

βάλλω [βαλ, βλα], βαλῶ, 2 aor. ἔβαλον,
βέβληκα, βέβλημαι, ἐβλήθην (25),
throw, throw at, pelt (w. dat. of
thing thrown). [para**ble**, prob-
lem, em**bl**em, sym**bol**]

βαρβαρικός, ή, όν (25), *foreign* (non-
Greek), *barbarian.* τὸ βαρβαρικόν,
the barbarian army.

βάρβαρος, ον (11), *not Greek, foreign,
barbarian;* as noun, ὁ βάρβαρος,
foreigner, οἱ βάρβαροι, *the bar*

barians, usually the Persians.
Cf. booby. [**barbarian,** rhu**barb**]

βασιλεία, ᾱς, ἡ (9), *kingdom, sovereignty.*

βασίλειος, ον (35), *belonging to a
king, royal;* as noun, generally
in plu., τὰ βασίλεια, *royal abodes,
palace.* [**basilica**]

βασιλεύς, έως, ὁ (31), *king;* when the
article is omitted, the king of
Persia is meant. [**basilisk,
Basil**]

βασιλεύω, βασιλεύσω, ἐβασίλευσα (10),
be king, rule.

βιάζομαι [βιαδ], βιάσομαι, ἐβιασάμην,
βεβίασμαι, ἐβιάσθην (59), mid. dep.,
but has also aor. pas., *force,
compel.*

βίος, ου, ὁ (2), *life.* [**bio**logy]

Βοιώτιος, ου, ὁ (23), *a Boeotian,* an
inhabitant of Boeotia, a division
of Greece.

βουλεύω, βουλεύσω, ἐβούλευσα, βεβού-
λευκα, βεβούλευμαι, ἐβουλεύθην (10),
counsel; mid., *counsel for oneself, plan, take counsel.*

βούλομαι [βουλ], βουλήσομαι, βεβού-
λημαι, ἐβουλήθην (ἠβουλήθην) (7),
pas. dep., *will, wish, be willing.*

Γ

γάρ (12), conj., postpos., *for, because.*
In introducing narration, *now,
then.* καὶ γάρ, *for* or *for indeed*
(with implied ellipsis, cf. Lat. et
enim); ἀλλὰ γάρ, *but then.*

γέ, intensive particle, enclitic,
postpos., usually emphasizes the
preceding word (ch. 3), *indeed,
surely, at least,* often rendered
by emphasis.

γέλως, ωτος, ὁ (47), *laughter.*

γέρων, οντος, ὁ (13), *old man.*

γέφῡρα, ᾱς, ἡ (4), *bridge.*

γῆ, γῆς, ἡ (14), *earth, land, country.*
κατὰ γῆν, *by land.* [**ge**ography,
geology, apo**ge**e]

γίγνομαι [γεν], γενήσομαι, 2 aor. ἐγενόμην, 2 pf. γέγονα, γεγένημαι (7), *come
into being, be born, become, be,
happen, occur;* meaning largely
determined by context. Cf. Lat.
gigno, genus. [oxy**gen**, **genus,
genitive**]

γιγνώσκω [γνο], γνώσομαι, 2 aor. ἔγνων, ἔγνωκα, ἔγνωσμαι, ἐγνώσθην (56),
know, recognize, learn, think.
Cf. Lat. nosco, Eng. know. [a**g-
nostic,** dia**gnosis**]

γνώμη, ης, ἡ (ch. 3), *opinion, plan.*
[**gnome**]

γνῶναι, γνώσομαι, see γιγνώσκω.

γράφω [γραφ], γράψω, ἔγραψα, γέγραφα, γέγραμμαι, ἐγράφην (24),
make a mark, draw, write.
[**graph**ic, photo**graph**]

γυμνάζω [γυμναδ], γυμνάσω, ἐγύμνασα,
γεγύμνασμαι, ἐγυμνάσθην (2), *train
(naked), exercise.* [**gymnastic**]

γυμνής, ῆτος, ὁ (29), or γυμνήτης, ου,
ὁ, *light-armed foot-soldier.*

γυνή, γυναικός, ἡ (36), *woman, wife.*
[miso**gyny**]

Δ

δακρύω, δακρύσω, ἐδάκρυσα, δεδάκρῡμαι
(ch. 3), *shed tears, weep.* Allied
to Lat. lacrima (dacruma), Eng.
tear.

δαπανάω [δαπανα], δαπανήσω, ἐδαπάνησα, δεδαπάνηκα, δεδαπάνημαι, ἐδα-
πανήθην (16), *spend money, consume.*

δᾱρεικός, οῦ, ὁ (17), *daric*—a Persian gold coin worth about
$3.50.

Δᾱρεῖος, ου, ὁ (3), *Darius,* king of
Persia.

δασμός, οῦ, ὁ (16), *tax, tribute.*

δέ (8), conj., postpos., *but, and;* less
emphatic than ἀλλά. μέν . . . .
δέ, *on the one hand . . . . on
the other,* or the contrast may
be shown by the voice in reading.

δέδια, δεδιώς, see δέδοικα.

δέδοικα, δέδια, first and second perfects with present meaning, from
δείδω, which is not used in present; fut. δείσομαι, 1 aor. ἔδεισα (48),
fear, dread, of reasoning fear;
cf. φοβέω.

δέη, δεηθῆναι, δεῖ, see δέω.

δείκνῡμι, δείξω, ἔδειξα, δέδειχα, δέδειγμαι, ἐδείχθην (33), *show, point out,
indicate.* [para**digm**]

δεινός, ή, όν (44), *fearful, terrible,
wonderful, powerful, able, clever.* [**dino**therium]

δέκα, indeclinable, *ten;* allied to
Eng. ten. [**decade, deca**logue]

δένδρον, ου, τό (53), *tree.* [rhodo-
dendron, dendroid]

δεξιός, ά, όν (44), *right.* ἡ δεξιά (χείρ),
the right hand. Cf. Lat. dexter,
Eng. dexterous.

δέον, neut. of pres. ppl. of δέω.

δέρμα, ατος, τό (37), *hide, skin.*
[epi**dermis**]

δεῦρο, adv. (ch. 3), *hither, here.*

δέχομαι, δέξομαι, ἐδεξάμην, δέδεγμαι,
ἐδέχθην (39), *receive, accept,
await.* [synec**doche,** pan**dect,
dock**]

δέω, δεήσω, ἐδέησα, δεδέηκα, δεδέημαι,
ἐδεήθην (22), *need* (rare in act.);
middle (pas. dep.), *want, need,
desire, beg,* gov. gen. δεῖ, impers., *it is necessary, one must.*

δή (11), intensive particle, postpos., used to give emphasis, usually to the preceding word; it often marks an entire statement as obvious, *now, to be sure, exactly, as you know.*

δῆλος, η, ον (41), *evident, clear, plain;* δῆλός εἰμι w. ppl., *am plainly;* δῆλον ὅτι (*it is plain that*), *evidently.*

δηλόω, δηλώσω, ἐδήλωσα, δεδήλωκα, δεδήλωμαι, ἐδηλώθην (15), *make clear, show, declare.*

διά (32), prep., w. gen., *through;* w. acc., *through, on account of.* [**dia**meter]

διαβάλλω [διαβαλ], διαβαλῶ, 2 aor. διέβαλον, διαβέβληκα, διαβέβλημαι, διεβλήθην (9), *throw across, throw* [words] *at, accuse falsely, slander,* [**diabolical, devil**]

διάγω [διαγ], διάξω, 2 aor. διήγαγον, διῆχα, διῆγμαι, διήχθην (41), *pass* [time], *live, continue.*

διᾱκόσιοι, αι, α, *two hundred.* δύο + ἑκατόν.

διαπορεύομαι, διαπορεύσομαι, διαπεπόρευμαι, διεπορεύθην (33), *pass through* or *over.*

διαρπάζω [διαρπαδ], διαρπάσω, διήρπασα, διήρπακα, διήρπασμαι, διηρπάσθην (49), *tear asunder, pillage, devastate.*

δίδωμι [δο], δώσω, ἔδωκα, 2 aor. ἔδοτον, δέδωκα, δέδομαι, ἐδόθην (42), *give.* [anec**dote**, **dose**, anti**dote**, Theo**dore**]

δίκαιος, ᾱ, ον (ch. 3), *just, right, lawful, fitting.* [**dicast, syndic**]

δίκη, ης, ἡ (ch. 3), *justice, right, penalty, punishment, deserts, lawsuit.*

διό (52), adv. for δι' ὅ, *therefore.*

δισχῑλιοι, αι, α (20), *two thousand.*

διώκω, διώξω, ἐδίωξα, δεδίωχα, ἐδιώχθην (30), *pursue, follow.*

διῶρυξ, διώρυχος, ἡ (18), *trench, canal.*

δοκέω [δοκ], δόξω, ἔδοξα, δέδογμαι, ἐδόχθην (25), *have an opinion, think.* Intrans., both pers. and impers., *seem, appear, seem best.* ταῦτα ἔδοξε, *this seemed best, was agreed,* fol. by dat. [**dogma**, ortho**dox**]

Δόλοπες, ων, οἱ (34), *Dolopians,* a tribe in Thessaly, or Δόλοψ, οπος, ὁ, *a Dolopian,* an inhabitant of Dolopia in Thessaly.

δοῦναι, see δίδωμι.

δραμοῦμαι, ἔδραμον, etc., see τρέχω.

δρόμος, ου, ὁ (47), *run, running.* [hipp**odrome**]

δύναμαι [δυνα], δυνήσομαι, δεδύνημαι, ἐδυνήθην (31), imperf. ἐδυνάμην, pas. dep., *be able, can.* [**dynasty, dynamite, durable**]

δύναμις, εως, ἡ (30), *ability, power, force, troops.* Cf. δύναμαι.

δυνάστης, ου, ὁ (50), *powerful man, nobleman, prince.*

δυνατός, ή, όν (ch. 3), *powerful, able, capable, possible.*

δύο, δυοῖν (8), *two.* Lat. duo. [hendiadys]

δώδεκα, indeclinable, *twelve.* δύο + δέκα.

δῶρον, ου τό (2), *gift.* [Pan**dora**]

E

ἐάν (22), conj., εἰ + ἄν, *if, if haply,* with subj. in conditional sentences.

ἑαυτοῦ (αὑτοῦ), ῆς (35), reflex. pro. third pers., *of himself, of herself, of itself;* οἱ ἑαυτοῦ, *his own men.*

ἐάω, ἐάσω, εἴασα, εἴακα εἴαμαι εἰάθην, imperf. εἴων (30), *let, permit, allow, let go.*

ἑβδομήκοντα, indeclinable, *seventy.*

ἐγκέλευστος, ον (ch. 3), *urged on, instigated.*

ἐγώ (35), pers. pro., *I.* [ego**tism**]

ἔδεισα, see δέδοικα.

ἔδραμεν, see τρέχω.

ἐθέλω (or θέλω) [ἐθελ], ἐθελήσω, ἠθέλησα, ἠθέληκα (58), *be willing, wish.* Cf. βούλομαι. [mono**thelite**]

εἰ (28), conj., proclitic, *if;* in indirect questions, *whether;* εἰ μή, *if not, except, unless.*

εἴα, εἴασα, see ἐάω.

εἶδον, see ὁράω.

εἴκοσι (32), indeclinable, *twenty.* Cf. Lat. viginti, Eng. twenty. [**icosa**hedron]

εἴληφα, see λαμβάνω.

εἶλον, εἰλόμην, see αἱρέω.

εἰμί [ἐσ], ἔσομαι (10), *be, exist;* ἔστι, *it is possible.* Cf. Lat. sum; allied to Eng. is, are. [par**usia**]

εἶμι [ἰ] (38), *go, come,* pres. has force of fut. Cf. Lat. eo.

εἶναι, infin. of εἰμί.

εἶπον (used as 2 aor. to λέγω), ἐρῶ, εἴρηκα, εἴρημαι, ἐρρήθην, *say, tell, speak, order;* fol. by ὡς or ὅτι; in meaning *order,* has infin.

εἰς (2), prep., proclitic, gov. acc., *into, against;* with numerals, *to the number of, as many as.*

εἷς, μία, ἕν (19), numeral, *one.* [hyp**hen, ace**]

εἰσβάλλω [εἰσβαλ], εἰσβαλῶ, 2 aor. εἰσέβαλον, εἰσβέβληκα, εἰσβέβλημαι, εἰσεβλήθην (51), *throw into, invade* (of an army), *empty* (of a river).

εἰσβολή, ῆς, ἡ (51), *invasion, entrance, pass.* εἰς + βάλλω.

εἰσελαύνω [εἰσελα], εἰσελῶ, εἰσήλασα, εἰσελήλακα, εἰσελήλαμαι, εἰσηλάθην (57), *drive into, march into.*

εἰσέρχομαι [εἰσερχ, εἰσελθ or -ελυθ], 2 aor. εἰσῆλθον, 2 pf. εἰσελήλυθα (51), *come* or *go in, enter.*

εἴσω (52), adv., *inside;* with gen., *inside of.* [**esoteric**]

εἶτα (45), adv., *then, next.*

ἐκ, see ἐξ (2).

ἕκαστος, η, ον (44), *each, every.*

ἑκατόν, indeclinable, *one hundred.* [**hecatom**b]

ἐκβάλλω [ἐκβαλ], ἐκβαλῶ, 2 aor. ἐξέβαλον, ἐκβέβληκα, ἐκβέβλημαι, ἐξεβλήθην (25), *throw out, expel, exile.* ἐκπίπτω is sometimes used as a passive.

ἐκδέρω [ἐκδερ], ἐξέδειρα, ἐκδέδαρμαι, 2 aor. ἐξεδάρην (37), *flay, skin.*

ἐκεῖ, adv. (ch. 3), *there, in that place.*

ἐκεῖνος, η, ο (10), demon. pro., *that;* like Lat. ille.

ἐκκαλύπτω [ἐκκαλυβ], ἐκκαλύψω, ἐξεκάλυψα, ἐκκεκάλυμμαι, ἐξεκαλύφθην (45), *uncover.*

ἐκκλησία, ᾶς, ἡ (60), *assembly.* [**ecclesiastic**]

ἐκλείπω [ἐκλιπ], ἐκλείψω, 2 aor. ἐξέλιπον, 2 pf. ἐκλέλοιπα, ἐκλέλειμμαι, ἐξελείφθην (55), *leave, abandon.* [**eclipse**]

ἐκφεύγω [ἐκφυγ], ἐκφεύξομαι, 2 aor. ἐξέφυγον, 2 pf. ἐκπέφευγα (60), *flee out of, escape.*

ἐλάττων, ον, comp. of μικρός and ὀλίγος, *smaller, fewer, less.*

ἐλαύνω [ἐλα], ἐλῶ, ἤλασα, ἐλήλακα, ἐλήλαμαι, ἠλάθην (55), *drive, ride, march.* [**elastic**]

ἐλάχιστος, superl. of μικρός or ὀλίγος, see ἐλάττων.

ἑλεῖν, ἑλέσθαι, see αἱρέω.

ἐλθεῖν, ἐλθών, see ἔρχομαι.

Ἑλλάς, άδος, ἡ (38), *Hellas, Greece.*

Ἕλλην, ηνος, ὁ (18), *a Greek;* as an adj., *Greek.*

Ἑλληνικός, ή, όν (12), *Hellenic, Greek;* τὸ Ἑλληνικόν, *the Greek army.*

Ἑλλησποντιακός, ή, όν (19), *Hellespontian.* [*pont.*

Ἑλλήσποντος, ου, ὁ (18), *Helles-*

ἐλπίς, ίδος, ἡ (13), *hope, expectation.*

ἐμαυτοῦ, ῆς, reflex. pro., *of myself.*

ἐμβάλλω [ἐμβαλ], ἐμβαλῶ, 2 aor. ἐνέβαλον, ἐμβέβληκα, ἐμβέβλημαι, ἐνεβλήθην (37), *throw in, attack* (of an army), *empty* (of a river). [**emblem**]

ἐμβαίνω, ἐμβήσομαι, 2 aor. ἐνέβην, ἐμβέβηκα (ch. 3), *go into, embark.*

ἐμός, ή, όν (35), *my, mine.*

ἐν, prep., proclitic (2), *in, on.* [**en**ergy, **em**piric, **em**blem, **em**porium] Governs dat.

ἕνδεκα, indeclinable, *eleven.* [**hendeca**syllable]

ἐνενήκοντα, indeclinable, *ninety.*

ἔνθα (55), adv., *there, then, thereupon.*

ἐννέα, indeclinable, *nine.* [**enne**agon]

ἐνοικέω [ἐνοικε], ἐνοικήσω, ἐνῴκησα, ἐνῴκηκα, ἐνῴκημαι, ἐνῳκήθην (55), *live in;* οἱ ἐνοικοῦντες, *the inhabitants.*

ἐνοράω, ἐνόψομαι, ἐνεῖδον, ἐνεόρακα or ἐνεώρακα, ἐνεώραμαι or ἐνῶμμαι, ἐνώφθην (ch. 3), *see in, observe in, see.*

ἑνός, ἑνί, see εἷς. [*upon.*

ἐνταῦθα (26), adv., *here, there, there-*

ἐντεῦθεν (34), adv., *from here, from there, afterward.*

ἐντυγχάνω [ἐντυχ], ἐντεύξομαι, 2 aor. ἐνέτυχον, ἐντετύχηκα or ἐντέτευχα (58), *happen upon, meet, find* (w. dat.); ἐν + τυγχάνω.

ἐξ (ἐκ bf. a consonant) (2), prep., proclit., gov. gen., *out of, from.* ἐκ τούτου, *after* or *in consequence of this.* Cf. Lat. ex. [an**ec**dote, **ec**logue, **ex**odus, **exoter**ic]

ἕξ (20), indecl. numeral, *six.* Cf. Lat. sex. [**hex**ameter]

ἐξελαύνω [ἐξελα], ἐξελῶ, ἐξήλασα, ἐξελήλακα, ἐξελήλαμαι, ἐξηλάθην (32), *drive out;* intrans., *march forth, march, proceed.*

ἐξέρχομαι, ἐξῆλθον, ἐξελήλυθα (ch. 3), *come* or *go forth, depart.*

ἐξέτασις, εως, ἡ (39), *inspection, examination, review* (of an army).

ἐπαινέω, -έσω, ἐπῄνεσα, etc. (ch. 3), *approve.*

ἐπεί (8), conj., *when, after, since.*

ἐπειδάν (60), conj. (ἐπειδή + ἄν), *when, whenever, as soon as,* with subj.

ἐπειδή (46), conj., *when, after, since.*

ἔπειμι (46), *go on, advance, attack.* ἐπί + εἶμι.

ἔπειμι [ἐπεσ], ἐπέσομαι (33), *be upon, be over.* ἐπί + εἰμί.

ἔπειτα (ch. 3), adv., *then, in the second place.*

ἐπί (9), prep., w. gen., *on;* w. dat., *on, at, near, in the power of* (a person); w. acc., *on, to, against* (w. verbs of motion). [**epi**taph, **epi**dermis, **ep**och]

ἐπιβουλεύω [ἐπιβουλευ], ἐπιβουλεύσω, ἐπεβούλευσα, ἐπιβεβούλευκα, ἐπιβεβούλευμαι, ἐπεβουλεύθην (9), *plan* or *plot against* (gov. dat.). ἐπί + βουλεύω.

ἐπιβουλή, ῆς, ἡ (15), *a plan against some one, plot.*

ἐπιδείκνῦμι [ἐπιδεικ], ἐπιδείξω, ἐπέδειξα, ἐπιδέδειχα, ἐπιδέδειγμαι, ἐπεδείχθην, imperf. ἐπεδείκνῦν (44), *point to, exhibit, show*, gov. acc. and dat.

ἐπικίνδῦνος, ον (ch. 3), *dangerous*.

ἐπίπονος, ον (ch. 3), *toilsome, laborious*.

ἐπίρρυτος, ον (53), *flowed upon, well watered*. ἐπί + ῥέω.

ἐπίσταμαι, ἐπιστήσομαι, ἠπιστήθην (ch. 3), *know, know how* (w. infin.), *understand*. [epistemology]

ἐπιτήδειος, ᾱ, ον (ch. 3), *suitable, fit, proper*. τὰ ἐπιτήδεια, *provisions*.

ἐπιτίθημι, ἐπιθήσω, ἐπέθηκα, ἐπιτέθεικα (ch. 3), *put upon, impose* (a penalty), *inflict*; mid., *fall upon, attack* (w. dat.). [epithet]

ἐπιτρέπω [ἐπιτρεπ], ἐπιτρέψω, ἐπέτρεψα, ἐπιτέτροφα (49), *hand over to, intrust to, allow, permit* (w. dat. and infin.).

ἐπιχωρέω [ἐπιχωρε], ἐπιχωρήσω, ἐπεχώρησα, ἐπικεχώρηκα, ἐπικεχώρημαι, ἐπεχωρήθην (46), *move on, advance*.

ἕπομαι, ἕψομαι, 2 aor. ἑσπόμην, imperf. εἱπόμην (49), *follow, accompany, pursue* (w. dat. or σύν).

ἑπτά (33), indecl. numeral, *seven*. Cf. Lat. septem. [heptarchy]

Ἐπύαξα, ης (42), *Epyaxa*, wife of Syennes s, king of Cilicia.

ἔρημος, η, ον (ch. 3), *desolate, deserted, desert, deprived of* (w. gen.). [hermit]

ἐρίζω [ἐριδ], imperf. ἤριζον (37). In prose used only in pres. and imperf.; gov. dat., *strive with, contend, quarrel*. [eristic]

ἑρμηνεύς, έως, ὁ (46), *interpreter*. [hermeneutic]

ἐρυμνός, ή όν (36), *strongly built, fortified*.

ἔρχομαι [ἐρχ, ἐλθ, ἐλυθ], ἦλθον, ἐλήλυθα (20), *come, go*. Used chiefly in indic. The future is supplied by εἶμι. [pros**elyte**]

ἐρῶ [εἰπ, ἐρ, ῥε] future; φημί or λέγω is used as its present; 2 aor. εἶπον, εἴρηκα, εἴρημαι, ἐρρήθην (32), *say, speak, tell*. Allied to Lat. verbum and Eng. word.

ἐρωτάω, ἐρωτήσω, ἠρώτησα or ἠρόμην (from ἔρομαι), imperf. ἠρώτων (59), *ask about, inquire, ask*, gov. two acc. [erotesis]

ἐσπόμην, see ἕπομαι.

ἔσται, ἔσοιτο, etc., see εἰμί.

ἐσταλμένος, see στέλλω.

ἔστην, ἑστηκώς, ἔστησαν, ἑστώς, see ἵστημι.

ἑστώς, second perfect participle from ἵστημι.

ἔσχατος, η, ον (40), *last, extreme*. [eschatology]

ἕτερος, ᾱ, ον (50), *other* (of two), *the other* (of two), *another* (without article). [hetero**dox**]

ἔτι (10), adv., *still, yet, besides, longer*.

ἕτοιμος, η ον, or ἕτοιμος, ον (19), *ready, prepared*.

εὖ (30), adv., *well*; εὖ ποιεῖν, *benefit*. [e**ulogy**, e**uphemism**]

εὐδαίμων, ον (29), gen. εὐδαίμονος, *happy, prosperous*; c. εὐδαιμονέστερος, s. εὐδαιμονέστατος. εὖ + δαίμων.

εὐήθεια, ᾱς, ἡ (ch. 3), *simplicity, stupidity, folly*.

εὐήθης, ες (ch. 3), *good-hearted, simple, stupid, foolish*.

εὑρεῖν, εὑρών, see εὑρίσκω.

εὑρίσκω [εὑρ], εὑρήσω, ηὗρον, ηὕρηκα, ηὕρημαι, ηὑρέθην (57), sometimes written εὗρον, etc., *find, discover;* mid. *get for oneself, procure.* [**eureka**]

εὖρος, ους, τό (32), *width, breadth.* [an**eurism**]

εὐώνομος, ον (44), *of good name, good omen.* Euphemism for *left*, hence τὸ εὐώνομον, *the left wing* (of an army). εὖ + ὄνομα.

ἐφ', see ἐπί.

ἐφάνην, see φαίνω.

ἔφασαν, ἔφη, etc., see φημί.

ἐχθρός, ά, όν (ch. 3), *hated, hostile;* as noun, *enemy* (private); cf. πολέμιος (public enemy); irreg. comp., ἐχθίων, s. ἔχθιστος.

ἔχω [σεχ], ἕξω or σχήσω, 2 aor. ἔσχον, ἔσχηκα, ἔσχημαι (1), *have, possess, keep;* mid., *be next to* (w. gen.); with an adv. has value of εἰμί and corresponding adj. [ep**och**, **hectic**]

ἑώρᾱ, ἑώρᾱκα, ἑώρων, see ὁράω.

ἕως, conj. (58), *until, till, while, so long as.*

Z

ζεύγνῡμι [ζυγ], ζεύξω, ἔζευξα, ἔζευγμαι, ἐζεύχθην (33), *yoke, join together,* esp. of bridges, with dat. of means. γέφῡρα ἐζευγμένη πλοίοις, a bridge made by joining boats. Cf. Lat. jugum. [**yoke, zeugma**]

H

ἤ, conj. (11), *than;* cf. Lat. quam.

ἡ, article (3), fem. of ὁ, ἡ, τό, *the.*

ἡγεμών, όνος, ὁ (ch. 3), *leader, commander.* [**hegemony**]

ἡγέομαι [ἡγε], ἡγήσομαι, ἡγησάμην, ἥγημαι, ἡγήθην (pas.) (31); mid. dep., *lead* (dat.), *have command of* (dat. or gen.), *think, consider,* followed by accusative and infinitive. [ex**egesis**]

ᾔδειν, ᾔδεσαν; see οἶδα.

ἡδέως (29), adv., *gladly;* comp., ἥδῑον; sup., ἥδιστα. From ἡδύς, allied to Eng. sweet.

ἤδη (25), adv., *already, now, at once.*

ἥδομαι [ἡδ], ἡσθήσομαι, ἥσθην (48), *be pleased, delight in* (dat.), pas. dep.

ἡδύς, ἡδεῖα, ἡδύ, (29), *sweet, agreeable, pleasant.* [**hedonism**]

ἥκιστα, see ἥττων.

ἥκω [ἡκ], ἥξω (27), *have come, have arrived.* Pres. tense shows completed action.

ἤλασε, see ἐλαύνω.

ἦλθον, see ἔρχομαι.

ἡμεῖς, see ἐγώ.

ἡμέρᾱ, ᾱς, ἡ (4), *day.* ἅμα τῇ ἡμέρᾳ, *at daybreak.* [ep**hemeral**]

ἡμέτερος, ᾱ, ον (35), *our, ours.* τά ἡμέτερα, *our affairs, our interests.* From ἡμεῖς.

ἡμιδᾱρεικόν, οῦ, τό (ch. 2), *half-daric.*

ἡμιόλιος, ᾱ, ον, *half as much again.*

ἤν, contracted form of ἐάν.

ἦν, ἦσαν; see εἰμί.

ἧς, rel. pro. (8), gen. sing. fem. of ὅς, ἥ, ὅ, *who, which.*

ἦσαν, see εἰμί.

ἥσθη, see ἥδομαι.

ἡττάομαι, ἡττηθήσομαι or ἡττήσομαι, ἡττήθην (38), *be less, be inferior, be defeated;* pas. dep. used as pas. of νῑκάω.

ἥττων, ον, comp. of κακός.

Θ

θάλαττα, ης, ἡ (4), *sea.* κατὰ θάλατταν, *by sea.*

θαρρέω, θαρρήσω, ἐθάρρησα, τεθάρρηκα (ch. 3), _be bold, be confident._

θᾶττον, adv., comparative of ταχέως.

θαυμάζω [θαυμαδ], θαυμάσομαι, ἐθαύμασα, τεθαύμακα, ἐθαυμάσθην (48), _wonder at, be astonished; often fol. by clause w._ εἰ _or_ ὅτι. [**thauma**turgy]

θεός, οῦ, ὁ (30), _god, deity._ [**theo**logy, **Theo**dore]

Θετταλία, ᾶς, ἡ (22), _Thessaly._

Θετταλός, οῦ, ὁ (20), _Thessalian,_ an inhabitant of Thessaly.

θεωρέω, θεωρήσω, ἐθεώρησα, τεθεώρηκα, τεθεώρημαι, ἐθεωρήθην (40), _view, inspect._ [**theory**]

θηρεύω, θηρεύσω, ἐθήρευσα, τεθήρευκα, ἐθηρεύθην (35), _hunt wild animals, hunt._

θηρίον, ου, τό (35), _wild animal, animal._ [**Ther**on, treacle, mega**therium**]

Θόανα, ων, τά (50), _Thoana,_ a city of Cappadocia.

Θρᾷξ, Θρᾳκός, ὁ (18), _a Thracian._

Θύμβριον, ου, τό (43), _Thymbrium,_ a city of Phrygia.

θύρα, ᾶς, ἡ (4), _door;_ allied to Eng. door. [**thyr**oid]

θύω [θυ], θύσω, ἔθυσα, τέθυκα, τέθυμαι, ἐτύθην (6), _sacrifice;_ mid., _seek for omens_ (by sacrifice). [**thyme, thurible**]

θώραξ, ᾱκος, ὁ (39), _breastplate, cuirass._ [**thorax**]

I

ἰδεῖν, ἰδών, etc., see ὁράω.

ἴδιος, ᾱ, ον (ch. 3), _one's own, private._ τὸ ἴδιον, _one's own property_ (interests). [**idiom**]

ἰδιώτης, ου, ὁ (ch. 3), _private person, private soldier._ [**idiot**]

ἰδών, 2 aor. ppl., see ὁράω.

ἱκανός, ή όν (27), _sufficient, able, enough, fit._

Ἰκόνιον, ου, τό (48), _Iconium,_ a city of Phrygia.

ἴλη, ης, ἡ (45), _crowd, troop_ (of horse). κατὰ ἴλας, _by squadrons._ [**hom**ily]

ἵνα, conj. (22), _that, in order that;_ fol. by subj. or opt.

ἱππεύς, έως, ὁ (31), _horseman;_ plu. _cavalry._

ἱππικός, ή, όν (ch. 3), _of a horseman, cavalry._ τὸ ἱππικόν, _the cavalry._

ἵππος, ου, ὁ (3), _horse._ [**hippo**potamus, **hippo**drome, Phil**ip**]

ἴσθι, ἴσμεν, etc., see οἶδα.

Ἰσσοί, Ἰσσῶν, οἱ (56), _Issi_ or _Issus,_ a city of Asia Minor.

ἵστημι [στα], στήσω, ἔστησα, 2 aor. ἔστην, ἔστηκα, ἔσταμαι, ἐστάθην; act. (exc. 2 aor. perf. and plup.), _make stand, set, stop;_ mid. (exc. 1 aor.), 2 aor., perf., plup. act., _take one's stand, halt._ Cf. Lat. sto, Eng. stand, state. [**sy**stem, **stat**ics]

ἰσχῡρῶς, (51), adv., _strongly, violently, exceedingly._

ἰχθύς, ύος, ὁ (19), _fish._ [**ichthy**ology]

Ἰωνία, ᾱς, ἡ (12), _Ionia,_ a country of Asia Minor.

K

καθ', see κατά.

καθεύδω, καθευδήσω (ch. 3), _lie down to sleep, sleep._

καθηδυπαθέω, καθηδυπαθήσω, καθηδυπάθησα (ch. 3), _waste in pleasure._

κάθημαι, imperf. ἐκαθήμην or καθήμην (ch. 3), _sit down, be seated, be encamped_ (of soldiers).

καθίστημι, καταστήσω, κατέστησα, 2 aor. κατέστην, καθέστηκα, καθέσταμαι, κατεστάθην (40), *set down, station, appoint, establish,* 2 aor., perf. act., and the mid. (exc. 1 aor.), *take one's place, be established.* κατά + ἵστημι.

καί (3), conj. and adv., *and, also, even,* adds emphasis to following word. καί .... καί, *both* .... *and.* τε .... καί, *both* .... *and* or *not only* .... *but also;* emphasizing the latter. καὶ γάρ, *and in fact.* καὶ δή, *and especially.*

κακός, ή, όν (30), *bad, cowardly.* [**caco**phonous]

καλέω [καλε], καλῶ, ἐκάλεσα, κέκληκα, κέκλημαι, ἐκλήθην (28), *call, summon.* [ec**cl**esiastic, **cal**endar]

καλός, ή, όν (2), *beautiful, good, honorable, noble;* c. καλλίων, s. κάλλιστος. [**cal**isthenics, **kal**eidoscope, **Call**iope]

καλῶς (28), adv., *beautifully, honorably, nobly, rightly.*

καπηλεῖον, ου, τό (55), *huckster's shop, store, tavern.* Cf. Lat. caupo, Eng. cheap.

Καππαδοκία, ᾶς, ἡ (50), *Cappadocia,* a country of Asia Minor.

κατά (14), prep., with gen., *down from, down;* acc., *down along.* κατὰ γῆν καὶ κατὰ θάλατταν, *by land and sea.* [**cat**arrh, **cata**logue, **cath**edral]

καταβαίνω, καταβήσομαι, 2 aor. κατέβην, καταβέβηκα, καταβέβαμαι, κατεβάθην (53), *go down, descend.*

κατάγω, κατάξω, 2 aor. κατήγαγον, κατῆχα, κατῆγμαι, κατήχθην (28), *lead down or back, restore.*

καταδύω, καταδύσω, κατέδυσα, 2 aor. κατέδυν, καταδέδυκα, καταδέδυμαι,

κατεδύθην (ch. 3), *sink down, sink, drown.*

κατακόπτω, κατακόψω, κατέκοψα, κατακέκοφα, κατακέκομμαι, κατεκόπην (57), *cut down, cut to pieces, slay.* [apo**cope, comma**]

καταλαμβάνω, καταλήψομαι, 2 aor. κατέλαβον, κατείληφα, κατείλημμαι, κατελήφθην (ch. 3), *seize upon, take possession of, capture.*

καταλείπω, καταλείψω, 2 aor. κατέλιπον, 2 pf. καταλέλοιπα, καταλέλειμμαι, κατελείφθην (47), *leave behind, abandon.*

καταλύω, καταλύσω, κατέλυσα, καταλέλυκα, καταλέλυμαι, κατελύθην (22), *unloose, end, make peace.* con̄ts̄ terms̄ ⁊ ṗositⁱ

κατανοέω, κατανοήσω, κατενόησα, κατανενόηκα, κατανενόημαι, κατενοήθην(31), *observe well, perceive, consider.*

καταπετρόω, καταπετρώσω, κατεπέτρωσα, καταπεπέτρωκα, καταπεπέτρωμαι, κατεπετρώθην (60), *stone to death.*

καταπράττω, καταπράξω, κατέπραξα, 2 pf. καταπέπραχα or καταπέπραγα, καταπέπραγμαι, κατεπράχθην (28), *do well, accomplish, achieve.*

κατατίθημι (ch. 3), *put down,* mid., *lay away.*

Καΰστρου πεδίον, ου, τό (41), *plain of Cayster, Caysterfield,* a city of Phrygia.

κέγχρος, ου, ὁ (54), *millet.*

Κελαιναί, ῶν, αἱ (34), *Celaenae,* a city of Phrygia.

κελεύω, κελεύσω, ἐκέλευσα, κεκέλευκα, κεκέλευσμαι, ἐκελεύσθην(12), *request, order, command.* [pro**celeusmatic**]

Κεράμων ἀγορά, ᾶς, ἡ (40), *Ceramon Agora,* a city in Phrygia.

κεράννῡμι [κερα, κρα] ἐκέρασα, κέκρᾱμαι, ἐκεράσθην or ἐκράθην (43), *mix.* [**crater, crasis**]

κῆρυξ, ῡκος, ὁ (36), *heıald.* In the Greek army he was public crier, summoned assemblies, kept order, and carried messages.

Κιλικία, ᾱς. ἡ (49), *Cilicia,* a country of Asia Minor.

Κίλιξ, ικος, ὁ (42), *a Cilician,* an inhabitant of Cilicia.

Κίλισσα, ης, ἡ (42), *Cilician woman.* ἡ Κίλισσα, *the Cilician queen.*

κίνδῡνος, ου, ὁ (59). *danger, risk.*

Κλέαρχος, ου, ὁ (17), *Clearchus,* a Greek general.

κλώψ, κλωπός, ὁ (18), *thief.*

κνημίς, ίδος, ἡ (45), *legging, greave.*

Κολοσσαί, ῶν, αἱ (33), *Colossae,* a city of Phrygia.

κράνος, ους, τό (50), *helmet.*

κρατέω, κρατήσω, ἐκράτησα, κεκράτηκα, ἐκρατήθην (44), *be strong, master, rule, conquer.* [demo**crat**, aristo**cracy**]

κράτιστος, η, ον, superl. of ἀγαθός, *strongest, most powerful.*

κραυγή, ῆς, ἡ (47), *cry, shout.*

κρείττων, ον, comp. of ἀγαθός, *stronger, more powerful;* s. κράτιστος, *strongest.* From κρατέω.

κρεμάννῡμι [κρεμα], κρεμάσω or κρεμῶ, ἐκρέμασα, ἐκρεμάσθην (37), *hang hang up.*

κρήνη, ης, ἡ (43), *spring, fountain.* [Hippo**crene**]

Κρής, Κρητός, ὁ (38), *a Cretan,* an inhabitant of Crete.

κρῑθή, ῆς, ἡ (54), *barley.* [**crith, crith**omancy]

Κύδνος, ου, ὁ (55), *Cydnus,* a river of Cilicia.

Κῦρος, ου, ὁ (2), *Cyrus,* a Persian prince.

κωλύω, κωλύσω, ἐκώλῡσα, κεκώλῡκα, κεκώλῡμαι, ἐκωλύθην (14), *hinder, oppose, prevent.*

κώμη, ης, ἡ (3), *village;* allied to Eng. home.

Λ

λαβεῖν, λαβών, etc., see λαμβάνω.

λαθεῖν, λαθών, etc., see λανθάνω.

λάθρᾳ (12), adv., *secretly, without knowledge of* (gen.).

Λακεδαιμόνιος, ου, ὁ (17), *a Lacedaemonian,* an inhabitant of Lacedaemon (Sparta).

λαμβάνω [λαβ], λήψομαι, 2 aor. ἔλαβον, 2 pf. εἴληφα, εἴλημμαι, ἐλήφθην (12), *take, capture, obtain, enlist.* [pro**lepsis**, epi**lepsy**, syl**lable**, di**lemma**]

λαμπρότης, ητος, ἡ (48), *brilliancy, splendor.* [**lamp**]

λανθάνω [λαθ], λήσω, 2 aor. ἔλαθον, 2 pf. λέληθα, λέλησμαι (22), *lie hidden, escape notice of* (acc.); mid., *forget;* with ppl. often has value of adv., *secretly.* Cf. Lat. lateo. [**lethe, leth**argy, **latent**]

λέγω, λέξω, ἔλεξα, λέλεγμαι, ἐλέχθην (6), *say* (ὅτι-clause), *tell* (infin. clause); pas. is fol. by infin. clause. [dia**lect, lexicon,** horo**loge, logic**]

λείπω [λιπ], λείψω, 2 aor. ἔλιπον, 2 pf. λέλοιπα, λέλειμμαι, ἐλείφθην (6), *leave, abandon, forsake.* Allied to Eng. leave. [ec**lipse, ellipsis**]

λιμήν, ένος, ὁ (17), *harbor.*

λόγος, ου, ὁ (6), *word, speech.* [bi**ology, log**arithm, **logo**machy]

λόχος, ου, ὁ (56), *ambush, armed men,* a division of an army (about 100 men).

Λῡδίᾱ, ᾱς, ἡ (32), *Lydia,* a country of Asia Minor.

Λύκαια, ων, τά (40). *The Lycaea,* or *The Lycaean Festival,* a festival in honor of Ζεὺς Λυκαῖος, so named from a mountain in Arcadia.

Λυκᾱονίᾱ, ᾱς, ἡ (49), *Lycaonia,* a country of Asia Minor.

λῡμαίνομαι, λῡμανοῦμαι, ἐλῡμανάμην, λελύμασμαι (ch. 3), *insult, destroy, ruin.*

λῡπέω, λῡπήσω, ἐλύπησα, λελύπηκα, λελύπημαι, ἐλῡπήθην (ch. 3), *pain, vex, trouble, grieve.*

λύω, λύσω, ἔλῡσα, λέλυκα, λέλυμαι, ἐλύθην (1), *loose, set free, destroy;* mid., *get freed, ransom.* Allied to Eng. lose. [analysis]

M

Μαίανδρος, ου, ὁ (32), *Maeander,* a river of Asia Minor. [meander]

μάλα, adv., *much, very greatly, exceedingly;* comp., μᾶλλον, *more, rather;* superl. μάλιστα.

μάλιστα, superl. of μάλα.

μᾶλλον (11), adv., comp. of μάλα. μᾶλλον . . . . ἤ, *more (rather)* . . . . *than.* Superl., μάλιστα, *most, especially.*

Μαρσύᾱς, ου, ὁ (36), *Marsyas,* a satyr.

μάχη, ης, ἡ (3), *battle, fight.* [logomachy]

μάχομαι, μαχοῦμαι, ἐμαχεσάμην, μεμάχημαι (36), *fight, fight with* (dat.).

Μεγαρεύς, έως, ὁ (30), *a Megarian,* an inhabitant of Megara.

μέγας, μεγάλη, μέγα (31), *great, large, tall.* μέγα (acc. n. sing.), adv., *greatly.* c. μείζων, s. μέγιστος. τὸ μέγιστον as adv., *chiefly.* Cf. Lat. magnus. [megaphone, omega]

Μεγαφέρνης, ου, ὁ (50), *Megaphernes,* a Persian nobleman.

μείζων, ονος, comp. of μέγας.

μεθ', see μετά.

μείων, ον, comp. of μῑκρός, *smaller, less.* [miocene]

μελίνη, ης, ἡ (54), *panic,* a kind of millet.

μέν (8), postpos. part. Sometimes confirmative, *truly, indeed,* usually fol. by δέ to show contrast between sentences or parts of a sentence, *on the one hand . . . . on the other,* often best shown by the inflection of the voice.

μέντοι (ch. 3), conj. adv., *in truth, assuredly, still, however.*

μένω [μεν], μενῶ, ἔμεινα, μεμένηκα (25), *remain, stay.* Cf. Lat. maneo, Eng. mansion, remain.

Μένων, ωνος, ὁ (34), *Menon,* a Greek general.

μέσος, η, ον (35), *middle, in the middle (or midst)* of, gen. in pred. position. τὸ μέσον, *the center, the middle.* μέσαι νύκτες, *midnight.* Allied to Lat. medius, Eng. mid. [Mesopotamia]

μετά (7), prep., w. gen., *in company with, with;* w. acc., *with, after.* [method, metaphysics, metaphor, meteor]

μεταπέμπω, μεταπέμψω, μετέπεμψα, 2 pf. μεταπέπομφα, μεταπέπεμμαι, μετεπέμφθην (7), *send for* or *after;* usually in mid., *send after, summon.*

μή (22), adv., *not*, used with imperative, infinitive, in conditions, etc.; after verbs of fearing, *lest*.

μηδέ (ch. 3), adv., *but not, and not, not even, not either*.

μηδείς, μηδεμία, μηδέν (37), *not one, no one, none*. μηδέν, adv. acc., *in no respect, not at all*. μηδέ + εἷς.

μηκέτι (58), adv., *no longer, not again*.

μήν, μηνός, ὁ (17), *month*. Allied to Lat. mensis, Eng. moon, month.

μήποτε (20), adv., *never*.

μήτε (ch. 3), adv., *and not*. μήτε . . . . μήτε, *neither . . . . nor*.

μήτηρ, μητρός, ἡ (17), *mother*. Allied to Lat. mater, Eng. mother.

μία, see εἷς.

Μίδας, ου, ὁ (43), *Midas*, a mythical king of Phrygia.

μῖκρός, ά, όν (4), *small, little*. [**micro**scope]

Μιλήσιος, ά, ον (24), *Milesian*, of Miletus.

Μίλητος, ου, ἡ (13), *Milētus*, a city of Ionia.

μισθοδότης, ου, ὁ (ch. 3), *paymaster*.

μισθός, οῦ, ὁ (20), *pay, wages;* allied to Eng. meed.

μισθόω, μισθώσω, ἐμίσθωσα, μεμίσθωκα, μεμίσθωμαι, ἐμισθώθην (59), *hire out;* mid., *hire;* pas., *be hired*.

μύριοι, αι, α (17), *ten thousand*. [**myriad**]

Μῡσία, ᾱς, ἡ (40), *Mysia*, a country of Asia Minor.

N

ναῦς, νεώς, ἡ (36), *ship;* cf. Lat. navis. [**nausea, nautilus,** aero**naut,** arg**onaut**]

ναυτικός, ή, όν (ch. 3), *naval*. [**nautical**]

νέος, ā, ον, *young, new;* c. νεώτερος; s. νεώτατος. Allied to Eng. new. [**neo**phyte, **neo**teric, **Nea**politan]

νεώτερος, comp. of νέος (8).

νεῶν, see ναῦς.

νῑκάω, νῑκήσω, ἐνίκησα, νενίκηκα, νενίκημαι, ἐνῑκήθην (37), *conquer, be victorious*. ἡττάομαι w. gen is used as its passive. [**Nicolas**]

νομίζω [νομιδ], νομίσω or νομιῶ, ἐνόμισα, νενόμικα, νενόμισμαι, ἐνομίσθην (7), *regard as a custom, consider, think, believe;* pas., *be customary*.

νόμος, ου, ὁ (44), *custom, law*. [eco**nom**y, astro**nom**y]

νῦν (30), adv., *now, at present*. τὸ νῦν εἶναι, *for the present*. Allied to Eng. now.

νύξ, νυκτός, ἡ (13), *night*. μέσαι νύκτες, *midnight*. Cf. Lat. nox. [**night**]

Ξ

ξενικός, ή, όν (27), *foreign*. τὸ ξενικόν, *the hired troops*.

ξένος, ου, ὁ (20), *stranger, guest-friend*. ξένοι, *hired soldiers, mercenaries*.

Ξέρξης, ου, ὁ (38), *Xerxes*, king of Persia.

ξίφος, ους, τό (49), *sword*. [**xiph**oid, **xiphias**]

O

ὁ, ἡ, τό (3), definite article, *the*. ὁ δέ at beginning of sentence or clause usually shows change of subject, *but he, and he*. ὁ μέν . . . . ὁ δέ, *the one . . . . the other;* οἱ μέν . . . . οἱ δέ, *some . . . . others;* frequently with value of pos. pro., *his, her, its*.

ὀγδοήκοντα, indeclinable, *eighty*.

ὅδε, ἥδε, τόδε (12), dem. pro., *this, the following, as follows.*

ὁδός, οῦ, ἡ (43), *road, way, journey.* [meth**od**, ex**odus**]

ὅθεν (37), conj., *whence, from which place, from where.*

οἱ, οἵ, οἷ, see ὁ, ὅς, οὗ.

οἶδα, 2 pf. w. present force; other moods, εἰδῶ, εἰδείην, ἴσθι, εἰδέναι, εἰδώς, 2 plupf. ᾔδειν (=imperf.), fut. εἴσομαι (59), *know* (have seen), *perceive, understand.* χάριν εἰδέναι, *be grateful.*

οἴκαδε (28), adv., *homeward, home.*

οἰκέω, οἰκήσω, ᾤκησα, ᾤκηκα, ᾤκημαι, ᾠκήθην, imperf. ᾤκουν (18), *inhabit, dwell;* pas., *be situated.* [**ec**umenical, **eco**nomy, dio**cese**]

οἰκία, ᾱς, ἡ (4), *house.* [**parish**]

οἰκοδομέω, οἰκοδομήσω, ᾠκοδόμησα, ᾠκοδόμηκα, ᾠκοδόμημαι, ᾠκοδομήθην, imperf. ᾠκοδόμουν (38), *build a house, build.*

οἴκοι (20), adv., *at home.* οἱ οἴκοι, *those at home.*

οἶνος, ου, ὁ (43), *wine;* cf. Lat. vinum, Eng. wine. [**oeno**mel, **oeno**philist, **oeno**mania]

οἴομαι or οἶμαι, οἰήσομαι, ᾠήθην, imperf. ᾤμην (45), *think, suppose, believe.*

ὀκτακόσιοι, αι, α, *eight hundred.* ὀκτώ + ἑκατόν

οἷος, ᾱ, ον (ch. 3), rel. pro. with correl. (τοῖος, τοιοῦτος), *as;* correl. usually omitted, when οἷος takes meaning of both, *such as, of such a kind as;* in indir. quest., *of what sort, how great.*

οἷοσπερ, οἵαπερ, οἷονπερ (ch. 3), stronger form of οἷος with same meanings strengthened, *just such as,* etc.

ὀκνέω, ὀκνήσω, ὤκνησα (ch. 3), *hesitate, shrink from, fear.*

ὀκτώ, indeclinable, *eight;* cf. Lat. octo. [**oct**opus]

ὄλεθρος, ου, ὁ (57), *destruction, death, loss.*

ὀλίγος, η, ον (51), *little, small;* plu., *few;* c. ἐλάττων, s. ἐλάχιστος or ὀλίγιστος. [**olig**archy]

ὅλος, η, ον (46), *whole, entire, all, in a body.* [c**a**t**holic, holo**caust]

Ὀλύνθιος, ου, ὁ (36), *an Olynthian,* an inhabitant of Olynthus.

ὁμοίως (ch. 3), adv., *alike, in like measure.*

ὅμως (ch. 3), adv., *nevertheless, yet, still, however.*

ὄν, ὄν, see εἰμί, ὅς.

ὄνομα, ατος, τό (13), *name.* [an**ony**mous, syn**onym**, patr**onym**ic, **onomasticon**]

ὅπῃ or ὅπη (ch. 3), conj. adv., *by which way, where, wherever.*

ὁπλίτης, ου, ὁ (29), *hoplite, heavy-armed foot-soldier.*

ὅπλον, ου, τό (29), *implement;* plural, *arms, armor.* [**pan**oply]

ὁπόσος, η, ον (27), relative pro., *as great as, as many as;* in indir. quest., *how much, how many, how great.*

ὁπότε (35), conj., *when, whenever.*

ὅπου (ch. 3), conj. adv., *where, wherever.*

ὅπως (10), conj., *how, in what way, as;* in purpose clauses, *that.*

ὁράω [ὁρα, ὀπ, ἰδ], ὄψομαι, 2 aor. εἶδον, ἑόρακα, or ἑώρακα, ἑώραμαι or ὦμμαι, ὤφθην, imperf. ἑώρων (48), *see, perceive;* fol. in ind. disc. by ppl., infin., or (rarely) a ὅτι-clause. [**op**tic, pan**orama**, **idea**, trapez**oid**, eph**or**, aut**opsy**, spher**oid**] ὀργίζομαι, ὀργίσομαι or ὀργιοῦμαι, ὠργίσθην (57), pas. dep., *be angry* (dat.)

ὄρθιος, ᾱ, ον (51), *straight up, steep.*

ὁρμάω, ὁρμήσω, ὥρμησα, ὥρμηκα, ὥρμημαι, ὡρμήθην (18), *start, hasten.* Usually dep. mid. or pas., *start oneself, set out.*

ὄρνῑς, ὄρνῑθος, ὁ, ἡ (36), *bird.* [**or**-**nitho**logy]

ὄρος, ους, τό (52), *mountain.* [**ore**ad, **or**ology, **Or**estes]

ὅς, ἥ, ὅ (26), rel. pro., *who, which, what.*

ὅσος, η, ον (26), rel. pro., *as great as, as many as, all who.* Correlative with τοσόσδε or τοσοῦτος or πᾶς; antecedent often omitted.

ὅταν (60), conj., w. subj., *when, whenever.*

ὅτε (38), conj., *when, while.*

ὅτι (12), conj., *that, because;* used to introduce substantive clauses.

οὐ (οὐκ before vowels, οὐχ before rough breathing) (6), adv., proclitic, *not;* absolute negative. [**U**topia]

οὗ (53), adv., *where,* gen. of ὅς.

οὗ (35), pers. pro., *of himself.* οὗ is used only as indir. reflexive; its place as pro. of third person is taken by αὐτός.

οὐδέ (45), conj., *nor;* emphatic adv., *not even, not either, but not.* οὐδέ .... οὐδέ, *neither .... nor.*

οὐδείς, οὐδεμία, οὐδέν (37), *not one, nobody, nothing.* οὐδέν (acc. n. sing.), adv., *in nothing, not at all.*

οὐκέτι (52), adv., *no longer, no more.*

οὖν (8), postpos. particle, *therefore, so, now.*

οὔποτε (ch. 3), adv., *not at any time, never.*

οὔτε (58), conj., *and not.* οὔτε ... οὔτε, *neither .... nor.*

οὗτος, αὕτη, τοῦτο (12), dem. pro., *this, the aforesaid.* Often used as a pers. pro., *he, she, it, they.*

οὕτω (οὕτως before vowels) (19), adv., *so, thus, as aforesaid.* Cf. οὗτος.

ὀφείλω [ὀφελ], ὀφειλήσω, ὠφείλησα, 2 aor. ὤφελον, ὠφείληκα, ὠφείλημαι, ὠφειλήθην (41), *owe;* pas., *be due;* 2 aor. ὤφελον (fol. by infin.), *ought,* implies a wish which cannot be realized=*would that,* etc.

ὄφελος, τό, used only in nom. and acc.(ch.3), *advantage, profit, use.*

ὀχυρός, ά, όν (54), *tenable, strong, fortified.*

Π

παῖς, παιδός, ὁ, ἡ (36), *child, boy, son.* Cf. Lat. puer. [**ped**agogue, encyclo**pedia**]

πάλιν (9), adv., *back again, a second time.* [**palin**ode, **palim**psest]

παντάπᾱσι(ν) (25), adv., *all in all, entirely, altogether.*

πάντῃ or πάντη (54), adv., *in every way, on all sides.*

παντοδαπός, ή, όν (53), *of all kinds, of every kind.*

παρά (11), prep., *beside;* w. gen., *from beside, from;* w. dat., *beside, with, at;* w. acc., *to the side of, beside, to.* [**para**digm, **para**graph]

παραγγέλλω [παραγγελ], παραγγελῶ, παρήγγειλα, παρήγγελκα, παρήγγελμαι, παρηγγέλθην (26), *pass the word along, announce, command, order;* gov. dat. or acc. and infin. παρά + ἀγγέλλω.

παραγίγνομαι, παραγενήσομαι, παρεγενόμην, παραγέγονα, παρηγεγένημαι
(23), *become beside, be near, be
present* (gov. dat.); fol. by εἰς,
arrive at. παρά + γίγνομαι.

παράδεισος, ου, ὁ (35), *park.* [**paradise**]

παραπλήσιος, ᾱ, ον (ch. 3), *near by,
similar, like* (w. dat.)

παρασάγγης, ου, ὁ (32), *parasang,* a
Persian measure of distance, 30
stadia, between 3⅓ and 3½
miles. [**parasang**]

παρασκευή, ῆς, ἡ (31), *preparation,
equipment.*

πάρειμι, παρέσομαι (8), *be by, be near,
be present;* fol. by εἰς and acc., *arrive at.* τὰ παρόντα, *the present
circumstances.* παρά + εἰμί

παρεῖναι, see πάρειμι.

παρελαύνω, παρελῶ, παρήλασα, παρελήλακα, παρελήλαμαι, παρηλάθην
(45), *ride by, march by, review.*
παρά + ἐλαύνω.

παρέχω, παρέξω or παρασχήσω, 2 aor.
παρέσχον, παρέσχηκα, παρέσχημαι
(17), *have at hand, provide, furnish.* παρά + ἔχω. *supply, give*

παρῆν, see πάρειμι.

Παρύσατις, ιδος, ἡ (8), *Parysatis,*
mother of Artaxerxes and
Cyrus.

πᾶς, πᾶσα, πᾶν (38), *all, every, whole.*
[di**apason, pan**-American, **pan**a-
cea, **pan**orama, **Pan**dora, **panto**-
mime]

Πασίων, ωνος, ὁ (30), *Pasion,* a
Greek general.

πάσχω (παθ), πείσομαι, ἔπαθον, πέπον-
θα (ch. 3), *experience, suffer.* As
pas. of ποιέω, εὖ πάσχειν, *be well
treated.* [**pathos,** homeo**pathy**]

πατήρ, πατρός, ὁ (17), *father;* cf.
Lat. pater, Eng. father. [**patri**-
arch, **patriot**]

πατρίς, πατρίδος, ἡ (ch. 3), *father-
land, native land;* cf. Lat. pa-
tria.

παύω, παύσω, ἔπαυσα, πέπαυκα, πέπαυμαι, ἐπαύθην (28), *make stop,
cause to cease;* mid., *make oneself stop, stop, cease.* [**pause,
pose**]

πεδίον, ου, τό (2), *plain.*

πεζός, ή, όν (ch. 3.), *on foot.* ὁ πεζός,
foot-soldier. πεζὴ δύναμις, *in-
fantry.*

πείθω [πιθ], πείσω, ἔπεισα, πέπεικα, 2
pf. πέποιθα, πέπεισμαι, ἐπείσθην (7),
persuade (acc.); mid. (and pas.),
be persuaded, obey (dat.)

πειράω, πειράσω, ἐπείρασα, πεπείραμαι,
ἐπειράθην (14), used chiefly as
mid. or pas. dep., *try, attempt;*
fol. by infin. [em**pirical, pirate**]

πείσομαι, see πάσχω, and πείθω.

Πελοποννήσιος, ᾱ, ον (12), *Peloponnesian,* an inhabitant of the
Peloponnesus.

Πέλται, ῶν, αἱ (39), *Peltae,* a city of
Phrygia.

πελταστής, οῦ, ὁ (30), *peltast,* a
light-armed foot-soldier, one
who carries a πέλτη.

πέμπω, πέμψω, ἔπεμψα, 2 pf. πέπομφα,
πέπεμμαι, ἐπέμφθην (3), *send.*
[**pomp**]

πεντακόσιοι, αι, α (29), *five hundred.*

πέντε, (37), indecl. numeral, *five.*
[**pent**agon]

πεντήκοντα, indeclinable, *fifty.*
[**Pentecost**]   [*concerning.*

περί, prep. (gen., dat., acc.), *about,*

περιγίγνομαι, περιγενήσομαι, περιεγενόμην, περιγέγονα, περιγεγένημαι

(20), *be superior to, conquer.*
περί + γίγνομαι.

περιέχω, περιέξω or περισχήσω, 2 aor.
περιέσχον, περιέσχηκα, περιέσχημαι
(54), *surround, encompass.* περί
+ ἔχω.

περιπλέω, περιπλεύσομαι or -οῦμαι,
παριέπλευσα, περιπέπλευκα, περιπέπλευσμαι (52), *sail around.* περί
+ πλέω.

Πέρσης, ου, ὁ (50), *a Persian.*

Περσικός, ή, όν (58), *Persian.*

πηγή, ῆς, ἡ (35), *spring, source* (of
a river or fountain). [pego-
mancy]

Πίγρης, ητος, ὁ (46), *Pigres,* a Greek
interpreter.

πιέζω [πιεδ], πιέσω, ἐπίεσα, πεπίεκα,
πεπίεσμαι, ἐπιέσθην (20), *press hard,
oppress;* pas., *be hard pressed.*
[piezometer]

Πισίδης, ου, ὁ (23), *a Pisidian,* an
inhabitant of Pisidia.

πιστεύω, πιστεύσω, ἐπίστευσα, πεπί-
στευκα, πεπίστευμαι, ἐπιστεύθην (29),
trust (dat.), *believe.*

πίστις, εως, ἡ (58), *trust, good faith,
pledges* (of good faith). [pistic]

πλανάομαι, -ήσομαι, etc. (57), *wander.*

πλέθρον, ου, τό (33), *plethron,* about
100 feet (Greek) or 97 1/12 (Eng.)

πλεῖστος, see πολύς. [pleistocene]

πλείων or πλέων, see πολύς.

πλήν (13), conj., *but, except, except
that;* sometimes as prep. w. gen.,
except.

πλήρης, ες (35), *full, full of, abounding in* (gen.). [plethora]

πλήττω [πληγ], πλήξω, ἔπληξα, 2 pf.
πέπληγα, πέπληγμαι, ἐπλήγην or
ἐπλάγην (54), *strike, hit;* allied to
Eng. plague. [apoplexy, plec-
trum]

πλοῖον, ου, τό (33), *boat.*

ποιέω, ποιήσω, ἐποίησα, πεποίηκα, πε-
ποίημαι, ἐποιήθην (15), *make, do.*
[poet, onomatopoeia]

πολεμέω, πολεμήσω, ἐπολέμησα, πεπο-
λέμηκα, πεπολέμημαι, ἐπολεμήθην
(16), *war, be at war with, fight*
(dat.).

πολέμιος, ᾱ, ον (49), *hostile.* οἱ πολέμιοι, *the enemy.* [polemic]

πόλεμος, ου, ὁ (36), *war.*

πολιορκέω, πολιορκήσω, ἐπολιόρκησα,
πεπολιόρκηκα, πεπολιόρκημαι, ἐπολι-
ορκήθην (28), *besiege.*

πόλις, εως, ἡ (19), *city, state.* [po-
lite, police, cosmopolitan]

πολλάκις (41), adv., *many times,
often.*

πολλοί, πολλή, etc., see πολύς.

πολύς, πολλή, πολύ (38), *much, many,
large;* c. πλείων or πλέων, s. πλεῖστος. [polygamy, polytechnic,
pleonasm]

πορεύομαι, πορεύσομαι, πεπόρευμαι,
ἐπορεύθην (7), *advance, march.*

πόρρω (ch. 3), adv., *far from* (gen.).

ποταμός, οῦ, ὁ (2), *river.* [hippo-
potamus, Mesopotamia]

πού (58), adv., enclitic, *somewhere,
anywhere;* to qualify a statement, *perhaps, suppose.*

ποῦ, interrog. adv., *where?*

πούς, ποδός, ὁ (37), *foot.* Cf. Lat.
pes, Eng. pedal. [antipodes, tri-
pod, pea]

πρᾶγμα, ατος, τό, (23), *thing done,
deed, act, matter;* in plu., sometimes, *difficulty, trouble,* πράγματα παρέχειν, *to cause trouble.*

πρᾶξις, εως, ἡ (ch. 3), *undertak-
ing, action, enterprise.* From
πράττω.

πράττω [πραγ], πράξω, ἔπραξα, 2 pf.
πέπρᾱγα or πέπρᾱχα, πέπρᾱγμαι,
ἐπράχθην (42), *do, accomplish,
perform.* εὖ or καλῶς πράττειν,
fare well, be fortunate; κακῶς
πράττειν, *fare ill.* [**practical**]

πρεσβύτερος (8), comparative of
πρέσβυς, which does not occur
in the Anabasis, *old.* [**Presbyterian, priest**]

πρίν (22), conj., *before, until.* After
affirmative clauses πρίν means
before and is followed by the in
finitive; after negative clauses,
until, followed by finite moods.

πρό (6), prep., gov. gen., *before, in
front of, in behalf of.* [**pro-
logue, programme**]

προβάλλω, προβαλῶ, 2 aor. προύβαλον,
προβέβληκα, προβέβλημαι, προυβλήθην (46), *throw before, hold be
fore oneself, present arms* (ὅπλα).
[**problem**]

προδίδωμι, προδώσω, προύδωκα, προδέ-
δωκα, προδέδομαι, προυδόθην (ch. 3),
give up, betray, abandon. forsake

πρόειμι (47), *go forward, advance.*

προεῖπον (46), used as 2 aor. of προαγορεύω (*announce*), *speak forth,
order, proclaim.*

πρόθῡμος, ον (ch. 3), *eager, willing,
ready.*

προκαταλαμβάνω, προκαταλήψομαι,
προκατέλαβον, προκατείληφα, προ-
κατείλημμαι, προκατειλήφθην (ch. 3),
seize in advance, preoccupy.

Πρόξενος, ου, ὁ (23), *Proxenus,* a
Greek general.

πρός (9), prep., *in the presence of;*
w. gen., *from before* or *facing,
before, in the sight of;* w. dat.,
before or *facing;* w. acc., *to a*
position before or *facing.* [**pros-
ody, proselyte**]

προσαιτέω, προσαιτήσω, προσῄτησα,
προσῄτηκα, προσῄτημαι, προσῃτήθην
(ch. 3), *ask besides, ask for more.*

προσέρχομαι, προσῆλθον, προσελήλυθα
(ch. 3), *come to* or *toward, ap-
proach* (w. dat.). [**proselyte**]

πρόσθεν (22), adv., *before, formerly.*
τὸ πρόσθεν, *the van.* πρόσθεν . . . .
πρίν, *before.* πρόσθεν . . . . ἤ,
sooner . . . . than.

προσποιέομαι, προσποιήσομαι, προσ-
εποιησάμην, προσπεποίημαι, *make
for oneself, assume, pretend.*

πρόσω (59), adv., *forward.*

πρότερος, ᾱ, ον (56), comp. of πρό
(πρῶτος is used as superl.), *former,
earlier.* πρότερον, adv., *formerly.*
πρότερον . . . . πρίν, *before.*

πρόφασις, εως, ἡ (25), *pretext, excuse.* [**prophet**]

πρῶτος, η, ον (45), superlative corresponding to πρότερος, from πρό,
first. πρῶτον, adv., *first, in the
first place.* [**proto**plasm, **prot**agonist, **proto**col]

πῡρός, οῦ, ὁ (54), *wheat* (gen. in plu.).

πώ (58), adv., enclitic, *yet, hitherto,
ever;* with neg., *not yet, never.*

Ρ

ῥέω, ῥυήσομαι or ῥεύσομαι, ἐρρύηκα, 2 aor.
ἐρρύην (act. in force) (35), *flow.*
Allied to Eng. stream. [cat**arrh**,
rheumatism]

ῥήτωρ, ῥήτορος, ὁ (17), *orator.* From
ἐρῶ. [**rhetoric**]

Σ

σαλπίζω [σαλπιγγ], σαλπίγξω, ἐσάλπιγξα (46), *sound the trumpet,
signal with the trumpet.*

Σάρδεις, εων, αἱ (29), *Sardis*, a city of Lydia

σατράπης, ου, ὁ (5), *satrap, governor of a Persian province.*

Σάτυρος, ου, ὁ (43), *Satyr*, a woodland divinity. ὁ Σάτυρος, *the Satyr, Silēnus*, attendant of Dionȳsus, god of wine.

σαυτοῦ = σεαυτοῦ.

σεαυτοῦ, ῆς, reflex. pro., *of thyself, of yourself.*

σέσωμαι, see σώζω.

σήσαμον (or σησάμη), ου, τό (54), *sesame.*

σιωπάω, σιωπήσομαι, imperf. ἐσιώπων (ch. 3), *be silent, keep silent.*

σκέπτομαι, σκέψομαι, ἐσκεψάμην, ἔσκεμμαι (pres. and imperf. supplied from σκοπέω)(ch. 3), *look carefully at, consider, reflect.* [**skeptic**]

σκευοφόρος, ον (ch. 3), *baggage-carrying;* as noun, *baggage-carrier, pack animal.*

σκηνή, ῆς, ἡ (3), *tent.* [**scene**]

σκοπέω, used only in pres. and imperf. (for other tenses use σκέπτομαι) (51), *look at, watch for, consider.* [epi**scopal**, micro**scope**]

Σόλοι, ων οἱ (56), *Soli*, a city of Cilicia. [**solecism**]

σός, σή, σόν, *thy, your.*

σοφία, ᾶς, ἡ (37), *wisdom, skill, ability.* [**sophist, soph**omore, philo**sophy**]

Σοφαίνετος, ου, ὁ (24), *Sophaenetus*, a Greek general.

σπεύδω, σπεύσω, ἔσπευσα (ch. 3), *urge, hasten, be in haste.*

σταθμός, οῦ, ὁ (32), *stopping-place, station, day's march.* Cf. ἵστημι.

στλεγγίς, ίδος, ἡ (40), *flesh-scraper, strigil.*

στολή, ῆς, ἡ (58), *robe, dress.* Cf. στέλλω. [**stole**]

στόλος, ου, ὁ (31), *equipment, journey, army.* Cf. στέλλω.

στράτευμα, ατος, τό (13), *army, force.*

στρατεύω, στρατεύσω, ἐστράτευσα, ἐστράτευκα, ἐστράτευμαι, ἐστρατεύθην (14), *conduct a campaign, make war* (of officers and soldiers); mid. dep., *serve in a campaign, march* (of soldiers).

στρατηγέω, στρατηγήσω, ἐστρατήγησα, ἐστρατήγηκα, ἐστρατήγημαι, ἐστρατηγήθην (ch. 3), *be general, command, lead.*

στρατηγία, ᾶς, ἡ (ch. 3), *generalship, command.* [**strategy**]

στρατηγός, οῦ, ὁ (2), *general.* [**strategy**]

στρατιά, ᾶς, ἡ (4), *army.*

στρατιώτης, ου, ὁ (5), *soldier.* ἄνδρες στρατιῶται, *fellow-soldiers.*

στρατοπεδεύω, στρατοπεδεύσω, ἐστρατοπέδευσα, ἐστρατοπέδευκα, ἐστρατοπέδευμαι, ἐστρατοπεδεύθην (ch. 3), *encamp*, usually mid. dep.

στρεπτός, ή, όν (58), *twisted.* ὁ στρεπτός, *necklace, collar.* Cf. στρέφω. [**strophe**]

Στυμφάλιος, ου, ὁ (24), *a Stymphalian*, an inhabitant of Stymphālus.

σύ (35), pers. pro., *thou, you.*

συγγίγνομαι, συγγενήσομαι, 2 aor. συνεγενόμην, 2 pf. συγγέγονα, συγγεγένημαι (17), *be with, meet, associate with* (dat.). σύν + γίγνομαι.

Συέννεσις, ιος, ὁ (42), *Syennesis*, king of Cilicia.

συλλαμβάνω, συλλήψομαι, 2 aor. συνέλαβον, συνείληφα, συνείλημμαι, συνελήφθην (9), *take with, sieze, arrest.* σύν + λαμβάνω. [**syllable**]

συλλέγω, συλλέξω, συνέλεξα, 2 pf.
συνείλοχα, συνείλεγμαι, συνελέγην
(14), *gather together, collect,
assemble.* σύν+λέγω. [**syllogism**]

συμβουλεύω, συμβουλεύσω, συνεβούλευσα, συμβεβούλευκα, συμβεβού-
λευμαι, συνεβουλεύθην (22), *plan
with, advise, counsel* (dat.); mid.,
*consult together, get one's advice,
deliberate.* σύν+βουλεύω.

σύμμαχος, ον (ch. 3), *fighting along
with;* as noun, *ally.*

σύμπᾶς, σύμπᾶσα, σύμπᾶν (39), *all
together, entire.* τό σύμπᾶν, adv.
acc., *on the whole, altogether.*

συμπέμπω, συμπέμψω, συνέπεμψα,
συμπέπομφα, συμπέπεμμαι, συνεπέμφθην (50), *send with.* σύν+πέμπω.

σύμπλεως, ων (53), *full, abounding
in* (gov. gen.). For declension
see p. 118.

συμπορεύομαι, συμπορεύσομαι, συμπεπό-
ρευμαι, συνεπορεύθην (ch. 3), *go
with, journey with, join in an
expedition.*

συμπράττω, συμπράξω, συνέπραξα, 2 pf.
συμπέπρᾱχα(γα), συμπέπρᾱγμαι, συν-
επρᾱχθην (15), *do with, help do,
co-operate with, assist.* σύν+
πράττω.

σύν (24), prep., gov. dat., *along with,
with, with the aid of.* Used
more frequently by Xen. than by
other Attic writers. Cf. μετά.
[**sym**pathy, **asyn**deton, **syn**tax,
synagogue]

συνάγω, συνάξω, 2 aor. συνήγαγον,
συνῆχα, συνῆγμαι, συνήχθην (60),
lead together, call together. σύν+
ἄγω. [**synagogue**]

συναλλάττω [συναλλαγ], συναλλάξω,
συνήλλαξα, συνήλλαχα, συνήλλαγμαι,
συνηλλάχθην or συνηλλάγην (26),

*change by bringing together,
reconcile;* mid., *make terms with*
(πρός).

συναναβαίνω, συναναβήσομαι, 2 aor.
συνανέβην, συναναβέβηκα (ch. 3),
go up with, march up with.

συνέπομαι, συνέψομαι, 2 aor. συνεσπό-
μην, imperf. συνειπόμην (ch. 3), *follow along, follow* (w. dat.). *with accompany*

σύνοιδα (ch. 3), *share in knowledge,
be conscious that* (w. dat.).

συντάττω [συνταγ], συντάξω, συνέταξα,
συντέταχα, συντέταγμαι, συνετάχθην
(44), *arrange together, form in
line of battle.* σύν + τάττω.
[**syntax**]

Συρᾱκόσιος, ον, ὁ (39), *a Syracusan,* an inhabitant of Syracuse.

συσκευάζω [συσκευαδ], συσκευάσω,
συνεσκεύασα, συνεσκεύακα, συνεσκεύασ-
μαι, συνεσκευάσθην (ch. 3), *get
ready together, pack up;* mid.,
pack baggage.

συστρατιώτης, ον, ὁ (57), *fellow-
soldier.* σύν + στρατιώτης.

σφεῖς, σφίσι, see οὗ.

σώζω or σῴζω [σωδ], σώσω, ἔσωσα,
σέσωκα, σέσωσμαι, ἐσώθην (39), *save,
rescue;* mid., *save oneself,
escape.* [creo**sote**, **sozo**dont]

Σωκράτης, ους, ὁ (24), *Socrates,* a
Greek general; for declension,
see 609.

Σῶσις, ιος, ὁ (39), *Sosis,* a Greek
general.

T

Ταμώς, ώ, ὁ (52), *Tamos,* commander of Cyrus' fleet; for declension, see 432.

τάξις, εως, ἡ (45), *order, array, line
of battle.* [**taxi**dermy]

Ταρσοί, ῶν, οἱ (55), *Tarsus,* a city
of Cilicia.

τάττω [ταγ], τάξω. ἔταξα, 2 pf. τέταχα, τέταγμαι, ἐτάχθην (1), *arrange, station, draw up in battle line, appoint.* [**tactics**]

ταχέως (46), adv., same meaning as ταχύ. [**tacho**meter]

τάχιστα, superl. of ταχύ.

ταχύ, adv., *quickly, swiftly;* c. θᾶττον, s. τάχιστα. ὡς (ὅτι) τάχιστα, *as quickly as possible.*

ταχύς, ταχεῖα, ταχύ (31), *swift.* ταχύ, acc. neut., adv., *swiftly;* c. θάττων, s. τάχιστος. τὴν ταχίστην ὁδόν, adv. acc., *the quickest way.*

τε, (17), conj., enclitic, *and.* τέ . . . καί, *both . . . . and;* emphasis on second member. Cf Lat. que.

τεῖχος, ους, τό (59), *wall, rampart, fort.*

τελευτή, ῆς, ἡ (3). *end, death.* τελευτὴ τοῦ βίου, *end of life, death.* [**teleo**logy]

τετρακισχίλιοι, αι, α (20), *four thousand.*

τετταράκοντα, indeclinable, *forty.*

τέτταρες, α (19), *four.* [**tetra**hedron, **tetr**arch]

τίθημι [θε], θήσω, ἔθηκα, (2 aor. ἔθετον), τέθηκα, τέθειμαι, ἐτέθην, imperf. ἐτίθην (40), *put, place;* mid., *place for oneself, arrange.* κεῖμαι is used as passive. [**thesis, theme,** apo**thecary**]

τιμάω, τιμήσω, ἐτίμησα, τετίμηκα, τετίμημαι, ἐτιμήθην (14), *honor, value, esteem.* Allied to Eng. title. [**timo**cracy, **Timo**thy]

τίμιος, ᾱ, ον (58), *valued, honored, esteemed, honorable.*

τιμωρέω, τιμωρήσω, ἐτιμώρησα, τετιμώρηκα, τετιμώρημαι, ἐτιμωρήθην (ch. 3), *avenge, punish;* mid., *avenge oneself on, punish.*

τὶς, τὶ (50), indefinite pro., enclitic, *some, any, a, someone, anyone, a certain one.* τὶ, adv. acc., *somewhat.*

Τισσαφέρνης, ους, ὁ, *Tissaphernes,* a Persian satrap, enemy of Cyrus. Declined, Τισσαφέρνης, ους, ει, ην, η.

τοιόσδε, τοιάδε, τοιόνδε (ch. 3), dem. pro., *such,* reg. fol. by οἷος (*as*); used alone, *such as.* τοιάδε, adv. acc., *as follows;* not so precise as τάδε.

τοιοῦτος, τοιαύτη, τοιοῦτο (ch. 3), dem. pro., *such,* such as precedes.

τοξότης, ου, ὁ (38), *bowman, archer.*

τοσοῦτος, τοσαύτη, τοσοῦτον (ch. 3), dem. pro., *so much, so great, so many.* τοσοῦτον, adv., *so much, so far, thus much.*

τότε (13), adv., *then, at that time.*

τοῦ, τόν, see ὁ.

τράπεζα, ης, ἡ (6), *table.* τέτταρες+πέζα. [**trapez**oid, **trapeze**]

τρεῖς, τρία (19), *three.* [**tri**angle, **tri**pod]

τρέφω [τρεφ], θρέψω, ἔθρεψα, τέθραμμαι, ἐτράφην (22), *nourish, support, maintain.*

τρέχω [τρεχ, δραμ], δραμοῦμαι, 2 aor. ἔδραμον, δεδράμηκα, δεδράμημαι (49), *run.* [**troch**ee, **trecho**meter]

τριάκοντα (39), indeclinable, *thirty.* [**triaconter, triaconta**hedral]

τριήρης, ους, ἡ (36), *trireme,* warship with three banks of oars. [**trier**arch]

τρόπος, ου, ὁ (17). *turn, way, manner, character.* τόνδε τὸν τρόπον, adv. acc., *in the following manner.* [**trope, tropic**]

τροφή, ῆς. ἡ (19). *support, maintenance.* [a**trophy**]

τυγχάνω [τυχ], τεύξομαι, 2 aor. ἔτυχον, τετύχηκα (20), *hit upon, happen upon, happen, gain, find* (w.gen.) Often with suppl. ppl.; see 585.

Τυριάειον, ου, τό (43), *Tyriaeum, a city of Phrygia.*

Y

υἱός, οῦ, ὁ (2), *son.*

ὑμεῖς, see σύ.

ὑμέτερος, ā, ον (35), *your, yours.* τὰ ὑμέτερα, *your affairs, interests.*

ὕπαρχος, ου, ὁ (50), *under officer, lieutenant.*

ὑπάρχω, ὑπάρξω, ὑπῆρξα, ὑπῆργμαι, ὑπήρχθην (11), *be at the beginning, make a beginning, exist, assist, favor* (w. dat.).

ὑπέρ (18), prep., *over;* w. gen., *over, in behalf of, for the sake of;* w. acc., *over, beyond* (more than). Allied to Eng. over. [**Hyper**ion, **hyper**critical]

ὑπερβολή, ῆς, ἡ (56), *a crossing-over, passage, mountain pass.* [**hyperbole**]

ὑπισχνέομαι [ὑποσεχ], ὑποσχήσομαι, 2 aor. ὑπεσχόμην, ὑπέσχημαι (28), *hold oneself under, undertake, promise.* ὑπό + ἴσχω (ἔχω).

ὑπό (20), prep., *under;* w. gen., *from under, at the hand of, by* (of agency); w. dat., *under, at the foot of;* w. acc., *under, to a place under.* Cf. Lat. sub. [**hypo**thesis, **hypo**dermic, **hypo**crite]

ὑποζύγιον, ου, τό (60), *under the yoke, pack-animal, baggage-train.*

ὑπολείπω, ὑπολείψω, 2 aor. ὑπέλιπον, 2 pf. ὑπολέλοιπα, ὑπολέλειμμαι, ὑπελείφθην (57), *leave behind, remain behind.* ὑπό + λείπω.

ὑποπτεύω, ὑποπτεύσω, ὑπώπτευσα, ὑπώπτευκα, ὑπώπτευμαι, ὑπωπτεύθην (3), *suspect, apprehend, fear.*

ὑποψίā, ᾱς, ἡ (ch. 3), *suspicion.*

ὑστεραῖος, ā, ον (52), *later, following, next.* τῇ ὑστεραίᾳ (ἡμέρᾳ), *on the following day.*

ὕστερος, ā, ον (60), *comparative, later, behind;* s. ὕστατος. ὕστερον, adv., *later, afterward.* [**hyster**on-proteron, **hyster**ology, **hyster**ics]

ὑψηλός, ή, όν (54), *high, lofty.*

Φ

φαίνω [φαν], φανῶ, 1 aor. ἔφηνα, πέφαγκα or πέφηνα, πέφασμαι, ἐφάνην or ἐφάνθην (25), *cause to appear, show;* mid. and. pas., *show oneself, appear, seem.* [**phenomenon**]

φάλαγξ, αγγος, ἡ (18), *phalanx, battle line.* [**phalanx**]

φανερός, ā, όν (ch. 3), *in plain sight, visible.* ἐν τῷ φανερῷ, *openly, publicly.* [**phaner**ogamous]

φέρω [φερ, οἰ, ἐνεκ, ἐνεγκ], οἴσω, 1 aor. ἤνεγκα, 2 aor. ἤνεγκον, 2 pf. ἐνήνοχα, ἐνήνεγμαι, ἠνέχθην (54), *bear, carry, bring, produce.* Cf. Lat. fero, Eng. bear. [meta**phor**, Christo**pher**, sema**phore**]

φεύγω [φυγ], φεύξομαι or φευξοῦμαι, 2 aor. ἔφυγον, 2 pf. πέφευγα (47), *flee, run away, be in exile.* οἱ φεύγοντες, *the exiles, the fugitives.* Cf. Lat. fugio. [apo**phyge**]

φημί [φα], φήσω, ἔφησα, imperf. ἔφην, rare except in pres. and imper., *say, affirm, assert.* οὔ φημι, *say no, deny, refuse, say that not.*

φθάνω [φθα], φθήσομαι, ἔφθησα, ἔφθην (ch. 3), *anticipate.* Cf. 585.

φιλέω, φιλήσω, ἐφίλησα, πεφίληκα, πεφίλημαι, ἐφιλήθην, imperf. ἐφίλουν (55), *love*. [**Phil**adelphia]

φιλία, ᾱς, ἡ (ch. 3), *friendship*.

φίλος, η, ον (3), *friendly*; c. φίλτερος; s. φίλτατος. ὁ φίλος, *a friend*.

φίλος, ου, ὁ (7), substantive use of the adj. φίλος, η, ον, *friend*. [**philo**sophy]

φλυᾱρίᾱ, ᾱς, ἡ (ch. 3), *nonsense, foolishness*.

φοβέω, φοβήσω, ἐφόβησα; usually pas. dep., φοβέομαι, φοβήσομαι, πεφόβημαι, ἐφοβήθην (48), *frighten*; mid., *fear, dread, be afraid*, of unreasoning fear. Cf. δέδοικα.

φόβος, ου, ὁ (47), *fear, fright*. [hydro**phobia**]

φοινῑκιστής, οῦ, ὁ (50), *a wearer of the purple*, a Persian officer of high rank.

φοινῑκοῦς, ῆ, οῦν (45), *dark red, purple*. Cf. phoenix.

φρούραρχος, ου, ὁ (12), *commander of a garrison*.

Φρυγίᾱ, ᾱς, ἡ (33), *Phrygia*, a country of Asia Minor.

Φρύξ, υγός, ὁ (43), *a Phrygian*, an inhabitant of Phrygia.

φυγάς, άδος, ὁ (17), *exile, fugitive*.

φυλακή, ῆς, ἡ (42), *guard, garrison*. [**phylactery**]

φύλαξ, ακος, ὁ(18), *watchman, guard*.

φυλάττω [φυλακ], φυλάξω, ἐφύλαξα, 2 pf. πεφύλαχα πεφύλαγμαι, ἐφυλάχθην (27), *watch, guard, defend*; mid., *be on one's guard against*. φυλακὰς φυλάττειν, *keep watch*. [pro**phylactic**[

X

χαλεπός, ή, όν (49), *hard, difficult, severe, stern*.

χαλεπῶς (ch. 3), adv., *hardly, with difficulty*. χαλεπῶς φέρειν, *bear ill, be troubled*.

χαλκοῦς, ῆ, οῦν (45), *of bronze, bronze*. [**chalco**graphy]

χαρίεις, ίεσσα, ίεν (38), *graceful, clever, pleasing*.

χείρ, χειρός, ἡ (36), *hand*; for declension, see 611. [**chiro**graphy, **surgeon** (old spelling chirurgeon)]

χείρων, ον, comp. of κακός, *worse, inferior*; superl. χείριστος.

Χερρόνησος, ου, ἡ (17), *Chersonesus*, a peninsula in Thrace.

χίλιοι, αι, α (29), *a thousand*. [**chiliad, kilo**gram]

χιτών, ῶνος, ὁ (45), *chiton, tunic*, a Greek undergarment.

χράομαι, χρήσομαι, ἐχρησάμην, κέχρημαι, ἐχρήσθην (pas.), mid. dep., *use, make use of, employ*; contract forms have η for ᾱ. W. dat.; cf. Lat. utor. [cata**chres**is, poly**chrest**]

χρή, -χρήσει, -ἔχρησε, imperf. χρῆν or ἐχρῆν (χρή is really a noun, sc. ἐστί; imperf. χρῆν = χρὴ ἦν, which came to be regarded as a verb, hence augmented, ἐχρῆν) (43), *it is necessary, one must, ought*, with infin., or acc. and infin.

χρῄζω (ch. 3), pres. system only used in Att., *wish, need, desire*.

χρῆμα, ατος, τό (18), *useful thing*; τὰ χρήματα, *things, property, money*.

χρόνος, ου, ὁ (50), *time, season, period*. [**chrono**logy, **chronic**]

χρῡσίον, ου, τό (18), *gold coin, money*. [**chrys**alis]

χρῡσοῦς, ῆ, οῦν (40), *golden, gold*. [**chrys**anthemum]

χρῡσοχάλῑνος, ον (58), *with gold-mounted bridle*.

χώρᾱ, ᾱs, ἡ (4), *country, land*. [enchoric, chorepiscopus]

χωρίον, ου, τό (55), *place, fortress, stronghold*.

Ψ

ψέλιον, ου, τό (58), *bracelet* worn by Persians of rank.

ψεύδω, ψεύσω, ἔψευσα, ἐψευσμαι, ἐψεύσθην (ch. 3), *deceive, cheat, prove false*. [pseudonym]

Ω

ὦ (3), interj. w. voc. *O*.

ὤνιος, ᾱ, ον (47), *for sale*. τὰ ὤνια, *wares, goods*.

ὥρᾱ, ᾱs, ἡ (ch. 3), *time, season, hour, proper time*. [hour, horoscope]

ὥσπερ, adv. (ch. 3), *just as, even as, just as if*.

ὡς (8), conj., proclitic, *as, just as, as if; how, as, when, because, since;* often used with a ppl. to show that the ppl. contains the thought of some other person than speaker or writer, *as if, on the ground that*. It often represents the action as pretended or assumed. ὡς with superlatives indicates the highest degree, ὡς τάχιστα, *as quickly as possible;* w. numerals, *about, approximately*.

ὡς (31), preposition (same word as preceding), gov. acc., *to*, used only with the name of a person.

ὥστε (15), conj., w. infin. (introducing result), *so as, and so;* w. indic., *so that*, emphasizes the result as a fact.

ὠφελέω, ὠφελήσω, ὠφέλησα, ὠφέληκα, ὠφέλημαι, ὠφελήθην, imperf. ὠφέλουν (18), *benefit, aid, help* (acc.).

INDEX

INDEX

[References are to sections.]

241